WAGING PEACE

WAGING PEACE

How Eisenhower

Shaped an

Enduring

Cold War

Strategy

ROBERT R. BOWIE

RICHARD H. IMMERMAN

OXFORD
UNIVERSITY PRESS

Oxford University Press

Oxford New York
Athens Auckland Bangkok Bogota Buenos Aires Calcutta
Cape Town Chennai Dar es Salaam Delhi Florence Hong Kong Istanbul
Karachi Kuala Lumpur Madrid Melbourne Mexico City Mumbai
Nairobi Paris São Paulo Singapore Taipei Tokyo Toronto Warsaw

and associated companies in
Berlin Ibadan

Copyright © 1998 by Robert R. Bowie and Richard H. Immerman

First published in 1998 by Oxford University Press, Inc.
198 Madison Avenue, New York, New York 10016

First issued as an Oxford University Press paperback, 2000

Oxford is a registered trademark of Oxford University Press

Library of Congress Cataloging-in-Publication Data
Bowie, Robert R. (Robert Richardson), 1909–
Waging peace : How Eisenhower shaped an enduring cold war strategy /
p.   cm.
Includes index.
ISBN 0-19-506264-7; 0-19-514048-6 (pbk.)
1. United States—Foreign relations—1953–1961.   2. Eisenhower,
Dwight D. (Dwight David), 1890–1969.   3. United States—Foreign
relations—Communist countries.   4. Communist countries—Foreign
relations—United States.   5. National security—United States—
History—20th century.   I. Immerman, Richard H.   II. Title.
E835.B66   1997
327.73—dc21   97-8447

For Teddy and Marion

9 8 7 6 5 4 3 2 1

Printed in the United States of America
on acid-free paper

Foreword

General Andrew J. Goodpaster
U.S. Army, Ret.

In our country, each presidential administration has a character of its own, and the Eisenhower administration was no exception. It bore the imprint—both direct and indirect—of Eisenhower himself. Its character was well displayed, in its broader outlines, by what was reported to the public at the time, but in later years it has been disclosed more fully and more deeply as records, interviews, and historical accounts give added insight and greater detail as to just how the major issues were handled, and how the major policies were pursued.

In this book, the reader will see Eisenhower in action, and is likely to come away with a quite different perception from what may previously have been held concerning his leadership. The reader will also be given a deeper understanding as to what the significance of the Eisenhower administration really was in terms of America's security and cold war strategy.

One key early finding, foreshadowed in Eisenhower's service as commander of NATO in 1951 and 1952, was that the National Security Council document NSC 68, a legacy of the Truman administration, would not be sustainable on a long-term basis as the foundation for American security and military planning. As a result, Eisenhower devoted himself as a top priority to the development of policy and doctrine for dealing with the realities of security that *would* be sustainable. In this process his views and conceptions were of central importance.

The authors of this volume make contributions of unique value. Each brings his own set of special qualifications to their combined task: Robert Bowie served as head of the State Department Planning Staff and senior advisor and assistant to Secretary of State John Foster Dulles, and he was the State member of the NSC Planning Board; Richard Immerman, through his background of previous scholarly work on both Eisenhower and Dulles, has equipped himself well for his part in this endeavor.

The circumstances with which Eisenhower and his administration had to deal on coming into office were dangerous and demanding. The war in Korea needed to be brought to an end. The confrontation with the Soviet Union centering on the future of Germany had become highly militarized, and both sides were rapidly arming with nuclear weapons in increasing numbers. Stalin's early death left the Soviet Union under the control of untested leaders. The challenge was to manage the relation in a way that would avoid a third world war while keeping our allies confident and secure. It was necessary as well to forestall any loss of independent nations to Soviet communism at a time when many less developed countries, newly freed from colonialism, were undergoing the challenges and traumas of nation-building and were threatened by communist subversion and encroachment.

Drawing on my own opportunity to see Eisenhower in action, I think it is first of interest to recall how well he was equipped by outlook and experience — including his direct contact with top Russian leaders in the postwar period — to deal with problems of such gravity and complexity. His methods — bringing diverse points of view to bear, looking at problems through the eyes of others, understanding the value Russian leaders placed on holding onto their hard-won personal positions, awareness of nationalist feelings in the less developed world such as he knew from his prewar service in the Philippines with Douglas MacArthur — combined with the attributes of a seasoned strategic thinker.

A few further comments recalling Eisenhower's own approach to his responsibilities as president may add to an understanding of the decision-making process he put into practice during his administration, and may throw added light on the decisions made and actions taken, as presented in these pages. Two aspects seem particularly worthy of note: the method — primarily organization and process — that Eisenhower established at the outset and maintained throughout his two full terms in office, for the conduct of the business of government within the executive branch; and the role he himself took in the ongoing day-to-day, week-to-week activities in which he engaged as he carried out the responsibilities of his office.

He had given close attention following his election to the organizational structure that he thought would best serve his administration — both at the White House/executive office level and between that level and the cabinet departments and major agencies, that is, between himself and his operating "lieutenants," as he liked to call them. Careful regard for organization was nothing new to him. He often expressed himself in almost identical terms, "Organization cannot make a genius out of a dunce. But it can provide its head with the facts he needs, and help him avoid misinformed mistakes."

Eisenhower likewise established a systematic process closely bound to the organizational structures. At his own level he gave emphasis to developing policy and foresighted planning, delegating operations and implementation, insofar as possible, to the operating echelons of the executive branch. A constant aim was to keep matters of a straightforward or routine nature out of the White House, to the extent action could be taken by the departments or agencies under the policy guidelines once established. He himself would address those issues that he deemed to be of major importance, or that had not been fully foreseen, with the full participation of his responsible subordinates in Oval Office meetings wherein the particulars of these complex questions could be thoroughly aired, and courses of action thoroughly deliberated. In doing so, he would draw upon the policy and planning work that had been done, while frequently reminding all those present that decisions should deal with actual realities, which habitually vary from even the best planning assumptions. He would typically revert to a quotation he attributed to the elder von Moltke, pointing out that at the time of decision "The plans are nothing, but the planning is everything."

His week was carefully structured around four regular meetings. Tuesday morning was his meeting with the legislative leaders of Congress, normally with those of his own party, but with those of both parties when international issues were involved. Wednesdays were his press conferences, which followed a meeting with his senior staff beforehand. Thursdays were devoted to National Security Council meetings and Fridays to meetings with the cabinet. For all of these he insisted on careful staff preparation, of which the work of the National Security Council Planning Board was the most intensive and thorough. To these were added long sessions in the Oval Office with Secretary Dulles, Secretary Humphrey of Treasury, the director of the Bureau of the Budget, and on occasion the secretary of Defense and the Joint Chiefs of Staff to deal with specific issues and crises. His long series of meetings with Secretary Dulles during the first year of his presidency were so thorough that he later said he thought, as a result, that he knew the inside of Dulles's mind as well as he knew his own. In addition, he met often with members of his own staff, and with others from within the government as well as from without on issues of wide range and variety.

The meetings would bring together all who shared significant responsibilities in the matter. The purpose was examination of the particular issue by "each in the presence of all" (to borrow a phrase) and with the understanding that there should be "no non-concurrence through silence." It often came with surprise to those at their first meetings with him to see the intensity and authority with which he led the discussion. He would often shape the discussion with one simple-sounding question, "What's best for America?" His aim was to induce his advisors to rise above their parochial interests and approaches. Once a decision was made, it was well understood that it defined what was to be done, and that it was to be followed up to assure faithful execution.

The range of activities in which President Eisenhower and his executive branch associates engaged left a record of leadership methods and results well worth studying, notably with respect to each of the three facets of policy and action that experience shows to be of principal importance: defining America's interests, devising policies and actions to serve and safeguard those interests, and building public and congressional understanding and support for the interests, policies, and actions. There is learning to be derived from examining each of these in the context of the specific issues and policy challenges of Eisenhower's time, and this book will aid greatly in that process.

An administration will ultimately be known by its works, and in assessing such works, two questions have a special value with respect to a particular president. The first is what happened on his watch, with what resulting effect on the well-being of the people of the United States, and the second—admittedly more difficult and speculative—is what might have happened but did not, and (if possible to discern), *why* it did not. On both counts, Eisenhower's record is impressive. He put in place the basic elements of a viable cold war strategy and he effectively managed East-West and allied relations, defusing a series of crises, including Korea, Vietnam, Suez, Berlin, and Sputnik, which could have been disastrous if mishandled.

A further question is how the character that the president gave to his administration affected both these outcomes. The complex issues President Eisenhower confronted on his inauguration and those that required decision and action as time went on were enough to provide ample basis for judgment, and ample food for retrospective analysis. It is hoped that the presentation by these authors of the Eisenhower administration's handling of the issues they have selected will give added understanding to the nature of the American presidency in general and to the work of the American executive branch under President Eisenhower in particular in the fulfillment of his constitutional responsibilities.

Acknowledgments

Both of of us have been interested in Eisenhower's policy-making process and national security strategy for many years: Bowie ever since serving as director of the Policy Planning Staff of the State Department and its member on the National Security Council Planning Board from 1953 to 1957; and Immerman since the torrent of new archives from the administration began to become available in the mid-1970s. We discussed our shared interest when attending conferences on the Eisenhower foreign policies; and in 1987 we decided to undertake this study. Our aim has been to produce an analysis of the policy-process and its resulting strategy, drawing on both direct experience and the documentary record.

For help in pursuing our study, we owe thanks to many more institutions and individuals than we can name. Because Immerman was a Social Science Research Council/MacArthur Foundation Fellow in International Peace and Security, we are grateful to both organizations. And we are grateful to the editors of Oxford University Press for their patience.

For providing access to documents and books, we express appreciation for the invaluable assistance of archivists and librarians at the National Archives, Seeley G. Mudd Library at Princeton University, the Eisenhower Library, the Johns Hopkins University's Paul H. Nitze School for Adanced International Studies, and the U.S. Department of State. We are particularly indebted to Milton Gustafson, John Taylor, Wilbert Mahoney, Steven Tilly, Mary Ronan, Nancy Bressler, Ben Primer, and most especially, David Haight. We also thank the many individuals who processed and reviewed our countless Freedom of Information Act requests.

We benefited immensely from the suggestions and criticisms of friends and colleagues. General Andrew Goodpaster has been extremely helpful in many ways: in interviews and discussion, in reading and commenting on the entire manuscript, and not least in writing the foreword. We also profited greatly from the comments and criticisms of Professors Ernest May, Robert Jervis, and Melvyn Leffler, and Max Hall, all of whom read the full manuscript as well. We are in addition much in debt to Paul Nitze and Luke Battle, who were intimately involved in the Truman administration, for reviewing our chapter on the Truman legacy, and to Professors Fred Greenstein and David Rosenberg, who read various chapters and otherwise encouraged and shared their expertise with us. Professor Rosenberg was also kind enough to provide us with documentation, as was Professor Tami Davis Biddle, and Heather L. Shaffer prepared the index. None, of course, is responsible for any errors which remain or for the judgments expressed.

Finally, we must express our deepest gratitude to our families for bearing with us in this lengthy endeavor.

Contents

WAGING PEACE

Introduction

The ending of the cold war, with the disintegration of the Soviet regime and its empire in Eastern Europe, gives special relevance to a fresh analysis of the origins of the basic strategy pursued by the United States and its allies for three decades, which contributed to that outcome.

I

The thesis of this study is that credit for shaping that strategy belongs to President Dwight D. Eisenhower. While the cold war originated under Harry S. Truman, it took its mature form under Eisenhower. He developed the first coherent and sustainable cold war strategy suitable for the basic conditions that would prevail during the following decades.

Eisenhower did not inherit such a strategy from Truman. The latter's containment policy evolved by stages between 1945 and 1953, largely as a reaction to crises that shaped American perceptions of Soviet purposes and the measures deemed necessary to counter them. After the North Korean attack in mid-1950, the Truman administration adopted a more aggressive strategy, known as NSC 68, to counter the grave threat posed by a Soviet Union then developing a nuclear arsenal. The ambitious objectives and programs of NSC 68 had the goal of coercing "rollback" of Soviet power through military predominance before the Soviets achieved nuclear plenty—estimated to be 1954, the year of "maximum danger." This policy led to the tripling of the defense budget, the establishment of integrated North Atlantic Treaty Organization (NATO) forces, and the decision to rearm West Germany. By the time Truman left office, the effort to pursue this strategy had produced a confused legacy of objectives, policies, and programs in disarray.

Moreover, in devising an alternate strategy for the period ahead Eisenhower confronted conditions more typical of an extended cold war than those of the Truman years. The most salient of these were the following:

a) Within weeks of Eisenhower's inauguration, the death of Joseph Stalin brought to a close his nearly 30 years of dictatorship. Eisenhower, therefore, had to reassess the Soviet threat in the context of a post-Stalin Kremlin. How far might the new collective leadership modify Soviet policy and its relations with the outside world? To what extent did Stalin's death present a "chance for peace"?

b) Eisenhower presided over two revolutions in strategic weapons systems: the advent of nuclear plenty, including the hydrogen bomb, and the emergence of the ballistic missile for both sides. How should this condition of mutual nuclear plenty and missiles affect grand strategy, NATO, and security in general?

c) For all of its problems Western Europe was recovering and regaining confidence. Yet a divided Germany and Eastern Europe dominated by Moscow seemed almost certain to remain so for years to come. The implications for Europe's stability, its economic and political future, and NATO would be critical in shaping the international environment for the rest of the cold war.

d) The inexorable collapse of colonialism was rapidly spawning dozens of emerging nations—almost all of which were poor and unstable. Resentful of past Western domination, they seemed to offer fertile soil for Soviet propaganda and subversion. At the same time, the wars of liberation and other manifestations of nationalist hostility severely taxed the resources of America's major allies and created serious tensions within the North Atlantic alliance, particularly between the United States and the colonial powers.

e) The Korean conflict had shown the difficulty of conducting, and maintaining public support for, a protracted ground war in the developing world. To provide substance to the maxim "No more Koreas," Eisenhower and his advisors had to devise alternatives for dealing with such threats on the periphery.

II

Eisenhower and Dulles were convinced that an effective foreign policy required an explicit and integrated grand strategy. This was not to be a blueprint for the future that would provide mechanical answers for specific issues and problems as they arose. Such issues would be decided in the Oval Office in consultation with key advisors. But a strategic concept should establish longer term purposes and priorities that would ensure consistency in day-to-day decisions and coherence for the actions of the United States and its allies over time.

For Eisenhower, a systematic process was imperative for analyzing alternatives and making sound policy decisions. He designed the National Security Council (NSC) mechanism to obtain the full benefit of the expertise and data from the various departments and agencies, and the judgment and recommendations of his principal advisors and other inputs. In the end, however, after all the staff work, deliberations, and debate, the ultimate strategy reflected the president's own decisions. These decisions, in turn, were molded by the values, beliefs, images, and predispositions Eisenhower brought to the Oval Office and the impact on him of the advice, deliberation, and debate produced by the policy process.

In preparing his basic national strategy, commonly called the "New Look," Eisenhower used this process to the full for exploring alternative courses and their implications, and for arriving at decisions regarding his strategy. In the end he rejected the objective of coercive rollback and the concept of a time of peak danger from the Soviet threat. In his view the task of preventing war and Soviet expansion, seeking to induce and encourage change in Soviet hostility, and mitigating the risk of war would require cooperative action by a vigorous free world over many years before the eventual decline of the Soviet system and threat. The strategy must be effective for these purposes and sustainable for the "long haul."

This study analyzes the fundamental questions about the strategy. What were its premises, its objectives, and the means for achieving them? What methods did Eisenhower use to design his "New Look"? How valid was Eisenhower's strategy for the conduct of the cold war in the light of its ultimate outcome? Are there lessons for policy making in the radically changed international environment of today? The focus is on the substance of Eisenhower's strategy and the process by which he formulated it, which took place mainly in 1953 but for some components extended through 1954. It is, therefore, not a history of foreign policy during the Eisenhower years. In fact, even for the period it covers, significant episodes such as the Korean War and the East German uprising are discussed only as they relate to the evolution of the Eisenhower strategy.

III

Today, there is no need to justify treating Eisenhower as a serious and able policy maker. For his part, the president never had any doubts on this score. He was fully confident of himself and, for that matter, of his chief foreign policy advisor, Secretary of State John Foster Dulles. Dulles knows "more about foreign affairs than anybody I know," Eisenhower said during his second term in office. "In fact," he continued, "I'll be immodest and say that there's only one man I know who has seen *more* of the world and talked with more people and knows more than he does—and that's *me*."[1]

Until a decade and a half ago, Eisenhower's legion of critics would have dismissed this appraisal as not merely immodest but self-delusionary. While the public trusted and respected him, most politicians, scholars, and journalists depicted Eisenhower as a political innocent and intellectual lightweight with neither the requisite knowledge nor skill to navigate the rapids and tides of the cold war, and as largely disengaged from policy making, giving Dulles free rein. Dulles, the consensus held, was brighter than the president, but his thinking and judgments were severely distorted by his moralism, dogmatism, and egotism. Thus Eisenhower's unfounded confidence in himself and his chief advisor, it was said, led to the administration's stubborn pursuit of ill-conceived and ineffective policies and programs.

The last 15 years have seen a reversal of this caricature of both men. Documents from the 1950s reveal an Eisenhower actively in charge and informed.[2] He, not Dulles, made the decisions, and the secretary of state always acted according to Eisenhower's directives. This does not diminish Dulles's importance. He was the president's trusted advisor, relied on to help generate and execute policy and to negotiate with America's allies and adversaries. The archives also show Eisenhower and Dulles to be much more subtle, imaginative, and sophisticated than their contemporary public image.

What is certain is that Eisenhower now enjoys new—or renewed—respect. Whereas historians of the presidency once rated him slightly better than Andrew Johnson but a tad inferior to Chester Arthur, they currently rank him among the top 10 chief executives in the nation's history, and his stature is rising.[3] The esteem in which Eisenhower is now held is based largely on the belated recognition of the leadership and decision-making skills with which he orchestrated policy and evaluations of the policy outcomes, especially when compared with those of his successors. Later events—the Bay of Pigs fiasco, the Cuban Missile Crisis, the Vietnam War, the Iran hostages and botched rescue, huge budget deficits, and Irangate—have enhanced appreciation of his prudence and sober judgment.[4] In a turbulent and dangerous stage of East-West relations, with an untested and erratic Soviet leadership and a changing strategic environment, Eisenhower managed a succession of crises and set a course that preserved both security and peace. Moreover, because he assumed that the cold war would continue for decades, his goals and the means for their pursuit were designed to be sustainable by the Western coalition until internal pressures ended the Soviet threat. To attribute to Eisenhower—or for that matter the United States—primary credit for the radical transformation since 1989 would be simplistic and ahistorical. But to deny the legacy of the 1950s would be equally mistaken.

IV

In examining and analyzing the production and substance of Eisenhower's initial national security strategy, our study draws on the exceptionally rich archives the administration bequeathed to scholars. Because Eisenhower paid so much attention to systematic decision making, and because that decision-making system enveloped so many inputs, the president placed a premium on accurate record keeping. As a result, there is available an extraordinary amount of reliable material that identifies the issues that Eisenhower and his advisors debated and traces the steps through which the debates were resolved. Especially valuable are the memoranda of the discussions in the NSC by S. Everett Gleason, a historian serving on the NSC staff, which he used to debrief its Planning Board. Although recorded in indirect discourse, Gleason's notes faithfully reflect the words of the NSC members, and we treat them as such in extensive quotations relating to the Council meetings.[5] The full records of the NSC and its Planning Board illuminate the interdependence between Eisenhower's strategy and the process that produced it. Interpreting these materials and putting them in context, moreover, has been facilitated by the recollections of one of us (Bowie), who was intimately involved in the policy process.

In the main this strategy was embodied in the Basic National Security Paper approved on October 30, 1953. NSC 162/2, as it was known, resulted from months of study, discussion, and decision making. It took account of the administration's formal review of existing national security programs and its own reappraisal of the Soviet threat, U.S. objectives, and the available and potential resources of the United States and its allies. In addition to NSC 162/2, however, certain issues were dealt with in other papers, and some were not finally settled until a year or more of further debate. This study embraces all these components. The strategy, moreover, was subject to regular reappraisal as the cold war unfolded, in order to update it each year of Eisenhower's tenure. We do not attempt to trace these revisions. With a few exceptions noted in the concluding chapter, however, the key elements of the strategy remained intact.

Part one (chapters 1–4) serves as a prologue to the Eisenhower presidency. The first chapter analyzes the security policies and programs he inherited from Truman. We then examine the outlook, premises, and convictions that Eisenhower and Dulles brought to office on the basis of their earlier experiences and the positions taken in the 1952 campaign.

Part two (chapters 5–9) examines the processes and inputs used to produce the New Look national strategy. The prompt reform of the NSC system created the machinery for reshaping national strategy (chapter 5). Before tackling that directly, however, two specific tasks related to it demanded immediate attention. The first was the revision of the pending fiscal year (FY) 1954 budget, especially the defense component, as submitted earlier by Truman (chapter 6). The other was the necessity to respond to Stalin's death in March 1953 (chapter 7). Finally, as a major input to the strategic review, Eisenhower mounted the elaborate Solarium exercise to compare alternative approaches to the Soviet Union (chapter 8).

Part three (chapters 10–14) analyzes the premises and substance of the strategy's main components. We consider the appraisal of the Soviet threat, the clarification of U.S. objectives, the definition of the military and other means to pursue them, the emphasis placed upon maintaining a cohesive noncommunist world, and efforts for arms control.

In part four (chapter 15) we briefly offer our appraisal. It evaluates the suitability of Eisenhower's premises and policies, how far they provided enduring elements of cold war strategy for the following three decades, and whether his approach to policy making has relevance for the very different future the United States will confront.

PART I

PROLOGUE

The Truman Legacy

The review [NSC 68] recommended a greatly expanded program
. . . for the purpose of creating the necessary military shield behind
which a positive program designed to bring about a modification in Soviet intentions and behavior could be developed. . . .

At one time it was hoped to accelerate the program to a target date of
1952 [instead of 1954] in order to lay the basis for taking increased risks of
general war in achieving a satisfactory solution of our relations with the
U.S.S.R. while her stockpile of atomic weapons was still small. For various reasons this acceleration was not, or could not be carried out.[1]

Paul Nitze (1954)

Eisenhower decided to run for the presidency for two principal reasons; both
were directly related to the Truman legacy.[2] The first was to prevent the election of Senator Robert Taft, the Republican frontrunner, who Eisenhower believed
would reverse the basic Truman strategy of cooperation with allies and collective
security for containing the Soviet Union. Taft had opposed the Marshall Plan and
the NATO Treaty and endorsed the call by Herbert Hoover after the Korean attack
for an "American Gibraltar" relying on unilateral nuclear defense and isolation.[3]
Eisenhower's second reason was his conviction that the Truman policies and programs for carrying out his strategy had to be reshaped to make them more coherent
and sustainable for the "long haul" of the cold war. While supporting many of Truman's actions, Eisenhower was appalled by the erratic decison-making process and
confused policies and implementation.[4]

Thus an understanding of Truman's legacy in foreign and security policy is critical to appreciating the situation Eisenhower inherited and the strategy that he developed. How then did Truman's policies and programs answer the strategic questions of the cold war: What was the nature of the Soviet threat? How did it endanger
U.S. interests? What should be U.S. objectives in seeking security? What means
were most feasible and effective for pursuing them? Our concern is where the answers stood as Truman left office. But because they changed over time, it is necessary to consider their evolution. As will appear, the Truman legacy was far less coherent or clear than is usually assumed as his term ended.

By that time the cold war had been underway for six years. By 1947 George Kennan's "Long Telegram" of February 1946, Winston Churchill's "Iron Curtain"

speech the next month, Soviet actions in Eastern Europe, Iran, and Turkey, and the Clark Clifford–George Elsey report for Truman in September on the Soviet Union had produced a consensus among U.S. policy makers that the Soviet Union was implacably hostile to the noncommunist world, was dedicated to steady expansion toward global domination, and posed a grave security threat which had to be resisted. In mid-1947 Kennan's "X" article in *Foreign Affairs* outlined the containment doctrine, which was already being followed.[5]

At that point, however, "containment" was only a general concept. It provided a framework for concrete measures yet to be devised and implemented. That process took place largely in reaction to specific threats or crises, going through two distinct phases: the first from 1947 to mid-1950, and the second from then to January 1953.

Containment, 1947 to Mid-1950

The first phase, guided largely by Secretary of State George Marshall and Kennan, then heading the State Department Policy Planning Staff (PPS), focused mainly on the threat from Soviet political warfare and subversion. The challenge was to build up the political and economic strength of the vulnerable non-Communist nations to enable them to resist this threat. In March 1947 the Greek-Turkish crisis prompted the "Truman Doctrine," pledging U.S. support for "free peoples who are resisting attempted subjugation by armed minorities or by outside pressures"; and stagnation in Europe led in June to Marshall's initiative for the European Recovery Program (ERP). The North Atlantic Treaty of 1949 was designed to reassure the Europeans after the Berlin crisis, the Point Four program for technical assistance to developing countries to help them make economic progress. The danger of Soviet military aggression was discounted: the U.S. atomic monopoly, though weapons were few, was expected to neutralize the very large Soviet conventional forces. Truman kept a tight ceiling on defense spending.

NSC 20/4

The first formal statement of national security strategy was prepared during the second half of 1948. In July, seeking to justify the higher defense budget he considered necessary, Secretary of Defense James Forrestal requested that the NSC prepare a strategic analysis of the security threats facing the United States, and of its interests, objectives, and means of coping with them, as a guide to budgeting and planning for forces and for making other security decisions.[6] Truman, while authorizing the study, told Forrestal to proceed with preparing the defense budget within a $14.4 billion ceiling. Over the next four months George Kennan and his PPS submitted to the National Security Council (NSC) several interim papers and a final document, NSC 20/4, the conclusions of which the president approved on November 24, 1948.

NSC 20/4 reflected the prevailing views based on nearly two years of containment. The gravest threat, it reaffirmed, stemmed "from the hostile designs of the USSR, and from the nature of the Soviet system." The Soviets were expected, however, to pursue their expansionist goals primarily through efforts short of war: to seek to subvert other states by exploiting political and economic weakness and discontent through tactics such as disruption, propaganda, and covert action, and through support of local Communist parties. While their large armed forces could probably overrun Europe and the Middle East and severely damage the United Kingdom in six months, the Soviets would be inhibited from initiating war involving the United States (unless by miscalculation) by the U.S. atomic monopoly and economic potential as well as their own domestic weaknesses.

To counter the Soviet threat the United States must pursue various measures "short of war," taking care not to permanently impair the U.S. economy and its fundamental values and institutions by "excessive" military spending.[7] To resist Soviet political warfare, it should assist nations able to contribute to U.S. security "to increase their economic and political stability and their military capability" and orientation toward the United States, and seek to discredit the Soviet Union and communism. In prudence, the United States should also maintain long-term military readiness as a deterrent to Soviet aggression, as support for U.S. foreign policy, as reassurance to nations resisting Soviet pressure, and for defense and rapid mobilization if necessary. Finally,

> our general objectives with respect to Russia . . . should be:
> a. To reduce the power and influence of the USSR to limits which no longer constitute a threat to the peace, national independence and stability of the world family of nations.
> b. To bring about a basic change in the [Soviet] conduct of international relations.

For this purpose, the United States should aim peacefully to promote "the gradual retraction of undue Russian power and influence," to foster dissent, and "to create situations which compel the Soviet government to recognize the practical undesirability of acting on the basis of present concepts." The goal should be to "place maximum strain on the Soviet structure of power" and especially on its satellite relations.[8]

Strategic Nuclear Retaliation

One of Truman's major legacies—creation of the Strategic Air Command (SAC) and heavy reliance on strategic nuclear retaliation for deterrence and defense—had its origins in this first phase of containment. The U.S. nuclear monopoly made this reliance natural, Truman's rigid ceiling on defense spending made it inevitable, and the pace of technology fostered its primacy during the rest of Truman's tenure.

Initially, the risk of Soviet attack was greatly discounted, despite the U.S.S.R.'s massive conventional forces. Truman's budget for FY 1949, submitted in mid-January 1948, requested only $9.8 billion for defense, with a 55-group Air Force compared with the 70 groups recommended by a special Air Commission he had appointed. During 1948, however, the Communist coup in Czechoslovakia in February and the Soviet Berlin blockade in June raised the spectre of possible hostilities and prompted serious war planning against a Soviet attack on Europe. The FY 1949 defense budget was raised to about $13 billion.[9]

The war plans against a Soviet attack on Europe called for responding at once with the atomic air offensive. Truman was deeply troubled by this reliance on atomic bombing. In May 1948, when briefed on these plans, he expressed his desire for an alternative "without using atomic bombs." Again, during the Berlin crisis, he vented his horror of the bomb: "I don't think we ought to use this thing unless we absolutely have to. . . . It is used to wipe out women and children and unarmed people, and not for military uses."[10] In September, nevertheless, he assured his advisors that "if it becomes necessary [to use the bomb] no one need have misgivings but that he would do so," although praying it could be avoided.[11] Yet conventional defense in Europe was clearly out of the question even within the increased budget.

This dilemma was reflected in NSC 30, adopted at about this time in response to a Joint Chiefs of Staff (JCS) request for guidance on the use of nuclear weapons. It provided 1) that the military in case of war "must be ready to utilize promptly and effectively all appropriate means available, including atomic weapons, in the interest of national security and must therefore plan accordingly"; but 2) that the "decision as to the employment of atomic weapons in the event of war is to be made by the Chief Executive when he considers such a decision to be required."[12]

Growing Primacy of SAC

In preparing the FY 1950 defense budget during 1948, Forrestal sought to persuade the president of the necessity for larger defense funding to allow for more balanced forces. On March 13 Truman had notified him and the JCS that the FY 1950 defense budget would be limited to $14.4 billion.[13] The defense secretary's July request for the NSC national strategy paper (NSC 20), discussed earlier, was prompted by the hope of an increase. Meanwhile, in an effort to cope with JCS dissension over the total budget and service shares, Forrestal finally decided also to prepare an alternative budget of $16.9 billion, but he was unable to enlist the support of Secretary of State George Marshall, who gave higher priority to the ERP and assisting European forces. To Forrestal's dismay, Truman found no grounds in NSC 20/4 for relaxing his strict constraint on the defense budget. When Forrestal presented his $16.9 billion alternative along with the prescribed $14.4 billion version, the president promptly adopted the lower budget.

Forrestal, giving up on balanced forces, now recognized that the only feasible strategy must be based on strategic air power, using nuclear weapons. In late December he urged Truman to provide $580 million more to add six bombing groups. Truman refused.[14] JCS war planning continued to be virtually immobilized by bitter disputes over allocating resources that all services considered inadequate, and especially between the Navy and Air Force over control of the strategic nuclear offensive. (Eisenhower, brought in to mediate, was dismayed by the service feuding but believed that a reliable $15 or $16 billion budget would be needed for adequate security forces.)[15]

During 1948–49 many other factors greatly enhanced the primacy of the nuclear air offensive as the mainstay of U.S. defense strategy. To begin with, nuclear weapons were in the course of becoming much more plentiful, more varied in design, and far greater in yields, as a result of major technological advances confirmed by spring 1948. As a result, the nuclear stockpile could be increased from 50 in mid-1948 to 400 by the end of 1950 instead of 1952.[16]

The Air Force was also actively improving its capacity for strategic bombing. In October 1948 General Curtis LeMay was named commanding general of SAC, largely neglected until then. Forceful and dedicated, LeMay built SAC into an elite service, highly motivated and trained, well equipped for its mission, and enjoying top priority in budgets and programs. LeMay took steps to improve targeting data, and in February 1949 persuaded the Air Force to cancel programs for light and medium planes in order to procure 75 more intercontinental B-36s. Truman approved in May. By early 1949 the Air Force had available 120 B-29s and B-50s adapted for nuclear weapons (compared with 30 a year before).[17]

In late April 1949 Truman had asked Forrestal's successor, Louis Johnson, to look into how effective the strategic nuclear offensive would be in case of general war with the Soviets. Two studies initiated earlier by the JCS sought to provide an answer, based on the joint war plan approved in December 1948, which called for attacks with 133 bombs. Both concluded that such attacks would not be decisive. Reporting in late May 1949, the committee headed by General H. R. Harmon estimated that if perfectly executed, they would reduce Soviet industrial capacity by 30 to 40 percent but not "bring about capitulation, destroy the roots of Communism, or critically weaken the power of Soviet leadership to dominate the people." Nor would the attacks seriously impair the Soviet ability to overrun most of Western Europe, the Middle East, and some of the Far East. Yet the Harmon committee concluded that the early use of SAC was "the only means of inflicting shock and serious damage to vital elements of the Soviet war making capacity."[18]

The second report, submitted in January 1950 by the Weapons Systems Evaluation Group (WSEG), dealt with the feasibility of such an attack. It advised the JCS that under the most favorable assumptions 70–85 percent of the U.S. aircraft would reach their urban/industrial targets and damage one-half to two-thirds of the targeted facilities beyond repair. But U.S. aircraft losses would be extremely costly—about one-third in the case of night raids and one-half in daylight. In view of logistical problems and plane losses, the report questioned whether the attack on the scale planned was feasible.[19]

On December 8, 1949, the JCS adopted the Joint Outline Emergency War Plan code-named OFFTACKLE. Under this concept the immediate U.S. response to a Soviet attack would be a full-scale nuclear strike by SAC against Soviet urban/industrial targets to disrupt its war-making capacity. (In deference to the European allies, the JCS had also assigned SAC the task of slowing the Soviet advance into Western Europe, but that mission was infeasible until more weapons were available.) The resulting damage, while severe, was not expected to knock the Soviets out of the war or even prevent its huge land army from overrunning most of Western Europe and the Middle East. The United States and its allies, it was hoped, would be able to retain a damaged Great Britain and footholds on the continent, North Africa, and the Cairo-Suez area. From these, after mobilizing U.S. resources for two years or so, the JCS planned to conduct an extended war not unlike World War II to retake Europe and defeat the Soviets.[20] Although the scale of forces steadily increased during the next two years, the basic OFFTACKLE strategy remained unchanged through 1952.

Reaction to the Soviet Atomic Test

The first Soviet nuclear test, detected in September 1949, was a severe shock. By ending the U.S. nuclear monopoly earlier than expected, it threatened to undercut the main pillar of U.S. strategy.

Yet the Soviet test had no effect on preparation of the defense budget for FY 1951, which was then under way. Early on Truman had told the services they could plan on a $15 billion budget, about the same amount as in FY 1950. Eisenhower, who at the time was president of Columbia University but also serving as an ad hoc JCS chairman, had been struggling with the services through June to work out a budget on this basis.[21] Facing a deficit of $5–7 billion, however, Truman had planned with the budget director in April to drop the ceiling nearly $2 billion to $13 billion, but he did not advise the JCS of the cut until July 1. Eisenhower complained in his diary that "one of our greatest troubles is inability to plan for a given amount of money . . . in spite of prior commitments by the President himself. . . . We work like the devil on an agreement on a certain sized budget, and then are told to reduce it."[22] Thus, the defense budget Truman sent to Congress in January 1950 requested $13 billion for the fiscal year starting on July 1 and remained unchanged until the Korean invasion in June.

On the nuclear front, however, the response to the Soviet test was immediate and far-reaching. Two months before the test Truman had told his advisors, "Since we can't obtain international control we must be strongest in nuclear weapons." Accordingly, in October he approved a JCS proposal for substantially expanding nuclear production facilities.[23]

Much more consequential was Truman's decision in January 1950, after several months of heated debate, to develop the hydrogen bomb. Strongly opposed were the Atomic Energy Commission (AEC) General Advisory Committee and a majority of the AEC. Vigorously in favor were scientists like Edward Teller, the JCS, AEC member Lewis Strauss, and influential congressmen. Approval was finally recomended by a special committee, composed of Acheson, Johnson, and AEC chairman David Lilienthal, although he had reservations. At his meeting with the committee on January 31, President Truman took only seven minutes to decide to go ahead with the hydrogen bomb development. His only question: "Can the Russians do it?" Five weeks later, reacting to the discovery of Klaus Fuchs's espionage, Truman authorized AEC and the Department of Defense (DOD) not only to develop but to prepare to produce the fusion bomb.[24]

Drafting NSC 68

In addition, the hydrogen bomb special committee recommended a broad strategic review. Thus, also on January 31, 1950, the president directed the secretaries of state and defense to reexamine "our objectives in peace and war and . . . our strategic plans, in the light of" the prospective Soviet fission and hydrogen bomb capability.[25]

Their report, prepared during February and March by a State-Defense working group headed by Paul Nitze, Kennan's successor as director of the PPS, was submitted to Truman in early April as NSC 68. While calling urgently for a massive build-up of defense forces and related measures, the report purposely omitted any cost estimates, although privately Acheson and Nitze foresaw annual defense spending more than tripling to $40 or $50 billion. After reading NSC 68 but before acting on it, Truman requested further information on the "implications of the conclusions . . . [and] a clear indication of the programs which are envisioned in the Report, including estimates of the probable cost of such programs." And in the interim "existing programs should not be postponed or delayed." Meanwhile, in early May he said, "The defense budget next year will be smaller than it is this year," and three weeks later reaffirmed the $13 billion cap on defense spending.[26]

National Security Policy, mid-1950 through 1952

The North Korean attack of June 25, 1950, moved U.S. national security policy into a radically new phase, which was the source of most of the policies and programs inherited by Eisenhower. Responding to the North Korean aggression and managing the conduct of the war inevitably preoccupied Truman and his key security advisors during the rest of his term. Yet the impact on the broader strategy for the cold war itself was much more consequential. The attack was seen as validating the analysis, conclusions, and recommendations of NSC 68. The costing process requested by Truman was overtaken by a huge defense expansion that quickly blew the lid off the defense budget. NSC 68's conclusions were formally approved by the president on September 29 as "a statement of policy to be followed over the next four or five years."[27]

Interpreting NSC 68

Ominous in tenor and polemical in style, NSC 68 devoted over 50 pages to analyzing the implications of prospective Soviet nuclear capabilities for the communist threat, U.S. objectives, and the character and timing of the U.S. response required. The premise was that the Soviet Union would be able to deliver a crippling surprise nuclear attack on the United States by 1954 (the year of "maximum danger" assuming existing defense programs). In its conclusions, NSC 68 repeated verbatim and reaffirmed as valid ("allowing for the immediacy of the danger") the conclusions (regarding threat, objectives, and means) contained in NSC 20/4 adopted in 1948. The gravely intensifying struggle must be pursued, however, with far greater urgency and much larger resources, especially for military purposes. A massive U.S. defense build-up across the board was required to achieve preponderance in order 1) to deter war and, if attacked, to survive and go on to win; and 2) to support other U.S. foreign policy objectives outlined in the report.[28]

Interpreting NSC 68 and appraising its significance has become a cottage industry for historians and others.[29] In his memoir, Nitze rejects as "erroneous" the contention that NSC 68 recommended a sharp departure in U.S. policy.[30] His claim is too modest. There was, of course, continuity: NSC 68 continued the basic objective of developing the political and economic strength of the noncommunist nations and fostering their cooperation and cohesion in order to resist Soviet subversion and intimidation. In the context set out in NSC 68, however, the words of NSC 20/4 took on a totally different import than they had in 1948, when Soviet political subversion was perceived as the main threat, nuclear weapons were a U.S. monopoly, and internal ferment and decay were the eventual nemesis of Soviet power.

According to NSC 68, the prospective Soviet nuclear capacity transformed the severity and immediacy of the Soviet threat, the U.S. objectives necessary to meet it, and the requisite means for doing so, especially in the role and scale of military capability. Kennan, who had drafted NSC 20/4, vigorously protested against the premises and proposed policies of NSC 68. And in his memoir, Acheson entitled the chapter on NSC 68 "A New Definition of Foreign Policy" and treated it in those terms. In explaining its style, he called NSC 68 a "bludgeon" to facilitate a presidential decision, while conceding the merit of one reader's bon mot that it was "the most ponderous expression of 'elementary ideas' he had come across."[31]

For our purpose of assessing Truman's legacy, the important question is how far the actual policies and purposes at the end of his tenure reflected the premises, aspirations, and recommendations of NSC 68. Its implementation was significantly affected by continuing challenges and reappraisals, practical difficulties, conflicting priorities, and service feuding. What was the outcome in practice after two and one-half years?

To that we now turn. With respect to the basic strategic components—threat, objectives, and means—we will first analyze what NSC 68 proposed and then examine how it had been implemented, modified, and evolved by the end of Truman's tenure.

The NSC 68 Strategy

The Soviet Threat

The radical shift in U.S. strategy embodied in NSC 68 was driven primarily by its reappraisal of the Soviet threat. As depicted in NSC 68, the Soviet Union was far more menacing than it was in the view that prevailed from 1947 to mid-1950 and that underlay NSC 20/4. In both periods policy makers accepted that the Soviets were implacably hostile to the noncommunist world and would actively seek to expand their influence and control with the ultimate objective of world domination. Beyond that, the appraisals diverged sharply. In the earlier phase, as already discussed, the danger was viewed primarily as Soviet subversion of noncommunist countries through political warfare—using propaganda, economic and political leverage, indigenous Communist parties, and intimidation to exploit their vulnerabilities. But while persistent, Soviet leaders were cautious and patient, and especially careful to avoid any risk to the security of the regime, in keeping with communist doctrine, Russian tradition, and the impact of World War II. Despite their superiority in ground forces in Europe, the Soviets would almost surely not initiate deliberate military action in the face of the U.S. atomic monopoly and its industrial potential, though war might occur by accident or miscalculation. Nor did Kennan expect that attaining atomic weapons would make the Soviets appreciably more aggressive.[32] Truman's defense cap of $13–14 billion until the Korean War had reflected this appraisal.

NSC 68 portrayed the Soviet threat in ominous terms. "[T]his Republic and its citizens in the ascendency of their strength stand in their deepest peril. The issues that face us are momentous, involving the fulfullment or destruction not only of this Republic but of civilization itself." The analysis made it "apparent . . . that the integrity and vitality of our system is in greater jeopardy than ever before in our history." The "risks we face are of a new order of magnitude, commensurate with the total struggle in which we are engaged."[33]

These judgments flowed from a much more aggressive concept of the Soviet Union. The U.S.S.R., according to NSC 68, was "inescapably militant because it possesses and is possessed by a world-wide revolutionary movement, because it is the inheritor of Russian imperialism, and because it is a totalitarian dictatorship." The Kremlin, "animated by a new fanatic faith," was dedicated to imposing "its absolute authority over the rest of the world . . . by violent or non-violent methods in accordance with the dictates of expediency." This "design, therefore, calls for the complete subversion or forcible destruction of the machinery of government and structure of society in the countries of the non-Soviet world and their replacement by an apparatus and structure subservient to and controlled from the Kremlin."[34]

As the main obstacle to Soviet ambitions, the United States was its principal target. In the memorandum "Recent Soviet Moves," written while NSC 68 was being drafted, Nitze concluded, "In the aggregate, recent Soviet moves reflect not only a mounting militancy and increased confidence, but they suggest a boldness that is essentially new—and borders on recklessness." They had shown willingness to use "any maneuver or weapon which holds promise of success. For this reason, there appeared no reason to assume that the Soviets would in the future make a sharp distinction between 'military aggression' and measures short of military aggression."[35]

For NSC 68, the projected Soviet nuclear capability "greatly intensified the Soviet threat" and made it "more immediate" than estimated by NSC 20/4. "For the moment our atomic retaliatory capability is probably adequate to deter the Kremlin from a deliberate direct military attack against ourselves or other free peoples." But once the Kremlin leadership "calculates that it has sufficient atomic capability to make a surprise attack on us, nullifying our atomic superiority and creating a military situation decisively in its favor, the Kremlin might be tempted to strike swiftly and with stealth." They would surely do so if confident of knocking the United States out. Mutual atomic plenty "might well act, therefore, not as a deterrent, but as an incitement to war."[36]

NSC 68 predicted that this situation would arise by 1954, when the Soviets would have about 200 nuclear weapons; of these some 100 might be deliverable on the United States (by one-way missions). Thus 1954 would be the year of "maximum danger." By then, NSC 68 warned, their growing atomic arsenal would give the Soviets various options despite U.S. numerical superiority. A Soviet surprise attack could severely damage "vital centers of the U.S.," seriously curtail its retaliatory capacity, and greatly reduce its economic superiority for an extended war. And no longer would Soviet ground forces be neutralized by the U.S. nuclear monopoly. They might also be emboldened to embark "on a more violent and ruthless prosecution of its design" by subversion and intimidation, as well as "on piecemeal aggression against others, counting on our unwillingness to engage in atomic war unless we were directly attacked." Yet "our present weakness would prevent us from offering effective resistance at any of several vital pressure points," where the only choice would be between capitulation and a global war of annihilation. And while the "preferred Soviet technique is to subvert by infiltration and intimidation, . . . [it] is seeking to create overwhelming military force, in order to back up infiltration with intimidation."[37]

The NSC 68 conception of the Soviet threat was challenged by the two top Soviet experts. Kennan's rejection of the premises and prescriptions of the paper has already been mentioned. The critique of Charles ("Chip") Bohlen was more specific and more persistent (and ultimately effective, as will be discussed later). While supporting a military buildup to balance Soviet forces, Bohlen took strenuous issue with the depiction of Soviet priorities and their proclivity to take risks for expansion that underlay the analysis and strategy of NSC 68. He first voiced his criticisms in April 1950, when he was briefly recalled from his Paris post to comment on the completed draft.[38] His objections failed to persuade Acheson.

NSC 68: U.S. Objectives

Truman's directive leading to NSC 68 was specifically to reexamine "our objectives" in the light of Soviet nuclear prospects. As already mentioned, that review had concluded that the objectives of the Truman strategy should continue to be the same as those set out in NSC 20/4 in 1948 and reaffirmed them verbatim. They were, in short,

1) to prevent the expansion of Soviet control and influence by political warfare, subversion, or military force; and

2) "to reduce the power and influence of the USSR to limits which no longer constitute a threat to the peace, national independence and stability of the world family of nations," and "bring about a basic change" in its conduct of international relations.[39]

But the identity was purely verbal or formal. NSC 68 stressed that the emerging Soviet nuclear capacity had "greatly intensified the Soviet threat" and the "immediacy of the danger."[40] In this ominous new context, NSC 68 gave these two U.S. objectives a profoundly different content from the previous period.

Achieving "preponderant power" as soon as feasible took top priority under NSC 68 for both objectives. For "reasonable assurance that the free world could survive an initial attack" by 1954, and still eventually attain its objectives, "it appears to be imperative to increase as rapidly as possible general air, ground, and sea strength, and that of our allies to the point where we are not so heavily dependent on atomic weapons." Enhancing our retaliatory power to deter a possible surprise attack would also provide more time for "our policies to produce a modification of the Soviet system."[41]

Deterring and if necessary defeating Soviet aggression and expansion, however, was only half of the NSC 68 strategy. "In a shrinking world, which now faces the threat of atomic warfare," it read, "it is not an adequate objective merely to seek to check the Kremlin." The "intensifying struggle requires us to face the fact that we can expect no lasting abatement of the crisis unless and until a change occurs in the nature of the Soviet system."[42]

Defensive containment was, therefore, not sufficient to cope with the threat from a nuclear-armed Soviet Union. The United States could no longer afford the risk of relying on the eventual retraction of Soviet power and influence primarily as the result of internal forces of decay and ferment with only limited Western nurturing. The United States must have a vigorous affirmative program: "[W]e should take dynamic steps to reduce the power and influence of the Kremlin and the other areas under its control. The objective would be the establishment of friendly regimes not under Kremlin domination."[43]

In pursuing this course, "the immediate objectives — to the achievement of which such a build-up of strength is a necessary though not sufficient condition — are a renewed initiative in the cold war and a situation to which the Kremlin would find it expedient to accommodate itself, first by relaxing tensions and pressures and then by gradual withdrawal."[44]

This objective was central to the strategy of NSC 68, as was stressed in its analysis and repeated in its conclusion: "The only sure victory lies in the frustration of the Kremlin design by the steady development of the moral and material strength of the free world and its projection into the Soviet world in such a way as to bring about an internal change in the Soviet system." For this purpose military supremacy was indispensable. "Without aggregate military strength in being and readily mobilizable, a policy of 'containment' — which is in effect a policy of calculated and gradual coercion — is no more than a policy of bluff."[45] Acheson stressed this point: "Many people thought that we were trying to hold a ring around the Soviet Union. In fact, we were endeavoring to see to it that freedom of choice rested with us, not the Russians."[46]

NSC 68 was vague, however, on how the "coercion" would be applied or would end the nuclear danger, as will be examined in the next section. Mostly, NSC 68 simply called in general terms for a "renewed initiative in the cold war," or "dynamic steps," or "a vigorous political offensive" against the Satellites, coupled with the rapid and massive buildup. It spoke of gaining "time for the process of accommodation, withdrawal and frustration to produce the necessary changes in the Soviet system." The basic premise was that Soviet "dynamism can become a weakness if it is frustrated, if in its forward thrusts it encounters a superior force which halts the expansion *and exerts a superior counterpressure.* . . . [Then] the seeds of decay within the Soviet system would begin to flourish and fructify."[47]

In retrospect (see the epigraph heading this chapter), Nitze spoke of "a positive program" based on "taking increased risks of general war in achieving a satisfactory solution of our relations with the USSR while her stockpile of atomic weapons was still small." But the content of the "positive program" remained unspecified.

As its proponents recognized, the rollback objective entailed risks until the overall buildup was achieved. The Soviet Union could exploit it in its peace campaign to divide the free world. Or fearing future rollback, the Soviets might be provoked into preventive military action, despite the damage to them, in order to overrun

Western Europe to augment their strength. Therefore the buildup and other measures should be presented as "essentially defensive."[48]

Preponderant Power

The central policy message of NSC 68 was that the United States and its allies must achieve preponderant power by a massive and rapid buildup, especially of military capacity across-the-board, before the Soviet Union acquired the capacity for a crippling nuclear surprise attack—estimated to be 1954. U.S. nuclear superiority must be maintained and supplemented by a great expansion of conventional forces, mainly by the NATO allies, to offset those of the Soviet Union and to reduce the dependence on nuclear weapons. The "maintenance of a strong military posture is deemed to be essential for two reasons: (1) as an ultimate guarantee of our national security, and (2) as an indispensible backdrop to the conduct of the policy of 'containment,' including 'roll-back.'"[49]

NSC 68 did not specify what forces would be needed or define the concrete strategy for achieving these goals. That was left to implementing programs. While no costs were mentioned, Acheson and Nitze, as mentioned, foresaw a tripling of U.S. defense spending.

Pursuing Rollback

To reiterate, NSC 68 was not clear on just how the preponderant power of the United States and its allies would bring about Soviet retraction or reduce the atomic threat. Preventive war was explicitly disavowed.[50] Yet coercion or pressure was assumed. For instance: "If the U.S. develops a thermonuclear weapon ahead of the U.S.S.R., the U.S. should for the time being be able to bring increased pressure on the U.S.S.R." (The converse was also recognized.)[51] NSC 68 seemed to expect that such a "situation of strength" would induce the Soviets virtually to capitulate or negotiate an end to the cold war on Western terms.

More generally, it asserted that in waging the cold war "[t]he integrity of our system will not be jeopardized by any measures, covert or overt, violent or non-violent, which serve the purpose of frustrating the Soviet design." Yet in the catalog of measures for a "comprehensive and decisive program to win the peace and frustrate the Kremlin design," the only specifics are "[i]ntensification of affirmative and timely measures and operations by covert means in the field of economic warfare and political and psychological warfare with a view to fomenting and supporting unrest and revolt in selected strategic satellite countries."[52]

Negotiations

NSC 68 discussed the role of negotiation in relations with the Soviet Union at some length, but the basic thrust of the analysis and argument was clear and simple.[53] In essence, it was that no effective agreement for atomic disarmament (or on other major issues) "can be negotiated unless and until the Kremlin design has been frustrated to a point at which a genuine and drastic change in Soviet policies has taken place."[54] Negotiated agreements therefore depended on the success of the buildup in achieving retraction of Soviet power and fundamental change in the Soviet system and could merely record such success. Meanwhile, the Soviets would take advantage of any agreements by bad faith and use negotiations to lull Western publics into delay or inaction on needed measures.

Still, the United States and its allies must have sound negotiating positions and be ready to negotiate "on terms consistent with our objectives," even though agreement at present "would reflect present realities and would therefore be unacceptable, if not disastrous, to the United States and the rest of the free world." This is "an essential element in the ideological conflict," a tactic "to gain public support for the program and to minimize the immediate risks of war," and a means to demonstrate Soviet intransigence.[55]

Implementation

U.S. Defense Buildup

While triggered by the Korean attack, the military buildup was expected to be guided by NSC 68. The attack was at once interpreted by policy makers as validating their estimate of Soviet readiness to take greater risks and to resort to force in pursuit of their "design." Thus the committee named by Truman in April 1950 to program and cost NSC 68 joined the JCS in preparing force targets for rearming against this broader threat, with a December deadline. Meanwhile, the Communist Chinese intervention in November sharply intensified the fear of greater Soviet boldness in pursuing "aggressively their world wide attack on the power position" of the United States and its allies.[56]

This sense of grave danger and great urgency was reflected in the program set out in NSC 68/4, approved by Truman on December 14. To accelerate the buildup, it advanced the initial target date for achieving the force levels from June 1954 to June 1952.[57] The force goals for FY 1952 were set at 18 divisions; 397 combat vessels; and 95 air wings, compared with pre-Korea goals for FY 1952 of 10 divisions, 281 naval vessels, and 58 wings. The total number of military personnel would be more than doubled to 3,211,000.[58] And on December 16 Truman declared a national emergency.[59] By June 30, 1951, Congress had approved four Supplemental Appropriation Acts, bringing the total amount of funds authorized and appropriated for FY 1951 to $49,364,524,250.[60]

Impressive progress in rearming had been made within a year after the Korean attack. By then, the Army had 18 divisions, the Navy 342 combatant vessels, and the Air Force 87 wings, with 3,243,000 men under arms. But there were serious shortfalls: the Munitions Board "estimated that at least 30 percent of the NSC 68/4 programs," especially for "critical weapons systems," could not "be completed by mid-1952."[61] Moreover, NSC 114/1, the review of the status of the buildup approved by Truman in August 1951, concluded that NSC 68 had underestimated the Soviet threat and that since April 1950 Bloc military power had probably grown more than that of the West. It estimated that the Soviets would probably have a stockpile of 200 nuclear weapons (which NSC 68 judged sufficient for a crippling attack on the United States) by mid-1953 instead of mid-1954. Much greater pace and scale of effort would be required to meet the target date for NSC 68/4 programs, or the 1954 goals of NATO's Medium Term Defense Plan (MTDP).[62] In consequence, the "US and its allies are already in a period of acute danger which will continue until they achieve a position of strength adequate to support the objectives defined in NSC 68." In October 1951 Congress responded by passing a defense appropriation of nearly $57 billion for FY 1952 plus another $4.5 billion for military construction.[63]

Primacy of SAC

Meanwhile, during the summer of 1951 an intense controversy developed among the services regarding force levels and priorities. The initial post-Korea surge in rearming had essentially funded each service about equally to produce "balanced forces." In May 1951, when the JCS asked for force projections for FYs 1952–1954, the Air Force requested 140 wings (not counting transport and troop carriers) for FY 1954. General Hoyt Vandenberg, Air Force chief of staff, argued that under the war plans, the strategic air force would soon have three missions: to destroy Soviet war-making industry, to neutralize its atomic delivery capacity, and to delay the Soviet advance into Western Europe. These tasks were essential for ultimate victory in case of general war, and only the Air Force could perform them. Thus these missions, and the Air Force, should enjoy top priority in building the necessary capability. "Balanced forces" ignored the relative urgency of these missions.

After the JCS had futilely debated for several months, Deputy Secretary of Defense Robert Lovett intervened and worked out a compromise in which the Air Force force levels for June 30, 1952, would be stated as "possible expansion to 138 [combat wings] by end of FY 1954." Secretary of Defense Marshall accepted the "principle" but not specific objectives, and Truman approved in August. Shortly thereafter, when force levels were being set for FY 1953, the Air Force figure was 143 wings (which, however, included 17 troop carrier wings). As the JCS official historian comments: "These debates and decisions may justly be termed momentous. Plainly the Air Force had been granted priority; it was allowed to swell greatly while the other services grew only slightly. . . . The 'New Look' of the Eisenhower Administration, and especially the emphasis on massive retaliation, was foreshadowed by the choices made in the autumn of 1951."[64]

The expansion of facilities to produce nuclear materials had also proceeded rapidly. As we have seen, in October 1949, well before NSC 68 and the Korean War, Truman had authorized the first nuclear facilities expansion, and in January 1950, the development of the hydrogen bomb. The following October, after the Korean attack, he approved building another U-235 and three more plutonium facilities. Finally, in January 1952 he ordered a third major expansion.[65]

The significance was profound. As David Rosenberg explains:

> By January 1953, a construction program was underway which would add eight pluto-
> nium production reactors and ten gaseous diffusion U-235 production plants to the

five reactors and two gaseous diffusion plants operating in mid-1950. These plants and reactors were capable of supporting an enormous expansion in the nuclear weapons stockpile [which grew from about 1000 in mid-1952 to 18,000 by 1960]. . . . No subsequent administration found it necessary to authorize any further expansion of nuclear production facilities to meet weapons requirements.[66]

Meanwhile, improved design was increasing the yield of fission weapons up to 25-fold, and the hydrogen bomb, successfully tested in October 1952, would enter the stockpile during 1954, with yields up to 15 megatons. The combined effect would be to multiply the yield of the stockpile nearly 150 times by 1955–1956. Although the Soviets tested a thermonuclear device in August 1953, their capability lagged well behind.

The role of SAC was underscored by the justification given for the third nuclear facilities expansion of January 1952. In urging it, Vandenberg told the president that there were "perhaps five or six thousand Soviet targets which would have to be destroyed in the event of war."[67] Though the U.S. nuclear stockpile would reach about 1,000 warheads in 1952, he explained that SAC, while a "powerful deterrent," could not yet deliver a knockout blow to the U.S.S.R. due to the improved Soviet "protective measures" against strategic air attack. "In light of this, I am convinced that the combat effectiveness of my forces from the standpoint of atomic warfare has tended to stand still, notwithstanding the gradual numerical increase in the size of the stockpile."[68]

Rearming NATO

To achieve military superiority and reduce reliance on nuclear weapons, as envisaged in NSC 68, most of the conventional forces needed to offset the huge Soviet ground forces would have to be provided by the European members of NATO. Yet when North Korea attacked, NATO was still getting organized and had little more than ambitious paper plans for defense. Suddenly, when a Soviet invasion of Europe loomed as a possibility, the sense of impotence created near-panic among many Europeans. Serious military planning in cooperation with the United States began in earnest to revise NATO's Medium Term Defense Plan. For Truman and his advisors, the conflict in Korea did not shake their priority for Western Europe as the critical area for U.S. security. Recognizing at once that the Europeans would need substantial assistance in equipping expanded forces, the president on July 26 requested that Congress appropriate an additional $3.5 billion for military assistance for Europe to supplement the $1 billion already approved. A survey showed huge European shortages in artillery, tanks, half-tracks, and aircraft.

During the summer and fall of 1950 the NATO members debated measures to convert the alliance into an effective, integrated defense coalition, including a West German contribution that preoccupied the JCS and deeply troubled the French. By December 1950, after extended negotiations at and after a critical September NATO Council (NAC) meeting, the Allies had taken major decisions: 1) the formation of an integrated defense force had been approved; 2) the post of Supreme Allied Commander (SACEUR) was created, with Eisenhower the first appointee; 3) the United States had agreed to deploy four more divisions in Europe; 4) an MTDP

(DC-28) had been adopted, setting 1954 force goals of 49 1/3 ready divisions (excluding reserves and any German forces) and rising to 95 1/3 by D + 90, 556 combat vessels, and 9,200 aircraft; and 5) Germany would in principle be allowed to rearm and participate, though the manner remained to be worked out.[69] In November 1951 the mid-1954 force goals were revised by MC 26/1 to 46 D-day divisions and 98 D + 30.[70]

The issues of force goals and the German contribution, however, continued to plague the Alliance to the end of Truman's tenure. Both were intimately linked to the imperatives of NATO war planning. For the Europeans, a strategy like OFF-TACKLE, which called for withdrawing to bridgeheads after the SAC strike and liberating the continent after mobilizing, was little better than capitulation. Thus only a "forward" strategy based on defending as far east of the Rhine as possible was acceptable to the continental countries. Since the NATO MTDP assumed (as did OFFTACKLE) that the SAC offensive would not be "decisive," a "forward" strategy would require very large NATO forces on the ground to counter the Soviet advance.

When Eisenhower, as SACEUR, met with President Truman and others in January 1951, he outlined such a preliminary "strategic conception" based on a force of 50–60 divisions, supported on the flanks by strong naval and air forces in the North Sea and Mediterranean. In SHAPE he allowed planning only on the basis of holding the Rhine-Ijssel line. But the JCS refused to accept this "Continental Strategy" as the last line of NATO defense in U.S. planning. The U.S. Joint Outline Emergency War Plan that was approved in September 1952 still embodied the OFFTACKLE concept for withdrawing after the SAC strike from the Rhine to the Pyrennes and from Northern Europe to Norway, and in the South, trying to hold as much of Southern Italy as possible.[71]

The 1950 MTDP soon proved to be too ambitious for the Europeans. By mid-1951 the increased defense spending imposed excessive strain on their economies, causing declines in industrial output and rising trade and balance of payments deficits. Moreover, U.S. military assistance (MDAP) shipments were lagging badly.[72] Consequently, in September 1951 the NAC appointed a Temporary Council Committee (TCC), with Averell Harriman, Jean Monnet, and Edwin Plowden as a Working Group, to undertake a study and report on reconciling European defense spending with what their economies could sustain. On the basis of the TCC report, the council at its Lisbon meeting in February 1952 adopted lower force goals for 1954 of nearly 41 2/3 divisions of ready forces (89 2/3 for D + 30) including 8 ready (and 12 for D + 30) to come from the Federal Republic of Germany. The effect was to reduce the earlier MTDP goals by 30 percent for other members.[73] The military leaders were convinced the revised force goals carried serious risks, but accepted them as stages to the full MC 26/1 goals. General Bradley refused Harriman's request to endorse the proposed forces as adequate to defend Western Europe, but at Acheson's suggestion he did say that they would strengthen the deterrent and defense capability.[74]

The results of Lisbon left Acheson "exuberant" at the prospects for "a more united and stronger Europe and an integrated Atlantic defense system."[75] His confidence, however, was short-lived.

U.S. Stretch-Out

In preparing the FY 1953 defense budget, to be submitted in January 1952, Truman had two reports on the security programs. In August 1951, NSC 114/1, as already discussed, assessed the current programs and stressed the urgency of the continued military buildup. In October the second report (NSC 114/2), concerned with proposals for policy and programs, also emphasized that the United States and its allies, while stronger, were "far from an adequate position of strength" and would face "heightening of tensions" and perhaps greater risk of war during the next several years as Western strength was being built and the Soviet nuclear stockpile grew. This prospect underlay the JCS force goals for FY 1953: 21 Army divisions and 3 Marine, 408 major combat vessels, and 143 Air Force wings, including 57 for SAC, with total personnel of 3,914,400. The estimated cost for FY 1952–53 was $108 billion.[76]

Meanwhile, pressures to slow the pace of the U.S. defense buildup were beginning to emerge. The Korean truce talks, although not productive, were relaxing tensions and fear of general war, despite two more Soviet atomic tests in October. The Bureau of the Budget was projecting a deficit of $10 billion for FY 1952, and $12 billion for FY 1953, which aroused Truman's conservative fiscal instincts. At mid-1951 some $38 billion from earlier defense appropriations remained uncommitted, and materials shortages constrained some higher arms output. Congressional critics were becoming more vigorous, and Truman's popularity had plummeted.[77] Thus the demand of NSC 114/2 for more defense buildup clashed with budgetary pressures for restraint.

Truman embraced both horns of the dilemma. As a basis for preparing the FY 1953 defense budget, he approved the increased force goals but imposed a tentative ceiling of $45 billion. The conflict between the approved force goals and the budget limit soon became apparent. With $45 billion, the current forces could be maintained but not expanded. Lovett managed to squeeze the New Obligational Authority (NOA) for FY 1953 to about $51.5 billion (plus $3.5 billion for military construction). Then, on December 28, 1951, Truman decided "to stretch out the build-up" in order to restrain defense *spending* to $44 billion in FY 1952 and $60 billion in FY 1953, thereby abandoning the approved FY 1953 force goals. Excluding military public works, the president's defense budget for FY 1953 called for $48.1 billion of NOA (with 43 percent for the Air Force) and estimated spending at about the same amount. The JCS advised the secretary of defense that "the general period of 1954 [would be] the most dangerous for the security of the U.S. in the foreseeable future. Adoption of the reduced program postpones until 1956 our military capability to meet this threat." Congress, however, cut the president's budget by almost $2 billion, mostly at Army expense, while slightly increasing the Air Force share, bringing it to nearly 46 percent of the $46 billion appropriation. MDAP fared even worse: the president's request for $5.3 billion was reduced to $4.2 billion, and defense support for Western Europe was cut by about 30 percent.[78]

Covert Action

The United States actively conducted an expanded covert program against the Soviet bloc, as proposed by NSC 68, but without significant results. From 1949 to 1953 it air-dropped agents into the Soviet Union; it kept contact with the Lithuanian resistance until 1952 and the Ukranian until 1953. From 1950 to 1952 it supported an opposition in Poland, which turned out to be controlled by the secret police. With the United Kingdom, it failed in an operation from 1948 to 1952—run by Kim Philby, who proved to be a Soviet agent—to overthrow the Albanian regime. And in 1950–1951, the United States initiated Radio Free Europe and Radio Liberty, broadcasting into Eastern Europe and the Soviet Union.[79]

Strategic Reappraisal Deadlocked: 1951

The effort to reappraise NSC 68 during the second half of 1951 was stalled by deep divergences regarding the premises and conclusions. In mid-July Truman had requested the NSC to produce such a reappraisal by October 1 to assist in preparing the FY 1953 defense budget.[80]

Bohlen, now counselor in the State Department and its member of the NSC Senior Staff that was charged with drafting the NSC report (NSC 114/2), vigorously pressed his criticisms of NSC 68 on Acheson and Nitze.[81] In a series of memoranda and meetings, he insisted (1) that "the guiding thought" of the Soviet leaders has always been "that under no circumstances and for no revolutionary gains must the Soviet state be involved in risks to the maintenance of Soviet power in Russia;"[82] (2) that "the [Soviet] internal situation is the single greatest controlling factor in its foreign policy" but is "virtually ignored in the entire [NSC] 68 series, in which" the opportunity, risk, and strength of its opponents are considered the only factors controlling and affecting Soviet actions; and (3) that

> any war, whether the prospect of victory be dim or bright, carries with it major risks to the Soviet system in Russia. The fact of war alone, its attendant mobilization, added strain on an already strained economy, exposure of Soviet soldiers to external influences, the entire problem of defection, the relationship of party to Army, the question of the peasantry and many other factors, which I am convinced are predominantly present in Soviet thinking on any question of war, are either ignored or treated as insignificant [in the NSC series].[83]

Nitze defended the analysis of NSC 68 and sought to rebut Bohlen's criticism.[84] On September 24, 1951, the dispute between Bohlen and Nitze led to a meeting with Acheson. The next day, feeling that the discussion had been clouded by extraneous issues, Bohlen wrote to Acheson, *"The only issue here is whether the NSC 68 analysis of the Soviet Union is sufficiently accurate to serve as a guide for U.S. Government interpretation of Soviet actions and for an estimate of probable future Soviet moves. My entire position is that it is not."* Korea did not reflect greater Soviet boldness in taking risks, but a gross miscalculation as to the U.S. reaction.[85]

Bohlen therefore proposed that the NSC 68 series be confined to justifying the U.S. military programs needed for balancing Soviet power (which he supported). For the broader purpose of "a guide to probable Soviet actions," he recommended "that a more balanced and exhaustive study might be undertaken separately with the help of some consultants who have had experience in the Soviet field."[86]

Acheson was impatient with this debate, later calling it a "stultifying and, so I thought, sterile argument between the Planning Staff and the Soviet experts."[87] Yet as will appear in our discussion of Eisenhower's strategy, it was central to the issue of deterrence.

The issue was not resolved when NSC 114/2 came before the NSC on October 17 in two parts: part I (policy review) and part II (proposed agency programs). While approving the *programs* in part II as the basis for budget submissions for FY 1953, the president deferred action on the disputed part I and instructed the NSC Senior Staff to submit to the NSC "at the earliest practicable date" a reappraisal of the policies and programs in the NSC 68 and 114 series, "in light of (1) the second Soviet atomic explosion and (2) the current evaluation of the net capabilities of the USSR to injure the continental United States."[88] Protracted dispute and debate delayed submission of the reappraisal for nearly a year.

Finale: Assessment

The last six months or so of the Truman administration brought to the fore the contradictions, clashes of view, and disarray in many of its security policies and programs, and the underlying NSC 68 strategy.

In assessing the Truman legacy, we have the benefit of two major reappraisals made by top officials of the administration near its close: one was NSC 135/3, "Reappraisal of U.S. Objectives and Strategy for National Security," which was approved on September 25, 1952; the second was NSC 141, a report by Secretary Acheson, Secretary of Defense Robert Lovett, and Director of Mutal Security W. Averell Harriman, on "Reexamination of U.S. Programs for National Security," submitted to the president on January 19, 1953.[89] Both will be discussed later in context. Also significant for this purpose are actions taken in this period in relation to NATO and continental defense.

Drafting NSC 135/3 and NSC 141

Reappraisal of NSC 68 proved an extremely contentious and protracted process. As already mentioned, the first attempt (NSC 114/2, part I) was so controversial that it was withdrawn by the NSC Senior Staff before consideration by the Council, which then directed the Senior Staff to prepare a revised reappraisal "at the earliest practicable date."[90] That process took about a year, involving even more bitter dispute, to produce NSC 135/3. The divergences were especially sharp between the NSC Senior Staff, on which Bohlen represented State, and Nitze and his PPS. In May, for example, a memorandum by Robert Tufts of the PPS referred to an early draft of the paper as "almost wholly irrelevant," ill-informed, "misleading in some respects, and inaccurate in others."[91]

By early July 1952 the NSC Senior Staff had an interim draft of NSC 135 ready for discussion and revision. Its form reflected its contentious origins. The draft consisted of a policy paper (and appendix) supported by a staff study in two parts. Part I of the staff study on "The Bases of Soviet Action" had been drafted by Bohlen and expanded his basic thesis that the Soviet leaders would be inhibited from taking any aggressive action that might entail a significant risk to their regime. Aside from war by miscalculation or accident, or in theory by a "decisive" blow if feasible, Soviet actions were most likely to be confined to cold war exploitation of Western weaknesses.[92]

When Bohlen circulated the draft of NSC 135 within the State Department for comment, Nitze wrote a slashing attack on it, supported by a more detailed PPS memorandum. The PPS director vehemently objected that the draft underestimated the risks and U.S. capabilities; set inadequate U.S. goals and strategy; gave deficient, unclear, or mistaken guidance for specific security programs; and was internally inconsistent and defeatist. More specifically, Nitze objected, it would abandon "any attempt now or later to roll back the Iron Curtain" or to get "preponderant power." Contrary to the draft, he asserted, the risks of war remained great; the United States with its allies must and "can within the next several years gain preponderant power"; and as they did so, according to the PPS memorandum, "opportunities will arise for inducing or compelling a retraction of Soviet power, not, of course, without any risk but at acceptable risk." Moreover, the PPS warned, announcing "rollback" as an overt goal prematurely would risk provoking the Soviets into overrunning Europe to augment their strength before it could be defended.[93]

These memoranda graphically displayed the depth of disagreement. Nitze and the PPS, at least, remained fully convinced of the analysis and policies of NSC 68. After further give-and-take at staff levels, Secretary Acheson held several meetings with Bohlen, Nitze, and others to settle the State Department position. As finally approved by him, the policy paper was submitted to the NSC as 135 in mid-August. In his meetings Acheson also considered and specifically approved part I of the Staff Study—Bohlen's analysis of the "Bases of Soviet Action."[94] After NSC consideration on September 3 and 24, the president approved the report on September 25, 1952, as NSC 135/3.[95]

The final appraisal of the Truman national security programs was a study called for by NSC 135/3.[96] Prepared by Acheson, Lovett, and Harriman, this report examined "whether the allocation of our resources under existing programs is appropriately related to the threats we face and to our strategy for meeting these threats." It was submitted as NSC 141 on January 19, 1953, Truman's last day in office.[97] The authors stressed that their report focused on the inadequacies of existing programs for meeting the dangers ahead and was not an overall balanced appraisal, including past achievements.[98] NSC 141, NSC 135/3, and related actions were of critical import in defining the national security legacy of Truman. In essence, while the "basic purposes and policies" of NSC 68 were nominally reaffirmed, its analysis, objectives, and policies were in fact radically modified or abandoned.

The Soviet Threat

Bohlen's view of the Soviet threat and priorities was finally adopted in NSC 135/3, two and one-half years after his initial criticism of that aspect of NSC 68. Part I of the staff study for NSC 135/3, explicitly approved by Acheson, contained an extended exposition of his thesis that the top priority of the Soviet leaders was the security of the regime. They would therefore not initiate major war or take any other action to expand Soviet influence or control if it entailed any significant risk to the maintenance of the regime.[99]

The final success of Bohlen's persistent effort was far more than an academic victory. It went to the heart of Soviet readiness to take risks in pursuing expansion even in a period of nuclear plenty. And it was therefore critical in determining what would provide an effective deterrent against aggressive Soviet actions.[100] This was explicitly recognized by NSC 135/3. With the growth of the Soviet nuclear arsenal, it read, the "vulnerability of the U.S. to direct attack, which is now serious, will in a few years, probably assume critical proportions." Deterrence, however, required only that the "over-all strength" of the United States and its allies be sufficient to "continuously confront the Kremlin with the prospect that a Soviet attack would result in *serious risk to the Soviet regime*, and thus maximize the chance that general war will be indefinitely deterred." The "year of maximum danger" was not mentioned. The "most immediate danger" was Soviet cumulative piecemeal expansion by subversion, political and economic warfare, or possibly local aggression, against unstable areas, especially on the Soviet bloc periphery, which could ultimately leave the United States isolated and vulnerable.[101]

Rollback

As for the NSC 68 objective of "retraction of Soviet power," NSC 135/3 displayed the marks of the underlying dispute. While repeating the objective in language similar to that used in NSC 68, NSC 135/3 actually abandoned aggressive rollback in favor of Kennan's pre-1950 position by the critical qualifications it imposed. In stating the objective it sounded both themes. The United States would seek, "[w]ithout deliberately incurring grave risk of general war, to induce a retraction of the Kremlin's control and influence, and so to foster the seeds of destruction within the Soviet system that the Soviet bloc is brought to . . . modifying its behavior to conform to generally accepted international standards." The "over-all strength" of the United States and its allies must be such as, inter alia, to "permit the exploitation of rifts between the USSR and other communist states and between the satellite regimes and the people they are oppressing."[102]

If further Soviet expansion were blocked, "the internal conflicts of the Soviet totalitarian system should, with positive effort from us, subsequently cause a retraction of Soviet power and influence and *eventually* cause that system *gradually* to weaken and decay, *although no time limit can be established by which these objectives will be achieved*."[103]

As for "positive efforts," NSC 135/3 provided that "without involving unacceptable risks, the United States should pursue and as practicable intensify positive political, economic, propaganda, and paramilitary operations against the Soviet orbit," especially those "designed to weaken Kremlin control over the satellites and the military potential of the Soviet system." But most significant were the caveats that followed: "However, we should not over-estimate the effectiveness of the activities we can pursue within the Soviet orbit, and should proceed with a careful weighing of the risks against the possible gains in pressing upon what the Kremlin probably regards as its vital interests." The appendix of NSC 135/3 was even more blunt: such operations alone, it warned, "however vigorously pursued against the Soviet orbit cannot be counted on drastically to reduce" the Soviet threat.[104]

That caveat was fully supported by the experience during 1949–1952. In that period the Central Intelligence Agency's (CIA's) Office of Policy Coordination (OPC), responsible for covert activities, grew enormously: from 302 to 6,000 in personnel; from $4.7 to $82 million in budget; and from 7 to 47 in overseas stations. From January 1951 to 1953, the number of operations increased by 16 times.[105] Yet the impact on Soviet power or the bloc was negligible. In "Estimate of the World Situation through 1954," issued in November 1952, the CIA concluded, "The Soviet regime is firmly entrenched in power, and there is no apparent prospect of its control being threatened or shaken." Moreover, "Soviet control over the European Satellites, now virtually complete, will probably be maintained" by its military, police, political, and economic controls. Discontent would persist and might increase, but would present only "a minor impediment to the Soviet program."[106] Bohlen, in his analysis of the Soviet Union, warned that it would "use military action to defend areas presently under its control deemed vital to Soviet security interests."[107] Finally, in its review of allocations for security programs, NSC 141 recommended against added resources for covert actions against the Soviet system because Western capabilities were so limited.[108] Essentially, NSC 135/3 was a return to the pre-1950 policy.

Work on NSC 141 brought an even crueler blow to Nitze: he found that the military never accepted rollback as a criterion for setting force goals or strategy. In his memorandum of January 12, 1953, to Acheson on NSC 141 Nitze said:

> Our national security programs have never actually been consistent with our objectives as those objectives have been repeatedly stated in NSC papers (20/4, 68, 114, and most recently 135/3). This became clear in the course of work on this project [NSC 141] when the Defense representatives stated time and again, in answer to the point that the defense program could not produce the situation of strength defined in 135/3, that the defense program had never been designed to produce any such situation of strength.

Doggedly, Nitze continued,

> The issue here is whether we are really satisfied with programs which in fact have the objective of making us a sort of hedge-hog, unattractive to attack, but basically not very worrisome over a period of time beyond our immediate position, or whether we take the objectives stated in NSC 20, 68, 114, and 135 sufficiently seriously as to warrant doing what is necessary to give us some chance of seeing those objectives attained.[109]

Appropriately, Truman had the last word. Whether he had fully understood or accepted the rollback objective of NSC 68 is not known. In his farewell address on January 15, 1953, however, he sounded more like Kennan than like NSC 68 (and Nitze) on this issue:

> As the free world grows stronger, more united, more attractive to men on both sides of the Iron Curtain—and as Soviet hopes for easy expansion are blocked—there will then have to come a time of change in the Soviet world. Nobody can say for sure

when that is going to be, or exactly how it will come about, whether by revolution, or trouble in the satellite states, or by a change inside the Kremlin. . . . With patience and courage, we shall some day move on into a new era.[110]

But this issue was not dead. As we shall see, it was aggressively reopened by the JCS in the making of Eisenhower's strategy.

U.S. Defense Strategy and Forces

Through 1952 the JCS adhered to the OFFTACKLE strategy and its premise that the SAC nuclear offensive, despite the growing nuclear arsenal, would not seriously impede a Soviet advance in Europe during the first ninety days. Thus NATO ground forces on the scale called for by MC 26/1 were still essential to prevent the overrunning of most of the continent. Yet the prospect of achieving the requisite forces seemed ever more doubtful and more remote as 1952 wore on.

U.S. Forces

With the "stretch-out" for FY 1953 already discussed, the U.S. buildup seemed to have reached a plateau. In late April 1952 Acheson expressed his concern in instructing a newly appointed Panel of Consultants on Disarmament:

[L]ook at our current armament program to see where it is headed and the consequences. We are moving faster in the atomic field than in other fields but in our general build-up effort it is very possible that we may be breaking ourselves in an effort to do what really can't be done. In short, can we accomplish what we are now undertaking? If not, what alternative roads are open to us?[111]

And in another context about the same time, Secretary of Defense Lovett said "that unless it were possible to rely more and more on atomic weapons as a means of shrinking the size of the military budget, we may well find ourselves running into astronomical rearmament cost figures."[112]

The NSC 135/3 reappraisal in September also found the security situation unsatisfactory. To deter the Soviets, with their expanding nuclear arsenal, from initiating or risking general war, it reaffirmed that the United States and its allies must have "the capability to inflict massive damage on the Soviet war-making capacity," to provide "reasonable initial defense," and to protect the nation during mobilization. "[S]ubstantially improved civil defense" ("air" was dropped) was also essential. Moreover, facing the increased danger that local communist aggression might now present the choice of defeat or general war, the United States must be willing and better prepared to cooperate with allies and strengthen indigenous forces for collective military response, or even to act unilaterally, when in the U.S. interest.

Current efforts, it said, were not sufficient in view of the rapidly growing Soviet atomic capability and the threats in Korea, Southeast Asia, Iran, Egypt, and Berlin. "All of these portents," NSC 135/3 concluded, "underline the risks involved in the projected rates of delivery and in adhering to presently programmed force levels [i.e., the 'stretch-out']." National security programs, it said, could be speeded up and expanded, if necessary, "without serious adverse effects on the U.S. economy."

Consequently, the paper recommended the reexamination of the amounts and allocations of resources for these programs (which became NSC 141). And meanwhile, it urged accelerating the output of "selected military end items."[113]

Despite this call for greater effort, the Truman budget for FY 1954 submitted in January 1953 chose "economy over expansion," in the words of the JCS history. It requested New Obligational Authority of about $40.3 billion for the armed forces, with nearly 42 percent earmarked for the Air Force, though postponing its 143 wings for another year. It estimated defense spending in FY 1954 at $45.5 billion, thereafter falling to about $35–40 billion per year.[114]

In essence, the NSC 141 review concluded that existing security programs were inadequate. Notwithstanding the massive increases in U.S. war-making capabilities, they would not, it asserted, produce the "situation of strength required to attain the objectives of NSC 135/3," nor would greater efficiency or any reallocating of current resources do so. That objective would require selective increases in security programs, which would raise outlays for FY 1954. Thereafter, whether spending would be at the FY 1954 level or higher was uncertain. Even then, however, NSC 135/3 objectives "could not be fully attained within the next two or three years." Indeed, "For some years to come the deterrent power of the United States will reside largely in its ability to deliver an atomic attack of tremendous force upon the Soviet Union." To safeguard that capacity against the growing Soviet nuclear capability would require large additional resources for continental and civil defense (as will be discussed later).[115]

In light of the political and economic constraints on the resources of the NATO partners, moreover, NSC 141 urged the new administration to accept the necessity to assume much of the responsibility for Europe's defense over the next several years, regardless of the United States' own political and economic constraints. Indeed, it recommended that rather than pressuring the European allies to increase their military contributions, the U.S. should concentrate on preventing cuts in their current programs and agree to allocate more military equipment for their use. Further, in order to cope with the "most immediate threat" for the next few years, the United States should also commit greater resources to strengthening indigenous forces in the Middle East and, even more so, in the Far East.[116]

NATO Strategy and Forces

During 1952, according to the official JCS history, "A loss of momentum became apparent in every aspect of NATO's activities."[117] Soon after the February meeting in Lisbon, the Europeans were retreating from the reduced force goals adopted there. The French, suffering the steady drain from their involvement in Indochina, pressed the concept of burden sharing in NATO to increase U.S. military assistance. In Great Britain, Prime Minister Winston Churchill was determined to reduce British defense spending to ease the severe strain on the balance of payments and the economy. For months during the summer and fall, the Treasury, Defense, Foreign Office, and Chiefs of Staff debated how far the defense budget could be curtailed without undue risk. The British Global Strategy Paper (discussed later) was in part prompted by this crisis. U.S. MDAP aid was lagging seriously: shipments to the Europeans through January 1953 amounted to only $3.2 billion of the $11.2 billion allocated.[118]

And the plans for rearming West Germany were virtually stalled. The European Defense Community (EDC) treaty and the related contractual agreements ending the German occupation regime had been signed on May 26 and 27, 1952. By the end of 1952, however, the ratification of the EDC treaty was blocked in France by the Gaullists and opponents of rearming Germany, and in Germany, by the maneuvering of the Social Democratic Party (SPD).[119]

Nuclear Weapons and NATO Strategy

Inevitably, the steady slippage in meeting NATO's conventional force goals heightened interest in the potential role of nuclear weapons in NATO defense. In fact, the final resolution at Lisbon noted that "the TCC report and other NATO studies to date have not taken into account in detail the effects" of nuclear weapons and techniques and directed that NATO planning should do so as soon as possible.[120]

Actually, Eisenhower, as SACEUR, had sought at least since October 1951 JCS authority and an agreement on procedures for integrating into NATO conventional defenses tactical nuclear weapons, as available, and SAC's retardation mission. These efforts were impeded by the strict secrecy and ban on sharing restricted data with foreigners imposed by the McMahon Act. Moreover, U.S. civilian leaders and the JCS also preferred to downplay this prospect for fear of reducing the pressure on the Europeans to fulfill the conventional force goals, especially since tactical nuclear weapons were not expected to be available in quantity until 1955–56.[121]

To carry out the Lisbon resolution, however, the Standing Group (SG) at NAC request prepared a study of the effect of "new weapons" on NATO force requirements and asked the JCS to review it. In June the JCS response (SG 201) essentially reiterated the concepts underlying OFFTACKLE: that new (i.e., strategic and tactical nuclear) weapons did not justify any "great change at present in force requirements" because massive Soviet forward stockpiles were adequate to support their advance into Europe for 90 days or more despite the SAC nuclear offensive. And tactical atomic weapons, while not yet tested under combat conditions, were unlikely to reduce materially force requirements for the first phase of the land battle.[122] In effect, the JCS reaffirmed the force goals of MC 26/1 for 1954: 98 divisions (ready and reserve) and 9,285 aircraft.

Meanwhile, the British Chiefs of Staff completed their 1952 Global Strategy Paper, a critique of NATO strategy for Churchill. Its conclusions clashed sharply with those of the JCS. Its thesis was that the OFFTACKLE strategy and the NATO force goals did not take due account of the impact of the SAC offensive, which would so devastate Soviet "vital centers" in the first few weeks as to render the Soviets incapable of "waging a full scale war." Thus the conventional force goals set by the MTDP or those agreed to at Lisbon were higher than needed to repel the Soviet advance, as well as beyond the NATO members' resources. "The Allies cannot afford — nor should they attempt — to superimpose a new atomic strategy upon the old traditional strategy." Moreover, even with the growing Soviet nuclear arsenal, the prospect of devastating retaliation would be an effective deterrent. "The likely prospect is for a long, drawn-out cold war."[123]

Yet to enhance the deterrent and insure against war by miscalculation, "the Free World must make proper preparation against a possible war" on a basis that could be sustained indefinitely. Thus the SAC offensive must be complemented by sufficient "land and air forces in a high state of readiness in Western Europe, supported by atomic air power," to convince the Soviets that their advance will be retarded enough to "enable the Allied air offensive to be effective before Europe has been over-run." Some increase in the present allied strength would be essential.[124]

In July 1952 Marshal John Slessor of the Royal Air Force presented the Global Strategy Paper to the JCS. The service chiefs were not persuaded that the SAC would be "decisive" in view of "modern defensive measures"; and atomic weapons would not be plentiful enough for tactical use until 1955.[125] Bradley agreed, however, to instruct General Matthew Ridgway, who had succeeded Eisenhower as SACEUR, to study the effect of tactical nuclear weapons on NATO force goals after 1956. Contrary to British hopes, Ridgway made it clear that his report would not be ready in time to influence the force goals for 1953 and 1954.[126]

This issue, nevertheless, shaped the agenda for NATO's December 1952 Annual Review, which had been expected to assess progress and set force goals for 1953 ("firm"), 1954 ("provisional"), and 1955 ("planning"). Substantial progress had been achieved on the 1952 force goals; the M-day goal of 25 divisions had been been met, the M-30 goal of 51 2/3 was about 10 percent short, and aircraft about 20 percent below target. While the United States was ready to approve future force goals 10 to 15 percent below Lisbon, resistance by Britain and others forced the Americans to agree to postpone setting these goals until a later meeting.[127] Moreover, the meeting brought out the serious divergences on major issues affecting future NATO strategy and the buildup among the NATO members, especially between the views of the United States and SACEUR and those of the United Kingdom. The unresolved disputed issues included the risk of deliberate Soviet aggression, the impact of nuclear weapons, the balancing of military security against economic constraints, and whether NATO should focus mainly on fighting a short, hot war or deterrence for a long, cold one. The conclusion of the official JCS history was sweeping: "Thus, during 1950–1952, strategic dilemmas [of NATO] remained unresolved."[128]

The December 1952 meeting left Acheson profoundly distressed. "It was plain to us that a reaction was underway in NATO from the high moment of renewed energy and hope at Lisbon." The force goals planned for 1953 and 1954 would not be met; there was a "growing belief that military plans were outgrowing the economic means to execute them." For Acheson, the outlook was grim: "Now momentum in Europe was being lost and retrogression had set in to the point of threatening disaster. . . . [I]f the European effort [to create a strong unified community] should fall apart, the whole business of our supporting effort would disintegrate."[129]

Nitze was equally troubled by the unresolved strategic dilemmas. In his memorandum of January 12, 1953, commenting on NSC 141, he wrote that "its tone" did not reflect his "serious concern about the implications of atomic developments." He said:

For some time to come (perhaps indefinitely assuming a continuance of present programs), the U.S. would be heavily dependent on the atomic threat to deter the Soviet Union from attempting to expand into areas of vital importance and on the strategic use of atomic weapons if it is to achieve military victory in the event of a general war.

While Soviet nuclear capacity to injure the United States was growing rapidly, the growth of America's offensive capacity was being offset by the improving Soviet defenses against SAC penetration. Further, a vulnerable SAC might never leave the ground in case of surprise attack. These facts were not generally realized within the government, Nitze claimed. Would its growing vulnerability inhibit the United States from threatening or using such weapons except against a direct atomic attack? And would allies in Western Europe and Japan, too near to Soviet bases for effective warning or defense, become unwilling to face a Soviet threat? These ominous implications, though of the "utmost delicacy," should be frankly confronted: "[T]he survival of the nation may depend on our preparedness to deal with [such] a situation." NSC 141, Nitze wrote, did not deal with the implications for U.S. forces, such as dispersal of airfields, or new tactics and techniques.

It would be in the interest of the United States and its allies, Nitze advised, "to develop such conventional forces that we would not be dependent for victory in the event of global war on the use of atomic weapons, particularly against strategic targets. . . . It will be a large task to overcome this dependence, but I believe it can be done." Strangely, he made no mention of the experience since mid-1950.

NSC 141, Nitze wrote, also did not discuss whether atomic plenty would allow such weapons to be used tactically to enhance the capability of limited conventional forces, especially in local situations. America's "great superiority in numbers" would make it to our advantage. Still, he added, "[i]t is difficult to see, however, how a precise dividing line can be drawn, or lived up to, separating tactical from strategic uses."[130]

The memorandum transmitting NSC 141 to the president expressed regret that lack of time prevented consideration in greater depth and precision of such "basic questions" as the "impact on our strategy and programs of modern atomic weapons."[131] That, of course, had been the mandate for NSC 68.

Default on Continental Defense

NSC 68 stipulated that it was essential "to provide an adequate defense against air attack in the United States."[132] Yet by the fall of 1952, despite the concern about Soviet surprise attack, little had been achieved on air defense. The capabilities for early warning and air defense were "extremely meager," according to the NSC "Key Data Book" prepared for the president.[133] NSC 135/3 called for "substantially improved civil defense" while warning against devoting undue resources to this purpose, apparently reflecting the JCS concern that air defense might divert resources from offensive forces.[134]

In September 1952 the serious neglect of continental defense was brought to the fore during the discussion of NSC 135 by Jack Gorrie, head of the National Security Resources Board (NSRB), which was responsible for civil defense. In memoranda to the NSC on September 2 and 24, he insisted 1) that civil defense was futile without adequate active continental defense against an attack; 2) that present and planned active defenses were entirely inadequate; 3) that such a defensive system would be an essential complement to offensive forces to deter and prevent decisive nuclear surprise; and 4) that according to qualified scientific and engineering studies, an effective system for three to six hours of warning and defense in depth could be constructed at reasonable cost within two to three years. It should be built, he urged, with "utmost urgency" and "highest priority."[135]

At the NSC meeting on September 3, Secretary Lovett queried the feasibility and effectiveness of a defensive system, said that Defense had for two years enlisted some of the best scientists to work on the problem, but insisted that progress was slow and difficult. The president said he had been "startled" that morning by a briefing on the problem and concluded that "there wasn't very much of a defense in prospect except a vigorous offensive." Lovett favored accelerating the nation's offensive capacity.[136]

At the September 24 NSC meeting, Gorrie circulated his second memorandum and forcefully restated his points. The president now "thought the subject of Mr. Gorrie's remarks and his memorandum, was of greatest importance." The deputy secretary of defense said that "other scientists of equal repute" disputed the technical feasibility and that the costs were greatly underestimated. The president directed the Department of Defense (DOD) to make an urgent survey "of the feasibility and cost of such an improved continental early warning system."[137]

On October 14 the NSC met to hear and discuss the DOD briefing on their study of a Continental Early Warning System. The DOD recommended equipping and manning four experimental warning stations, using new technologies, but did not favor the "crash implementation" advocated by Gorrie and some scientists. Instead, the DOD recommended "a somewhat slow expansion of the funds" for this purpose. The president closed by asking the DOD and NSRB to prepare a joint recommendation for him. Afterward, Undersecretary David Bruce, who attended for State, urged the president to instruct the DOD to give "an overriding priority" to the project.[138] In mid-November a PPS paper recommended that the DOD be directed to install an early warning system by December 31, 1954, using up to $120 million from FY 1953 funds.[139]

The NSC returned to the subject when it met on November 26 to consider a report on a net evaluation of the Soviet capability to injure the United States, which had been commissioned 15 months earlier. When that report was found inadequate, an interagency Special Evaluation Subcommittee, headed by Lt. General Idwal H. Edwards, was appointed on January 19, 1953, to prepare a more comprehensive evaluation by May 15, 1953.[140]

Finally, NSC 141, the report by Acheson, Lovett, and Harriman on resource allocations among security programs, concluded that continental and civil defense programs at current levels involved "critical risks" and recommended "large additional resources" for those programs. But they stressed that these were "new and distinct requirements" that must have new, *additional* funding. Echoing the DOD, NSC 141 warned that "we must not sacrifice our capacity of projecting our power abroad by concentrating too heavily on the purely defensive aspects of our security." Amazingly, they had reached no conclusion, they conceded, as to how far these programs should be undertaken if new funding was not provided.[141] This judgment—in such sharp contrast to the priority urged by Gorrie, Bruce, Nitze, and others—suggests that these officials really did not grasp the urgency of the issue. With these mixed messages, the Truman administration passed the problem to Eisenhower, having launched a study essential for its solution.

Reprise

The Truman legacy was a mixture of great achievement and serious flaws. In his farewell address in January 1953 Truman took legitimate pride in having confronted the Soviet threat. During its first phase, particularly from 1947–1950, his administration had put in place critical components for the containing the U.S.S.R. Having identified the Soviet Union as hostile and expansionist, Truman and his advisors, especially Kennan as head of PPS and Marshall as secretary of state, recognized that the first essential was to strengthen the noncommunist nations to enable their governments and societies to frustrate Soviet efforts at subversion, infiltration, and intimidation. Focusing initially on Western Europe and Japan, the United States helped to restore prosperity, stability, and confidence by the Truman Doctrine, the Marshall Plan, the Berlin airlift, and the North Atlantic Treaty. By early 1949 Truman had extended U.S. concern to include the developing countries with the modest Point Four program for technical assistance to help them to overcome their poverty and bolster their capacity for resistance to Soviet subversion.

In its effort to strengthen the West and its cohesion, the Truman administration skillfully moved to integrate the former enemies, West Germany and Japan, into the West, and to foster steps toward European unity. That the ultimate failure of EDC did not derail this initiative or the rearming of Germany was testimony to the basic soundness of this course. In this first period, the U.S. nuclear monopoly had neutralized concern about a Soviet military threat and led to Truman's tightly constrained defense budgets.

By mid-1950, however, the Soviet nuclear test, the Communist takeover of China, and the Korean War opened a new stage in the cold war, and in the Truman strategy, with the adoption of NSC 68 and the frantic military buildup by the United States and NATO. During the final two and one-half years the record became much more confused and much less coherent. The North Korean invasion had been defeated; U.S. forces had more than doubled; and NATO had been transformed into a well-organized coalition whose military strength, though well short of its goals and imposing severe strains on European economies, had been enhanced. But if Europe was more secure, many less developed nations were unstable and in ferment, and therefore potentially vulnerable to Soviet subversion. Among the more troubling areas as Truman left office were Iran, Indochina, Egypt and the Middle East, and Guatemala.

As the defense buildup proceeded, there developed growing disparity between the avowed objectives of NSC 68 and the actual forces, priorities, and budgets. In the end, the objectives of NSC 68—notably across-the-board preponderance, less reliance on nuclear weapons, and rollback—proved impractical or illusory, producing disarray and incoherence in policies, programs, and strategy.

Eisenhower was fully cognizant of Truman's contribution in establishing the basic containment strategy. Indeed, the next chapter will develop his substantial role in and support for much of it. But it will demonstrate as well his keen awareness of the contradictions and disarray in the objectives and implementing policies, especially in the second phase. His task, as he saw it, was to adapt the positive legacy to new conditions and clear away the confusion, in order to develop a coherent strategy to maintain a secure peace on a basis sustainable by the United States and its allies for the long haul.

2

The Prepresidential Eisenhower

My first day at the president's desk. Plenty of worries and difficult problems. But such has been my portion for a long time—the result is that this just seems (today) like a continuation of all I've been doing since July 1941—even before that.[1]

Dwight D. Eisenhower (1953)

The convictions and preferences Eisenhower brought to the White House derived from his reflections during a long and varied prepresidential career. With much broader experience in military and foreign affairs than any twentieth-century U.S. president, he developed strong opinions about the meaning of national security and how best to achieve it, the hierarchy of American interests and the threats to them, the requisites of national and international leadership, the nature of war, and even the future of civilization. As a consequence, he shared many of the fundamental premises of the Truman administration, in which he was actively involved. But, as foreshadowed in the previous chapter, he disagreed sharply with others, and was personally frustrated by the short-comings in consistency and implementation.

Eisenhower's preexisting beliefs and core values provided a framework for but did not determine the New Look strategy. He instituted, managed, and responded to a policy-making process that drew heavily on his bureaucratic expertise and ensured consideration of situational factors—both foreign and domestic. What Eisenhower believed prior to becoming president, nevertheless, and what he felt and thought influenced how he interpreted the world around him and acted to shape it.[2]

Eisenhower's Formative Experience

Raised in America's rural heartland and gifted with a highly analytical and logical mind, Eisenhower found that his peripatetic career after graduating from West Point constituted a prolonged tutorial. He served under the leading military minds of the era—Generals John J. Pershing, Fox Connor, and Douglas MacArthur—and graduated first in his class of 275 from the Fort Leavenworth Command and General Staff School. Following Japan's attack on Pearl Harbor, Army Chief of Staff

41

General George Marshall chose Eisenhower to head the War Plans Division of the War Department. Soon thereafter President Franklin Roosevelt named him to lead the assault on North Africa and the campaign in Italy. In 1944 Roosevelt selected Eisenhower the Supreme Allied Commander in Europe, charged with Operation Overlord, the cross-channel invasion of France. Long before he marched triumphantly down the Champs-Elysées and led the drive into Germany, Eisenhower was a household name with political magic.[3]

The experience Eisenhower gained from his diverse posts extended well beyond that normally associated with military service. He once described his duties as MacArthur's chief aide, both in Washington and the Philippines, as "beginning to verge on the political, even to the edge of partisan politics."[4] From the start in North Africa, moreover, his World War II command responsibilities grew. "Soldiering is no longer a simple thing of shouting 'Turn boys turn!'" he wrote his wife in mid-1942. I "must be a bit of a diplomat—lawyer—promoter—salesman—social hound—*liar* (at least to get out of social affairs)—mountebank—actor—Simon Legree—humanitarian—orator—and incidentally (sometimes I think most damnably incidentally) a soldier!"[5]

Eisenhower's on-the-job training did not end with the war. Following the Nazi surrender and Truman's succession to the presidency, he remained in Germany as military governor at the start of the period of occupation. His duties placed him at the center of the controversies that intensified in proportion to Soviet-American hostility. Already stung by criticism for having refused to race the Russians to Berlin, Eisenhower came under more fire after he relieved General George Patton for defying the official policy of denazification and, pursuant to the Yalta agreements, he ordered the repatriation of Soviet soldiers from America's zone of occupation. He did not need additional schooling in the relationship between politics and national security; he received it nonetheless.

Eisenhower's education continued, and his discontent with the policy-making process intensified, after he reluctantly agreed in late 1945 to succeed Marshall as Army chief of staff. He was constantly confronted, he said, with "personal hatreds, political and partisan prejudices, ignorance, [and] opposing ideologies." He estimated the consequences as "far more frustrations than progress."[6] He was too modest. Although he failed to persuade Congress to enact a program of universal military training, Eisenhower orchestrated the demobilization of America's armed forces at a rate compatible with their peacetime missions but unsatisfactory to impatient Americans. More significant, in his view, was his role in helping to craft the provisions of the 1947 National Security Act intended to promote better coordination within the Armed forces by institutional reform. For this purpose, the Act created the Department of Defense and placed within it the Departments of the Army, Navy, and Air Force (now separate from the Army). Although it gave DOD less authority over the services than Eisenhower considered necessary, he hoped it would foster the kind of teamwork among them that he had long considered essential for their efficiency, effectiveness, and ultimate power, and could be stengthened later.

The increased unification of America's military, in Eisenhower's judgment, came none to soon. While Eisenhower was Army chief of staff, the cold war erupted in earnest. As discussed, in response to the Soviet-American face-off in Iran,

the progressive descent of the Iron Curtain in Europe, and the increasing vulnerability of Greece and Turkey, President Harry S. Truman announced the Truman
Doctrine and promulgated the European Recovery Program.[7] Even as his anxiety
over Truman's strategic sophistication heightened, Eisenhower's hope that the
Moscow-Washington wartime entente could endure evaporated.

In 1948, the year of the Communist coup in Czechoslovakia and the Soviet
blockade of Berlin, Eisenhower retired from active duty to assume the presidency
of Columbia University. He intended to devote himself to educating Americans to
be better citizens of the nation and the world. His divorce from the military, however, was hardly complete. Within months he agreed to Secretary of Defense James
Forrestal's request that he temporarily chair the Joint Chiefs of Staff until Congress
legislated the creation of a permanent one. Eisenhower shuttled back and forth between New York and Washington for much of 1949, negotiating successfully a compromise budget between the Truman administration and the warring service chiefs.
The process reinforced his contempt for institutional parochialism and his growing
conviction that future defense planning must stress the deterrent value of strategic
air power.

Duty called again in 1950. At the end of the previous year the Soviets successfully tested an atomic bomb and China fell to the Communists. Then in June came
the outbreak of war in Korea. Fearful that the Kremlin would perceive the American deployment to the Far East as an opportunity to attack Europe, Truman asked
Eisenhower to serve as the first supreme allied commander (SACEUR) of the em-
bryonic North Atlantic Treaty Organization's (NATO's) armed forces. Already an
avid proponent of collective security, Eisenhower was convinced by events that he
must continue to serve the nation and its allies as the U.S. defense budget spiraled
and the rise of Joseph McCarthy and the firing of General Douglas MacArthur exacerbated partisan divisions. There existed the danger, Eisenhower feared, that the
Republican Party would call into question America's commitment to Europe at the
very time that it was most needed. To avoid this catastrophe, he finally conceded,
he had to run for the presidency. In 1952 he returned to the United States to campaign for the Republican nomination.

Eisenhower was not one of the key figures—the so-called "wise men"—who formulated America's foreign policies in the immediate postwar era.[8] But in one capacity or another, he spent the years prior to running for the presidency intimately
involved with designing, budgeting for, and executing them. In doing so he sharpened beliefs and skills that had been germinating over three decades. They provide
the context for examining his conduct and policies as president.

Eisenhower's Concept of National Security

Eisenhower's guiding principle was that specific policy decisions had to be made
within the framework of a coherent strategic concept. That concept, moreover, had
to result from a realistic examination of threats, objectives, and priorities, and an
objective appraisal of the means and support required to achieve them. It had to be
articulated, moreover, with sufficient clarity to generate the understanding and

backing of the national and international public, and with the precision necessary to inform deliberations at subordinate as well as top levels of government.

The foundation of America's strategic concept, it followed, must be an enlightened appreciation of what constituted national security. And in Eisenhower's view, strategists must recognize that national security embraced a broad range of interests, especially a healthy economy. His years in the Pentagon caused him to worry that Americans would fail to "face up to the problem arising out of the conflicting considerations of national security on the one hand and economic and financial solvency on the other." As he wrote his wartime aide Walter Bedell ("Beetle") Smith in 1947, there was "very obviously a definite limit to our resources." He feared, therefore, "internal deterioration through the annual expenditure of unconscionable sums on a [defense] program of indefinite duration, extending far into the future."[9] In short, because the American economy could crumble under the "crushing weight of military power," strategists must recognize that "national security and national solvency are mutually dependent."[10]

Along with the economy, what also could crumble were the core values and democratic institutions that government programs were intended to promote and protect. The imposition of price controls, rationing, and even censorship that would surely result from a peacetime defense posture that was as expensive as it was unenlightened could "do permanent damage to our system" by making a mockery of "the assurances and safeguards of our Constitution."[11] In a long, soul-searching letter to a private in the infantry, Eisenhower waxed eloquent. "True human objectives comprise something far richer and more constructive than mere survival of the strong," he wrote. "The theory of defense against aggressive threat must comprehend more than simple self-preservation; the security of spiritual and cultural values, including national and individual freedom, human rights, and the history of our nation and our civilization, are included."[12] To a joint session of Congress Eisenhower spoke similarly: When "we talk about defending the free world, we are not merely talking about defense in the terms of divisions and battleships and planes. We are talking about what is in our hearts, what we understand with our heads, and what we are going to do as a body."[13]

It was in fact while serving as Army chief of staff in 1947 that Eisenhower conceptualized what would be known as the "Great Equation," which included a list of variables more expansive than the military and economic ones written about during his presidency.[14] He worried that the Truman administration failed to appreciate this breadth. "Assistance to Greece and Turkey is important to the security of the United States," he told to his Pentagon bosses within a day of Truman's declaration of the doctrine that would bear his name. But this assistance must encompass "political, economic, and psychological" as well as military "factors." Of these the "greatest factor of all," Eisenhower concluded, is "the human spirit. . . . Without this, no amount of military strength can preserve freedom."[15]

The outbreak of the Korean War and difficulties of his NATO command led Eisenhower to refine his formula. By the time he made up his mind to run for office, it had become elegant in its simplicity. "Spiritual force, multiplied by economic force, multiplied by military force, is roughly equal to security," he said to Lucius Clay. "If one of these factors falls to zero, or near zero, the resulting product does likewise."[16] What concerned Eisenhower was that the guardians of the national security would forget that "[t]he purpose of America is to defend a way of life rather than merely to defend property, homes, or lives."[17]

National Defense

Not that Eisenhower was unconcerned with American and allied defense capabilities or the strategic balance. During the early years of the cold war, no one was more committed to the tenet of peace through strength. "We must hew to the line of principle and be in position to sustain our strength," Eisenhower said shortly after accepting the offer from Columbia's trustees in 1947. "Anything less will mean merely a succession of new Munichs, finally war under conditions least favorable to us."[18] His memoir of World War II, published the next year, ended with a warning of the dangers inherent in deficient military capability.[19]

Yet Eisenhower was acutely aware that his definition of strength differed fundamentally from the majority in the Pentagon. Because he was so intimately familiar with orthodox strategic algebra, he was skeptical of it. As Eisenhower put it with typical understatement a year before his inauguration, "I know something of the *methods* of making such [military] estimates."[20]

He also knew something about military planning. Eisenhower had learned during his years in Washington that bureaucrats normally requested greater appropriations than they expected to receive. He was convinced, nevertheless, that the inflated amount of the military's requests was due to more than standard negotiating tactics. Each service chief resisted correlating his budgets with an integrated strategic concept. The root cause, Eisenhower argued, was institutional loyalty. Indeed, he characterized the military's opposition to unification as "the most intensive campaign of special interest that I have seen in Washington."[21] The implications for the budgetary process became that much more apparent to Eisenhower when, as previously mentioned, he sought to fashion a compromise when he temporarily chaired of the JCS in 1949. Each service, according to Eisenhower, measured "its importance to the country in terms of the size of its" appropriations. As a consequence, each devoted more effort to "selling" than "critical analysis & logical conclusion."[22]

The result, from Eisenhower's point of view, was that defense spending became the barometer for national security. Strategists, and not just those in the military, paid too little attention to the other variables in his equation: America's morale, its economic vitality, and the like. Further, the incessant battle among the services for a larger share of defense appropriations undermined long-range planning and was inimical to efficient and rational procurement and production.[23] Eisenhower was so frustrated by the ordeal of negotiating the miltary budget in 1949 that he threatened—at least in private—to "quit & begin criticizing."[24] Of course he did not; not long thereafter he returned to active duty. But before embarking for Europe he testified again to Congress. "We have to devise a scheme that we can support," he said, "if necessary over the next 20 years, 30 years, whatever may be the time necessary, as long as the threat, the announced threat of aggression remains in the world."[25]

Assessing the Soviet Threat

Along with a sophisticated concept of national security and proper management of the military, sound strategy requires a realistic estimate of the enemy threat. According to Eisenhower, the military's proclivity for basing its planning on worst-case scenarios militated against arriving at one. Too often it exaggerated its estimates of adversaries' intentions as well as capabilities. That this was an understandable response to the tragedy of Pearl Harbor and the time it took to retaliate did not in Eisenhower's view make it any less pernicious. Its effect was to underestimate America's strength while simultaneously eroding it.

At the end of World War II, Eisenhower shared the hope of many that a peaceful international order could be structured according to a balance of power among the World War II allies.[26] Gradually, however, he became convinced by Soviet behavior, especially in Eastern Europe, that this hope was unrealistic. History would look favorably on Forrestal's warnings, he wrote as an informal eulogy to the first secretary of defense. In the years ahead the Kremlin would seek continually to expand its influence and control.[27] Like Bohlen, nevertheless, Eisenhower adamantly rejected the thesis that it would rely heavily on military means that increased the risk of general war.

Eisenhower's experience, particularly during the war, deterred him from demonizing the Soviets. Long after the breakdown of the Grand Alliance, Eisenhower considered Marshal Georgi Konstantinovich Zhukov, who led the Soviets' wartime forces, a genuine "friend." In general, he moreover believed, "In his generous instincts, in his love of laughter, in his devotion to a comrade, and in his healthy, direct outlook on the affairs of workaday life the ordinary Russian seems to me to bear a marked similarity to what we call an 'average American.'" He is "naturally friendly."[28]

Eisenhower did not recklessly generalize. He counseled Washington to "distinguish sharply between those who rule and those who are ruled." To fail to make this distinction would be a grave mistake, a lesson Eisenhower learned painfully after Zhukov's banishment to an obscure provincial outpost not long after the war's end.[29] Still, he was persuaded by the brief time he spent with Joseph Stalin in 1945 that even the Soviet dictator had a humane side and concerns other than expansion. As Eisenhower described a four-hour conversation, "damn near all [Stalin] talked about was all the things they needed, the homes, the food, the technical help. He talked to me about 7 people living in a single room in Moscow just as anxiously as you or I'd talk about an American slum problem." This meeting made an indelible impression on the future president. Eisenhower recalled it repeatedly, and years after the event.[30]

Eisenhower was probably more impressed by what he had seen of the cost to Russia of the German invasion, a cost that surely heightened the Soviets' sense of vulnerability. He vividly recollected his flight back to Berlin after his August 1945 visit with Stalin in Moscow. The general could not get over the devastation he witnessed from the air. "From the region of the Volga westward," Eisenhower wrote in his memoir, "almost everything was destroyed. . . . I did not see a house standing between the western borders of the country and the area around Moscow."[31]

These scenes of destruction, combined with his image of the Soviets and the inferences he drew from "Marxist-Leninist-Stalinist doctrine," convinced Eisenhower that Stalin and his subordinates would not resort to war to achieve expansionist objectives. "These Communists are not early Christian martyrs," Eisenhower wrote. They were too rational and pragmatic to jeopardize their country's or their regime's security (and "their necks") after having barely survived the Nazi onslaught. "Make no mistake, they like their jobs," Eisenhower said of Stalin and the Kremlin. They also "know the lesson of Napoleon, of Hitler, of Mussolini." This could lead to but one conclusion: "I cannot see them starting a war merely for the opportunity that such a conflict might offer their successors to spread their doctrine." Instead, they would, he forecast, cautiously bide their time, probing, subverting, "poisoning men's minds" through "lying propaganda," "false promises," and other means of manipulating international opinion.[32] In a January 1951 lecture to the National War College Rear Admiral Leslie C. Stevens argued that the "national strategy" of the Soviets "does not contemplate any g[l]obal war of her own choosing" because the "risk of losing is too great." Eisenhower wrote in the margin of his copy of the text, "I've preached [this] for 5 years!"[33]

Eisenhower's confidence in his ability to take the measure of America's adversaries buttressed his faith that the United States would ultimately prevail in the bipolar contest.[34] He never swerved from his conviction that the free world was stronger than the Soviet bloc and that Communist Russia itself would inevitably explode — or implode. The "tyranny and threat represented in the announced and implacable antagonism of Communism to our form of goverment *will not always be with us*," he predicted. "The practice of their Godless doctrine of Communism carries within itself the seed of its own destruction."[35]

In this regard Eisenhower believed as firmly in inexorable historical processes as did any Marxist. "Communism and slavery are synonymous," he said, and "the history of mankind proves that all systems of slavery sooner or later are destroyed, usually from internal convulsion." History likewise taught, he told Bedell Smith after the latter took up his post as ambassador in Moscow, that "all conquerors, from the days of the Persians . . . finally absorb so much territory that the dissident populations cannot be digested." Americans should keep these "lesson[s] of the past . . . before our eyes constantly."[36]

Because of his definition of national security and the Great Equation, Eisenhower was certain that in "total assets" the United States is "immeasurably stronger than the Iron Curtain countries." America's strength derived from its "(1) complete devotion to democracy, which means a faith in men as men (essentially a religious concept) and practice of free enterprise . . . ; (2) industrial and economic strength; (3) moral probity in all dealings; (4) [and only lastly] necessary military strength." The Kremlin's need to rule the "backward" Soviets by "organized threat," conversely, would remain a source of inherent weakness. "If we can be strong enough," he was therefore confident, "if we endure enough, we can wait for the inevitable explosive process to take effect."[37]

But victory in the cold war would not come quickly. Americans would be foolish, Eisenhower felt, to expect "Communistic Russia" to "relax its pressure against us as long as we were exponents of free government."[38] Except "to gain time," the

Soviets would never accept "a reasonable and practical basis for living together in the world," he advised President Truman.[39] Temporary settlements, nevertheless, including those achieved through formal negotiations, could make less dangerous the "colossal problem" of "co-existence between free government and dictatorship." And if the United States and its allies behaved intelligently as well as vigorously, if they husbanded and exploited their assets, in the end the Soviet system would collapse under the weight of its inherent contradictions and "imperial overstretch."[40]

Eisenhower on War

Eisenhower's prognosis for the outcome of a hot war was, in contrast, unambiguously grim. He was among the first of the postwar strategists to acknowledge that with the dawn of the atomic age, the ultimate certainty of mutual vulnerability to intolerable destruction inverted the relationship between force and diplomacy. As Army chief of staff in 1946 he read a draft of Bernard Brodie's seminal treatise on the nuclear revolution, which he distributed to his staff.[41] By the time he ran for president, he had concluded that "[m]odern [general] war" was no longer "a conceivable choice in framing national policy."[42] Deterrence, therefore, of both Soviet aggression and general war, had to be America's number one priority.

Eisenhower arrived at this point of view incrementally and logically. The lesson he learned from reading Clausewitz's *On War* three times as a young officer in Panama serving under Fox Connor was that the maxim that war is but the extension of politics by other means must not be divorced from the parallel one: the means must be in proportion to ends.[43] What Eisenhower came to realize was that the nuclear revolution made this proportional relationship impossible. As he wrote to his son, John S. D. Eisenhower, as early as 1946, "The readiness of people to discuss war as a means of advancing peace . . . is a contradiction in terms."[44]

Although Eisenhower did not participate in Truman's decision to drop the atomic bomb on the Japanese, he recalled that at a meeting with Secretary of War Henry Stimson following the successful test in New Mexico he "voiced to him my grave misgivings." Indeed, years after the fact he still doubted that it had been "necessary to hit them with that awful thing."[45] These doubts, however, had nothing to do with the viewpoint on atomic warfare he formulated between Hiroshima and the White House. One could not define America's national security as Eisenhower did and sanction a general war with the Soviet Union that, he was sure, would entail the use of nuclear weapons, as a viable means to protect it. General war "would do unthinkable damage to every moral and material value we cherish," he said. Not only was it the "greatest cancer that continues to consume the substance of human society" and "the most dreadful thing to which men can resort," war in the atomic age was also "completely stupid" and "futile." After all, "even the physical destruction of the centers of Communistic authority and industrial production would still leave us a chaotic world."[46]

Yet Eisenhower saw a silver lining. Driven by his perception of the Soviets and estimate of the threat they posed, he argued, as discussed earlier, that Stalin and his Kremlin cohorts shared his horrific outlook on general war. The "possibility of total destruction, terrible though it is, could be a blessing," he said. "Confronted by that outcome to another world war, all of us, East and West, are in the same boat." To Eisenhower the logic was inescapable. The Russians will not "engage in global war because nobody would win it," he predicted to the journalist Arthur Krock.[47]

America's policy makers, however, either underestimated Kremlin's pragmatism or for political reasons chose to minimize it. Either way, their alarmism approached—and created throughout the nation—a "hysterical fear" that undermined the nation's strategic superiority by generating policies and postures that sapped America's most vital assets. "Fear, induced by peril is a climate that fosters militarism," Eisenhower explained in a public address. Fear also "nourishes bankruptcy in dollars and morals alike" and "is as costly in its toll on material resources, on lives, on the spirit of men as defeat in war. In an era of chronic fear can be heard the death rattle of a nation."[48]

Intertwined with these concerns was Eisenhower's anxiety over a potential "powder keg" war, a war that would arise through miscalculation as opposed to deliberate initiation. Or panic could lead to overreaction. With talk of a preventive war circulating in Washington, he could only assume that the same was true in Moscow. Even before the Soviets successfully detonated an atomic device in 1949, Eisenhower considered this thinking absurd. "[T]here is no such thing as preventive war," he remarked, "at least against a great and monolithic power such as exists in Eurasia today." But it was equally absurd to contemplate seriously that the United States either retreat from the Soviet menace or simply succumb to wishful thinking.

What was required, according to Eisenhower's logic, was a strong defense posture that signaled resolve and foreclosed windows of opportunity. He saw "no recourse for the free world," Eisenhower wrote, "but [to] develop a security situation which Russia *must* respect, which it will not attack." If that posture exceeded what was required for these purposes, however, it might be misconstrued as evidence of aggressive intent. Insecure to begin with, and largely ignorant of all things Western, the Kremlin was particularly susceptible to this "security dilemma."[49]

Strategy for the Atomic Age

The riddle confronting America's national security planners, then, was how to prevail in a cold war while preventing it from turning hot. Eisenhower conceded that there "is no completely clear cut solution." His experience and reflections about the variables that comprised the national security equation, nevertheless, produced for him a creed: the United States needed a comprehensive, integrated, and coherent strategy that established objectives for the long and short term, set priorities, exploited opportunities and assets, and took into account America's finite resources and the limits on what it could expect to accomplish. Security managers in Washington must "put our consoli[d]ated professional brains to the job" of devising a general plan based on "the areas in which we can concentrate most advantageously."[50]

That plan must be also based on a "middle line" between "desirable strength and unbearable cost."[51] Because this middle line required the contributions and cooperation of America's allies, Eisenhower dismissed talk about a U.S. "Gibralter" as "nonsense." The "simple and stark" reality of the "polarity of world power," from his point of view, demanded military outposts throughout the globe, and these outposts must be manned primarily by the native populations. Even more important, "as democracy is weakened anywhere else in the world, it is weakened here." It "would be impossible," he argued, "for even a country so great as ours to live as an island of democracy in a surrounding sea of dictatorship." Consequently, the United States as well as the other world "democracies must learn that the world is now too small for the rigid concepts of national sovereignty that developed in a time when nations were self-sufficient and self-dependent for their own well being and safety," Eisenhower wrote in his World War II memoir. "None of them today can stand alone."[52]

Eisenhower devoted one of his most inspirational and eloquent speeches—his Guildhall address in London in June 1945—to the theme of collective security, and the rivalries and distrust within Western Europe became his constant postwar lament.[53] It is a "sad commentary on the state of the world that we had to spend so much of our energy at this time on building up [the] defenses of Europe," he said to Truman and Acheson in January 1951. In light of its "350 million people, tremendous industrial capacity, and highly skilled and educated population," why "is there so great a fear of Russia?" he asked. The "answer was simple: There is unity on the part of the Russians and disunity on the part of the West."[54]

Eisenhower feared that Europe's endemic rivalries would render it perpetually weak and vulnerable. As the ultimate solution, he championed the efforts of Jean Monnet and others to foster European integration. "I think there is no real answer for the European problem until there is definitely established a United States of Europe," the general noted in his diary while commanding NATO's forces. Without a concert of Western Europe, which had to include the former German enemy, the billions of dollars spent by the United States for economic recovery and military assistance was "sheer waste." Eisenhower considered the possibility of a unified Europe at least as early as 1948. By the time he ran for president he was wondering—in private—whether the United States should insist on "political and economic federation" among West Germany, the NATO countries, and "(I think) Sweden, Spain, & Jugoslavia, with Greece definitely in if Jugoslavia is. (If *necessary*, U.K. could be omitted)."[55]

But the first order of business had to be to strengthen NATO's military capabilities. Following his appointment as SACEUR, Eisenhower had committed all his energy, resources, and prestige to this goal. For two weeks in January 1951 he publicly toured NATO's European capitals and West Germany, encouraging the military and civilian leadership of each to sacrifice for the common good. Everywhere he preached greater cooperation and contribution. To Eisenhower, a credible NATO defense would do more than deter a Soviet attack. More important, it would create a foundation of confidence and harmony on which the free world could build during the years of East-West conflict that lay ahead.

Indeed, it was primarily as a means to rejuvenate Europe's morale and lubricate its collaboration that Eisenhower implored Washington to commit additional men and materiel to NATO. The United States must lead by example, he told the White House and Congress. He had faith that the Europeans would follow. "What we are trying to do," Eisenhower explained, "is to start a sort of reciprocal action across the Atlantic. We do one thing which inspires our friends to do something, and that gives us greater confidence in their thoroughness, their readiness for sacrifice. We do something more and we establish an upward-going spiral which meets this problem of strength and morale." Once this plan was successful, "most of the danger would end."[56]

Even as he worked to build up NATO Eisenhower expected that the United States would redeploy its forces in inverse proportion to Europe's contribution.[57] He feared that the permanent stationing of U.S. troops on the continent would not only impede the growth of Europe's self-confidence, but it would also generate resentment and friction. No less deleterious to the free world's long-term security would be the excessive drain on America's resources. Over time, Eisenhower was sure, "our people progressively [would have] to accept voluntarily a constantly lowering standard of living." He was equally sure they would not, and their resistance would pose a greater threat to national security than would the Soviet military. A "nation that cannot make a living cannot afford to maintain an adequate strength in military formations," he said. Worse still, "the question would surely occur as to whether there was anything in the country worth defending."[58]

For someone with Eisenhower's beliefs, of course, this question should never arise. And it would not if Washington and its allies followed his prescriptions. That done, the West could concentrate on exposing the hollowness and duplicity of the communist philosophy. Because Eisenhower equated the national interest with the defense of the nation's core values, he defined the cold war as a contest between two visions, two ways of life. Communism should not be able to compete, but the free world was providing the Kremlin and its apostles with the opportunity. Just as in the economic and defense arenas, America was squandering its ideological capital. As a consequence, the "Russians are getting closer to the masses than we are."[59]

By "the masses" Eisenhower meant primarily the peoples of the newly emergent countries and discontented colonies—what became known as the Third World. Consistent with his previous experiences, especially as supreme commander in World War II and in NATO (the Supreme Headquarters Allied Expeditionary Force and Supreme Headquarters Allied Powers in Europe commands) and service as Army chief of staff, Eisenhower concurred with the postwar geopolitical consensus that control over Europe was the sine qua non for control of the Eurasian land mass, and control of Eurasia would be decisive to the cold war's outcome. America's stake in Europe, he therefore held, was of central importance.[60]

These same experiences, nevertheless, impressed upon Eisenhower the increasing interdependence between the world's core and peripheral regions. The inseparability of political economy and strategic concerns, he said, required the developing regions to link their future to the developed ones and to each other. The West's industrial base and potential, the very infrastructure from which so much of its power flowed, was "acutely dependent upon numerous other areas for indispensable raw materials." Many of these existed in virtually inexhaustible supply in Asia, the Middle East, Africa, and Latin America, and access to them "requires, at the very least," that they be kept "outside the domain or control of the [West's] enemies in the Kremlin."[61] Increased economic, political, and cultural intercourse between the core and periphery, moreover, would promote cohesion, prosperity, and confidence to their collective benefit.

Although Eisenhower's direct exposure to the Third World had been limited, it was nevertheless instructive. In particular, his posting to the Philippines in the 1930s, where he engaged in nation-state building as well as defense planning, taught him about the importance of winning the heartfelt allegiance of the indigenous population if security programs were to be at all effective.[62] This conviction drove his prescription for meeting the communist challenge. No less vital than the military instruments of containment would be the expansion of trade and extension of financial and technical assistance. More important still, the West "must not appear before the world as a combination of forces to compel adherence to the status quo." So strongly did Eisenhower feel about the need to embrace the Third World that, if necessary, he was prepared to distinguish the position of the United States from that of European allies who remained wedded to "old prejudices or instinctive reaction." Before taking office, in fact, he expressed the secret hope that Winston Churchill would turn the reins of the Tories over to "younger men" who thought more progressively.[63]

Eisenhower had great faith that by appealing to the cause of freedom, democracy, and individualism, the free world could unmask communism for the oppressive system that it was. But success demanded "our deeds as well as our words" and radically new programs. While the Soviets were experts in the use of agents, skillful propaganda, and bribery, Eisenhower, owing to his wartime experiences, was expert too. He had learned that covert and psychological warfare, as much as the more orthodox type, demanded a strategic concept, detailed planning, careful organization, and skilled personnel. Unfortunately, in this area the U.S. "effort has been far too weak, and probably not directed with the intelligence that we could use now," Eisenhower told Congress. "We have been amateurs in the field and we have not been experts like some of our opponents have been. The minds of men are what we are trying to win." Eisenhower recommended that the United States increase its effort "ten times," but as late as 1952 he said that "the 'typical' military approach was to forget about such unpleasant and such unmilitary activities." He would as president consequently promote psychological warfare and other unconventional tactics.[64]

An illuminating example of Eisenhower's abiding commitment to prosecuting an ideological campaign against the Soviet Union was his acceptance in 1949 of future CIA legend Frank Wisner's invitation to become a sponsoring member of the National Committee for Free Europe, an organization devoted to organizing, supporting, and inspiring "captive peoples" living behind the Iron Curtain.[65] Among the committee's initial activities was the sponsorship of a series of lectures, whose concluding speaker was John Foster Dulles. The organization, Dulles said, reflected his "oft-expressed view that we can only win this 'cold war' if we take the *offensive*; and that we can only win *peacefully* if we take the offensive with moral, and not merely material, weapons." This was Eisenhower's "oft-expressed view" as well.[66]

National Security Management

Eisenhower believed fervently that no strategy could be effective without careful management and strong leadership. And despite the institutional innovations of the Truman presidency — the establishment of the State Department Policy Planning Staff, the National Security Council, the Department of Defense, and the Central Intelligence Agency, for example — he remained dissatisfied with the organization and rigor of the process.[67] In Eisenhower's judgment, the flaws in Truman's advisory structure exacerbated the president's personal limitations. "[P]oor HST," he lamented privately months after the outbreak of the Korean War, "a fine man, who in the middle of a stormy lake knows nothing of swimming. Yet a lot of drowning people are forced to look to him as a lifeguard. If his wisdom could only equal his good intent."[68]

Every policy, every program, and every expenditure, Eisenhower explained during his presidential campaign, must be consistent with "broad national purposes" and "so timed and directed at a principal target, and so related to other government actions, that it will produce a maximum effect." The decisions reached on these purposes and targets, in turn, must guide all subsequent behavior. Thus coordinated implementation must go hand in hand with formulation and planning. Dozens of "criss-crossing and overlapping and jealous" departments, agencies, and bureaus, each of which contributed to the national security agenda, had to act in concert "under an overall scheme of strategy."[69]

But an overall scheme of strategy must not be confused with inflexibility. The fluidity of the environment and unpredictability of circumstances was particularly pronounced in the realm of international and military affairs, especially in light of rapidly changing technologies. As a veteran strategist Eisenhower was acutely aware of the limits of strategy. It must provide direction but not become a straitjacket. Specific decisions and tactics had to be contingent on specific conditions. "Rely on planning," Eisenhower frequently told his associates, "but never trust plans."[70]

Eisenhower was convinced that a methodical and orderly policy-making process allowed the strategist to anticipate as many scenarios as possible. There had to be a chain of command, but there must be no obstacle capable of denying the commander the counsel of each link. Nor must there be any question that the commander was in complete charge. "The one quality that can be developed by studious reflection and practice is the leadership of men," Eisenhower wrote in an unpublished draft of his World War II memoir.[71] Throughout these years he had more opportunities than he wanted for reflection and practice. The difficulties Eisenhower experienced at SHAEF asserting his authority over all elements in his theater, including air power, not to mention his need to control and even override the preferences of field generals like Montgomery, reinforced the distinction between collaboration in decision making and collective decision making. It was standard procedure for Eisenhower to sound out all of his advisors, making every effort to elicit dissent and ensure that each felt satisfied he had had his day in court. But afterward, Eisenhower insisted, only he could choose among the alternatives.

Moreover, only by meeting regularly with his chief subordinates, and sometimes with theirs, could he instill the esprit de corps and sense of involvement essential to promote loyalty—and candor. There must be ample opportunities for the uninhibited, face-to-face exchange of ideas from which all parties would learn. Furthermore, for Eisenhower an orderly process was the sine qua non for protecting a decision against poor execution because of misinterpretation, miscommunication, or ignorance.

Much has been made of the attention Eisenhower paid—both before and after his election as president—to selecting and delegating authority to his subordinates, and rightly so. Certainly influenced by his unique perspective on the contrasting styles of MacArthur and Marshall, he concluded that a leader's effectiveness is dependent on the ability, initiative, self-confidence, and selflessness of his lieutenants, as well as on their respect for their leader. He accordingly considered it critical to assess individual strengths and weaknesses when choosing advisors. He used these same criteria when assigning them their respective functions and responsibilities. To Eisenhower teamwork was the key to the success of any bureaucracy. And, he advised Forrestal, in "organizing teams, personality is equally important with ability. . . . I simply cannot over-stress this point."[72]

3

The Presecretarial Dulles

[John Foster Dulles is] an intensive student of foreign affairs. He is well informed and, in this subject at least, is deserving, I think, of his reputation as a "wise" man. Moreover, he is a dedicated and tireless individual—he passionately believes in the United States, in the dignity of man, and in moral values.[1]

Dwight D. Eisenhower (1953)

E isenhower had voted for Dulles in New York's 1949 special senatorial election primarily because he respected the Republican candidate's lengthy involvement in and study of foreign affairs and his commitment to U.S. internationalism and collective security.[2] The general harmony between their diagnoses and prescriptions, nevertheless, was not as foreordained as might at first appear. They had traveled in very different milieus and had little contact prior to 1952. Indeed, Dulles's formative experiences could not have been more different from Eisenhower's. Yet as president and secretary of state, they cooperated and collaborated to an exceptional degree. Eisenhower made the decisions, but never unilaterally. As will emerge in this study, he sought the counsel of all his advisors, but he valued Dulles's most of all, taking it fully into account. An assessment of the Eisenhower administration strategy, therefore, must examine the beliefs and contributions of both men.[3]

Dulles's Formative Experience

Born a few years before Eisenhower, in 1888, Dulles was raised in upstate New York, the son of a Presbyterian minister. Offsetting this rural and religious upbringing, however, was his frequent contact with and devotion to his maternal grandfather, former Secretary of State John Watson Foster, who instilled in young Dulles the cosmopolitan, secular vision of America's turn-of-the-century elites. Reinforcing this outlook were Dulles's early travels to Europe, his Princeton education, where he studied with Woodrow Wilson, a year's tutelage under Henri Bergson at the Sorbonne, and law school at the George Washington University.[4]

Dulles began his legal career with the Wall Street law firm of Sullivan & Cromwell in 1911. He was introduced to the world of diplomacy even earlier. In

1907 Dulles served as secretary for his grandfather, who represented China, at the Second Hague Peace Conference. But his formal diplomatic career started the year the United States entered World War I, when President Woodrow Wilson asked Dulles to negotiate an arrangement between Panama and its neighbors for the defense of the Panama Canal. And at the end of the war Wilson, whose secretary of state at the time was Dulles's uncle, Robert Lansing, appointed the young lawyer to the U.S. delegation to the Paris Peace Conference. As counsel to the Reparations Commission, Dulles drafted the clauses in the treaty that reflected the administration's effort to limit German compensation to the victors. The refusal of the other peacemakers to adopt what he considered the only enlightened policy profoundly impressed the youthful Dulles. For the remainder of his life he would cite the Versailles negotiations as an object lesson in counterproductive diplomacy.[5]

Dulles, like many disappointed and displaced Wilsonians, retreated to the private sector following the failure to achieve a "just and durable peace." He returned to Sullivan & Cromwell and was soon named executive partner. But he never strayed far from public affairs nor lost his ambition to become secretary of state himself. At the same time that Eisenhower's military assignments took him to peripheral outposts across the United States and the globe, Dulles extended his roots in the "Eastern Establishment." He became an active participant in the Council of Foreign Relations, the Foreign Policy Association, the Carnegie Endowment for International Peace, and similar organizations. These forums provided Dulles with opportunities to refine his long-germinating beliefs about the United States and its role in the world. He expressed them in countless speeches and publications, including a book, *War, Peace, and Change*, published in 1939, the year Germany invaded Poland.[6]

While rejecting the views of America's pre–World War II isolationists, Dulles initially was more restrained in urging U.S. assistance to the opponents of the Axis nations than most of his fellow internationalists.[7] The behavior during the 1920s and 1930s of France and Britain in particular gave him little confidence that their appreciation for Wilsonian principles was greater than it had been at the time of the Versailles conference. He made clear in *War, Peace, and Change* that London's and Paris's appeasement of Hitler was symptomatic of their bankrupt values. Indeed, his evenhanded treatment of the European powers, combined with his writings on international relations and counsel that the United States refrain from any involvement on the continent, made Dulles vulnerable to the charge that he was not entirely unsympathetic to Germany's "dynamic" objectives.[8]

In truth, Dulles detested everything fascism stood for. The problem, from his perspective, was that the democracies' efforts to reinforce the status quo bred the environment in which a Hitler could flourish. Predictably, then, postwar planning became Dulles's consuming interest as soon as U.S. belligerency appeared unavoidable. In 1940 he accepted the chairmanship of the Commission to Study the Bases of a Just and Durable Peace, appointed by the Federal Council of the Churches of Christ in America. Summoning his prodigious energy and displaying almost evangelical fervor, Dulles took full advantage of representing a constituency made up of some 25 million Protestants and 120,000 churches. In 1943 he personally presented to President Franklin D. Roosevelt the commission's blueprint for the systemic reform of the international order, the "Six Pillars of Peace."

The "Six Pillars" reflected, in addition to scores of study groups and meetings with domestic and foreign religious and political leaders, Dulles's conviction that World War II presented a second chance to follow Wilson's precepts. The program he outlined to Roosevelt, accordingly, was reminiscent of the Fourteen Points. It included establishing organizations to institutionalize international cooperation and economic interdependence, committing the great powers to pursuing arms control and accepting peaceful and legitimate changes in the global structure, and proclaiming the right of all peoples to religious, intellectual, and political freedom. Political freedom, moreover, was incompatible with colonialism, as the document made explicit.[9]

Dulles believed that the Christian and Wilsonian principles of the "Six Pillars"contained the solutions to the world's most serious problems.[10] Yet he conceived of the project primarily as an intellectual exercise. Although Dulles correctly interpreted Roosevelt's request that he leave a copy of "Six Pillars" at the Oval Office as evidence of the president's interest in its ideas,[11] he fully recognized that he lacked real influence with the government. Notwithstanding his diplomatic pedigree, the wide network of connections he established through Sullivan & Cromwell, and the many foreign policy organizations to which he belonged, at World War II's beginning Dulles remained a Washington outsider without power and with little cause to believe he would acquire it.

Dulles's commission work, however, brought him prominence as probably the Protestant Church's most influential lay spokesman on foreign affairs. It likewise brought him prominence as the internationalist wing of the Republican Party's most prolific speaker. This increased stature within the GOP, combined with his close relationship with Thomas Dewey, made him the logical choice as the 1944 Republican presidential candidate's chief foreign policy advisor. And had Dewey defeated Roosevelt in 1944, he surely would have appointed Dulles his secretary of state. As it was, Dulles became more involved in and committed to Republican politics, and in doing so he predictably aligned with the party's internationalists. Most notable of these was the ranking Republican on the Senate Committee on Foreign Relations, Michigan's Arthur Vandenberg. It was at Vandenberg's insistence that Roosevelt appointed Dulles a delegate to the United Nations conference at San Francisco, Dulles's first official government position since Versailles.[12]

Dulles's contribution to the founding of the UN was but the beginning of his return to the official diplomatic arena. Even more than Roosevelt, Truman needed the bipartisan support Dulles came to personify. As a consequence, Dulles played a more active and consistent role after 1945 than he had before. In his capacity as the Republican expert on foreign affairs most closely identified with the evolving Truman policy of global containment, he participated in some ten diplomatic conferences subsequent to San Francisco, virtually all of which involved the Russians, Western allies, or both. He also, despite reprising his role as Dewey's foreign policy advisor during the 1948 election, served as the chief negotiator for the Japanese Peace Treaty that ended the Occupation, guaranteed the United States military bases, and excluded the Soviet Union. In short, between 1945 and 1952 Dulles became the Republican most intimately involved in the formulation and implementation of Truman foreign policy—toward Asia as well as Europe—even as he was developing his own critique of it.

Dulles's Concept of National Security

In designing a grand strategy for the United States, Dulles, like Eisenhower, began by defining national security. And like Eisenhower's definition, Dulles's was not confined to simple military and geopolitical considerations and interests. But unlike Eisenhower's, his views evolved mainly from reading and thinking, not practical experience. Although greatly influenced by his grandfather and the political and historical teachings of Wilson, Dulles had majored in philosophy at Princeton. Indeed, he had graduated with the department's highest honors and won the Chancellor Green Fellowship in Mental Science, which financed his year at the Sorbonne. Dulles chose to study with Bergson because of the venerable French philosopher's arguments concerning the inevitability of change. Nothing in the world is fixed, Dulles came to believe fervently; the dynamic will prevail over the static. Peace and security, accordingly, required the progressive adjustment to evolving conditions. But this adjustment, in turn, required enlightened statesmanship.[13] Otherwise, Dulles felt compelled to concede, "even beneficial change cannot be accomplished except by force."[14]

Hence by the time Dulles began to devote so much of his time and energy to writing and speaking about foreign affairs in the 1920s, his intellectual development had brought him to the conclusion that international stability and prosperity depended on the acceptance of Bergson's laws by the leaders of the world's great powers. Rather than seek to protect their states' interests by relying on their respective military establishments to reinforce the existing balance of power, the strongest global actors should promote the integration of the world's peripheral peoples, including the downtrodden and colonized, into a multilateral framework. For Dulles, the devout Presbyterian, Wilsonian statesman, and corporate lawyer, this framework had to include the worldwide institutionalization of democracy and free enterprise, the liberal exchange of goods and ideas, the education of all peoples in Western-inspired norms of behavior, the realization of legitimate national aspirations, and, ultimately, the establishment of international organizations dedicated to promoting all the above. American security, it followed, was intertwined with progress toward this global community.[15]

Dulles's first book, *War, Peace, and Change,* as noted above published in 1939, was his most concentrated attempt to explain the international system's "cycle of recurrent violence" and to educate domestic and foreign leaders about what was necessary to break it. Predictably, he drew heavily on those who most influenced his worldview: John Calvin, Henri Bergson, and Woodrow Wilson. Because human beings were inherently selfish and greedy, Dulles argued, each had an insatiable appetite for wealth, power, and position. The drive to dominate the zero-sum, anarchic global system reflected this appetite. Those nations who had, wanted to have more and, even worse, they wanted to deny anything to the have-nots. The static resisted the dynamic. The consequence was endemic competition that, inflamed by passion and unreason, meant endemic war.[16]

The allegations that *War, Peace, and Change* provides evidence of Dulles's sympathy for fascism are groundless. But *in toto*, the book is an abstract exposition of his thesis. The "Six Pillars," produced during World War II, and much more pragmatic in its prescriptions for international peace and security, appropriately reflected his transition from intellectual to active participant in foreign affairs. Still, Roosevelt did not pursue the commission's proposals vigorously at the 1943 Tehran summit. The president's subsequent efforts to promote the inchoate Four Policemen concept as a means to preserve the Grand Alliance, combined with Stalin's insistence on spheres of Soviet interest and Churchill's determination to uphold the British empire and revive that of France, signaled to Dulles a collective failure to learn from the debacle at Versailles.[17]

The outbreak of the cold war with Russia provided Dulles with further confirmation of the need for the United States to take the lead in championing peaceful change in the international system and channeling it for the betterment of all nations and peoples. More specifically, his involvement in so many postwar conferences and negotiations reinforced his belief that Washington must not equate national security with "huge military power." Power, he felt it imperative that both Republicans and Democrats recognize, "is not merely the existence of material [i.e., military] power." Just as essential, he asserted with increased frequency in the years following World War II, were economic performance, world opinion, moral force, "the resources of diplomacy and conciliation," and parallel "intangibles," which, taken together, "determine what men do and the intensity with which they do it." Because of this perspective, Dulles shared Eisenhower's opinion that the United States possessed "assets for peace [and security] which no generation has ever had before."[18] Because of his experiences before and during the Truman presidency, he also shared Eisenhower's concern that policy makers too often defined national security too narrowly and therefore did not exploit these assets effectively and efficiently.

National Defense

Dulles shared Eisenhower's concern with the state of American military preparedness as well. World War II taught, he advised Dewey during the 1948 campaign, that "the enemies of human freedom are ever present and constantly looking for what seem to be soft spots." It also taught that aggressor nations "assume that the man who does not lock his house has nothing in it that he greatly values." Otherwise, he would maintain a force-in-being to protect it. The United States, it followed logically, must project its military power in order to demonstrate that "our people are resolute" and "united." By doing so it would send unequivocal signals throughout the world, thereby deterring potential aggressors, militating against their intimidating fence-sitters, and providing the allies with the reassurance necessary for their economic recovery and political stability.[19]

It was therefore axiomatic to Dulles that "[w]e need a strong military establishment and a backlog of citizenry with some rudiments of training, respect for discipline and recognition that continuing freedom calls for continuing sacrifice."[20] It was equally axiomatic that the United States needed to commit the required resources to develop its atomic power. Nevertheless, even in the years immediately following World War II, when the military's budget remained relatively low, Dulles feared it was too high. Like Eisenhower, he questioned whether America's economic well-being could withstand massive increases in defense spending. Also like Eisenhower, he knew of "no greater fallacy" than the belief that "a government can provide a successful foreign policy despite an unsuccessful domestic policy."[21]

Throughout the early years of the cold war, in fact, Dulles worried about the defense program's potentially deleterious effect on the nation's values and vitality. "We must maintain a strong military establishment and keep the will to use it if necessary," he said a month prior to the announcement of the Truman Doctrine. Yet in the next breath he warned, "We must make certain that our military establishment is not bought at the price of impairing the moral and educational development of our youth." More generally, he said, a state was secure only if it held the allegiance of its people. If the United States was no longer capable of providing expected goods and services and if the free enterprise system broke down as it had two decades earlier, the United States would forfeit its advantages over the Soviet Union. It would probably remain safe from direct attack, but, as in the 1930s, it would be unable to offer material support or leadership to its allies. Dulles felt it unnecessary to spell out the implications of this scenario.[22]

Inflated military spending, Dulles said, was due to more than the organizational interests Eisenhower so severely criticized. He traced the essence of the problem to the pervasive misunderstanding of national security. In the United States, he argued in the year of the Soviet blockade of Berlin, there is a "natural tendency to rush to arms in time of peril." This is because of the "many people who believe that force in itself can produce peace, and thus the only problem with which they are concerned is the creation of that force." Dulles said that this is "putting the cart before the horse."[23] A fundamental principle for Dulles by the time he took charge of the State Department was that it is "dangerous to let military factors determine foreign policy."[24]

Assessing the Soviet Threat

Dulles was confident of his understanding of America's national security and the dangers to it. In particular, he was confident of his estimates and image of the Soviets. This had not always been so. Despite his subsequent reputation, except for a brief period immediately following the Russian Revolution, prior to World War II Dulles had paid scant attention to the Kremlin. He detested what Moscow represented, but similar to most contemporaries he did not seem concerned that it might evolve into a real threat as opposed to occasional irritant. In fact, the Soviet Union is virtually a missing actor in Dulles's early writings about international relations.[25]

World War II and the Soviet-American alliance, of course, altered his perspective. For one thing, as was true with Eisenhower, the behavior of the Soviet troops elicited from Dulles undeniable if grudging respect. "The war and Russia's magnificent performance in it have somewhat allayed the very strong anti-Soviet feeling which existed up until 1940," he commented in the aftermath of the battle of Stalingrad. Indeed, he wrote Arthur Hays Sulzberger of the *New York Times* shortly before Roosevelt met with Stalin for the first time, "Russia's success against Germany has demonstrated in a way that none could question that there must have been very solid accomplishment under the U.S.S.R." As a result, he advised Dewey during the 1944 campaign, Americans have "come to a new understanding of Russia. The devoted and sacrificial and immensely successful effort of the Russian people shows values to which we had been blind."[26]

Among these values was "the cardinal virtue of being creative." The "leaders of the Soviet Union are dynamic," Dulles wrote, echoing his favorite theme. Consequently, the challenge they posed could force the noncommunist nations to abandon their counterproductive impulse to restore "things as they were" and then maintain "them as they are." Too much "security" could serve as a "sedative," he feared, citing Arnold Toynbee as his authority. As late as 1947 Dulles held out the hope that Soviet competition for world leadership would "be a stimulating thing for the whole world. It could lift us up out of the apathy into which we have fallen in recent years and restore our sense of mission in the world."[27]

The downside, to be sure, was that to Dulles the Soviet regime stood for "tyranny, ruthlessness, aggression, atheism, denial of individual freedoms, etc." As such, the expansion of its influence across the globe could become as dangerous to America's ideals and objectives as would have been a Nazi victory. Dulles did not rule out the possibility that the war itself would precipitate "some regeneration" within Russia. But he remained extremely skeptical. Notwithstanding the sense of harmony and common destiny produced by the combat experience, the "different Russian philosophy," Dulles concluded, "makes it extremely difficult to produce anything which Anglo-Saxons would regard as fundamentally sound and inspiring." What is more, nothing that the Soviets—or more precisely Stalin—did during the period of Soviet-American cooperation altered Dulles's belief that "provocation is inherent" in Moscow's and Washington's contrasting worldviews. Unless the Kremlin underwent radical change, therefore, the United States would find itself at war's end sharing the victor's table with an adversary whose goals were inimical.[28]

Yet Dulles was initially sanguine about the prospects for a "new era" in Soviet-American relations, particularly after the Yalta agreements.[29] But he soon changed his mind after he came face to face with Stalin's representatives for the first time at the April 1945 conference at San Francisco to establish the United Nations. Within a year, during which time period he had also attended the London and Moscow meetings of the Council of Foreign Ministers and the UN General Assembly's inaugural session, his hope for detente all but evaporated.[30]

Not only did Stalin's progressive subjugation of Eastern Europe convince Dulles that no tactic was too repugnant so far as the dictator was concerned, but he came to see something sinister in all Soviet behavior. The very fact that in London Molotov expressed the fear that Washington was practicing atomic diplomacy suggested to Dulles that if the tables were turned Moscow would have no compunctions about using—or at least threatening to use—atomic weapons to realize its objectives. After all, what other explanation was there for Molotov's raising an option that had "never entered our minds"?[31]

Dulles felt secure drawing such inferences. He repeatedly reminded his audiences that within a few short years of the Soviet-American encounter on the banks of the Elbe he had participated in numerous "major sessions with the Russians, including one [at the end of 1945] of nearly two months at Moscow with Stalin, Molotov, and Vishinsky." He had also held long discussions with Jan Masaryk and others intimately familiar with the Kremlin leadership, systematically reviewed translations of the Soviet press, and purchased four copies of Stalin's *Problems of Leninism*, the Communists' "bible," which he read studiously. The result of his labor: "[B]it by bit I have learned, and I think now know, why the Russian bear ticks the way he does."[32]

Dulles considered himself a quick study. As early as 1946 he composed a long article, "Thoughts on Soviet Foreign Policy and What to Do About It," published in two parts in *Life*. In his judgment, it was "more authoritative" than the works of "writers who try to be his [Stalin's] apologists" and "who for the most part have not had comparable access to original sources."[33] The article's premise was that the different ideals and beliefs that separate the United States and the Soviet Union were fundamental, and they would remain so. Thus tension and conflict lay ahead. History, regional interests, and logistics would dictate the flash points and tactics of this conflict, but it would have no boundaries.[34]

Yet Dulles's prognosis in 1946 was more hopeful than this diagnosis might seem to suggest. He agreed with Eisenhower that the Russian people were "inherently friendly."[35] Further, while the Soviets' ambitions were boundless, the weaknesses inherent in their totalitarian system, Dulles argued, particularly the centralized bureaucracy and reliance on repressive means of control, would frustrate the implementation of far-reaching programs and breed disloyalty and discontent. Moreover, the Kremlin's expansionist agenda reflected discernible geopolitical priorities, thereby allowing the West to predict their behavior and formulate countermeasures. And this behavior would not be reckless. Characterizing the contemporary Bolsheviks as "shrewd and realistic politicians," who "are not as fanatical as were their predecessors," Dulles, again paralleling Eisenhower, forecast that once Stalin and his "lackeys" recognized the futility of their aggression, "we can expect that they will, as a matter of expediency, desist from methods which cannot succeed and which probably will provoke disaster." Dulles said that Stalin especially would carefully calibrate the risks of his international actions, retreating and relieving tension whenever he encountered opposition. He was too cunning to pursue rashly a foreign program that would jeopardize his World War II gains. "Self-interest" remained the "dominant human motive." Therefore, Dulles argued, "it can be taken as certain that neither the Russian people nor their leaders have any conscious desire to plunge into another war."[36]

Dulles's increased contact with the Soviets after 1946, along with his rereadings of *Problems of Leninism* and close observation of Stalin's international conduct, increased his concerns. Even before the Communist coup in Czechoslovakia and the Berlin blockade, he was no longer so sure that the Kremlin would behave cautiously. Russia is run "by a small group of fanatical people who feel sure they are right and who are prepared to go to any lengths to make the rest of the world agree with them," he wrote for *Collier's*. Their strategic inferiority compelled them to bide their time, acting cautiously and on occasion even appearing reasonable. Once they had acquired atomic capabilities, however, they could be expected to become more belligerent and, because they lacked "moral restraints of the kind which tend to inhibit us," more dangerous.[37] In addition, Stalin's police state thrived on manufacturing external enemies. Hence, Dulles said, its reliance on terror for domestic control would inexorably spill over its borders.[38]

Notwithstanding his more critical assessment of Stalin and his cohorts, Dulles did not succumb to the growing fear that war with the Soviet Union was inevitable. "There is no doubt but what the Russian people want to have improved relations with the United States," he said in an interview as late as 1949. Schooled in Lenin, the Bolsheviks, moreover, "believe in violent means" but "do not believe in continuing violence," Dulles maintained. The threat to the free world, it followed, came not from "the destruction of men's bodies by new methods of material warfare, but the destruction of human liberty by Soviet Communist victory in class war." In addition, Marxist Leninism taught "tempo," that there is "a time to attack and a time to retreat." To assess accurately Stalin's intentions required thinking like him. "If you were in Stalin's place in the Kremlin," Dulles said in 1948, "I think you would figure out that it would not be expedient to start the Red armies marching throughout Europe and Asia." Stalin was predisposed toward "evil methods, diabolical methods," but "not war." Dulles described this strategy as "not war, not peace," a concept difficult for Americans, who think in terms of absolutes, to grasp. But they must, Dulles insisted, and once they do, they will be able to fashion effective countermeasures.[39]

Dulles on War

Dulles was not a student of Clausewitz, nor is there evidence that, like Eisenhower, early in the cold war he wrestled with the strategic implications of the nuclear revolution. Until 1950, in fact, he tended to minimize the role of atomic weapons.[40] He worried a great deal, nevertheless, about the relationship between means and ends and the potential consequences of a bipolar conflict. Even while the United States retained an atomic monopoly, he portrayed the obstacles to defeating the Soviets as no less formidable than those faced by Napoleon and Hitler. And once the Soviets successfully tested an atomic device, Dulles's perspective dovetailed with Eisenhower's. "A few people talk as though it would be smart for the United States to fight a so-called preventive war and to try to wipe out a nest of vipers by dropping a few well aimed atomic bombs," he remarked. "That would be folly. . . . War has become so pregnant with evil that no sane person would invoke it as a means of achieving good ends."[41] All peoples, he said, must "end any complacency about war and see it as it really is, namely, something which would engulf all of humanity in utter misery and make almost impossible the achievement of the ends for which we would profess to be fighting."[42]

As these comments indicate, however, Dulles was not confident that his was the unanimous opinion in the United States. Indeed, he was more concerned with the possibility of America's launching a preventive war than one might expect. For a long time he had worried over the influence of "hatreds, passions and false conceptions" — in short, "war fever" — on policy makers' thinking. And as the cold war escalated, he detected the symptoms. "We are seeing in this country" he told a 1948 audience, an increasing "danger that the people will be swept by mass emotionalism into doing reckless and unreasonable things."[43] Dulles feared that Americans — including government leaders — were especially vulnerable to this phenonenon during such an election year. "It seems to me that the immediate pre-election mood is not best calculated to produce the calm thinking and wise decisions which correspond to the gravity of the situation," Dulles wrote Arthur Vandenberg in the midst of Truman's comeback against Dewey.[44]

Dulles predictably worried more about the potential for the Soviets behaving rashly. After all, the Kremlin leaders were ruthless, violent men of unlimited ambition. Further, they were insecure and therefore that much more prone to panic when confronted by a well-armed adversary, especially when those arms included an atomic capability that the Communists lacked. Even while championing the formation of NATO in early 1949 Dulles warned that Stalin might perceive the Atlantic Pact's intent as offensive. "We must take into account," he wrote, that "the men in the Kremlin, as Russian leaders, inherit age-old suspicions of the West; as communists, they believe that capitalism seeks their encirclement; and as despots, they are told what frightened agents think they want to hear."[45]

What Dulles feared most, and to an extent that perhaps surpassed Eisenhower because of his greater worries about the Soviets behaving rashly, was a tinderbox war. "If we have another great war, that is probably the way it will come," said Dulles in his 1946 *Life* article. "It will be the result of miscalculating." In a speech he wrote for the Federal Council of Churches that same year he added, "The combination of fear and aggressiveness which determines the policies of each nation induces more fear and more aggressiveness. Unless that vicious circle can be broken, a third world war becomes not a possibility, but a probability." Just before the Korean War broke out, Dulles returned to this theme. "When acute tension exists between two nations. . . [t]here is always a risk of stumbling into war."[46]

Dulles reflexively agreed with the consensus that the Soviets were responsible for North Korea's attack on the South. Kim Il-Sung's assault "may mark a new phase of Bolshevik Communist aggression," he warned. "It may invalidate the assumption that the Soviet Union would not risk general war." He recommended an immediate military response. Yet Dulles's intent was not to initiate World War III. Rather, his primary purpose in recommending that the United States engage its forces was to make clear that the nation would not tolerate aggression, thereby bringing Stalin to his senses and lessening the chances that he would miscalculate. To "sit by while Korea is overrun by unprovoked armed attack," he advised Truman, "would start [a] disastrous chain of events leading most probably to world war." He was "confident" with that danger averted, "we shall find the ways to paralyze the slimy, octopus-like tentacles that reach out from Moscow to suck our blood."[47]

Strategy for the Atomic Age

To find the ways to paralyze Moscow's tentacles and to minimize the risk of general war required calm deliberation, intelligent planning, and a clear vision, Dulles told Thomas Dewey in 1948 when the White House appeared in the grasp of the Republicans. A "fresh approach on foreign affairs is imperative." Strategists must seek to counter Moscow's strengths and exploit its weakness, while keeping in mind at all times the ingredients of power. "Napoleon said that in war the material counted for one-quarter and the non-material for the other three-quarters," Dulles remarked. "I suppose that the disparity is even greater in a 'cold' war." What made the Soviet Union so menacing, then, was its leaders' understanding of what Dulles held to be the fundamental principle of international affairs: the dynamic triumphs over the static. The appeal of communism rested on "two imponderables"—hope and fear—he told the Senate Committee on Foreign Relations not long after Dewey's defeat and the Democrats regained the majority. Bolshevism offers "leadership to the discontented and the idealists who want to change radically the existing order, and it tries to frighten into inaction those who oppose such change."[48]

For the author of *War, Peace, and Change*, the strategic antidote was obvious albeit difficult to implement. Washington must beat Moscow at its own game. Reiterating his prewar preachings Dulles argued that "it is both futile and wrong to identify peace with a static condition." The failure of the United States and its Western allies to adapt their attitudes and institutions to accommodate nationalist aspirations, economic disparities, racial stratification, and similar items on the agendas of "dynamic" peoples would breed conflict and disorder. Conversely, acceptance of—indeed support for—change would benefit the United States and the entire noncommunist world. And in the long run, it would spell doom for the communist one.[49]

Military force, it followed, could contribute only a small part to victory in a cold war because it is powerless against the mass discontent and despair that the Depression and World War II, as well as centuries of imperialism and authoritarianism, had left in their wake. "The struggle that is," Dulles said, "is a struggle to be fought with food and fuel and with creative ideas and lofty ideals. . . . We should use the tested peacetime way which, for generations, has made our nation supremely productive, both materially and spiritually." Dulles anticipated the title of Eisenhower's future White House memoir. "Peace," he wrote for Thomas Dewey's use in the 1948 campaign, "must be waged just as war is waged."[50]

What was more, Dulles doubted that the American "way of war" could be effectively applied to those peripheral arenas where communists exploit subversive guerilla tactics.[51] The Truman Doctrine's rhetoric threatened to engage America's military—and American prestige—in quixotic campaigns that would fuel the communist charge that the United States was an aggressive imperialist and cause national and international grief. Washington should not "send U.S. troops and seem to nail the U.S. flag to an untenable masthead," Dulles told Undersecretary of Defense Robert Lovett during the initial planning for NATO.[52]

Despite his reservations about the military aspects of America's strategy and the defense budget, for the most part Dulles supported and, as discussed, actively contributed to the Democrats' foreign policies through 1950. He enthusiastically embraced the Truman emphasis on collective security and building an Atlantic Community. In this context Dulles judged the impact of the Marshall Plan and NATO's establishment, coupled with the collapse of the Berlin blockade, as particularly positive portends. For the near-term Dulles was content that Germany was still divided.[53] And as steps toward European unity, he welcomed the French proposals in 1950 to cooperate with West Germany in establishing the European Coal and Steel Community and the European Defense Community.[54] These initiatives, he believed, would insulate Europe from the Soviet challenge, while at the same time allowing for the restoration of West German sovereignty, the revival of its economy, and its rearmament and ultimate reunification in a way that would anchor it firmly to the West without alarming those with whom it had so recently fought.[55]

But even without supranational institutions, Dulles reported in 1949 after attending the Paris meeting of the Council of Foreign Ministers, the "tough fiber of resistance that has been built up in Western Europe" was paying dividends. By acting in concert and with resolve, the allies had blunted the Soviet offensive. In contrast, Dulles said, Stalin's avarice in Eastern Europe was already causing Moscow "indigestion."[56] Like all dictatorships, he wrote in his 1950 sequel to *War, Peace, and Change*, the Soviet empire presented "a formidable exterior," but inside it was "full of rottenness."[57]

There remained cause for apprehension, however. Dulles was still skeptical of Europe's capability to sustain its "tough fiber of resistance," and the Paris meeting notwithstanding, he doubted that through negotiations the West could induce the Soviet tiger to change its stripes.[58] Moreover, Truman's successes in Europe were masking his neglect of America's broader interests. "I do not believe that the lines that demark the American and Atlantic areas are intended to demark the limits of our vital interest," Dulles testified to Congress in 1949 in support of NATO. The United States had to build up the strength, coherence, vitality, and loyalty to the free world in the peripheral as well as core countries.[59]

Having prior to 1950 collaborated with the Democrats almost exclusively on policy toward Europe, Dulles was comfortable, even before the Republican campaign began, criticizing Truman for abandoning China to the communists. Policy makers, he now said, had to address the consequences. Juxtaposing the communists' success in China with the opposition they faced in Western Europe, Dulles predicted that Stalin would shift his attention to the less developed areas of the world, in particular Asia. The prize was "over one billion people to be 'amalgamated' into the Soviet Union." If successful, Japan would be easy prey. Tokyo's allegiance to the free world was too weak for it to swim long in a communist sea. It would defect, after which a strengthened Moscow would turn again to Europe. Were the communists to acquire the industrial capacities and trained manpower of just Japan and West Germany, Dulles told a study group of the Council of Foreign Relations shortly after Truman assigned him responsibility for the Japanese Peace Treaty negotiations in 1950, "the world's balance of power would be profoundly altered." The Kremlin could then "contemplate the Western World with equanimity."[60]

Dulles's recommendation that Truman respond militarily to North Korea's aggression was therefore predictable. No longer in his opinion did the United States enjoy the luxury of gradually "converting its economic potential into military reality." All the world must see Americans' "willingness to accept sacrifice and discipline so that their resolution may be potent unto the end." If "the rest of the world feels that we are today afraid to take a stand which would involve a risk of war," he said, "they would judge that almost certainly we will not take that risk tomorrow." Dulles did not seek a general war with the communists; but he was sure that the credible threat of one to deter Soviet aggression was the most effective preventive against its inadvertant outbreak. This reason, combined with his concern over the costs to U.S. resources and prestige of a land operation, especially outside of Europe, explains Dulles's stress on sea and air — especially atomic and soon thermonuclear — power.[61]

It was in fact in the aftermath of the outbreak of war in Korea that Dulles first publicly articulated his doctrine of "Massive" or "Instant" retaliation.[62] In subsequent chapters we will argue that the conventional criticism of his precept is misleading.[63] What Dulles advocated from the start, in essence, was that the United States rely more heavily and explicitly on its atomic superiority as a means to avoid getting "bogged down in an interminable and costly operation," to keep the communists off balance and deter aggression, and to decrease the possibility of a war of miscalculation. In addition to its strategic and economic benefits, Dulles added, this policy would have the further advantage of allowing the United States to manipulate the communists' estimate of the risk their behavior entailed. By doing so Washington would maintain relentless pressure on and thus exacerbate tensions between Moscow and its satellites.[64]

For Dulles "massive retaliation," moreover, could never be more than a single dimension of grand strategy. "To assume responsibility for *new* foreign policies apart from the possibility of their integration in a total national policy would be to risk failure," he said as early as 1948. This meant doing nothing to undercut America's ability to project the image necessary to generate domestic and international support. To appear as the atomic bully would do just that. Indeed, Dulles was greatly concerned with the impact a greater emphasis on atomic weapons would have on allied relations. Massive retaliation could never substitute for collective security and "local defense."[65]

What is more, deterrence — the purpose of the threat to retaliate massively — was fundamentally a guarantor of the status quo. The end of successful foreign policy must be change — dynamic, positive change. This reasoning drove Dulles's dissatisfaction with containment as a strategic framework and his rejection of those elements of Realist thought that precluded considerations other than stability and the balance of power. The "past dynamism of our nation has genuinely stemmed from a profound popular faith in such concepts as justice and righteousness and from the sense that our nation had a mission to promote these ideals," he wrote George Kennan shortly after the scholar-diplomat published his classic Realist treatise, *American Diplomacy*. The "so-called 'containment' policy," however, "is a current example of non-moral diplomacy" and "not healthy." America must not appear satisfied with holding the line against communism. Winning the cold war required a more positive, future-oriented strategy.[66]

This intellectual path led Dulles to espouse eventual liberation as the logical successor to containment. But he favored propaganda and psychological warfare as the means to pursue it. As a consequence, he said as early as 1948 that the Voice of America's "short-wave lispings are scarcely heard above the flood of communist propaganda." An early contributor to the National Committee for a Free Europe, as already discussed, he proposed that Truman create an "organization dedicated to the task of non-military defense, just as the present Secretary of Defense heads up the organization of military defense." This agency, he suggested, would through the radio and press, "tell adequately the story of what is happening." Although Truman did establish the Psychological Strategy Board in 1951, Dulles remained dissatisfied. There remained "a grave deficiency in our ability to carry on a 'Cold War' counter-offensive that would really crack the Iron Curtain," he said. The United States had to improve its "political or psychological efforts to extend its own creed and way of life."[67]

National Security Management

Dulles paid less attention than did Eisenhower to the organization and process by which these policies would be formulated. Unlike the future president, he had never needed to concern himself a great deal with the mechanics of policy making. Rarely had he had the responsibility for making decisions—or been in a position to make them. Instinctively he was more of an advocate than a deliberator. His diverse experiences, nevertheless, which included his close observations of Acheson's frustrations, predisposed Dulles to Eisenhower's style of leadership and policy management. Further, the greater his active participation in actual policy making, the greater became his appreciation of the complexity of problems and the need to examine them from a variety of informed perspectives.

Therefore Dulles shared Eisenhower's emphasis on structuring a process that improved teamwork and coordination among the various managers and dimensions of national strategy. One person—the president—must make the decisions, and he must have one primary foreign policy advisor and spokesperson—the secretary of state. Yet a mechanism must exist to facilitate the flow of information and advice, both horizontally and vertically, among and within the many agencies and departments that both the president and secretary of state must draw on. Otherwise, "dispersion and confusion" would plague the policy-making process. This confusion and dispersion "can throw almost insuperable roadblocks in the paths of even the most competent officials and seriously impede the attainment of important national objectives," he explained.[68]

Based on his own experiences, Dulles concluded that under Truman's leadership the NSC failed to eliminate this confusion and dispersion. In fact, in certain respects it exacerbated the problems. "The situation is so organized that the Secretary of State has an appearance of responsibility much greater than his authority," Dulles wrote shortly after the enactment of the 1947 National Security Act. In reality the locus of authority for conducting foreign affairs, he said, had come to rest in the DOD and NSC. "That division of authority and the question of what to do about it," Dulles concluded, is "worrying me greatly."[69]

Dulles's worries increased during the remainder of Truman's tenure. Particularly while stitching together the Japanese Peace Treaty, he had a front row seat as relations deteriorated between Acheson and Secretary of Defense Louis Johnson. Instead of promoting dialogue and exchange between Foggy Bottom and the Pentagon, Truman's ambiguous chain of command seemed to Dulles to breed conflict and competition between them. To rectify this condition required a president well versed in both arenas, a secretary of state who would insist on his prerogatives but value the counsel of others, and a process driven by concern for the national as opposed to bureaucratic interests, expertise, and a shared vision of what must be done. According to these criteria, by 1952 Dulles had become confident that both he and Eisenhower were highly qualified.

4

Campaigning for Security with Solvency

I did not become engaged in the current political fight out of any desire to promote a personal candidacy for the Presidency, but because I deeply and firmly believe that . . . America cannot live alone, and that her form of life is threatened by the Communistic dictatorship. These facts give rise to the problems we have in developing general policies applicable to the situation. All of these policies must conform to the yardstick of our enlightened self-interest.[1]

Dwight D. Eisenhower (1952)

By 1952 the nation was in a deeply frustrated and divided state. During Truman's last two years, a succession of events had contributed to this increasingly bitter political climate. General Douglas MacArthur had been fired as the military commander in Korea. The negotiations at Panmonjon were dragging on while fighting continued. The public anxieties about disloyal and subversive activities at home, fanned by the convictions of Klaus Fuchs and Alger Hiss, were being viciously exploited by the demagoguery of Joseph McCarthy and his supporters. Further, the Truman administration was being racked by serious scandals in the Internal Revenue Service, the Justice Department, and elsewhere.

As an overall consequence Truman's influence and power had plummeted to disastrously low levels. The Democratic Party was accordingly on the defensive and in disarray. And the Republicans, after 20 years out of power, were profoundly split. The so-called Eastern, internationalist wing of the party had largely supported Truman's security measures, especially the commitments to Europe. The GOP Old Guard, however, was basically unilateralist if not isolationist. Indeed, Herbert Hoover, the last Republican president, virtually called for a "Fortress America." This right wing proposed to rely almost solely on the U.S. retaliatory capacity and opposed collective security commitments.

Eisenhower's Decision to Run

Since 1948 Eisenhower had rejected appeals from both parties to stand for president. What changed his mind in 1952 was primarily the virtual certainty that Robert

A. Taft would win the GOP nomination.[2] He had little quarrel with Taft's conservative social agenda. If anything, he considered "Mr. Republican" too "leftish" on many domestic issues.[3] But as the minority leader in the Senate, Taft had spearheaded the sizable group of Republican legislators who opposed NATO and the Marshall Plan while at the same time virulently denouncing the Truman administration for not committing greater resources to assist the Nationalists in China. Indeed, Eisenhower deemed the combination of the Ohio senator's hostility to the U.S. commitments in Europe, on the one hand, and his preoccupation with the Far East, on the other, contrary to the national interest. What concerned him above all was that if elected Taft would adopt "nuclear retaliation" as a unilateral U.S. security policy and irresponsibly diminish U.S. participation in NATO and reduce financial assistance to the European allies.[4] The result would undermine the progress that had been made toward recovery, cooperation, and collective security. The damage, believed Eisenhower, would be irrevocable.

With this threat in mind Eisenhower, immediately prior to taking up the NATO command in January 1951, arranged a private meeting with Taft at the Pentagon in an effort "to kill two birds with one stone." Tucked in his pocket was a statement he had previously prepared committing the GOP front-runner to support the Atlantic alliance and the broad principle of collective security. Had Taft agreed to it, the general intended to make "a dramatic and flat announcement" that "my name may not be used by anyone as a candidate for President—and if any do I will repudiate such efforts." But Taft refused to commit himself. Instead, he confined the session to a discussion of whether a credible European defense posture really required the projected deployment of four additional U.S. divisions (which would bring the U.S. total to six). "This aroused my fears that isolationism was stronger in the Congress than I had previously suspected," Eisenhower wrote. He tore up the statement and "scrapped" his plan.[5]

On October 16, 1951, Taft officially declared his quest for the Republican nomination and shortly thereafter sent Eisenhower a letter designed to minimize the difference between them on NATO. Eisenhower was unpersuaded, reluctantly concluding that his candidacy was necessary to preserve America's commitment to collective security and its leadership of the free world. In February 1952 he notified a delegation of Republican internationalists that if nominated he would run, and in June he returned to the United States. After an acrimonious GOP convention in Chicago the next month he defeated Taft on the first ballot. "I know something of the solemn responsibility of leading a crusade," Eisenhower told the Republican delegates when accepting the nomination. "I accept your summons. I will lead this crusade."[6] Predictably he chose foreign policy as the subject of the speech that formally launched his candidacy on September 4.[7]

The Dilemmas for the Electoral Campaign

As the standard-bearer for the minority party, Eisenhower had to command a coalition almost as challenging as the one he managed in World War II.[8] Victory in November required the backing of both Republican wings, independent-minded

Democrats, and nonpartisan voters. Of these, generating and maintaining support among Taft followers presented the greatest difficulty. Shortly after his victory at the Chicago convention, at a meeting at the Morningside Heights residence he had occupied while president of Columbia, Eisenhower arranged a "truce" with Taft by reaching agreement on such domestic issues as support for the Taft-Hartley (National Labor Relations) legislation, flexible farm prices, and of course reductions in federal spending.

Yet their profound disagreements over foreign and security policy remained. Moreover, the two Republican wings diverged sharply over a proposed amendment to the Constitution first introduced in 1951 by Ohio senator John Bricker in response to Truman's unilateral decision to deploy the four U.S. divisions to NATO and forgo requesting from Congress a declaration of war in Korea. Its purpose was to curtail executive authority over foreign affairs far beyond what Eisenhower considered prudent.[9]

Most important of all, Eisenhower had to choose his words carefully lest he appear either to repudiate the essential elements of Truman's international course, which he advocated, or to approximate the "me-tooism" that had contributed to Dewey's downfall in 1948. In short, throughout his campaign Eisenhower confronted a complex dilemma: he needed to forge unity among the Republicans and to distance himself from the Democrats without renouncing the principles and programs of U.S. foreign policy that had driven his decision to run in the first place.

Eisenhower's electoral strategy, as a consequence, was to underscore themes that signaled his genuine and profound distress over what he considered Truman's mismanagement of the United States's strategic assets and interests and his inadequate leadership. This strategy enabled him to finesse what he described to Dulles as "widely divergent views" within his own party by downplaying the many components of the incumbent's foreign policy with which he agreed and had contributed to.[10] It was fortunate for Eisenhower, and to his credit, that the public's confidence that they could on faith entrust their fate to their World War II hero permitted him to keep his cards close to his vest.

Eisenhower's speeches demonstrate how selectively and carefully he handled the most contentious questions in order to sidestep issues that could disrupt the fragile harmony that his candidacy produced between the Republican factions.[11] The more specific their content, the greater the likelihood that the candidate would precipitate an internecine feud that would play right into the hands of the Democrats. Eisenhower, therefore, soft-pedaled his sympathy with the Atlanticist perspective so prevalent among the Democrats' strategists and Republican internationalists. It is remarkable, for example, how by allowing his record as SACEUR to speak for itself, Eisenhower successfully skirted the entire controversy attendant to the United States's participation in NATO, notwithstanding its catalytic role in his decision to run for office.[12] And he confined his criticism of Truman's China policy to allegations that the Democrats had "abandoned China to the Communists" and intended to "accept the loss of Formosa."[13] As to whether as president he would devote more resources to this theater, however, Eisenhower said only that the principle of "enlightened self-interest" would guide his administration's international commitments.[14]

In addition to such political considerations, Eisenhower studiously refrained from articulating specific policy proposals that might later prove constraining. For Eisenhower this rule was especially important. Notwithstanding his — and Dulles's — preferences and predispositions, he believed it premature in 1952 to commit himself to a comprehensive strategy of his own. He wanted first to assemble a national security team that would be free from electioneering imperatives to systematically "review and reappraise the present policies." Eisenhower intended to modify and improve upon Truman's foundation, not obliterate it. He never doubted this goal required patient, informed, and nonpartisan deliberation.[15]

The campaign allowed for no such deliberation. Eisenhower left it primarily to Dulles to devise acceptable formulas for the foreign policy planks in the Republican platform.[16] Nonetheless, the need to hold together the fractious GOP forced him to compromise his effort to stand above politics. While he accepted Truman's offer to send him weekly intelligence reports, he refused to meet with the president to receive a personal briefing from the incumbent and his CIA director — Eisenhower's World War II chief of staff, Bedell Smith.[17] And in retirement he characterized his "'prosecuting-attorney' style" attacks on the Truman legacy as "purple."[18]

Actually, compared to other Republicans Eisenhower's discourse was tame. It was his running mate, Richard M. Nixon, who labeled Eisenhower's opponent, Adlai E. Stevenson, "Adlai the Appeaser" and a graduate of "Dean Acheson's Cowardly College of Communist Containment." And it was McCarthy who indicted George Marshall for participating in "a conspiracy so immense and an infamy so black as to dwarf any previous venture in the history of man." But Eisenhower censored neither. Indeed, despite his intention to use a campaign speech in Milwaukee to defend his wartime mentor against McCarthy's charges of disloyalty, Eisenhower acquiesced to his advisors and not only dropped the reference to Marshall from the text but also delighted his Wisconsin audience by shaking the senator's hand.[19] For his part, Dulles acknowledged the Republicans' political gamesmanship at his confirmation hearing as secretary of state. He asked the Democrats on the Senate Committee on Foreign Relations to make "allowance, of course, for the bombast and exaggeration incident to a campaign."[20]

The Issues Discussed

Nuclear Weapons

On issues most likely to spark controversy, and most vulnerable to being misconstrued, Eisenhower generally allowed Dulles, or the generic Republican party, to be his mouthpiece. What role "special weapons" would play in his grand strategy, which was so fundamental to the split within the GOP, was one such issue. Eisenhower worried that the term "massive retaliation" could be interpreted as a euphemism — or code word — for the unilateral strategy supported by the Taft-wing Republicans.[21] He recognized that many of the international challenges the United States would confront in the years ahead would be tactical, whereas the primary utility of atomic weapons was strategic deterrence. He also understood and sympathized with the fears of a nuclear holocaust that pervaded—and could potentially divide—the United States and the free world. "Exclusive reliance upon a mere power of retaliation is not a complete answer to the broad Soviet threat," Eisenhower wrote Dulles in the midst of the campaign. "This means that we must be successful in developing collective security measures for the free world."[22]

Eisenhower learned early in the campaign that his position on nuclear weapons would have to be managed delicately. At the same time he identified one of Dulles's principal shortcomings. Dulles was frequently frustrated and distressed by the failure of both U.S. and foreign leaders to behave in a manner congruent with his beliefs and advice. Hence when he received opportunities to promote them, especially to a public audience, and most especially when the objective was to win a political victory, Dulles tended to paint issues in black and white and adopt the posture of an advocate. He employed provocative rhetoric intended to evoke emotion and forcefully presented one-sided arguments. As a consequence, Dulles was prone to reducing complex issues by eliminating considerations that were salient but either extraneous to or, worse, weakened his "case."

Over the course of the administration's first year, we will demonstrate, Eisenhower became sensitive to this characteristic of his secretary of state and expert in handling it. In 1952, however, the two men were only casually acquainted, and Eisenhower's initial impressions were not all positive. He flinched after reading in April a draft of Dulles's seminal salvo against the Democrats to be published in *Life*, as "A Policy of Boldness."[23] The prospective candidate, as did many contemporary readers, inferred from Dulles's underscoring of the words *"retaliate instantly against open aggression . . . by means of our choosing"* that his likely chief foreign policy advisor was too close to Taft-like neo-isolationism.[24] He immediately challenged Dulles to explain the utility of atomic weapons as a means to counter Soviet *"political* aggression, as in Czechoslovakia." To Eisenhower, "this is the case where the theory of 'retaliation' falls down."[25]

Dulles replied, "You [Eisenhower] put your finger on a weak point in my presentation," and he promised to try to "cover it in a revision."[26] In the revised version that was published he wrote explicitly that developing the capability and will to retaliate instantly "does not mean that old ways of defending the peace should be abandoned" and added also, "Everywhere free nations should have the ability to resist attack from within."[27] Yet Eisenhower remained dissatisfied. What is more, after reminding Dulles that "[p]eace is our objective" and "we reject all talk and proposals of preventive war," and complimenting him on his "understanding and determination," he demanded the deletion of the words "retaliatory striking power" from Dulles's first draft of the GOP platform because of the implications for Taft's supporters. The plank he approved read only, "[D]efense against sudden attack requires the quickest possible development of appropriate and completely-adequate air power and the simultaneous readiness of coordinated air, land, and sea forces, with all necessary installations, bases, supplies and munitions, including atomic energy weapons in abundance."[28]

Yet Eisenhower agreed with Dulles that, as a deterrent to aggression, security blanket for the noncommunist world, and unequivocal testimony to U.S. power, the capability of the United States to retaliate whenever, wherever, and however it chose had to be the centerpiece of U.S. strategy and doctrine. Anything less would increase the likelihood of Soviet miscalculation and undercut the confidence of America's allies by leaving in doubt U.S. resolve to exploit its technological advantage to the fullest. To develop and reserve the right to use whatever weapons the president chose did not mean the United States would rain nuclear bombs over Moscow at the slightest incident. It meant only that in the event of communist aggression the president would not have to exhaust all other options prior to deciding to retaliate massively, and that the Soviets could not discount the possibility from the start of any adventure. But such subtlety was inappropriate discourse for a presidential campaign. Predictably, therefore, as a candidate Eisenhower avoided the subject altogether, concerning himself only with their cost and production.[29]

Defense and the Economy

No aspect of Truman's national security program troubled Eisenhower more than its cost. The problem, Eisenhower charged, was that the Democrats relied on ever increasing spending on the military to compensate for the failings of its overall strategy. Hence the United States was becoming mired in a crippling economic swamp. He fully understood, of course, the appeal that a pledge to reduce the defense budget held for Old Guard Republicans. But he was determined that his criticisms of Truman's spending would be presented responsibly. I refuse "to go around this country making any stupid promises about slashing our defense costs," Eisenhower told his campaign staff. Nothing, "and I mean *nothing* — is going to come ahead of assuring the safety of the United States."[30]

What Eisenhower thought was integral to the safety of the United States, nevertheless, allowed him to lash out at Truman's spending with a clear conscience. Convinced as he was that economic strength played just as important a role in the nation's security as did military strength, and that the United States would have to engage the communists over the long haul, he made clear that the budget required to implement Truman's global posture exceeded what a sound economy could bear. And this extravagance was as unnecessary as it was dangerous. Eisenhower promised to better integrate advances in U.S. technology and capabilities and strategic planning. No less important, he would end the current "stop-and-start planning" produced by the incumbent administration's "swing[s] from optimism to panic." Eisenhower explained that effective national security management required "plan[ning] for the future on something more solid than yesterday's headlines."[31]

Liberation

Eisenhower was also caught in a quandary concerning the problem of liberation. On the one hand, he worried that liberation had become a code word for coercive "rollback." In truth even Republican polemicists would not associate the party with advocating the use of military force to roll back the Communist tide. After asserting that "[w]e should be *dynamic*," in his *Life* article Dulles underscored that the United States must make "*it publicly known that it wants and expects liberation to occur.*" But he acknowledged that "liberation from the yoke of Moscow will not occur for a very long time" and cited Tito's Yugoslavia to illustrate that "[t]here can be peaceful separation from Moscow." The people of the United States, he wrote, "do not believe that good ends can, in fact, be promoted by invoking the evil method of war."[32] Yet Dulles was criticized as if he invoked just that.[33] When linked to a Republican Party identified with repudiating the Yalta agreements and championing Chiang Kai-shek, liberation could easily be depicted as advocating armed intervention in Eastern Europe and China.

On the other hand, as an issue to which the Republican right wing was emotionally attached, liberation was fundamental to the GOP electoral strategy.[34] It appealed to ethnic minorities, Legionnaires, and other Republican target groups. Further, many Republicans believed the party could profit from depicting the Democrats as having abandoned Eastern Europe to the Soviets. Eisenhower also wanted to stress that in a cold no less than hot war, victory went to the side that seized the initiative. The safest and most effective way to start, Eisenhower sincerely believed, was by reaching out to "the roll of countries once independent, now suffocating under the Russian pall." The United States must signal unequivocally that it will never "rest content," he proclaimed, "until the tidal mud of aggressive Communism has receded within its own borders."[35]

In this sense, Eisenhower was willing to make the aspiration for liberation a theme on which he would personally campaign. As discussed, he left the political diatribes to Republican point men. But he acceded to the Republican platform's inflammatory and truculent rhetoric: Truman's "negative, futile, and immoral" policy of containment "abandons countless human beings to a despotic and godless terrorism," it charged. In order to "set up strains and stresses within the captive world which will make the rulers impotent to continue in their monstrous ways and mark the beginning of the end," a Republican administration would "revive the contagious, liberating influences." Indeed, the GOP platform promised to be content with nothing less than the "genuine independence of these captive peoples."[36]

By agreeing to run on this plank and delivering speeches that explicitly endorsed it, Eisenhower was unquestionably courting votes and placating his party's Old Guard. But he tried to minimize the cost. When the reaction of many sophisticated commentators in the United States and virtually all the NATO allies suggested a widespread unease with the GOP plank on liberation, its nominee moved quickly to clarify his position.[37] Following a postconvention Dulles press conference, Eisenhower admonished the Republican foreign policy spokesman for neglecting to qualify his reference to liberation with the words "by all peaceful means."[38] And in his own speeches Eisenhower explicitly stated that he perceived liberation as a long-range goal to be achieved without military force. The "passage of years," he explained, "will [not] put an end to the search for the *peaceful* instruments" of liberation."[39]

As to his thinking about what instruments for liberation *his* search would lead him to adopt, Eisenhower revealed little. In his *Life* article Dulles recommended some "specific acts" the United States might take to pierce the Iron Curtain, none of which entailed the use of force. They included efforts to create "political 'task forces' to develop a freedom program for each of the captive nations"; to "stimulate the escape from behind the Iron Curtain of those who can help to develop these programs"; or to "coordinate our economic, commercial, and cultural relations with the freedom programs." To avoid any hint that he approved a program of coercive rollback, Eisenhower would not get even this specific. The farthest he would go was to enumerate such "peaceful tools" as "[d]iplomacy, the spreading of ideas through every medium of communication, mutual economic assistance, trade and barter, friendly contacts through travel and correspondence and sport."[40]

Eisenhower was somewhat more specific when discussing what he (and Dulles) believed were the strongest weapons in the United States's arsenal — its ideals and moral magnetism. Indeed, "psychological warfare" was the focus of the most comprehensive and revealing speech on foreign policy the candidate delivered throughout the campaign. "Don't be afraid of that term just because it's a five-dollar, five-syllable word," he told a San Francisco audience in October. "'Psychological warfare' is the struggle for the minds and wills of men." No battle was more critical, yet Americans "have been dozing at the gate." He therefore announced that the "means we shall employ" to keep alive the hope of liberation among captive people and unmasking the "truth" about the Kremlin would be "psychological." This strategy, he promised, would produce a cold war "victory without casualties."[41]

Except for a cryptic reference to "the controversial 'Voice of America,'" however, and the promise to "choose a man of exceptional qualifications" to direct the "psychological effort," Eisenhower did not explain how. He avoided mention of the CIA or any other government agency. To the contrary, he stressed that improving the message was as critical as improving the messenger. The United States and its allies, Eisenhower said, must emphasize their support for freedom, not simply their opposition to repression. Victory in a cold war demanded strengthening the unity and morale of the free world nations and capturing the imagination of the global masses, whether they resided within or beyond the Soviet orbit. Rather than project the image of a nation in panic, the United States must appear self-confident, the epitome of the dynamism that, as Dulles had repeatedly preached, deserved the mantle of world leadership that the Soviets sought to usurp. It must communicate a renewed and revitalized sense of national mission — and destiny. The United States has "an appointment to keep with history," Eisenhower proclaimed. "We are not going to win the struggle for men's minds merely by tripling Congressional appropriations for a super-loud Voice of America. Rather, it will be the message which we give the Voice to speak. . . . We must realize that as a nation everything we say, everything we do, and everything we fail to say or do, will have its impact in other lands. It will affect the minds and wills of men and women there."[42]

Korea

Korea presented Eisenhower with his greatest challenge in terms of walking the tightrope across the chasm separating Republicans from one another. Both he and Dulles had unequivocally backed Truman's deployment of U.S. forces to this theater, and neither sympathized with those in their party who had sided with MacArthur during the controversy over his firing. MacArthur's sacking had galvanized the Asia-Firsters' disposition for taking the battle to China. Eisenhower was willing to hear MacArthur out, but he would have nothing to do with this kind of thinking. No one believed more strongly that broadening the conflict would alienate world opinion and jeopardize collective security in Europe.[43]

Moreover, in a large measure because of Dulles's efforts, progress had been made toward anchoring Japan to the free world orbit, and the role it played in the logistics of the U.S. military effort in Korea had provided a most welcome kick-start to its recovering economy. An attack on China would probably provoke direct Soviet military intervention. Just as probably Stalin would order an invasion of Japan. Thus might begin the very general war Eisenhower believed civilization's future required that it avoid.

Of course, had Eisenhower publicly revealed this thinking, he would have brought down the wrath of the GOP's Old Guard. By claiming that the Democrats' mishandling of the Far East invited opportunistic communist aggression, he made his most fundamental point without paying a political price. Eisenhower portrayed the Korean War as an object lesson in Truman's failed leadership, inept policy making, and geopolitical myopia. This "tragedy" was "a symbol—a telling symbol—of the foreign policy of our nation," he said, and a "sign—a warning sign—of the way the Administration has conducted our world affairs."[44] It reflected the "lack of imagination and firmness in the overall political direction which guides all security planning," as well as "the calamities that have come to our nation because of lack of . . . leadership of wisdom and courage."[45]

This approach allowed Eisenhower to indict Truman without crawling into bed with the Republican right wing. He zeroed in on Secretary of State Acheson's exclusion of Korea from the U.S. defense perimeter in his January 1950 address to the National Press Club on the crisis in Asia.[46] By implying that "this Administration had written off most of the Far East as beyond our direct concern," Acheson's speech, Eisenhower said, was tantamount to "psychological strategy in reverse."[47]

Eisenhower forthrightly conceded that while he was Army chief of staff the JCS had appraised Korea as not of vital strategic importance to the free world in the event of a future general war. In fact, he defended this advice. The estimate had been sound militarily, and it was still. Korea would not be militarily important in case of general war. But, Eisenhower continued, the Korean attack raised a different issue: would the United States allow the communists to expand by force in a limited area? In this context, Truman's decision to translate this military estimate about general war into a political decision regarding a specific locale was unsound, and Acheson's announcement of that decision to "a potential enemy," especially so soon after the withdrawal of America's occupation force, even more so. "Many an American family knows only too well how history has dealt with this policy decision of our government. The Communists hastened to exploit it. And we American are still paying dearly to redeem it."[48]

The task at hand, therefore, was to arrest the consequent bleeding of the United States's economy, domestic tranquility, and global force posture. This required an armistice, but its terms must not compromise the nation's strategic interests or credibility. "For this task a wholly new Administration is necessary," declared Eisenhower, because the "old Administration cannot be expected to repair what it failed to prevent."[49] Accordingly, "Without weakening the security of the free world," Eisenhower exclaimed on October 8, "I pledge full dedication to the job of finding an intelligent and honorable way to end the tragic toll of American casualties in Korea. No one can pledge you more."[50] Less than three weeks later, however, he did. "I shall go to Korea," he announced in Detroit on October 24.[51] Eisenhower's promise electrified the electorate, as if the missing piece in the Panmonjon peace-making puzzle was the personal intervention of their greatest wartime hero. Eisenhower knew better.[52]

Leadership and Strategy

The underlying thesis of Eisenhower's critique, then, was that the Truman administration had ineffectively exercised the leadership demanded of it by the American people and the global community and required by the severe and unprecedented challenge posed by the Soviet Union. As a consequence, the free world was less unified, less vibrant, and less creative than it needed to be in order to wrest the initiative from Moscow. The essential need was to remedy what he diagnosed as Truman's foreign policy pathologies. These were poor leadership and mismanagement, and the failure to develop a comprehensive, integrated, national strategy that encompassed the core and peripheral regions of the globe; established objectives for the long and short term, and set priorities; took into account America's finite resources and the limits on what it could expect to accomplish; and "harness[ed] military plans to a coherent political program."[53]

Eisenhower campaigned, in sum, on the most basic of themes: his administration, unlike the incumbent one, would formulate and pursue a coherent and effective "'cold war' national strategy."[54] This required certain reorganizations of the government's operations. As a minimum first step Eisenhower would establish "a commission of the most capable civilians in our land" to "critically review the political policies governing our military program" and the "military program itself in all its significant details." More fundamentally, Eisenhower would restructure the National Security Council. Describing Truman's NSC as "more [of] a shadow agency than a really effective policy maker," he expressly committed his administration to improving its effectiveness.[55]

But elections are not won over NSC mechanics. Besides, Eisenhower wanted to stress to the public that even more critical to an effective—and cost-efficient— strategy than improved planning and coordination was the type of leadership exercised in World War II by George Marshall—and Dwight Eisenhower. To navigate the perilous international waters, "we must have a firm hand at the tiller to sail the ship along a consistent course," he said.[56] He left no doubt that he considered it his duty to become that navigator. "If the experience of 40 years in the military service of my country can help bring security with solvency to my fellow citizens," he said, "I am yours to command."[57]

From Campaign to Governance

On November 4, 1952, Eisenhower defeated Stevenson by an overwhelming margin of some six and one-half million votes. Proportionally his victory in the electoral college was even greater: 442 to 89. The Democrats managed to retain their hold on

the Deep South. But Eisenhower was the first Republican since 1928 to carry
Florida, Tennessee, Texas, and Virginia, and overall he won all but nine states.[58]

Whether this landslide constituted a clear and positive "mandate for change," as
Eisenhower entitled the first volume of his White House memoir, is problematic.
Although his immense personal popularity transcended party affiliation, the rancor
of the campaign exacerbated the preexisting mood of angst. As the pollster Louis
Harris noted, voters saw in Eisenhower "a safety valve for [their] emotions." They
seemed to know only what they did not want—Korea, communism, and corrup-
tion—and the Republicans successfully tarred the Democrats with all three. Other
evils the electorate associated with the Democrats were budget deficits, high taxes,
and inflation. If Eisenhower did receive a mandate, therefore, it must be defined as
largely a demand for better execution and management of policy rather than a radical shift in its direction.[59]

This ambiguity meant that Eisenhower would have to work hard to educate the
public. And he would have to work even harder to get the 83rd Congress to cooperate. The election did return Republican control to both houses, but by a razor-thin
majority. In the House they outnumbered Democrats 221-214, and in the Senate by
only 49 to 47 (and although Oregon's Wayne Morse voted with the Republicans in
terms of the Senate's organization, he labeled himself an "Independent"). Furthermore, this majority was not only unreliably slim, but it was misleading. Because the
campaign had done nothing to bridge the chasm that divided the Republicans, and
because Eisenhower was determined not to yield to the right wing, he would have
to attract support from the other side of the aisle. It helped that both Democratic
leaders, Sam Rayburn and Lyndon Johnson, came from the conservative South
(and Eisenhower's birth state of Texas). Many Democrats subscribed to a Keynesian
view of fiscal affairs. And most felt entitled to exact revenge for their shameful treatment by Republican extremists.

While Eisenhower was acutely aware of the challenge that confronted him, he
was supremely confident that he possessed the experience and ideas to meet it.

PART II

PROCESSES AND INPUTS

5

Organizing for National Security

The President . . . said that he wanted every member of the [National Security] Council, both statutory and invited, to feel absolutely free to bring up any idea they wished for discussion at this table. As soon as possible, however, a written report on such a subject should be prepared and put through the Planning Board before the Council gave it final consideration. Freedom to discuss should not imply hasty decisions.[1]

Memorandum of NSC discussion (1954)

No American president believed more strongly than Eisenhower in an orderly system for strategic planning and policy making, and that a well-conceived organization was essential for such a system. "Organization cannot make a genius out of an incompetent" or "make the decisions which are required to trigger necessary action," he reflected in retirement. "On the other hand, disorganization can scarcely fail to result in inefficiency and can easily lead to disaster."[2] The cold war magnified the importance of this truism. "[S]ituations of actual or probable conflict change so rapidly and the weaponry of modern military establishments increase their destructiveness at such a bewildering speed," explained Eisenhower, that the U.S. president "will always need the vital studies, advice, and counsel that only a capable and well-developed staff organization can give him."[3]

Eisenhower developed these convictions, as discussed in chapter 2, over the course of his lengthy career in the military. During these years as well, he developed a critical perspective on the management styles of Presidents Herbert Hoover, Franklin Roosevelt, and, of course, Harry Truman. It was "inconceivable to me," he wrote later, "that the work of the White House could not be better systemized than had been the case during the years I observed it."[4] Hence if elected president, he vowed throughout his campaign, he would make certain that America's process for national security policy was indeed better systemized.

The Interregnum

Eisenhower lost no time, to borrow his campaign metaphor, taking hold of the tiller and setting sail—literally. On November 29, 1952, under the cloak of great secrecy, he went to Korea. His purpose was to jump-start his administration's discussions of strategy as much as to address the critical task of ending hostilities. Equally important, he wanted his national security advisors to get to know one another on a personal as well as official basis, and he personally wanted to better acquaint himself with them as soon as possible. Eisenhower had learned from his years of command the value of taking into account his subordinates' personalities. In his effort to best utilize them, he would even commit to paper his private assessments of their strengths and weaknesses. "Personally, I like and admire" Dulles, wrote Eisenhower in his diary, for example. "[M]y only doubts concerning him lie in the general field of personality, not in his capacity as a student of foreign affairs. . . . He is not particularly persuasive in presentation and, at times, seems to have a curious lack of understanding as to how his words and manner may affect another personality."[5]

Accordingly, in the brief period between the election and his departure Eisenhower made his top level appointments. Accompanying him on the flight to Korea were Herbert Brownell, political advisor and choice for attorney general; Secretary of Defense-designate Charles E. Wilson; press secretary James C. Hagerty; retired Major General Wilton B. (Jerry) Persons, who would serve as the White House liaison to Congress (a position first established by Eisenhower); and incumbent JCS chairman General Omar Bradley. They were joined at Iwo Jima by Admiral Arthur W. Radford, commander in chief, Pacific (CINCPAC).

The party reached Korea on December 2. Over the next three days they received detailed briefings on the military situation, listened to the recommendations of American and allied personnel, including South Korean president Syngman Rhee, and toured the countryside. What Eisenhower learned reinforced his belief that "we could not stand forever on a static front and continue to accept casualties without any visible results." He learned nothing, however, that promised an easy resolution to the war.[6]

While Bradley and Radford flew ahead to Pearl Harbor, for the return trip the president-elect chose to travel slowly by sea. At Guam he and the others transferred to the cruiser *Helena*. Off the coast of Wake Island on December 7 a helicopter brought other principals, including Dulles; Secretary of Treasury–to-be George Humphrey; Eisenhower's nominees for budget director, Joseph Dodge, and secretary of the interior, Douglas McKay; General Lucius Clay; speechwriter Emmet Hughes; and Charles (C. D.) Jackson, Henry Luce's longtime lieutenant at Time-Life, whom Eisenhower had known since World War II and would soon appoint the first White House assistant for cold war strategy.[7] Isolated in this relaxed atmosphere for the three days it took to reach Hawaii, Eisenhower and his advisors discussed primarily budgetary matters and the first State of the Union address. In Hawaii, however, where Radford learned of his impending appointment as Bradley's successor to chair the JCS, Eisenhower shifted the conversations' focus to national security affairs.[8]

Foreshadowing his leadership style, Eisenhower let Dulles initiate the discussions.[9] He rehearsed his grounds for pessimism. The Soviet aim, Dulles insisted, was to "extend our resources & our patience and divide us internally by mounting a series of local actions around the world at times and places of their choosing." In response the United States must no longer behave "like a boxer who abides by the Marquis of Queensbury rules" but take off the gloves and seize the initiative. "The way to stop him [the Soviets] is to be ready and able to beat him at his own game." This would entail accepting "risks," but "disaster is almost a *certainty*" if the United States refused to accept them and persisted along its present course.[10]

None of this was new or precise; but it posed for debate the central strategic issue: the nature of the Soviet threat and the appropriate U.S. response. Dulles's remarks, therefore, suited Eisenhower's purposes perfectly. In his view, only if he was exposed to vigorously articulated competing diagnoses and prescriptions, and only if he received candid information and advice, could he make the sound and informed decisions on which a consistent and coherent national strategy depended. Moreover, only if his advisors actively participated with him in the process that produced his decisions could he be confident that they fully understood and would loyally support them. Without this understanding and support, Eisenhower was acutely aware, he could not efficiently mobilize and orchestrate the resources necessary to implement the decisions over an extended period of time.

Accordingly, Eisenhower conceived of the *Helena* "retreat" above all as an opportunity to introduce his advisors to what he considered the two complementary essentials of an effective advisory process. First, they must engage in the "freest and fullest kind of discussion and argumentation, even in those cases where they found it impossible to reach an agreement."[11] Second, they must function as a team. Productive teamwork, his advisors had to understand, did not require the one to sacrifice for the many. What was required, to the contrary, was that the one contribute with enthusiasm and conviction while recognizing that through cooperation and coordination the total effort will always exceed the sum of the individual contributions.

Participants subsequently described the *Helena* meetings as "interesting," "enjoyable," "fine," "helpful," and "good." For his part, Eisenhower announced at one of his cabinet's first sessions that the talks constituted the "most satisfactory conference of his life."[12] Doubtless he exaggerated. Nevertheless, the president certainly believed that by the time the *Helena* docked in New York City on December 14, his national security planning process was well under way.

Reforming the NSC System

As a next step, between January 12 and 13, 1953, Eisenhower gathered around him at his Commodore Hotel headquarters his future NSC, cabinet, and White House staff. Together they completed work on the State of the Union address, and defined staff functions. In the process Eisenhower built upon the foundation of rapport laid during the campaign and aboard the *Helena*. "I hope," he began the Commodore meeting, "that before we have gone very long each one of you will consider the rest of you here your very best friends in the world so that you can call up and do your own coordinating. That is the perfect way."[13]

Eisenhower was no Pangloss. He would not depend solely on this ideal for the degree of coordination his management style demanded. Shortly after returning from Korea he had created a President's Advisory Commission for Government Organization (PACGO), composed of his brother and closest confidant, Milton S. Eisenhower, Arthur Flemming, and Nelson Rockefeller. It began immediately to solicit advice from experienced Washington hands on how to make executive operations more effective, and at the Commodore it made its initial report.[14] But, as memoranda from veteran NSC staffers indicated, the deficiencies in the national security machinery warranted more specialized attention than could be provided by PACGO, especially because that commission was resisted by those within the Republican Party who preferred that reorganization proposals come from a second Hoover Commission over which Congress would exercise control.[15]

Dulles, as discussed in chapter 3, shared Eisenhower's concern with the "dispersion and confusion" that he felt plagued Truman's national security organization. Shortly after Eisenhower had invited him to join the administration, Dulles prepared a memorandum on the state of foreign policy making. There was now so much overlap and competition between Foggy Bottom and the other departments and agencies that contributed to America's international activities, it read, that no longer was the role of the State Department, and its secretary, clearly defined. As a consequence, security policies and programs suffered from duplication, inefficiency, and incoherence. Making matters worse, efforts to clarify the relationship of State to other departments had led to unsound proposals. As an example, Dulles cited the first Hoover Commission's recommendation that the State Department "make foreign policy" but not "engage in operations"— an artificial division that in Dulles's opinion was a recipe for disaster.[16]

As would become manifest during his tenure in office, Dulles's remedy with respect to the secretary's role was to work hard at gaining and maintaining the president's esteem and confidence, to articulate as precisely as possible the prerogatives of his office and department, and to defend vigorously those prerogatives against any potential usurper. Regarding the more general issue of orderly policy making, he supported Eisenhower's effort to revamp the NSC. In contrast to his earlier view, by 1952 Dulles no longer identified the NSC as a challenger. Indeed, he fully endorsed Eisenhower's campaign promise to redesign and rationalize the NSC so that it could bring essential order to the national security process, to "transform this agency [the NSC] from shadow to substance."[17]

At the Commodore Eisenhower began making good on that promise by announcing his appointment of Robert Cutler to fill the new position of special assistant to the president for national security affairs. A Boston banker, Cutler had served on Marshall's staff during World War II, been a special assistant to Secretary of Defense James Forrestal, served on the Truman NSC senior staff as the deputy director of the Psychological Strategy Board (PSB), and been the resident expert on the NSC aboard the campaign train.[18] Eisenhower instructed him to present to the Commodore gathering a "dissertation" on this "subject in which I am vitally and deeply interested."[19]

Cutler reviewed the Council's organizational history since its creation in 1947, quoted from Eisenhower's campaign speeches, and outlined his duties. In his capacity as the president's special assistant, he would not, Cutler explained, offer substantive advice on policy. Rather, he would confine his responsibilities to improving the NSC's performance in order to ensure that it became the critical element in the administration's national security procedure. His goal was a process that ensured that Eisenhower's decisions on policies resulted from the merits of recommendations he received, not the bureaucratic acumen of the recommenders. Toward that end, Cutler would oversee the NSC's reorganization and then manage its operations. He would carry out these custodial functions, he added with emphasis, with a "passion for anonymity," making "no speeches except when ordered by the Cabinet or the President."[20]

Cutler immediately set to work reforming the NSC structure. Having already received copies of the recommendations sent to PACGO,[21] he organized "study groups" comprised of Truman veterans such as Paul Nitze, Sidney Souers, Gordon Gray, Allan Dulles, W. B. Leach, and W. Y. Elliott. These groups, in addition to presenting their individual and collective advice, reviewed past NSC papers, heard expert testimony, and compiled memoranda from such other experienced national security hands as Ferdinand Eberstadt, George Marshall, Robert Lovett, Charles Bohlen, and James Lay. Appropriately, Marshall, so familiar with the military's advising system and so much Eisenhower's mentor, set the tone. Truman's NSC was too "evanescent," the former Army chief of staff and secretary of state and defense testified. The meetings were "of busy men who had no time to pay to the business before them, and not being prepared, therefore took refuge in non-participation or in protecting their own departments." This shortcoming, said Marshall, was exacerbated by two additional serious weaknesses: the NSC's policy papers, on the one hand, "never presented alternatives to decide upon," and, on the other hand, President Truman was "not a leader, a force at the table to bring out discussion."[22]

The other experts echoed these themes and added supplemental criticisms.[23] An effective national security policy required an organic connection between different agencies from the domestic, diplomatic, and military spheres; and also the integration of ends, means, and financial resources. This necessitated, first of all, more direct and constant presidential involvement throughout the policy-making process. Further, the NSC's deliberations could be made more productive, according to these authorities, by broadening attendance at meetings within practical limits, improving coordination and liaison between the participants, and providing planners with more intelligence and information, particularly on military matters unfamiliar to many civilian advisors, than was the norm under Truman.[24]

In addition, the study groups' catalog of recommendations continued, the NSC must be supported by a full-time "nucleus" staff or secretariat that collaborated as a unit. Its members should have no responsibilities other than to serve a "senior staff," "advisory board," or "central substantive staff," comprised of delegates from each department or agency represented on the NSC. Ideas and recommendations must flow from this board up to the Council members as easily as in the reverse direction lest it end up only finding ex post facto justifications for already arrived at decisions. At both levels hard questions had to be asked, and policies must be continuously reviewed and reappraised. The advisory board had to prepare papers for consideration that explicitly stipulated the pros and cons of differing positions, rather than reflect compromises that presented the full Council with a fait accompli by papering over disagreements. In certain circumstances, moreover, knowledgeable civilians might be invited to participate in NSC discussions as a further safeguard against parochialism and premature closure.[25]

But even then, presidential leadership was pivotal. The president should be at the center, with ideas and views "moving centripetally from all sides to him."[26] Whenever possible he must attend NSC meetings in order to hear personally the advice and debate. This was because no matter how precisely the draft NSC papers spelled out differences among the departments and agencies and how well the White House special assistant for national security affairs performed his custodial role, only the president possesses the stature to make sure that conflicts are brought out into the open for debate. It was imperative that this open exchange take place in the Council itself in order to ensure that a wide spectrum of options was covered, to mitigate buck passing, and to instill within those departments and agencies responsible for implementation the understanding and loyalty that participation in the formulation would generate. Moreover, as one Harvard political scientist who participated in Truman's NSC system asserted, "It is impossible for the President to devolve to any other official in the Government sufficient authority to *force* a settlement where there is a strong divergence of views among his principal Cabinet [i.e., national security] officials."[27]

The recommendations Cutler received from the study groups were consistent with Eisenhower's own views as to what was required for the NSC to become, as Eisenhower demanded it become, "the most important policy-making body in government." By that he did not mean that the Council would decide policy. He alone would take the decisions; the Council would only offer advice. But its role would be critical to the process.[28]

Cutler's comprehensive and detailed plan for reorganizing the NSC system, reflecting his consultations with Eisenhower, his advice from the Truman NSC veterans, and his own experience, was submitted on March 16.[29] The next day the president approved it in toto and directed Cutler to present him promptly with the list of nominees for the NSC Planning Board proposed by the heads of the departments and agencies and endorsed by Cutler himself "so that I can decide on their appointments and the Planning Board can begin to function. I place great emphasis on the selection of men of high calibre for these positions, able to devote plenty of time to their Planning Board functions; for thereby the Council will be better able to operate promptly and effectively."[30]

Eisenhower's NSC System

Eisenhower's NSC system has often been depicted as a cumbersome bureaucratic machine that spewed out piles of useless paper. That is a caricature of its actual operation.[31] It did, of course, produce many policy documents. But the great value of the system lay in the vigorous and informed debate regarding national security policy that it generated among the key officials and the president, as well as among officials at lower levels of the agencies. The NSC papers and debates served several essential and interdependent needs.

By design the NSC papers and discussions normally concentrated on setting the basic guidelines necessary for coherent policy and planning. Eisenhower never intended the official statements of policy the Council produced to serve as blueprints for operations. They were intentionally general and strategic in that that they were driven by longer term premises and objectives. Eisenhower's experiences from the Kasserine Pass through the Battle of the Bulge impressed upon him that situations evolve in unique, not preconceived ways. For the day-to-day, tactical decisions that had to be made under ever-changing circumstances, especially during a crisis or emergency, Eisenhower planned from the start to convene a select group of advisors for informal meetings in the Oval Office.

Without question, however, the formal NSC deliberations and conclusions informed the informal meetings. "To my mind," Eisenhower wrote for posterity, "the secret of a sound, satisfactory decision made on an emergency basis has always been that the responsible official has been 'living with the problem' before it becomes acute." For this reason, the NSC was "the most important weekly meeting of the government," he advised his successor, John F. Kennedy. "Failure to use, on a continuing basis, the National Security Council," Eisenhower was convinced, "entails losing the capacity to make emergency decisions based on depth of understanding and perspective — that is, on a clear comprehension of the issues involved, the risks, the advantages to be gained, and the effects of this particular action."[32]

Eisenhower was also convinced that the scope of the president's responsibilities makes it essential for him to focus on issues that were strategic or of unusual importance. For less critical issues, therefore, and for much of the execution of policy, he must delegate authority to his subordinates. The NSC meetings, Eisenhower believed strongly, were the most effective means to school his subordinates about the guidelines he expected them to follow. The dissemination of NSC records of action following the meetings, moreover, provided the insurance against an official charged with implementation misinterpreting a decision or directive.[33]

The two factors most essential to the effective functioning of the NSC system were the president and the Planning Board.

The President's Role

As prescribed in Cutler's plan, the president was to chair the NSC meetings and to lead the discussion "by asking for views around the table so as to bring out conflicts" and to create a sense of participation.[34]

Eisenhower fulfilled these functions assiduously. Normally the president presided over a two-hour meeting once a week. Indeed, Eisenhower missed but six of the 179 meetings that took place during Cutler's nearly-four year tenure as special assistant for national security affairs; he received detailed briefings on those rare occasions when he was absent.[35]

"In order to make possible a genuine exchange of ideas and foster free discussion," Cutler's report had recommended, "there should not, as a general rule be more than *eight* persons who have the right formally to participate as Council members."[36] Including statutory and "standing-request" members, the Council initially consisted of the president, vice president, secretaries of state, defense, and treasury, and the directors of the Office of Defense Mobilization (ODM) and the Mutual Security Agency (renamed the Foreign Operations Agency in August 1953).[37] The CIA director, the chairman of the JCS, and the special assistant to the president for cold war operations (a position Eisenhower created to supervise psychological warfare) would attend meetings regularly as advisors. Other officials, such as the chiefs of staff, service secretaries, chairman of the AEC and attorney general would be invited when appropriate. In addition, because the NSC procedure required all policy proposals to include a budgetary annex, so, too, would the chairman of the Council of Economic Advisors (CEA) and director of the Bureau of the Budget (BOB). (Eisenhower later instructed the BOB director regularly to attend the NSC meetings.)

In addition, the reforms allowed "civilians without departmental responsibilities" on occasion to serve as consultants to the NSC on specific policies or programs. For this same purpose, the president could create temporary committees and commissions. Not only could these private citizens proffer potentially instructive counsel but also, to the extent their participation was revealed to the public, their involvement, in Eisenhower's judgment, would strengthen domestic and international "confidence in the adequacy of the nation's security." The president believed that maintaining congressional and allied political and economic support for his policies and programs hinged on developing this confidence.[38]

At the weekly NSC meeting the president was flanked by Secretaries Dulles and Wilson at a table just large enough to hold the regular NSC members and special invitees. Cutler, with two assistants, sat at the end of the table and presented the topics on the agenda one by one. A small number of observers sat along the wall but took no part in the discussion. CIA director Allen Dulles opened each meeting with a relevant intelligence summary. For each paper Cutler explained the "splits" before the discussion began. Typically, Eisenhower would turn to Secretary Dulles for the first comment. Again, in the main, discussion and debate took place between Dulles, Wilson, Admiral Radford for the JCS, who participated actively even though he was nominally an advisor, and Humphrey, with interventions by Harold Stassen, the director of the Foreign Operations Administration, Vice President Richard M. Nixon, and occasionally others.

As succeeding chapters will show, the debate was almost always vigorous and intense, with each of the major participants stating his arguments or rebuttals forcefully. The president took an active part in the debates, injecting comments, questions, and sometimes playing "devil's advocate," in order to probe the alternatives or implications of a proposed course. To make certain that such discussions were not mistaken for decisions, a formal record of action (decisions) was prepared after the meeting and approved by Eisenhower. Even if Eisenhower seemed during deliberation to favor of a course of action, he might ultimately reject it. "He could be very enthusiastic about half-baked ideas in the discussion stage," an impressed Nixon later explained, "but when it came to making a final decision, he was the coldest, most unemotional and analytical man in the world."[39] Indeed, Eisenhower had the unusual ability to shift his mind between two modes: policy discussion and decision making.[40]

The Planning Board

The policy papers that made up the NSC's agenda were prepared by its Planning Board. For Eisenhower, the Board was pivotal to the deliberative and informed policy-making process Eisenhower insisted on. "You Council members . . . simply do not have enough time to do what needs to be done in thinking out the best decisions regarding the national security," he explained at an early NSC meeting. "Someone must therefore do much of this thinking for you."[41] That was the task for the Planning Board, and to the president nothing was more vital. In a letter appointing a member of the Planning Board he wrote, "the effective functioning of the Council depends in good measure upon the sufficiency and the high quality of the support which it derives from the Planning Board."[42] He prohibited its members, except when absolutely necessary, from accompanying their principals on trips out of the country so that they could "stay on the job and supply a continuity of planning and thought."[43]

The Planning Board was composed of senior officials appointed by the president but nominated by and representing the regular members of the NSC (except for the vice president).[44] Each Planning Board member was to be the principal planning official for his department or agency head in order to assure that he have free access to his chief and the entire bureaucracy.[45] At the same time, however, Eisenhower insisted that just as the NSC members were to see themselves as part of a "corporate body" whose responsibilities were to the president, not to their department or agencies, so the members of the Planning Board were "to search and to seek with their background and experience statesman-like solutions to the problems of national security, rather than to reach solutions which represent merely a compromise of departmental positions."[46] Moreover, because the Planning Board would be taking "a new look at existing policies and programs," Eisenhower preferred that its members be "new faces" not identified with those policies and programs.[47]

The Planning Board's importance to the policy-making process cannot be exaggerated. It was the forum in which twice or more often a week officials of great "stature and calibre" interacted and collaborated with one another in an effort to analyze trends, anticipate as well as identify problems, consider proposed solutions' advantages and disadvantages, and confront—explicitly—questions of means and ends. The Board was also the channel for drawing on and integrating into the policy process relevant expertise, intelligence data, and experience from the rest of the government. The members not only had full access to their own departments and agencies, but they could request memoranda, staff studies, and other pertinent data from others when appropriate.[48]

The Planning Board sought to resolve disputes between the positions taken by different departments or agencies, but "never with a view to watering-down a basic split or to 'sweeping it under the rug.'" To the contrary, Cutler followed the study groups' advice and placed a premium on sending up to the NSC drafts that, by setting "splits" side by side in columns, expressed as sharply and precisely as possible whatever divergent views remained in order that the Council members understood the conflicts clearly. The papers, and debates that led to them, normally focused on establishing the general framework and goals of policy, as opposed to immediate brushfires, thereby, Cutler hoped, promoting the maximum degree of coherence and continuity.

The Planning Board meetings were extremely intimate and informal. They were held in a small room, at a table seating only nine or ten, and with others sitting around the wall as observers. Actually, the debate was carried on mainly by four or five members of the Board, representing State, Defense, the JCS, Treasury, and the CIA, with the Mutual Security, ODM, or other members intervening at times. This small number of discussants allowed direct give-and-take in argument. Further, the members were not constrained in their comments or proposals to the jurisdiction of their agency—Robert Amory, Jr., CIA deputy for intelligence, and the JCS member, while formally advisors, took full part in the general discussions. Cutler, in presiding, confined his role primarily to focusing the exchanges, clarifying papers, and ensuring that "splits" were clearly articulated. An average paper took three or more three-hour sessions and several redraftings to hammer out. One outside witness to Planning Board meetings remarked, "never have I seen a group of men keener, more sensitive in their instinct to understand what was said, more sympathetic to a presentation, or more penetrating in their questions."[49]

The NSC plan approved by Eisenhower also made sure that the NSC members came to the meetings adequately prepared to discuss the papers on the agenda. It provided that everyone on the Planning Board had "an unbreakable engagement to brief the head of his department or agency before every Council Meeting."[50] In the State Department, for example, Secretary Dulles always received a memorandum from Bowie, as his Planning Board member, explaining the issues on the NSC agenda. He also met for as much as two hours the afternoon before each NSC meeting with Bowie and the relevant regional or functional assistant secretaries and other experts from the department to discuss the upcoming papers, especially any splits. The secretary was not, of course, obliged to support his Planning Board delegate in the NSC, but he would understand the grounds for the positions taken by him and was aware of opposing views. The president also received similar briefings from Cutler and his staff, and he expected all the NSC members and advisors to be fully informed and prepared to express their considered opinions.

By identifying the core questions and highlighting differences, the papers focused the NSC debates. The debates themselves provided the opportunity for additional explanation and elaboration, and in most circumstances issues that remained contentious could be carried over to succeeding meetings. During the interim, the Planning Board prepared revised drafts as directed by the records of action. Concurrently, the principals consulted Eisenhower, their staffs, and one another. By the time Eisenhower approved a paper, therefore, his key subordinates—and theirs—were intimately familiar with its substance and rationale. Thus the papers produced by the Planning Board educated those officials charged with executing Eisenhower's decisions and enhanced their fealty to his policies.

The Special Assistant for National Security Affairs

The role of the special assistant was completely different from what it became during later administrations. Cutler was not a policy advisor but still an important official. His task was to manage the NSC system to ensure that it functioned as Eisenhower intended, and he had only a small staff to assist him. Thus he controlled the agenda of the NSC and the flow of work in the Planning Board. He chaired the Planning Board sessions in the fashion already described, making sure that the papers clearly articulated the disputed issues; and he briefed the president before NSC meetings. Perhaps his most important task, nevertheless, was to present the Planning Board papers at the NSC meetings, tending to concentrate on the splits which had to be resolved. At times, this had the effect of "short-changing" the discussion of broader issues, on which there was not disagreement but which would have deserved more consideration by the Council. Indeed, in 1958, during Cutler's second term as special assistant, Eisenhower expressed his "strong preference" that the Council meetings "focus *less* on discussion of papers and *more* on discussion of [provocative] issues . . . which required high level thought." Cutler agreed to do so although, perhaps not fully grasping the president's point, he stressed the value of the policy papers in focusing debate.[51]

The NSC process was undoubtedly time-consuming. Yet as any participant would attest, it virtually assured that the key policy makers, and especially the president, had become informed about the background of various issues and their implications, and had extensively discussed U.S. interests and possible actions before specific decisions had to be taken. This process created a context that greatly improved the odds that such decisions would be more rational, better informed, and coherent.

The Operations Coordinating Board

Even before Eisenhower adopted the new process of policy formulation, work had begun on improving the procedure for implementation. The result was the administration's creation of the Operations Coordinating Board (OCB) in September 1953. As Cutler explained, "just as [the] Planning Board on one side of NSC helps *draft* policy papers so the Operations Board on the other side of [the] NSC would help *coordinate* development to carry out such policy papers." Toward this end the OCB not only oversaw coordination but at intervals of three to six months transmitted to the NSC two-part progress reports that summarized those actions taken to execute a policy and evaluated the policy's "effectiveness, timeliness, and applicability." Cutler would include discussion of these reports on the NSC's agenda. For this reason he described the OCB as the "counterpart down-side" to the Planning Board's "upside."[52]

The NSC's secretariat traced the genesis of both the Planning Board and OCB to Eisenhower's October 8, 1952, campaign speech in San Francisco.[53] Although plans for both were discussed then, the OCB evolved later and less directly. In line with his stress on propaganda and psychological warfare, the new president felt an immediate need to develop greater capabilities in the field innocuously labeled "international information policies and activities." As one way to do so, he created the previously mentioned position of special assistant to the president for cold war operations. As another, shortly before the preinaugural cabinet meetings at the

Commodore Hotel, he asked William Jackson, a veteran of Truman's Psychological Strategy Board, to chair a committee composed of other experts in psychological warfare and propaganda and representatives of State, Defense, and the NSC to review and assess the Psychological Strategy Board's operations and responsibilities.[54]

The Jackson Committee[55] quickly decided, however, that the very term "psychological strategy" was a "misnomer" because it implied that propaganda programs and related means to influence how people thought and behaved could be separated from grand strategy. This implication "does violence to the recorded history of nations."[56] If policy makers placed too much emphasis on the "p[sychological]-factor," they might rely "too heavily on some magical formula of psychological strategy derived from a psychological approach," warned a British authority the Jackson Committee consulted.[57] This would be folly. "Political warfare is not a kind of activity separable from other activities of the government in the foreign field," another memorandum read, "but rather an aspect of the totality of action we call foreign policy." Indeed, "There are no distinctive instruments of political warfare apart from the traditional and the newer instruments of foreign policy." This premise could lead to only one conclusion: "[T]he place for consideration of political warfare problems is at the heart of the national strategic planning process, namely in the machinery of the NSC."[58]

This judgment drove the Jackson Committee to expand the scope of its examination to envelop all dimensions of the "machinery of the NSC." Already Cutler's study of Truman's NSC had identified pervasive shortcomings of execution, as well as the lack of a systematic mechanism for evaluation and reappraisal of current policies and programs.[59] The Jackson Committee heard the same complaints and, more than that, was advised that the problem could be traced to the operations of the PSB—the committee's focus.[60] As things currently stood, the PSB performed the function of overseeing policy implementation out of default, notwithstanding its limited charge and composition. This created confusion and, all too often, a breakdown. "[D]ivorced from the line operations of the responsible departments and agencies in the national security area," the PSB lacked sufficient authority to coordinate effectively the various departments and agencies involved in a program. It also lacked the staff and expertise to evaluate programs adequately.[61] Making matters worse, these efforts distracted the PSB members from exploiting the expertise they did have in psychological planning.

Accordingly, the Jackson Committee determined that "there exists a serious gap between the formulation of general objectives and the detailed actions required to give effect to them." This gap could not and should not be filled by the PSB. It would be more productive to create, "within the National Security Council structure, a group capable of assuring the coordinated execution of national security policies."[62] The committee, therefore, recommended that the president add to the NSC an organ that, like the Planning Board, represented at the highest level the agencies and departments with input into foreign policy. This organ—that is, the OCB—would coordinate implementation of operational plans and propose actions within the framework of approved policies in response to changed circumstances. It would likewise assume responsibility for preparing the aforementioned progress reports that summarized actions taken to execute a policy and evaluated the policies themselves.[63]

The Jackson Committee reported to the president on June 30.[64] Eisenhower's only concern was that with the abolition of the PSB, the "psychological factor" could be overlooked. C. D. Jackson assured him that a small "think tank" within the OCB would "keep track" of psychological dynamics. With that assurance, Eisenhower swiftly endorsed the recommendation, and on July 8 the White House issued a press release. "Establishment of such an Operations Coordinating Board," it proclaimed, "would complete what the President has described as 'the reconstitution and revitalization of the National Security Council' begun last March with the appointment of Robert Cutler as Special Assistant for National Security Affairs, the development of the NSC Planning Board, and the taking of other steps to strengthen NSC operations."[65] Eisenhower instructed Cutler, after consulting the Planning Board and budget director, to work out the details for the OCB's funding and composition, and it was established by executive order on September 2, 1953. To guard against the perception that planning and actions comprised two distinct areas, the Operations Coordinating Board was chaired by the undersecretary of state. It also included the deputy secretary of defense, the deputy director for mutual security, and a special assistant to the president. It would also have an executive officer who would attend Planning Board meetings.[66]

Over the subsequent months and years the administration continually tinkered with the OCB's organization and functions; still, its performance never met the president's expectations. But the OCB's important contribution to America's national security was never questioned, and Eisenhower and his advisors viewed his successor's decision to dismantle it as a grave mistake.[67]

6

How Much Is Enough?

[O]ur system must remain solvent, as we attempt a solution of this great problem of security. Else we have lost the battle from within that we are trying to win from without.[1]

Dwight D. Eisenhower (1951)

The formulation of any national security strategy premised on the long haul approach required an informed and systematic review of the threat assessment, defense plans, forces, and budget inherited from Truman. For this purpose, Eisenhower had distributed to the statutory members of the NSC and others whom Eisenhower intended to include in strategic planning summaries of each existing statement of basic national security policy.[2]

The summaries, explained NSC Executive Secretary James Lay in his covering memorandum, had "no official standing." Rather, they were solely "for the personal use of the recipients in preparing for and engaging in discussions at Council meetings." Accompanying the summaries, moreover, was a memorandum with an array of "major questions" the president's advisors would be asked to examine over the course of these discussions. They did not, Lay's memorandum read, "indicate any proposed policies." They did indicate, however, the basis on which policies should—and would—be proposed.[3] Consequently, they warrant quotation in full:

1. How far can we reduce Soviet power and influence without accepting grave risks of general war?
2. If we continue to contain Soviet power and build free world strength, will an unbearable stalemate ensue?
3. Can we reduce Soviet power and influence without deliberate subversion behind the iron curtain?
4. Do existing policies sufficiently weigh or consider the vulnerabilities of the Kremlin regime (such as indigestive results of swallowing such large areas and populations so rapidly), or the psychological aspects related thereto?
5. Should we support any government, even though totalitarian, provided only that it is independent of Soviet control and influence; or should we work only with "democratic groups"?
6. Under existing policies and programs will we ever be strong enough to negotiate a lasting agreement? What are the conditions, short of unconditional surrender, on

which we would settle? Is there any acceptable temporary accommodation short of ultimate settlement?

7. Can the free world with U.S. leadership, develop an international trade and financial pattern which will eliminate the necessity for U.S. aid or for trade with the Soviet bloc?

8. Despite our offensive capability, are we carrying out adequate programs for defense against atomic attack?

9. In case of general war what conditions, if any, should be placed upon the use of atomic weapons? Under what circumstances, short of general war, might atomic weapons be employed?

10. Do we still believe that the Soviets shun war:
    a. Because they believe they can gain their ends otherwise?
    b. Because of retaliatory power?

11. Should we devote additional resources to carry out our existing policies effectively?

12. Should we reallocate our existing resources among the various security programs? How?[4]

Eisenhower would have preferred that his administration discuss and settle these intimately related questions together and at one time. The pressure of the budget process, however, would not allow for this ideal. The new president had to submit his alternative to the FY 1954 budget already proposed by Truman before the start of the new fiscal year on July 1. Although that interim budget could and did anticipate some of the central aspects of the administration's strategic approach—its emphasis on the "long haul" and primary reliance on nuclear weapons, for example—it inevitably could not reflect a considered revision of overall U.S. defense strategy. In fact, that revision would not be completed until after Congress had approved the new FY 1954 budget, planning was well under way for one for FY 1955, Eisenhower had reconstituted the JCS, and the NSC had developed its first statement of Basic National Security Policy (BNSP). Like Eisenhower, therefore, we must consider the revision of Truman's estimate on defense spending before considering the comprehensive revision of Truman's national strategy.

The "Great Equation"

In seeking to reduce Truman's estimated FY 1954 military budget, Eisenhower proscribed economies that jeopardized U.S. and free world security. The task, as he had described it in congressional testimony as early as 1948, was to reconcile the "conflict" between the "mission of armed forces" and "the economic capacity of " the Nation."[5] That task preoccupied Eisenhower throughout his presidency. "It is the firm duty of each of our free citizens and of every free citizen everywhere to place the cause of his country before the comfort, the convenience of himself," he proclaimed in his inaugural on January 20, 1953. "We must be willing, individually and as a nation, to accept whatever sacrifices may be required of us." But because "economic health" was "an indispensable basis of military strength and the free world's peace," he went on, "only a United States that is strong and immensely productive can help defend freedom in our world."[6]

Eisenhower was confident he was up to solving what contemporary journalists dubbed his "Great Equation": balancing requisite military strength with healthy economic growth.[7] "I know better than any of you fellows about waste in the Pentagon and about how much fat there is to be cut," he told his speechwriters during the campaign.[8] It therefore followed that defense spending could be pared in the same responsible manner that successful businesses held down their overhead.

Toward this end Eisenhower had appointed General Motors president Charles Wilson secretary of defense with the mandate to reorganize the department in order to strengthen civilian authority and improve its administration. Eisenhower recognized Wilson's military and political inexperience. But he had plenty of advisors in these areas, in which he was expert himself. To direct the Pentagon behemoth, he wanted a skilled chief executive officer, and as head of the world's largest corporation, Wilson had a background in budgeting and procurement that seemed to qualify him for the position.[9] "In his field, he is a really competent man," Eisenhower wrote of Wilson a few months into the administration. "I have no slightest doubt that, assisted by the team of civilian and military men he has selected, he will produce the maximum of security for this country at minimum or near minimum cost."[10]

Eisenhower knew he could not bring down military costs to a level he regarded as acceptable solely by eliminating extravagance and duplication. He announced in his February 2 State of the Union address his intention to reassess critically every existing security program.[11] To the NSC the president explained why. "[T]ending to dodge the essential dilemma which faced the country," he remarked with regard to defense spending, "[w]e have been trying to have our cake and eat it at the same time."[12]

Since the outbreak of the Korean War and approval of NSC 68, it must be recalled, Truman had nearly quadrupled the defense budget. The estimate he submitted in January 1953 for FY 1954 anticipated spending more than $45 billion on the military and over $41 billion in new obligational authority.[13] What was more, NSC 141, the reexamination of his security programs that Truman's advisors had completed in January 1953, had called for a significant albeit unspecified increase in defense spending.

During the campaign Eisenhower had vigorously attacked the thinking that produced NSC 141. But once elected, he instructed his NSC to determine "whether NSC 141 is an accurate appraisal of the threat facing the United States and of the programs required to cope successfully with that threat."[14] The document was valuable "as a legacy from three important members of the previous administration who had no personal interest in having its proposals adopted," he explained to his national security advisors when they met in formal session for the first time on February 1.[15] More than that, the president continued, it clarified the "great problem" confronting the NSC: how "to discover a reasonable and respectable posture of defense." With the help of his advisors, Eisenhower vowed, he would "figure out a preparedness program that will give us a respectable position without bankrupting the nation" and "enable the world to reach a decent economic position."[16]

Eisenhower's introductory remarks triggered the first of many NSC debates over the capacity of the American economy to absorb the cost of present security programs, let alone to pay for the additional ones recommended in NSC 141. Not everyone was as pessimistic as the president and his fiscal watchdogs—Secretary of the Treasury George Humphrey and Director of the Bureau of the Budget Joseph Dodge. The meeting adjourned after accepting Cutler's suggestion that the NSC continue this discussion at the next meeting and that Humphrey and Dodge prepare written statements of their positions.[17]

Concurrently Wilson conducted a parallel exercise in the Pentagon. NSC 141 was not the only written evaluation of his security programs that Truman furnished Eisenhower. He had also requested an interagency report on the "Status of United States Programs for National Security as of December 31, 1952." Although the JCS did not complete the military's contribution to this multidimensional NSC 142 until March 1953, within the first two weeks of his tenure Wilson requested that the service chiefs provide him with their comments on the draft as well as their recommendation as to the force levels the Department of Defense (DOD) should use as the basis for revising Truman's estimated budget.[18]

The JCS's response was rapid—and discouraging. In the chiefs' collective judgment, "the current programs for allocation of resources to military purposes are generally inadequate to provide the forces which are desirable to meet the threat of Soviet military power predicted for the years 1954–1955, which is considered to represent a very dangerous period." Furthermore, they claimed, each of the already overextended services had a "vital need for some increase in its combatant forces and personnel to fulfill the missions for which it will be responsible in implementation of the United States Joint Outline War Plan (JOWP) for 1954 (JCS 2143/6) or NATO Medium Term Defense Plan [DC-13], due to the increased capability of the USSR."[19]

The sole dissent came from Admiral William M. Fechteler, the chief of naval operations. In his view the JCS overestimated the Soviet threat, especially the atomic threat to the United States, and underestimated the "retaliatory threat" that America and its NATO allies "posed to the U.S.S.R."[20] The other service chiefs rejected this argument. To the contrary, they warned, the administration must not "pursue a program which would emphasize any single concept at the expense of other well considered concepts, and which would permit the concept so favored to command a major portion of the total resources available to the military establishment." What is more, the Joint Strategic Plans Committee (JSPC), writing on behalf of the JCS, predicted that except for the probable termination of hostilities in Korea by the middle of 1954, there would be "no other significant change in the present world situation." The conclusion was inescapable. Wilson must budget for "continuous and progressive improvements in our military forces" at every rung of the escalatory ladder.[21]

Wilson, no doubt for tactical reasons, withheld this conclusion from the NSC when it reconvened on February 18. Instead, budget director Dodge, armed with detailed charts, took center stage. Dodge had earned a reputation for austerity as Eisenhower's financial advisor during the early occupation of Germany, and then MacArthur's in occupied Japan. Now, focusing on the national debt and taxes, the former Detroit banker "raised the crucial question as to whether we can afford to keep absorbing our resources at this rate and maintain our free and democratic way of life." He then distributed a Bureau of the Budget statement that answered emphatically in the negative.[22]

Dodge concluded his briefing by offering a solution that he and Humphrey had concocted through an exchange of letters following the February 1 meeting. In essence they proposed that the administration determine the defense budget in the context of an established ceiling on all expenditures during the fiscal year. "This means," Humphrey explained in a letter Dodge read out loud, "that the total cost of all present policies will be known before any are authorized so that if the total contemplated is more than we can afford, the various policy items [primarily military programs] . . . least necessary can be either curtailed or eliminated to bring total expenditures within the limits we want to set for the entire program." Officials *outside* the military, moreover, would screen every defense cost estimate, and except in time of "extreme emergency" the approval of any new program would be contingent on reducing or terminating enough existing ones to produce equivalent savings.[23]

As soon as Dodge completed his presentation, Eisenhower voiced his discomfort with the procedure's potentially deleterious effect on U.S. security. To be sure, the summary memorandum of the meeting read, the president "expressed firm agreement with the general position taken by the Director of the Budget." More specifically, he added that "[w]e must get the budget back into reasonable limits." Yet by asking whether "it might be possible, in looking at the budget, to make cuts in other areas than those of the national security and international relations," Eisenhower hinted at his concern that Dodge and Humphrey neglected to consider sufficiently that economic strength constituted only half of the "Great Equation."[24]

As it had at the February 11 meeting, the president's intervention sparked vigorous discussion in the NSC. Dulles in particular took Eisenhower's hint. The secretary of state argued that before the NSC could establish a ceiling on defense spending it had to agree to a general strategic concept that "brought together and looked at together . . . [a]ll these different pieces of the puzzle." Perhaps, he cited as an example, the development of an increased atomic capability would allow for scaling back America's conventional forces, and thereby produce savings without compromising the security posture. Eisenhower's comment that this approach would undermine current efforts to encourage the Western allies to meet their NATO commitments opened the door for JCS chairman General Omar Bradley, who had been Eisenhower's chief World War II lieutenant. Speaking for the first time, he stated matter-of-factly that "we had to do both things—develop our conventional forces and develop our atomic capabilities." Humphrey's response was equally matter-of-fact: his and Dodge's "whole point" was that this was impossible. With that the NSC agreed to carry over the discussion to the next meeting—and as many additional ones as would be necessary to forge a consensus.[25]

By the meeting on February 25 Dodge had calculated that even if none of NSC 141's recommendations were implemented, current military planning would carry a price tag of $44 billion for FY 1954. Such spending, the budget director forecast, would make it impossible to balance the budget before 1958. Eisenhower was "very clearly disturbed," by both Dodge's projections and the evident discrepancy between his assumptions and those of the Pentagon planners. Without better coordination between the BOB and Pentagon, he complained, the NSC would be paralyzed. It needed more precise figures.[26]

It also needed, or at least might profit from, a perspective less influenced by institutional interests. Eisenhower had just such a situation in mind when during the campaign he proposed to create at "the earliest possible date next year . . . a commission of the most capable civilians in our land to restudy the operations of our Department of Defense" in order to determine the "most economical way to fill the demonstrated needs of the nation."[27] That very morning he and Cutler agreed that the time had arrived to implement the proposal. Therefore as the NSC meeting drew to a close, he announced his decision to invite a panel of "distinguished Americans, broadly representative of the geographic areas and talents of the country," to come to Washington as soon as possible in order to "participate in this review" and advise the Council "on basic national security policies and programs in relation to their costs."[28] From some 20 names suggested by Cutler Eisenhower invited Dillon Anderson, James Black, John Cowles, Eugene Holman, Deane Malott, David Robertson, and Charles Thomas.[29]

The Battle Is Joined

On March 4, 1953, the NSC met to address what Humphrey succinctly labeled the "dilemma represented on the one hand by the demands of the national security programs and on the other by the necessity that this country live within its means." A scheduling conflict forced Eisenhower to leave the meeting early. He insisted, nevertheless, that instead of adjourning the Council continue its discussion. Cutler took this opportunity to brief the members on a revision of the Dodge-Humphrey proposed procedure that had been worked out between the BOB and NSC staff. The "latest device" called for Dodge to figure out what reductions in defense and mutual security spending would be necessary in FY 1954 in order to achieve a balanced budget by FY 1955. Wilson and Mutual Security Administration (MSA) director Harold Stassen would then report to the Council how they could produce these savings and what their impact would be.[30]

Dodge then threw down the gauntlet. In anticipation of the meeting, he prepared a formula to serve as a "springboard for measuring the effects of budget cuts on programs and objectives." As only a "dry run" and exercise "to grasp the essence and magnitude of the problem," he "was careful to point out," he intended to circulate a memorandum including a preliminary FY 1954 budget that deducted 10 percent ($7.8 billion) from Truman's total FY 1954 estimate. He targeted the military, he explained, for more than half of the savings ($4.3 billion), bringing spending down to a little over $41 billion for FY 1954. With further cuts of $15 billion during FY 1955, and again Dodge suggested the majority ($9.4 billion) would come from the military (which translated to reducing defense spending to $35.6 billion), the budget could be brought into balance by that fiscal year.[31]

Although Cutler interjected that the Council's consideration of Dodge's numbers did not imply anyone's acceptance of either the cuts or a commitment to a balanced budget by FY 1955, Wilson "indicated considerable anxiety." Still, with

Stassen concurring the defense secretary conceded that as an exercise the process could prove instructive. He agreed to explore with the JCS what program cuts would have to be made in order to meet Dodge's spending targets. Wilson would also ask the JCS to assess what impact these revisions would have on currently approved national security policies and objectives. The Council instructed Wilson to provide the NSC with a written statement of the results by the end of March.[32]

The service chiefs were prepared. The JCS had just completed the revisions of the military's contribution to NSC 142, the previously mentioned assessment of the status of America's national security programs as of December 31, 1952, commissioned by Truman for his successor. Its substance did not differ from the draft Wilson had read a month earlier. NSC 142 held that the mission of the military program was "(a) Protection against disaster; and (b) Support of our foreign policy." Because current U.S. forces in being were barely adequate for these purposes, military planners did not have the flexibility necessary to respond effectively to a new emergency. Moreover, even with its atomic superiority, "in case war occurs" the United States lacked the military capabilities to "give the nation a reasonable assurance of victory."[33]

Buttressed by an impressive array of tables and graphs that compared each service's force levels on hand and programmed, readiness, and mobilization potential with approved national security objectives, the report concluded that Truman's budget estimate was imperative as a minimum. The JCS recommended, in fact, the financial commitment to the buildup envisioned by the authors of NSC 141.[34]

NSC 142 drove the JCS's response to Dodge's "dry run." The memorandum Chairman Bradley wrote to Wilson in compliance with the NSC's instructions did not mince words. The "build-up of the military strength of the United States," it read, "is the keystone and, indeed, the very life blood" of the free world's strategy "to frustrate the Kremlin design of a world dominated by its will." To impose Dodge's spending limits, the memorandum continued, "would so increase the risk to the United States as to pose a grave threat to the survival of our allies and the security of this nation." In the judgment of the JSPC, the Army would have to reduce its strength from 20 to 12 divisions. The Air Force, which planned to expand from 98 to 143 wings, would have to downsize to 79. Only the Navy would be able to hold its own. It could not, however, redress its existing deficiencies. Therefore, America's armed forces would be incapable of executing the "minimum military tasks in the event of a general war," maintaining an "adequate mobilization base," or carrying out currently "approved policies and commitments."[35]

Bradley could not guarantee that even the current level of activity in Korea could be maintained if the administration reduced military appropriations, and he warned that with or without an armistice there, the United States would be helpless when other local wars erupted. And they surely would, as the communists would perceive America's retrenchment as an invitation to aggression. Hence the JCS prognosis was "a progressive and cumulative loss of positions of importance which could, in turn, eventually reduce the United States, short of general war, to an isolated and critically vulnerable position."[36]

Cutler scheduled the JCS to present their case to the NSC on March 25. At a meeting a week earlier, however, Wilson foreshadowed what the Council members should expect to hear. "[W]e will probably have to try to strike some kind of compromise between the figure for the Defense program set forth in the Truman budget and the figure which would result if the proposed cuts were to be made," he predicted.[37]

In his remarks on March 25 Bradley made clear the extent of Wilson's understatement. In the unanimous opinion of the JCS, he told the Council (whose members, already familiar with NSC 142, also received copies of his memorandum to Wilson), Dodge's formula for achieving a balanced budget and the military's mission to provide for the national security were incompatible. Therefore, even as an exercise the proposal was useless. In succession each of the service chiefs seconded their chairman.[38]

But Wilson offered them only qualified support. On the one hand, he described the military's problem as "extraordinarily difficult" and counseled against arbitrarily setting spending ceilings such as Dodge and Humphrey advocated. On the other hand, he expressed his confidence that by reducing overhead and duplication in programs, "economies could be carried out without producing quite such drastic effects on the nation's security as those which had been described by the spokesmen for the Defense Department." This was all Eisenhower, who had indicated his displeasure with the JCS, had to hear. He had asked them to trim costs and support personnel, not combat forces. No decision would be made on the military budget, the president instructed, until Wilson provided the NSC with a list of the "economies."[39]

NSC 149/2 and the Defense Budget

Wilson had the Defense Department's comptroller scrutinize the claim of each service regarding the impact of a reduced appropriation. By confirming Eisenhower's low opinion of the military's budget process, this review strongly supported the president's premise that major savings were feasible without impairing U.S. defense capabilities. It identified, among other shortcomings, exaggerated figures for procurement costs; failures to take into account existing stockpiles and the large backlog of unobligated funds accumulated from earlier appropriations; little effort to set priorities and "recognize economies in non-essential or less-essential activities and programs"; and no attempt to establish a division of labor among the services. Further, the potential for decreasing noncombatant personnel and increasing unit efficiency had not been examined, and military personnel costs "are perhaps 100 million dollars high in each year because of such factors as an increase in the grade structure of enlisted men." The comptroller thus advised Wilson, "In general the [services'] statement as to the military forces that could be achieved within the expenditure limitations is not valid."[40]

While this review took place in the Pentagon, Cutler scheduled a special session of the NSC from 9:30 to 6:30 on March 31 to hear the views of the civilian consultants.[41] The panel had convened in Washington on March 1 and received extended briefings from Cutler and the heads or their chief subordinates from all appropriate departments and agencies. "[P]robably the most important factor in pending Government decision on this basic national issue," commented Cutler in explaining to the group why Eisenhower sought their counsel, "is not an estimate of Soviet capabilities and intentions, but rather a judgment as to American capabilities and desires as a people."[42]

For the March 31 meeting the consultants prepared a written statement. Following presentations by Wilson, Dodge, Humphrey, and both Dulles brothers, Dillon Anderson read from it.[43] "We have bitten off more than we can chew," he said. The United States could not continue its current deficit spending "and at the same time maintain a strong economy and preserve our fundamental values and institutions." A balanced budget and national security, therefore, went hand in hand. Each member of the civilian panel, moreover, believed "that the Administration could balance the cash budget" in FY 1954. They further agreed that the NSC should proceed on the assumption that doing so was compatible with "a satisfactory national security posture."

The consultants felt that the U.S. mutual security program was significantly overextended, and while the atomic energy program required money for research and development, the production of more fissionable material was wasteful. They dwelt primarily, however, on the "excessive" cost of the military program. A "tightening up of expenditures and certain choices as to emphasis and timing in our preparedness program must be made." There was much too much overlap and duplication, a rigid adherence to force goals adopted in the post-1950 "atmosphere of haste and fear," and disregard for the impact of atomic weapons. The consultants also criticized the military for its "near profligate use of manpower" and for unnecessary stockpiling.

If the administration adopted a "more definitive policy as to scope, pace, and priority, and a consideration at the highest policy level of feasibility, costs and need," the "top figure" for the FY 1954 national security program (military, mutual security, and atomic energy), Anderson said, should be $45 billion. This amount will "produce forced selectivity and economy" but "should not impair our defense posture." In future years, moreover, an appreciably smaller appropriation would be all "reasonable security" should require. And this security could be maintained "on a *sustained* basis" (emphasis in original).

Although generally pleased with the consultants' advice, Secretary of the Treasury Humphrey remained unsatisfied. Having joined the cabinet after years as chair of Ohio's steel giant, M. A. Hanna Company, Humphrey saw a balanced budget, low inflation, minimal corporate taxes, market economies, and free trade as the solution to all national and international problems. He accordingly seized Anderson's presentation as an opportunity to win support for the "radical" changes in the formulation of security policies he and Dodge agreed were imperative. Simply put, Humphrey wanted the NSC to establish a "top limit" of only $40 billion for expenditures and then determine "what it could buy" with it.[44]

The other Council members, however, favored a more moderate approach. Since February they had supported fully the Humphrey-Dodge procedure that every proposed security program be accompanied by an estimate of its cost and recommendations as to where the necessary funding could be found.[45] But to set a ceiling—a low one at that—in advance of formulating a strategy seemed reckless. Dulles especially advised caution, reprising his argument that the "greatest single prevention of global war was a strong and vigorous United States . . . whose capabilities both our friends and our enemies would respect." The secretary of state also described as "absolutely indispensable" the U.S. programs of foreign assistance. Current defense and mutual security spending was appropriate and reasonable. To go beyond finding cost-saving measures, Dulles feared, would prove destabilizing and "produce panic."

Wilson added that he had anticipated many of the consultants' recommendations. Without mentioning the comptroller's criticism of JCS's projections, he notified the Council that in line with his instructions following the March 25 meeting DOD was working on a plan "to achieve expenditure cuts of a notable order." Wilson predicted that it would be "pretty tough" to find sufficient savings to achieve a balanced budget in FY 1955, let alone FY 1954. He said it could probably do so, however, by FY 1956.

Eisenhower expressed his sympathy with both Dulles and Wilson. Indeed, one might infer from the president's remarks and the publicity the White House afforded the "fresh point of view" these "seven prominent citizens" could provide that his true reason for requesting the consultants' input on the budget had more to do with convincing the Republican right wing and the American business community that he was doing everything he could to trim defense spending than with his respect for their advice on weighty strategic issues.[46]

Contravening to a degree Cutler's initial charge to the panel of consultants, Eisenhower said that he was concerned most of all with possibly inviting a Kremlin miscalculation. "If the Soviets attempt to overrun Europe" because they interpreted defense cutbacks as an indication of America's lack of resolve, he said, "we would have no recourse but to go to war." Eisenhower also wondered whether "the dangers to our economy which the Consultants had perceived and emphasized" required him to balance the budget so rapidly. Still not finished, he admonished Humphrey for failing to distinguish clearly between the development and maintenance of security programs. Eisenhower's "own belief" was that "we should now show our determination to move in the direction of a balanced budget rather than to make a sudden cut to achieve that objective now." There was "certainly no point," he continued, "in cutting off your leg because it was injured." All on the Council, save Humphrey, agreed. The NSC then referred the paper back to the Planning Board.

In light of the NSC discussion, the Planning Board drafted a statement on current basic national security policies and programs in relation to their costs. On April 3 it was circulated as NSC 149. "The survival of the free world depends on the maintenance by the United States of a sound, strong, economy," it began. "For the United States to continue a course of Federal spending in excess of Federal income will weaken and eventually destroy that economy."[47]

Following Eisenhower's lead, the draft nevertheless rejected the consultants' advice to target FY 1954 as the year the budget would be brought into balance. The United States "will annually balance its Federal expenditures with its Federal income," it read, only as "rapidly as is consistent with continuing our leadership in the free world." Further, because of existing commitments and responsibilities that must be met, the United States "can approach only gradually a balancing of its Federal Budget."[48]

The Planning Board also determined that the consultants' recommended $45 billion *total* national security budget was unreasonable, to say nothing of Humphrey's $40 billion ceiling. The draft did itemize a number of areas with the potential for substantial savings. These included settling the Korean War, placing more emphasis on "modern weapons," and cutting down on overhead and eliminating waste. NSC 149 also recommended that the administration reduce both U.S. and NATO force goals, that it more rigorously establish priorities among America's foreign interests, and that it scale back stockpiling and plan for a "floating D-Day" in contrast to a year of maximum danger. This last recommendation could produce significant savings by allowing for the purchase of expensive items, especially Air Force equipment, in gradual increments. As a result, military spending could be kept at $43.2 billion for FY 1954, which included $2 billion earmarked for the Korean War.[49] Add to this $6.5 billion in mutual security and $2.5 billion in atomic energy spending, and the total national security budget was slightly more than $52 billion (eclipsing the consultants' figure by some $7 billion). By FY 1955, however, military expenditures could be brought down to $40 billion, and to $35 billion by FY 1956. With corresponding cuts in the mutual security and atomic energy programs, a constant tax rate, and no increase in inflation, by this fiscal year the administration would have a budgetary surplus (which it did).[50]

The NSC discussed NSC 149 at its April 8 meeting. In principle all the members with the exception of Humphrey approved. He still hoped for greater cuts for FY 1954. Cutler gave him some cause for hope, explaining that the figures were not firm until the departments, especially Defense, had time to study them. The Council decided to defer action until the April 22 meeting, even though Foster Dulles, Wilson, Humphrey, Stassen, and Bradley would be in Europe for the NATO meeting.[51]

In the two weeks between the meetings the Office of the Secretary of Defense (OSD) finished its process of budget planning and evaluation of NSC 142 that had begun back in February. The conclusions were compatible with NSC 149's[52] recommendations. By reducing manpower requirements through increased efficiency, training, and weapons modernization, the Army could achieve a still-adequate combat strength of 18 divisions by FY 1956 or 1957. Similar cost-saving measures in the other branches would produce comparable figures. Even the Air Force, which would suffer the most severe cutbacks because of postponements in the purchase of capital equipment, would have the wherewithal to increase to 14 wings in FY 1954. These force levels were entirely consistent with the concept of a "floating" D-day demanded by the long haul.[53]

In fact, in a letter to Cutler prior to leaving the country Wilson suggested some additional savings, and at the April 22 meeting Wilson's deputy Roger Kyes said that it was quite possible that after further examination by his office "still further cuts could be made in the costs of the Defense Department program."[54] Because the JCS had not been consulted by the OSD since the comptroller's devastating review of their postion in late March, Bradley's stand-in, Air Force chief Hoyt Vandenberg, whose service bore the brunt of the cutbacks, was defenseless to object.[55]

Dodge, who participated in the discussion more actively with Humphrey not present, was evidently resigned to NSC 149's formula. He confined his remarks to proposing fewer appropriations for mutual security. When Eisenhower and Under-secretary of State Smith firmly opposed his recommendations, Dodge conceded defeat. With the president's support the NSC had firmly rejected his and Humphrey's—and the Panel of Civilian Consultants'—extreme fiscal conservatism but still pared $5.3 billion in new obligational authority for military programs and $2.3 billion in military expenditures off Truman's estimate. After one final meeting on April 28, the Council approved NSC 149 with only minor revisions as NSC 149/2.[56]

A day later, simultaneous with submitting to Congress his plan for reorganizing the Department of Defense, Eisenhower met with the Republican congressional leadership to explain and defend NSC 149/2 and its FY 1954 budget projections. With Humphrey and Dodge by his side he underscored his administration's recognition "that the time has clearly come when the United States must take conclusive account, not only of the *external* threat posed by the Soviets, but also of the *internal* threat posed by the long continuance and magnitude of Federal spending." Dramatically illustrated by NSC 141, he went on, Truman's quest to build up America's military strength "to a state of readiness on a *specified D-day*" had "largely overlooked or totally ignored the length of time over which this costly level of preparedness would have to be maintained."

NSC 149/2 and its spending program, the president said, redressed this mistake. "The new policy which we are proposing will give primary consideration to the external threat," as it must in an environment punctuated by wars in Korea and Indochina and a Western Europe that remained weakened from World War II. "But it will no longer neglect the second threat." His NSC determined that taxes had to remain at the current rate and the budget could not be balanced immediately because "too arbitrary or too precipitate" action could produce "dangerous and undesirable domestic and international repercussions." Still, by substituting a floating D-day for a specific one, revising downward NATO force goals, reducing overhead and eliminating waste, putting off premature purchases, and taking other cost-saving measures, his proposed budget cut billions off of Truman's and laid the foundation for an ultimate surplus that would permit reduced taxes.[57]

Taft, now the Senate majority leader, nonetheless vehemently charged Eisenhower with Democratic-style fiscal irresponsibility. He "could not possibly express the deepness of his disappointment at the program the Administration presented today," Taft said. The "net result" of Eisenhower's "puny" cuts would be "to spend as much as Mr. Truman spent." That would violate Congress's "responsibility as guardian of the purse-string," chimed in Indiana representative Charles Halleck. He predicted that the House Appropriations Committee would recommend additional cuts. When Eisenhower responded that his lengthy examination had turned up all prudent savings, Taft retorted that then "a whole new study was needed." With "all due respect for the NSC," he added, "he didn't believe that the members knew anything more than he about these problems."[58]

It was all Eisenhower could do to contain his legendary temper.[59] But his dependence on Taft's support in an evenly divided Senate provided him with sufficient incentive to succeed. After "quietly" reviewing the "essentials of U.S. global strategy" and surveying the international problems that drove it, the president "asserted that he could not endanger the security of the country by agreeing to any less than [an] adequate program." He also defended the "National Security Council's competency as being equal to that which any such group would have from living with the problem day after day and keeping it under constant study." He allowed, however, that he would entertain any reasonable congressional suggestion to reduce expenditures.[60]

In the congressional hearings on the budget, the JCS objected strenuously to the proposed cuts in their programs. Eisenhower probably benefited from their testimony. Still, the FY 1954 budget Congress finally approved did in fact reduce the administration's request in military spending from $43.2 billion to $40.3 billion (and mutual security financing from $5.8 billion to $4.5 billion). Eisenhower accepted this reduction. It was necessary price to pay for maintaining the support of Taft Republicans. Moreover, his process had generated valuable debate within the new administration on the most fundamental questions of national security. While many remained to be answered, and the extremes represented by Humphrey and Dodge on one side and the JCS on the other remained dissatisfied, NSC 149/2 reflected the president's insistence on balancing military and economic strength and planning for the long haul.[61]

7

A Chance for Peace?

The new leadership in Russia, no matter how strong its links with the Stalin era, was not completely bound to blind obedience to the ways of a dead man. The future was theirs to make. Consequently, a major preoccupation of my mind through most of 1953 was the development of approaches to the Soviet leaders that might be at least a start toward the birth of mutual trust founded in cooperative effort.[1]

Dwight D. Eisenhower (1963)

One other event dramatically interrupted Eisenhower's plans for an orderly review and revision of basic national security policy, and potentially changed the context. On March 5, 1953, Joseph Stalin died. Because the Kremlin's longtime autocrat had been perceived since the 1930s as the embodiment of the Soviet state, perceptions of him drove estimates of the communist threat. These perceptions produced an ironic mix of dread and comfort. On the one hand, analysts and policy makers alike viewed Stalin as ruthless, megalomaniacal, and quintessentially evil. On the other hand, he was known and considered cautious and predictable. As a consequence, Stalin's death complicated efforts to assess Soviet intentions even as it revealed deep divisons among the perspectives and priorities of Eisenhower's advisors—Dulles and C. D. Jackson in particular.

The Initial Debate

Stalin's sudden passing raised many questions. Who, or which factions, were likely now to exercise power, and what would be his or their motives and chief objectives? If there was a contest for power in the Kremlin, what would be its effect within the Soviet Union and throughout the communist bloc? What influence might the United States exert, and to what end? How would America's allies and nonaligned nations react? Was the world more or less dangerous because Stalin was dead, or should the United States expect little fundamental change?

To Eisenhower's distress, he discovered that Truman and his national security managers had given hardly any thought to these issues.[2] The CIA had not prepared a single intelligence estimate that took into account that Stalin would not live forever. Indeed, not until Moscow's public announcement on March 4 did Allen Dulles learn that Stalin had suffered a heart attack two full days earlier.[3]

On the day the Kremlin announced Stalin was critically ill, Cutler hastily convened a special meeting of the NSC. Although there had been no time to digest the implications,[4] at the outset Eisenhower made his predilection apparent. As a "psychological and not diplomatic move," he said, the "moment was propitious for introducing the right word directly to the Soviet Union." But was it? And what word was right? C. D. Jackson, whom Eisenhower had appointed his special assistant for cold war operations to implement his campaign promise to conduct psychological warfare more aggressively, did not hesitate. Jackson said that at long last the United States had the opportunity to launch an aggressive propaganda campaign to seize the initiative from the communists.[5]

Secretary of State Dulles, however, recommended caution. The department's Office of Research expected the Soviet system and its foreign policies to remain essentially the same whether or not Stalin died. Hence it estimated that Moscow's "unremitting hostility" toward the West and "hard" positions toward Korea, Germany, and all key sources of East-West contention would not lessen.[6]

Personally, moreover, Dulles feared that an aggressive propaganda campaign could boomerang whether Stalin's successors reacted more or less assertively. The former could heighten international tension. The latter could intensify congressional pressure to reduce defense spending and aggravate divisions within the Western alliance.[7]

Eisenhower saw some merit in the arguments of both Jackson and Dulles. With his advisors leading him in opposite directions, he wanted more information before making any decision. The president therefore directed, "as a matter of high urgency," the CIA to prepare an intelligence estimate of the scenarios Stalin's "disappearance" might precipitate and the State Department to draft a statement of the policy implications. Simultaneously, Eisenhower instructed Jackson to formulate a plan for the psychological exploitation of Stalin's death.[8]

Jackson had a head start. As chairman of the National Committee for a Free Europe (NCFE), in May 1952 he had called a meeting at his alma mater, Princeton University, to assess the committee's limited results. Based largely on the findings of a study by Max Milliken and Walt Rostow at MIT's Center for International Studies (CENIS), the group, which included Bohlen and Allen Dulles, concluded that the Soviet regime and its control of the satellites were vulnerable to psychological warfare. The problem lay in Washington. American policy "offered an inadequate foundation for talking persuasively" to the captive peoples of Russia and Eastern Europe. The conferees drafted a statement outlining the type of positive message that should frame future policy. The United States should insist that Moscow lift the Iron Curtain, permit the democratic unification of Germany, and negotiate worldwide arms reduction and control. During the campaign Jackson sent the Princeton statement to Eisenhower, a charter sponsor of the NCFE. "Can I count on it that you people are now going to go ahead and develop an actual plan?" the candidate reportedly responded.[9]

From Jackson's point of view, the NSC meeting of March 4 and Stalin's death on March 5 offered the chance finally to give Eisenhower an answer. He therefore immediately invited Rostow to come to Washington. Working around-the-clock the weekend of March 7–8, the two, with help from members of the Psychological Strategy Board, hammered out a plan. The administration would exploit Stalin's death by undertaking a "comprehensive and decisive program of action" toward achieving the "goal[s] set forth in the [Truman] NSC papers." As a first step, Eisenhower would deliver a "dramatic," well-publicized address that targeted audiences in the Soviet Union, the satellites, Western Europe, Asia, and, of equal importance, the United States.[10]

The speech's "strategic purpose," Jackson explained, would be fourfold. It would be 1) to create dissension within the new Soviet regime by forcing it to make difficult decisions, 2) to present a "vision" of U.S. purposes designed to inspire the Eastern bloc and neutral peoples to identify their aspirations with America's, 3) to foster greater unity throughout the free world, and 4) to rally Americans behind Eisenhower's leadership and programs. Hence, Jackson stressed, it must not be a "reiteration of pious platitudes." Rather, the address must put forth proposals that would "impress upon friend and foe" that the United States was serious about wanting to end the cold war.[11]

Jackson asked Rostow to draft a speech with the concrete proposals. Predictably he built upon the Princeton statement and the CENIS Soviet Vulnerability project.[12] He also incorporated a modification of a "Peace Plan" that had been circulating between the White House and State Department. In February Charles E. ("Electric") Wilson, Truman's director of defense mobilization, had recommended to Eisenhower that in an international broadcast the president advance solutions to the "problems heretofore preventing peace." The State Department would somehow arrange for the broadcast to be transmitted uncensored to the Soviet Union and its satellites and followed immediately by endorsements from the Allies. Dulles wrote Eisenhower that the idea "deserves careful consideration" and suggested that Jackson work up an outline "of exactly what should be said."[13]

The "guts" of the draft speech that Rostow produced for Jackson reflected these materials. Eisenhower would issue a public invitation to reconvene the Council of American, Soviet, British, and French Ministers, which had met for the sixth and last time in the spring of 1949. In doing so, the president would announce he was prepared to table measures to settle the Korean War, unify Germany, end the occupation of Austria, and promote general arms control and specific security regimes.[14]

Over this same weekend the Kremlin announced Georgiy Maksimilianovich Malenkov's appointment as chairman of the Soviet Council of Ministers. On Monday Jackson distributed to the NSC drafts of his plan and Rostow's address. The reception was universally negative. Writing in his private diary, speechwriter Emmett Hughes described the proposals as "incredible gobblydegook" [sic] that alternated between "the banal and the inane."[15] The State Department criticism was more substantive.

In Dulles's absence, the Policy Planning Staff met with Undersecretary Walter Bedell Smith and Bohlen, the administration's top Soviet expert, who while awaiting to be confirmed as ambassador to Moscow remained the department's counselor. While he had attended the Princeton meeting, Bohlen disputed the premises of Jackson's proposed initiative. His judgment was evidently decisive in the PPS's reaching a rapid consensus. The day after Washington learned of Stalin's death, Bohlen had written that a "direct frontal political or psychological assault on the Soviet structure or leadership would only have the effect of consolidating their position and postponing the possibility of dissension in the top leadership." Congruent with his long-held view that the foremost concern of Soviet leaders was the regime's security, he "confidently predicted that the first reaction of the Kremlin will be to pull itself together tightly and show no signs of weakness to the outside world." Bohlen also forecast that if Eisenhower delivered the speech within the two weeks Jackson recommended, the president's behavior would be regarded as in poor taste by the millions of communists everywhere who mourned the passing of a leader they viewed with genuine affection. Accordingly, wrote Bedell Smith in his memorandum supporting the Policy Planning Staff position, at this time a speech of the kind Jackson proposed would probably "prevent the later emergence of opportunities which could be exploited."[16]

In terms of grand strategy, Bedell Smith continued, Jackson leaped to conclusions about which Bohlen and the PPS were highly ambivalent or to which they were opposed. The United States should not propose a meeting of the Council of Foreign Ministers until the administration had considered the disadvantages as well as advantages and completed a great deal of advance planning. Without prior consultation with the French, British, and West Germans, the mere proposal could "create divisive tendencies."

So, too, might Jackson's ambitious agenda for negotiations, Bedell Smith continued. The State Department had consistently held that because they would involve parties whom the United States refused to recognize, Far Eastern problems were not subject to discussion by the Council of Foreign Ministers. It likewise held that a Korean armistice must precede all other settlements. Stalin's death should not affect these positions, nor should it affect the fundamental proposition that the most effective way to weaken the East was to strengthen the West. Hence the administration would have to formulate precisely any overtures to the Soviets concerning central Europe, lest they undermine collective security, particularly but not exclusively by delaying indefinitely European Defense Community (EDC) ratification. In sum, whereas Jackson advocated exploiting Moscow's vulnerabilities, the State Department feared that the Soviets would exploit Europe's to divide the West.[17]

Undoubtedly hoping to preempt the State Department's criticism, Jackson wrote a lengthy letter to Dulles timed to greet the secretary upon his return to Washington from New York. A "certain amount of hell has been popping here," it began. What followed was Jackson's summary of the draft plan and presidential address, review of the objections to both, and rebuttal. Jackson found it "inconceivable" that the administration was not prepared to advance specific proposals at a meeting of the Council of Foreign Ministers. The "actuality is that the United States has in fact thought profoundly about all these issues," he argued. "There is nothing new involved—except the will to bring fresh and imaginative thinking to bear in preparation for the new diplomatic offensive of the United States."

Indeed, to Jackson an "important by-product" of his initiative "would be a reinvigorated Department of State." In this same vein, it would provide the allies "with a unifying sense of purpose and destiny" more than would "dollars and guns." The PPS criticism demonstrated the extent to which it remained wedded to the static policy of containment that Dulles had declared bankrupt and immoral. What he was proposing had a "dynamic quality," Jackson wrote. It corresponded with the "fundamental change" in U.S. foreign policy that "the President and you yourself have wished."[18]

While this debate was simmering, on March 7, Bernard Baruch forwarded to Eisenhower a memorandum written by Samuel Lubell, the political journalist who had written a highly regarded analysis of the 1952 election.[19] Lubell recommended that Eisenhower should propose to the Kremlin a Soviet-American agreement that would set a ceiling on the resources each could devote to armaments, military research, war-related industries, and the like. If the the new regime ignored the proposal, Lubell maintained, its priorities would be revealed to its own and the world's populations. And should the Soviets sign the agreement and then violate the ceiling, they would disclose their aggressive intentions. Hence the West would be warned to mobilize for war, thereby ameliorating the aggressor's "terrifying advantage."[20]

Eisenhower questioned the feasibility of devising a formula for establishing the ceilings, and if ceilings were established, he doubted that the United States could detect Soviet violations.[21] Still, because of his interest in arms limitation, he was intrigued by the concept Lubell labeled "butter over guns." Eisenhower circulated the memorandum among his advisors. The concept, the president suggested, "might evolve into something worth while."[22]

This flurry of activity provided the backdrop for the March 11 NSC meeting.[23] It began with Allen Dulles's summary of the Intelligence Advisory Committee's just completed Special Estimate responding to Eisenhower's instructions at the March 4 meeting.[24] SE-39's judgments were inevitably speculative. Malenkov's rapid appointment to head the new government suggested that the Kremlin had planned in advance for the succession. As a consequence, although a power struggle could still erupt, the Communist Party's control remained secure and internal disputes were likely to be concealed. Hence there was little prospect of a diminution of the bases of state power or of a fragmentation of the Eastern bloc. Stalin's death might exacerbate strains in the Sino-Soviet relationship, but that would only increase the Communist People's Republic of China influence in Asia.

Like the State Department, therefore, the intelligence community foresaw few changes in Soviet foreign or domestic policy. Lacking a leader of Stalin's stature, and probably his skill, the new regime would have less room to maneuver and be loath to abandon established positions. Further, the United States should not expect allied support for proposals that challenged Moscow. The Special Estimate predicted that especially the leaders of Western Europe would urge Eisenhower to exercise restraint and caution, while at the same time hoping that the Kremlin's preoccupation with consolidating its rule would produce a relaxation of tensions.[25]

Jackson laid out his plan without reference to the intelligence estimate. Contrary to its conclusions, in fact, he described the new Kremlin regime as in "disarray" and "panic," and he followed the same line of argument as in his letter to Secretary Dulles. Everything in the draft address, which Jackson asserted had "real bite," derived from Eisenhower's campaign speeches and the Republican platform and "fit into the framework of this Administration's thinking on psychological strategy." As such, his program (which "linked closely" a presidential speech to "all the other facets of American power and influence") must be understood as both a "dramatic psychological move" and a "serious policy proposal." All Jackson needed was authorization; he was "ready to shoot."

When Jackson started to address State's objections, Dulles interrupted. He would speak for his department, the secretary insisted. With that, point by point he concurred with Bohlen and the PPS. Any bold initiatives at this time, Dulles said, would "enhance Soviet family loyalty." At a minimum the United States should delay until "the corpse was buried and the mourners gone off to their homes to read the will." More than that, while Dulles believed strongly that the United States should fan the flames of Eastern bloc nationalism and discontent that Stalin's death would ignite, he believed that the outcome of Jackson's program would be to disrupt the free world coalition. If in his speech Eisenhower called for a meeting of the Council of Foreign Ministers without prior allied accord on the specific agenda and negotiating positions, he would invite disaster.

Dulles took dead aim at Jackson's list of proposals. "[H]istory proved that the Soviets," he said, "would resort to all their devices for delay and obstruction." Dulles had learned from his own experience that the Kremlin's negotiators could be counted on to say anything in order to give "new heart" to "neutralists," divide the West, and extend the talks. He was "sure," for example, that they would tie together discussions of German unification and arms controls in an effort to "ruin every prospect" for EDC ratification, drive a deeper wedge between Bonn and Paris, and undermine those European leaders most friendly to the administration. For Dulles, the Soviet "Note" in 1952 proposing a Council of Foreign Ministers meeting designed to negotiate the neutralization and demilitarization of a unified Germany was an object lesson. It seemed to him that Jackson was disregarding this precedent simply because Stalin had died.[26]

Accordingly, Dulles opposed a Council of Foreign Ministers meeting at this time regardless of what prior agreements might be reached with America's allies. He would not, however, rule out Eisenhower's marking Stalin's death by delivering a speech. But in his opinion, the secretary of state concluded, a more "positive and constructive" speech than Jackson's draft would be one that avoided mention of the Council of Foreign Ministers and only renewed previous U.S. proposals for resolving the Korean and Indochina conflicts. This tack would avoid the pitfalls of "begin[ning] from the European end" and yet "satisfy American opinion that no attempt to cause the Soviet to change its spots had been le[f]t unexplored."

Neither point of view satisfied Eisenhower. He shared Dulles's assessment of a precipitous meeting of the Council of Foreign Ministers. A "formal multilateral meeting," he forecast in a letter to British Prime Minister Winston Churchill, "would give our opponent the same kind of opportunity he has so often had . . . to balk every reasonable effort of ourselves and to make the whole occurence [sic] another propaganda mill for the Soviet."[27] Yet like Jackson Eisenhower wanted to do "something dramatic to rally the peoples of the world around some idea, some hope, of a better future." The West "should give up any more appeals with regard to specific issues," he determined. But he could "say that he would be ready and willing to meeting with anyone anywhere from the Soviet Union provided the basis for the meeting was honest and practical."

The speech Eisenhower had in mind, then, differed from the recommendations of both Jackson and Dulles. Building on Lubell's concept, the president proposed that Jackson develop a new "psychological plan" and speech that focused "on the simple theme of a higher living standard for all the world." An appeal to this "universal desire," he said, "might really work." Jackson objected, but to no avail. He had had his "full day in court," and Eisenhower had delivered his verdict.[28]

A "Serious Bid for Peace"

Immediately after the meeting Jackson instructed Rostow to revise the speech, a task Rostow finished by the end of lunch.[29] Yet what he produced was hardly the new speech Eisenhower had asked for. Rostow did delete all references to a Council of Foreign Ministers meeting. Instead of omitting mention of specific issues, however, he simply changed the verb. Whereas the initial draft read that the United States would "propose" measures to unify Germany, end the occupation of Austria, terminate the Korean War, and control armaments, it would now merely "seek" measures toward these same ends. The draft discussed the relationship between the arms race and domestic welfare in one brief paragraph. It included not a word about converting military to consumer spending. Dulles's displeasure was palpable. "I just don't see [a] solid purpose in this," he said.[30]

Apparently Eisenhower agreed. He shifted primary responsibility for drafting the speech to Emmet Hughes. But before Hughes could make any progress, Malenkov stole a march on the administration. Having in his eulogy at Stalin's funeral raised the possibility of detente with the West, on March 15 the Kremlin's new leader proclaimed to the Supreme Soviet that all existing international disputes could and should "be decided by peaceful means, on the basis of mutual understanding." Their nuclear capabilities, he added shortly thereafter, obligated Moscow and Washington to reach an accommodation. His government, Malenkov declared, was prepared to negotiate with the United States toward this end.[31]

Virtually no one in the administration interpreted Malenkov's overture as anything other than a "peace offensive" designed to undermine Western unity.[32] Virtually no one, however, doubted its appeal. At a minimum, there was now the danger that Eisenhower would be perceived as engaging in a sterile competition to "out-offer" Malenkov.[33] The peace offensive, Dulles and Eisenhower agreed, made a major presidential address more imperative than ever.[34] But they were less certain than ever about what he should say. Clearly the plan to finesse such specific issues as German unification, ending Austria's occupation, and a Korean settlement by focusing on solely the universal desire to improve their standard of living was no longer viable.

Unable to receive adequate direction from either Dulles or Jackson, Hughes went directly to Eisenhower. "You know, it is so difficult," the president said. "We are in an armaments race. Where will it lead us?" Pacing around the Oval Office in a wide arc, Eisenhower grew more intense. "You come up to these terrible issues, you know what is in almost everyone's heart is peace, you want so much to do something—and then you wonder if there really is anything you can do by words or promises."

With the "air of a man . . . fast veering toward a conclusion," Eisenhower made clear that he had to try. "Let us talk straight," he told Hughes. On the one hand, Jackson's psychological plan offered only "double talk," "sophisticated political formulas," and "slick propaganda devices." On the other hand, if Dulles and "his sophisticated advisers . . . can *not* talk of peace seriously, then I am in the wrong pew." Eisenhower suggested that he could combine an appeal to the Soviets' interest in improving their standard of living with calls for troop withdrawals from and free elections in both Europe and Asia. This speech would "cut out all this fooling around and make a serious bid for peace."[35]

Eisenhower instructed Hughes to convene a meeting with Dulles and Jackson on March 17 to get their reaction to his giving a "speech just ASSUMING that Malenkov was a reasonable man with whom we had serious differences to iron out." Neither liked it, particularly after Eisenhower discussed his latest ideas for its contents. It would be useless for Eisenhower to "talk about schools and hospitals for the ignorant and sick" to the Soviets, responded Jackson, because "their idiom is totally different" from America's.[36] Dulles argued that any proposal to negotiate limits on conventional forces as well as atomic weapons would create serious difficulties with the allies and require the military to overhaul completely its plans. Eisenhower retorted to Jackson that he knew a lot more about Russia and the Russians than Jackson did.[37] As for Dulles's concerns, they were surmountable "provided we have a plan of action."[38]

Eisenhower Takes Charge

Dulles was not persuaded. Rather than continue the argument, however, he assigned Paul Nitze, who still directed State's PPS, to work with Hughes. They rapidly agreed on the wording of a proposal to reduce the level of U.S. and U.S.S.R. military spending to a percentage of each's gross national products. But each time Hughes drafted a section of the speech addressing a specific political or military issue, the PPS objected. Even though Eisenhower would not propose the Council of Foreign Ministers meeting, State Department planners held, the mere mention of German reunification and an end to the occupation of Austria would all but guarantee that the Soviet government would. Hence the administration could not avoid "getting into a corner on this willingness to meet with the Russian leader." If it refused, Moscow would portray the United States as militarist and obstructionist. If it agreed, the Kremlin would recycle its old proposals in an effort to neutralize Germany and end all hope for the EDC. Either way, free world unity and confidence in U.S. leadership would suffer. It would be far better to keep pressure on the Soviets. Eisenhower's insistence that an armistice in Korea precede any subsequent settlements could help, but this stipulation would probably impede the current negotiations.[39]

Nitze's reports to Dulles about the difficulties with the drafting reinforced the secretary's reservations. By the beginning of April he no longer believed Eisenhower could give any speech that served U.S. interests. The danger that it would encourage allied wishful thinking that the Malenkov regime posed less of a threat to the free world than had Stalin's was too great.[40] Nitze recognized this danger. Nevertheless, he still thought a speech designed to explore whether the new Soviet leadership had a genuine interest in seeking negotiated solutions to at least some outstanding issues could be valuable. Nitze therefore urged that Eisenhower postpone giving it until the State Department had more time to address the current draft's deficiencies and consult America's allies.[41]

The president opposed a delay, in part because his appraisal of allied cohesion differed from that of Dulles and the State Department. Virtually from the moment the Kremlin announced Stalin's death, Winston Churchill had implored Washington to reconsider its reluctance to negotiate with Moscow.[42] Encouraged by Malenkov's subsequent expressions of interest in peacefully resolving East-West differences, the division of Europe in particular, the British prime minister cabled Eisenhower on April 5 that the allies must "lose no time" in exploiting "the apparent change for the better in the Soviet mood" and "finding out" the extent of the new regime's commitment to "easing things up all around." In his reply the president discussed his planned speech. If he did not give it soon, Eisenhower did not doubt that Churchill would give his own. And in all probability he would call for the very four-power meeting that Eisenhower and the NSC had rejected.[43]

There was a more basic cause for Eisenhower's sense of urgency. The president considered it vitally important to investigate as rapidly as possible whether Malenkov was at all sincere in wanting to ease world tension. A speech indicating that the United States and its allies were "deadly serious in our search for peace and are ready to prove this with acts and deeds" was a means to produce evidence. The Kremlin might "retreat into their shell." That itself, Eisenhower said, would be revealing. But he would not rule out Malenkov's responding positively. That would show, Eisenhower stated clearly, that "some kind of *modus vivendi* might at long last prove possible."[44]

Eisenhower thus insisted that in time for delivery on April 16 Hughes complete a new draft that would "delineate, at least in outline, the specific steps or measures that we believe necessary to bring about satisfactory relationships with resultant elimination or lowering of tensions throughout the world." He wanted to offer Moscow the opportunity to signal its commitment to negotiating in good faith on issues ranging from ending the Korean War to reunifying Germany to permitting free elections in Eastern Europe to controlling the arms race. At the same time, he wanted to "make strong mention of the fact that we are going to go RIGHT AHEAD rearming until it's clear we no longer have to."[45] Nitze and other State Department representatives "worked over" Hughes's revisions "with the meticulousness of a treaty negotiation," and the speechwriter regularly sent Eisenhower and his brother Milton the updated versions. By April 10 the president was prepared to "freeze" the text.[46]

Dulles, however, continued to find fault with it.[47] Eisenhower decided to have one final meeting to iron out the remaining problems. Although Dulles was away from Washington, on April 1 the president asked Hughes and Bedell Smith to join him and Milton Eisenhower in the Oval Office. As soon as they arrived, Eisenhower showed them another cable he had just received from Churchill. Eisenhower had forwarded to him the latest speech draft, and the prime minister expressed concern about the terms it set for a Korean armistice. Raising such issues as the repatriation of prisoners, free elections aimed at unifying the country, and establishing a neutral zone in North Korea along the Yalu, Churchill worried, "might quench the hope on an armistice." Ironically, therefore, whereas a few days earlier Churchill's impatience had been seen as a reason not to delay his address, the prime minister was now urging the president to "bide your time. . . . [I] cannot see what you would lose by waiting till the full character and purpose of the Soviet change is more clearly defined." It would be a "pity," he followed up the next day, "if a sudden frost nipped spring in the bud."[48]

Bedell Smith jumped at the opening. With characteristic bluntness he told the president, "I've been opposed to a speech from the beginning." Further, Dulles's undersecretary continued, "so I think [h]as the State Department." Bedell Smith explained that however carefully worded, the speech could be used by the Kremlin to derail progress toward free world unity and collective security. For his part, he never thought it was a good idea to offer to negotiate with the new regime, no matter the specifics of the proposals, until the United States was sure that the negotiations would produce a retraction of Soviet power. "I don't think it's good strategy," Bedell Smith said to Eisenhower in the vocabulary of their special relationship, "to call on your GHQ artillery until you've got your target clearly sited—and I don't think we have it clear yet."[49]

Eisenhower was "shocked." He was also angry. "I don't know what I've got State Department advisors for," he fumed, "except to tell me things like this and not keep them to themselves all the time." What troubled him even more, it became evident, was the viewpoint Bedell Smith expressed and ascribed to all of his colleagues at Foggy Bottom. Not only did they appear uninterested in testing the new regime's intentions, but they also seemed opposed to resolving any East-West problems without prior guarantees of an imminent Soviet surrender. "[O]bviously we aren't going to liberate east Europe tomorrow," said Eisenhower in frustration. "[M]y god that's a job for ten years." But he could confine his speech to "the simple things. . . . THEN we can go ahead to the big things." A *modus vivendi* with the Soviets could never be the ultimate objective of U.S. national strategy. If one could be achieved, however, it would facilitate the consolidation of the West, thereby improving its financial, political, and strategic position so that it would be better prepared to take advantage of increasing discontent within the Soviet bloc as it progressively became more manifest. In the meantime, the world would be made less dangerous.[50]

Eisenhower had taken charge. He would give the speech and, to minimize future confusion and controversy, he personally supervised the final revisions. In an effort to strike a balance between Churchill and his State Department, the president drafted entire passages that he intended to sound neither "belligerent or truculent" to the Soviets nor too conciliatory to the West. Convinced that "it is primarily our growing and combined strength that is bringing about a change in the Russian attitude," Eisenhower wanted it understood throughout the world that he was not suggesting amendments to the West's current military plans. But he likewise wanted it understood that he was not presenting Moscow with ultimatums. He intended merely to state that he would "welcome" progress toward international peace and freedom. Indeed, the president would pledge that if his speech resulted in constructive Soviet behavior—with regard to Korea, Austria, Germany, wherever—the Eisenhower administration would "meet them half way." The fundamental message Eisenhower wanted conveyed to the Soviets was that "all we want is sincerity, sincere acts, not talk, sincerity — whatever they want to do . . . all they've got to do is DO them."[51]

For the next several days Eisenhower labored over the text. It was exceedingly difficult to produce a serious speech that the Kremlin could not exploit with only token gestures. Not until April 15 was Eisenhower satisfied. By this time, he had aggravated his stomach condition to the extent that some within the administration questioned whether he was in too much pain to deliver it. Those closest to the president, however, never doubted that he would and could.[52]

Not long before he signed off on the final draft, Eisenhower decided to call the speech "The Chance for Peace."[53] On April 16 he presented it to the American Society of Newspaper Editors. It was up to the Soviets, Eisenhower challenged, to join the United States in seizing the "precious opportunity" afforded by Stalin's death to "turn the tide of history." Even a few "clear and specific acts," he said, "would be impressive signs of sincere intent. They would carry a power of persuasion not to be matched by any amount of oratory."[54]

The speech was conspicuously devoid of details. As the State Department urged from the beginning, moreover, its initial focus was on the Far East. Eisenhower called upon the Kremlin, as a "first great step," to spare no effort in order to produce an "honorable" armistice in Korea that would lay the groundwork for free elections. But as a signal of Moscow's genuine interest in a "true and total" peace in Asia, even a constructive role in negotiations leading to a cessation of hostilities in Korea would be insufficient. The communists would also have to cease all "direct and indirect" aggression in Indochina and Malaya.

Eisenhower then moved on to discuss Europe. To end "the present unnatural division of Europe," he stressed, the Soviets could take initiatives that would generate the environment that the United States thought necessary for future negotiations—especially on arms control—to succeed. He cited as illustrations that the new regime could conclude a treaty with Austria to terminate the occupation, it could agree to a procedure for Germany unification that guaranteed the German people both their political and territorial integrity, and it could promise to recognize the "full independence" of each nation in Eastern Europe.

From one perspective, then, the address recycled most of America's claims to innocence and demands since the start of the cold war. In Eisenhower's own view, however, what distinguished his speech from, for example, Truman's cold war rhetoric, or even his own inaugural address, was its nonconfrontational tone. His intention was to articulate simply and objectively what had to be the ultimate bases for a stable peace and normal U.S. relations with the Soviet Union. He did not confront Moscow with a specific set of conditions or a timetable; he focused only on making a start toward improving relations. In addition, even as he presented the Soviets with a catalog of "deeds" that would provide the new leadership opportunities to demonstrate a genuine interest in relaxing tensions, he cataloged the "Costs of a World in Arms" and proposed concrete measures to reduce the "burden of armaments." In this manner, Eisenhower sought to indicate that his overarching objective was to generate the environment necessary to pursue disarmament agreements that would lessen the possibility of general war and related schemes by which the savings in money and resources could be applied to improve the global standard of living. He genuinely believed he was asking the Soviet leadership to choose between war and peace, fear and security, hunger and prosperity, and stagnation and productivity.

The administration arranged for "The Chance for Peace" to be translated into some 45 languages. It was broadcast over combined radio and television networks throughout the free world, carried over the Voice of America and Radio Free Europe, and distributed worldwide through press releases and more than three million pamphlets. The West uniformly applauded.[55]

But two days later, Dulles addressed the same Society of Newspaper Editors, and his abrasive tone may have worked at cross purposes with the president. Dulles focused exclusively on containment and deterrence.[56] Belittling Malenkov's peace offensive as a peace *defensive* prompted by the the free world's successes, Dulles said that "We are not dancing to any Russian tune." The secretary reaffirmed America's commitment to NATO, EDC ratification, and other military measures designed to "deter attack from without." America's first priority was peace in Korea, but, Dulles warned, in seeking an armistice "we will not play the role of supplicants." Nor would Washington allow the communists to exploit the cessation of hostilities in one Asian theater to "pursue aggressive war elsewhere in the Far East." As if to put the new Kremlin regime on notice, Dulles emphasized the administration's intention to increase its military and financial assistance to the French in Indochina and to tighten the blockade of communist China. This was necessary, he announced, because "our Eastern friends, from Japan, Korea and Formosa, to Indochina and Malaya, face a single hostile front."

The West must keep up its guard, Dulles explained, because the future "must always remain obscure so long as vast power is possessed by men who accept no guidance from the moral law." Stalin's death, accordingly, must not be allowed to affect America's duty. A people with "the tradition and power of the United States," he concluded, perhaps with allied opinion in mind, "must act boldly and strongly for what they believe to be right."[57]

Eisenhower apparently did not consider Dulles's text to be inconsistent with his own.[58] In the president's mind, the two speeches represented two sides of the same coin. Eisenhower had expressed his hope that Stalin's death created a "chance" for peace — not his confidence that it had. And he had made a special point of highlighting the West's need to continue to build up its military strength until concrete Soviet actions justified behaving otherwise. Notwithstanding his efforts to speak to a future in which negotiations replaced indictments and butter replaced guns, Eisenhower made clear that the prerequisites for normal East-West relations and a secure international peace required the Kremlin to reverse, even if incrementally, the fundamentals of Stalin's postwar policy.

The Soviets' tepid response did not provide Eisenhower with a basis for optimism. *Pravda* did carry a complete and accurate translation of the president's address and "an unprecedented" six-column article on the front page, a positive sign according to some observers.[59] But as Bohlen pointed out from Moscow, the article's content and tone could hardly be interpreted as positive. It placed the "onus" of the cold war squarely on the United States, defended the correctness of past Soviet foreign policy, accused the United States of delaying German reunification, and derided the idea of restoring "the reactionary regime[s] overthrown by [the Eastern European] peoples."[60]

What was more, the ambassador's analysis of *Pravda*'s evaluation of Eisenhower's and Dulles's addresses stressed that although the Kremlin seemed to think the two speeches were contradictory and reserved its "sharpest language" for the secretary's, it did not seem to welcome either enthusiastically. The new regime, Bohlen wrote, was careful to avoid "the appearance of throwing cold water" on the U.S. initiative. But by not suggesting any specific actions the Soviets would consider taking, it was "cautious and wary even to the point of indecision." Indeed, "the article gives no new information or clue concerning future Soviet positions in regard to specific subjects listed by the President." A Special Intelligence Estimate concurred and drew the inevitable conclusion: "The statement gives no indication that the rulers of the USSR will modify their stand on any of the issues outstanding between East and West" or "that they are prepared to make substantial concessions."[61]

Despite the assessment of later scholars, it was therefore not "curious" that Eisenhower refused to follow up his speech with any proposals to negotiate.[62] "We have so far seen no concrete Soviet actions which would indicate their willingness to perform in connection with larger issues," he wrote Churchill several weeks after delivering his address. Hence "[p]remature action" by the West "would risk raising hopes of progress toward an accommodation which would be unjustified." It also "might have the effect of giving the Soviets an easy way out of the position in which I think they are now placed."[63]

It would have been illogical for Eisenhower to react differently. Until the Soviets took some initiatives in response to his challenge to them, until they agreed to at least some of the measures he proposed, he could only assume that the new regime remained too wedded to the Stalinist past and the Soviet peace offensive was a charade. To assume otherwise would run the risks articulated so vigorously by Dulles and his State Department associates.[64] It would also risk irreparably damaging Eisenhower's relations with the Republican right wing. As a consequence, in the final analysis the speech became primarily a weapon in C. D. Jackson's campaign of psychological warfare.[65]

Although Eisenhower was disappointed, perhaps the Soviet response was inevitable. Recently uncovered evidence suggests that the Kremlin was never united in its peace overtures, and *Pravda*'s publication of Eisenhower's full text and the article evaluating it was a strained effort at a compromise. Dismissing Eisenhower's speech as specious propaganda in contrast to Dulles's expression of America's true intentions and goals, Malenkov's opponents, above all Foreign Minister Vyacheslav Molotov, exploited his efforts to forge a detente with the United States in order to cast doubt on his fortitude and undermine his leadership. And even Malenkov's purpose seems primarily to have been to build up his own authority and legitimacy as a statesman by forcing Eisenhower to agree to a summit meeting.[66] Most fundamentally, given the pervasive climate of fear and suspicion, probably nothing the president of the United States could have said in April 1953 could have induced the new regime to "do" what Eisenhower insisted it must to signify its sincere intent. Hence his position would remain as it had been since Stalin's death.

Nevertheless, the speech did shed light on several of Eisenhower's most fundamental strategic notions. Chief among these were what he considered the prerequisites for normal East-West relations, his conviction that abnormal relations did not preclude supporting partial measures for relieving tensions, and his profound interest in reaching some type of accord on arms control. Further, because neither the president nor anyone else could discount completely the possibility that "basic changes in Soviet policy were in the offing," Eisenhower insisted that "it behooved us to study the problem constantly." The burden was on the Kremlin to provide the evidence, and "we must do our best to anticipate absolutely everything that the Russians were likely to do in the next weeks and months."[67]

8

The Solarium Exercise

[D]on't talk about decisive action until all the facts are laid out cold and hard. . . . Against such a background the NSC would be qualified to come to a decision."[1]

Dwight D. Eisenhower (1953)

The debate and decisions over the 1954 defense budget and the "Chance for Peace" speech established some specific guidelines and clarified many of the priorities and attitudes of the president and his major advisors. The administration substituted a long-haul approach and made clear its determination to constrain spending, although without seeking to balance the budget so abruptly as to impair security programs and capabilities. The "Chance for Peace" address, moreover, laid out Eisenhower's concept of the conditions required for ultimate peaceful and normal relations with the Soviets, as well as his deep concern with the escalating arms race and willingness to negotiate for their limitation. Similarly, Dulles indicated the priority he placed on maintaining the cohesion of the alliance, his deep skepticism over negotiating with the Soviets, and his support for a robust defense posture as a foundation for foreign policy. The JCS insisted that this foundation required more military spending; Humphrey and Dodge insisted it would be solid even with much less.

The ground was now cleared for a systematic effort to elaborate a comprehensive national strategy by developing answers to the basic questions posed by Cutler's memorandum to the NSC at the start of the Eisenhower presidency. In May that effort began in earnest.

The Origins of Solarium

To assist the NSC's examination of his 12 questions, on May 1 Cutler instructed the Planning Board to draft a working paper that codified existing security policy. The members rapidly produced a synthesis of NSC 20/4, 68/2, and 135/3 from the Truman era and the Eisenhower administration's own 149/2. By the time the president approved this document as NSC 153/1 on June 10, however, the policy-making process had taken an extraordinary turn.[2]

On May 8, just a week after the Planning Board set to work on NSC 153/1, Eisenhower held an off-the-record meeting from 5:00 to 6:45 in the afternoon with the Dulles brothers, Humphrey, Smith, Jackson, and Cutler in the White House solarium for the purpose of generally discussing the state of East-West relations.[3] "It is difficult to conclude that time is working in our favor," the secretary of state began the discussion. "In the world chess game, the Reds today have the better position. . . . Practically everywhere one looks, there is no strong holding point and danger everywhere of Communist penetration." Therefore it was evident that the "course" mapped out by Truman is "a fatal one for us and the free world." Unless "we change this policy, or get some break, we will lose bit by bit the free world, and break ourselves financially."[4]

Dulles expected little help from the Western allies. Reminiscent of his pre–World War II analysis, he described Europe's leaders as "shattered 'old people'" who hoped that the "Soviets, like Ghenghes [sic] Khan, will get on their little Tartar ponies and ride back whence they came." Lacking "the strength, the dynamic" required to meet a threat more severe than that of Hitler's Germany, they "want to spend their remaining days in peace and repose." Consequently, they were "willing and glad to gamble" with the free world's future.

"[C]an Western civilization survive?" Dulles asked. Only if the administration accepted its "duty to take leadership at a fast and vigorous pace," he answered. Then he outlined what he saw as the available options. On a "grand scale," the United States could "draw a line and tell the Soviets that if one more country on our side of the line should succumb to Communism by overt or covert aggression from the outside or (more likely) by cultivated indigenous uprising from within, that would be a casus belli between the U.S. and the Soviets. This alternative risks global war."

On a "lesser scale," Dulles proposed limiting the line to Asia and warning Beijing and Moscow that "if one more country falls to Communism on our side of the line, we will take measures of our own choosing." In his judgment, "This alternative might not risk global war," especially if in support of it the United States could "work up an Asian NATO." To do so, however, "would take a long, long time," Dulles estimated.

Dulles's third option, which he indicated he preferred and was compatible with either of his first two, was "to attempt to restore the prestige of the West by winning in one or more areas a success or successes." The "Communists have won victory after victory in the post-war years," Dulles lamented. Consequently, "[a] success for the free peoples is badly needed." For this purpose, Dulles recommended that Eisenhower pursue the policy of "boldness" he had prescribed during the campaign. Even as it deterred further Soviet advances, this policy would revive morale in the West and promote liberation in the East. On the one hand, it would force the Kremlin to "think more of holding what it has" and "less of gaining additional territory and peoples." On the other hand, it would throw "Stalin's monolith" into disarray, transforming it into a "loose alliance" with greatly diminished capabilities and certain to break apart.

While the others remained mostly silent, a dialogue ensued between Dulles and Eisenhower. The president agreed that "the present policy was leading to disaster."

He disagreed that time was America's enemy, however, because he did not share Dulles's bleak assessment of the state of the alliance. Hence he rejected the need to accept the risk of general war that both of Dulles's "drawing the line" options entailed.

Moreover, in expressing his preference for his third option, and dropping the modifier "peaceful" that Eisenhower had insisted that he use during the campaign, the secretary of state seemed to the president to parallel the views of Nitze and NSC 68. The successes that Dulles considered so imperative to shift the cold war's momentum, Eisenhower said, would come about when the populations of both the East and the West "see freedom and communism in their true lights." That "will take time, but it must be done." When Dulles replied that "talk about 'liberty' doesn't stop people from becoming communist," Eisenhower fired back, "It's men's minds and hearts that must be won."

Eisenhower did not foreclose examination of Dulles's options. To the contrary, he proposed to turn the debate into an exercise that would analyze competing national strategies for dealing with the Soviet Union. He suggested that the administration assemble "teams of bright young fellows." Each team would "take an alternative" and "tackle" it "with a real belief in it just the way a good advocate tackles a law case—and then when the teams are prepared, each should put on in some White House room, with maps, charts, all the basic supporting figures and estimates, just what each alternative would mean in terms of goal, risk, cost in money and men and world relations."

Eisenhower's exchange with Dulles produced an exercise unique in the history of U.S. national security policy making: Project Solarium.[5] Cutler briefed the NSC about it on May 13, but it took several more weeks to arrange the mechanics.[6] A working committee comprising Cutler, Smith, and Allen Dulles supervised the organization, which included the appointment of a panel, chaired by General James Doolittle and including Robert Amory, Lt. General Lyman Lemnitzer, Dean Rusk, and Admiral Leslie C. Stevens (whose 1951 lecture to the National War College, it should be recalled, so impressed Eisenhower), to draft "precise and detailed terms of reference for each alternative." Among the factors each task force would be asked to consider were "forces needed, costs in manpower, dollars, casualties, world relations; intelligence estimates; time-tables; tactics in every other part of the world while actions were being taken in a specific area; relations with the UN and our Allies; disposition of an area after gaining a victory therein; influencing world opinion; Congressional action required."[7]

Also at issue was the phenomenon of atomic plenty. When, at the May 13 NSC meeting, Vice President Richard Nixon asked what the administration's policy would be once the Soviets had "amassed a sufficient stockpile of atomic weapons to deal us a critical blow and to rob us of the initiative in the area of foreign policy," Eisenhower responded "that Project Solarium was being initiated with this precise problem in mind."[8]

The Doolittle Panel formulated terms of references for the three task forces accordingly. The advocates of Alternative A were to develop arguments and propose programs that supported the existing policy summarized as follows: "(1) To maintain over a sustained period armed forces to provide for the security of the United

States and to assist in the defense of vital areas of the free world; (2) To continue to assist in building up the economic and military strength and cohesion of the free world; and (3) Without materially increasing the risk of general war, to continue to exploit the vulnerabilities of the Soviets and their satellites by political, economic and psychological measures." The policy defended by Task Force B would be "(1) To complete the line now drawn in the NATO area and the Western Pacific so as to form a continuous line around the Soviet bloc beyond which the U.S. will not permit Soviet or satellite military forces to advance without general war; (2) To make clear to the Soviet rulers in an appropriate and unmistakable way that the U.S. has established and determined to carry out this policy; and (3) To reserve freedom of action, in the event of indigenous Communist seizure of power in countries on our side of the line, to take all measures necessary to re-establish a situation compatible with the security interests of the U.S. and its allies."9

The objective of Alternative C would be rollback, a policy designed "to force the Soviets to shift their efforts to holding what they already have rather than concentrating on gaining control of additional territories and peoples and, at the same time to produce a climate of victory encouraging to the free world." Hence those assigned to it would recommend programs "(1) To increase efforts to disturb and weaken the Soviet bloc and to accelerate the consolidation and strengthening of the free world" and "(2) To create the maximum disruption and popular resistance throughout the Soviet Bloc." Task Force C's members, the Doolittle Panel made explicit, must recognize that "[w]hile this policy is not designed to provoke a war with the Soviet Union, it involves a substantial risk of general war."10

Consistent with the administration's concern with the Soviets' growing atomic capabilities from the perspective of both America's vulnerability to a surprise attack and the resolve of the Western allies, the Doolittle panel proposed a comparable examination of preventive war.11 Cutler and Solarium's other organizers, however, postponed staffing out this "Alternative D" pending the completion of an intelligence estimate of its "major premise": "[A] few years hence, the Soviet atomic capability might well present an unacceptable risk to the security of the United States." And by the time the task forces began work, preventive war had been excluded from consideration. Perhaps this was because SE-46 ("Probable Long Term Development of the Soviet Bloc and Western Power Positions"), which was not completed until July, concluded that although "it is likely that within the period of this estimate the West and USSR will each have the means of delivery with which to cripple the other, . . . neither side would be able to prevent powerful retaliation in kind."12 More probably, Eisenhower, even before receipt of SE-46, intervened to proscribe considering seriously what he long held would be suicidal atomic exchange.

The Cutler, Smith, and Allen Dulles working committee established the criteria for selecting the task force participants. Members of Task Force A were to have an "intimate understanding of the past policies and actions of the United States, the rest of the free world and of the U.S.S.R., and broad gauge political, military, economic and psychological planning for the future." The requirements for inclusion on Task Force B were an "intimate knowledge of communist reactions and methods; sound political and military judgment both regarding the Communist orbit and the free world; knowledge of United States military capabilities to wage general war, including the use of unconventional [i.e., nuclear] weapons; [and] ability to evaluate the economic capability of the United States and the rest of the free world to support the alternative." The qualifications for working on Alternative C included "imaginative military, political, psychological and subversive planning experience; profound experience on Soviet-Communist actions and reactions; knowledge of the military situation in Korea and Soviet satellite areas; and ability to evaluate the economic resources required to follow such a course."[13]

Eisenhower approved the final composition of the task forces.[14] Indeed, in certain cases the president evidently directly influenced the selections. For example, General (then-Colonel) Andrew J. Goodpaster learned from Cutler that "President Eisenhower had put me on Task Force C. He wanted the rollback option thoroughly evaluated, and he said he wanted somebody with common sense . . . on Task Force C to see that they didn't go completely off on their analysis." According to Goodpaster, in fact, Eisenhower's decision "against the rollback policy . . . was finalized at the time of the Solarium exercise."[15]

Eisenhower was probably also responsible for the role George Kennan played. The Solarium working committee initially nominated Paul Nitze, the primary author of NSC-68, for membership on Task Force A. But Nitze excused himself because of unspecified "other commitments."[16] Conversely Kennan, whose State Department career Dulles had terminated and who was left off the original list of candidates, was ultimately chosen to chair Task Force A.[17] As with Goodpaster, it is likely that Eisenhower, who respected Kennan greatly, insisted that the first PPS director prominently participate.[18]

The Task Force Reports

Cloistered in the National War College with a support staff and the latest intelligence reports, economic data, and other pertinent materials at their disposal, the task forces began to formulate their cases at the start of June. To promote rigor and symmetry, the Working Committee provided each with a list of questions parallel to but more detailed than those Cutler had developed for the NSC in early February.[19] The task forces met in plenary session on June 26.[20] On July 16 each presented its recommendations to a special meeting of the NSC.[21]

Although the memorandum of the meeting's discussion has disappeared, the presentations can be inferred from the written reports on which they were based (Task Forces B and C actually organized their written reports according to their planned oral presentations).[22] Notwithstanding the task forces' access to government documents, these reports, because of "limitations of time and considerations of security," relied "extensively on the peculiar knowledge and judgment of individual members of the group." No president before or after Eisenhower, however, ever received such a systematic and focused briefing on the threats facing the nation's security and the possible strategies for coping with them. Therefore the reports warrant detailed review with a focus on the fundamental issues and arguments.[23]

Task Force A

The argument of Task Force A reflected Kennan's overarching influence. He wrote the sections that established its "philosophical" thrust. Predictably, although the task force concluded that "there are areas in which significant improvements could be made within the framework of NSC 153/1," Kennan defended the original framework—NSC 20/4—that he had essentially designed for Truman. The task for the Eisenhower administration was "to rectify imperfections in our strategy; give it new confidence, boldness and constructiveness; recapture flexibilty; effect better integration; and improve implementation."[24] So long as the United States avoided the political, economic, and military mistakes of the interwar years, the report stressed, the strategic balance, the aspirations of peoples and nations, and time all favored the free world. Its "basic advantage can be maintained and exploited to bring about the diminution of Soviet-Communist external influence until it ceases to be a substantial threat to peace and security" (15).

The gravest danger confronting America's security, then, was atomic war. The Soviets, according to estimates, would within two to five years acquire the capability to inflict unacceptable damage directly on the United States. But Task Force A wrote that they would be deterred from doing so by America's superior capability — unless Eisenhower adopted the programs of Task Force B or C. "If confronted with Course B," it warned, the Soviet leadership "might sooner or later conclude that U.S. policy was becoming so rigidly committed as to eliminate all alternatives to eventual war, and it might thereafter proceed on the assumption that war would be desirable as soon as relative Soviet capabilities could be developed to their maximum." Similarly, should the program articulated by Task Force C "show promise of achieving the results intended for it, the Kremlin might in time perceive such threats to its essential security interests as would make general war appear the least undesirable of alternatives" (145–46).

According to Task Force A, therefore, the administration must "reject any policy based on acceptance of a calculated risk of general war, as being full of risk, empty of calculation, and unwarrantedly hazardous to the continued existence of the U.S." Certainly America's defense program must be sturdy and steady. Yet "military power, if properly designed and built, is power to enforce our national will without resort to hostilities — power for peace" (22–27).

Task Force A devoted most of its attention to Europe, which its members considered the most vital of America's global interests. While the Soviets firmly controlled their satellites, Europe was inherently unstable. Nevertheless, the report emphasized, the "Western coalition is in a better position with relation to Soviet power today than it was two or three years ago" (10). By building on its achievements, the administration could "assume the strategic offensive" (67).

As a first step, the task force recommended allowing increased trade (except in commodities that have "major strategic significance) with nations behind the Iron Curtain to lessen their dependence on the Soviet Union. Relaxing current restrictions, further, would "call the Russians' bluff" by falsifying their claim that U.S. policies, not the centralized communist system, was responsible for Eastern Europe's economic distress (76–79).

Indeed, Task Force A advocated that the United States formulate and implement a more systematic and dynamic campaign of political and psychological warfare. If "shrewdly and subtly carried out," this campaign should, "*in time* undermine the effectiveness of Kremlin control over the Soviet Orbit and sap the strength of the Soviet power machine." In "*certain circumstances*," moreover, it might "bring the liberation of some of the Satellites from Soviet domination." But "headstrong ventures" were more likely to "gravely discredit U.S. prestige or seriously involve U.S. interests in explosive situations." Even "spectacular tactical victories" often "do not contribute to long-range strategic purposes" (129–33; emphasis added).

Hence the primary aim of the psywar programs should be to convince Kremlin leaders that "in seeking to undermine and destroy the Free World, they are in fact steadily incurring burdens and risks which sooner or later will undermine and destroy Soviet Communism" and "will lead them into personal and national disaster." If the Kremlin leaders could be made to understand "the fallacy of the fundamental concepts upon which their policies are based, and without which these policies are neither intelligible nor intelligent," Task Force A predicted, they would change them. And as their policies changed, so would their goals (129–31). The "battle will be won because the pressures and examples from the Free World, acting on the spiritual and material weakness of the totalitarian system, will progressively cause that system to deteriorate — both absolutely and relatively to ours" (67).

Consistent with this perspective, Task Force A advanced its most dramatic proposal, the implications of which were far-reaching. It argued that the most effective means to pierce the Iron Curtain was to propose immediate negotiations with the Soviets for the purpose, initially, of allowing limited West German rearmament and, subsequently, reunifying Germany. As a maximum position, it recommended that Washington seek the removal of all foreign troops from German soil. A minimum position would be their concentration in select enclaves. Either scenario would greatly reduce the threat of a Soviet surprise attack and diminish their power to police East Germany. Yet neither would "confront the Soviets with such excessive and impossible demands as to make their discussion out of the question," especially if they were assured that for an agreed-upon period of time West German forces would not be integrated into either either EDC or NATO (88–95).

According to Task Force A, Soviet agreement to the U.S. proposals would lead to a rearmed, reunified German state, "ostensibly independent" of both blocs but "oriented toward the West." America's European allies would have to assume more responsibility for their defense, but the retraction of Soviet forces would instill more confidence among them. With U.S. troops no longer in Germany, moreover, the Soviets would have much more difficulty refusing to end the occupation of Austria and to scale back their presence in the satellites. Should they nonetheless resist all U.S. overtures, they would be saddled with the onus of sabotaging the negotiations, thereby exacerbating tensions within the Eastern bloc and generating the support still needed for EDC ratification (89–91, 95).

Generalizing from the particular, Task Force A emphatically endorsed negotiations as a fundamental component of the national strategy. "We must not nail our flag to the mast of rigid positions with regard to any of the great outstanding problems of our relations with the Communist Bloc, no matter how great the subjective appeal of such positions." Flexible negotiating postures not only undermined communist propaganda, but they also provided hope to captive people that their freedom need not come about through a general war that they could probably not survive. Without this hope they would not seek their liberation. In short, however the Soviets responded, Kennan's task force concluded, in "due course" and with minimal risk, by following this course of action Eisenhower would lay the foundation for the "roll back of Soviet hegemony over Eastern Europe" (139–40, 86–95).

Task Force A considered the West's position weaker in regions outside of Europe. In Asia it was especially vulnerable, and while necessary, assisting the development of indigenous forces was not sufficient. So long as Beijing remained aligned with Moscow, commitments would have to be made.

Direct military intervention, in fact, could not be excluded from the available repertoire of responses to communist or communist-inspired aggression where America's vital interests were engaged. The United States, for example, must be prepared for "possible offensive action in an expanded war situation in the Far East" (13). If unavoidable, this action should "be pressed with all necessary vigor and force to the end that U.S. prestige emerges enhanced." The likelihood of a war that warranted American participation was greatest in the areas bordering on China, such as Vietnam, which thus made the danger of its escalating into a general war omnipresent. Decision makers must assess this attendant risk, but, "except in the gravest and most exceptional circumstances," it must not "deter us from taking the steps necessary to win, and win decisively. . . . We must leave no room for Soviet blackmail, pressures, probes and possibly disastrous miscalculations" (125–26).

As it did with regard to Europe, nevertheless, Task Force A cautioned the administration not to allow military programs to drive strategy. "We believe we should guard against exaggerating the probability of peripheral war clearly *directed* by Moscow," counseled Kennan and his colleagues (26). The Kremlin would probably attempt to expand its influence through the "subtle weapons in the Soviet arsenal—diplomacy, economic pressures and inducements, political warfare, Communist 'front' methods, coups d'etat, etc." The United States should concentrate on defusing these weapons. The report recommended economic, political, and psychological programs designed to build confidence in and among indigenous anticommunists, to promote stability and development, to expose communism's bankruptcy and disingenuous exploitation of nationalist aspirations, and to sow dissension between Moscow and its dependents (17, 124–31).

The members of Task Force A appreciated the financial burden their proposed strategy placed on the United States. Indeed, their report repeated virtually verbatim the president's formula for the Great Equation. The basis of strength, their report read, was "the product—not the sum"—of spiritual, political, military, and economic variables. Consequently, "if any one of the factors falls to zero, the product becomes zero" (67).

But the task force did not appraise the threat of an economic collapse as severe—certainly not comparable to that stemming from the Soviet Union. The administration would have to increase the budget for all its security programs. Even the increased integration of nuclear weapons into the U.S. and NATO defense structure would not produce "a material reduction in cost." Military expenditures as a percentage of the gross national product, however, would progressively decline. Moreover, there was "no question that our country has the economic capacity to provide a high plateau of preparedness"—certainly the program envisioned by Task Force A—over a sustained period. In brief, the "United States could afford to survive" (45–56).

Task Force B

Task Force B's directive was also to accept containment as a viable policy. But its premise was that the policy would be more effective if pursued less timidly and more unilaterally. The approach of atomic plenty, it asserted, confronted the United States with the alternatives of either launching a preventive war or pursuing measures that insured the longest possible period of peace. Eisenhower's rejection of preventive war left only the second. And the foremost guarantee of enduring peace was a categorical declaration that any Soviet or Soviet-sponsored armed aggression would invite a general war.[25] General war meant that the United States would "apply its full power—whenever, however, and wherever necessary to defeat the main enemy, and to achieve its other war objectives." By removing all ambiguity in the minds of the communist leadership, Task Force B argued, this "warning of general war as the primary sanction against further Soviet-Bloc aggression is the best means available for insuring the security of the United States" (1–3).

The presentation was not as detailed or sophisticated as that of Task Force A. In part this was because Task Force B lacked an advocate who, like Kennan, was intimately familiar with and deeply committed to its charge. "In conformance with the directive we have presented our best advocacy," read the introduction. But none of its members would "assume personal responsibility for the conclusions expressed" (i). Further, the task force recognized that the "rigidity" of its recommended course of action could increase the risk of a Soviet-American exchange, which would be "terribly destructive even to the victor" (88–89, 12–13). The report also acknowledged that the threat of general war as a deterrent to aggression was largely irrelevant to many of the most serious concerns confronting policy makers (32–33, 65, I–2)

Nevertheless, as a support for containment, Task Force B concluded that its alternative "does merit serious consideration as a basic element in U.S. foreign policy" (i). To begin with, the report maintained that the current strategy has been less successful than Task Force A's evaluation suggested. Virtually all of Truman's accomplishments were confined to Europe. U.S. prestige and the strategic and economic interdependence of the free world, however, mandated that the Soviets at no point breach the line separating the communist from noncommunist spheres (I–6; 5–6).

Task Force B argued that the explicit threat of a nuclear response was the most effective way to hold that line—everywhere. Were the United States to put the communists on notice that it would not countenance aggressive behavior of any kind, and that the Soviets could not expect sanctuary, America's strategic superiority would "rob Moscow of the advantage it now possesses in being able to use the resources of a subordinate country in a war against the U.S. while conserving Russian resources" (22–23). Existing policy allowed the Kremlin "to indulge in the false comfort which comes from avoiding the real meaning of atomic weapons." It must be made to understand that Americans were prepared to make "the best possible use of their power and resources . . . to inflict decisive defeat on the Soviet Union if it continues its active policy of expansion" (3–4, 29).

Because the Kremlin leaders were rational opportunists who would not jeopardize the security of their regime, let alone their lives, by intentionally provoking U.S. military retaliation in order to expand, they would probe "at places and times of [their] own choosing and through employment of strategies and resources which are convenient to the Soviet bloc and are costly and risky to the United States." Task Force B warned that if the administration left open "until the last moment" the "question whether the United States would tolerate by inaction, or resist by general war" these probes, the Soviets would become more adventurous (I, 1–2, 83). This would increase the risk that Moscow would "blunder" into an atomic conflagration through accident or miscalculation (11, 49). Task Force B's proposal, the members asserted, decreased this likelihood "to the vanishing point" and virtually made the concept of a peripheral war obsolete (43).

Moreover, the guarantee that the United States would exploit its power and resources to the maximum in the event the communists trespassed on the free world did not mean that a nuclear holocaust would inevitably result if they did. "Bombs would not fall automatically on Moscow on H-hour." Circumstances would dictate the American choice of means. All that would be certain in advance of an incident, which by the definition of armed aggression could not be a "trifling" one, is that the United States would respond, and it, as opposed to the communists, would determine how high up the escalatory ladder that response would be (1–2, 13).

Task Force B further argued that its policy had the greatest potential for inducing the change in Soviet aims and the "mellowing" of the Soviet regime that was containment's objective. Without "peripheral wars to confuse the issue," the pacific nature of America's global posture would become progressively apparent to all behind the Iron Curtain (23). As it did, the Kremlin's subjects, whose "respect" the United States would have earned through its irrevocable commitment "under clearly defined rules which may be tough but which must be conceded to be just," would become increasingly skeptical of justifications for military spending and authoritarian rule and discontented with a regime whose ambitions placed them in the line of fire (54). The United States could pour salt on the wound by relaxing controls on East-West trade (9). The fear of losing control over its captives, coupled with the possibility of a general war that the Soviets could not win, might be enough to persuade Moscow "to value more highly the retention of the power and territory which it has acquired and to measure more realistically the risk of giving effect to its aims of further expansion" (83). Similarly, it might keep its clients on a shorter leash in Asia (17, 70–72).

Indeed, if U.S. strategists heeded its advice, Task Force B did "not reject the possibility that there will ultimately evolve in the Soviet Union a government *permanently inclined* to avoid the risk of aggression"(23, emphasis added). It wrote, "In the past the Soviet leadership has shown considerable flexibility in adjusting its immediate goals to changes in real and recognized power situations." It followed logically, then, that the task force's alternative "offers the best chance of using U.S. power to promote conditions favorable to the 'settling down' of the Soviet regime and gives time to internal Soviet factors of development to work in this direction" (82–84).

Task Force B did not expect America's anxious allies to accept this logic. Hence initially, and perhaps for the "foreseeable future," the United States would have to act unilaterally and accept criticism that it was reckless and irresponsible (1, 25, 34). Although unfortunate, this was preferable to projecting the image of a superpower fleeing "from its responsibilities in the face of the atomic reality." This image would result in "timid" nations becoming more vulnerable to Soviet "blackmail" and "fall[ing] successively by the wayside" (12–13, 61).

Besides, Washington could manage whatever problems ensued from its behavior through skillful public and private diplomacy. Allies would come to appreciate that "the U.S. does not hire others to fight its war for it" (13). More important, the "Free World knows that any general war which might follow the announcement of the new U.S. policy would come only by the deliberate choice of the U.S.S.R." (12). Likewise, it knows that what drove this new policy was "a Soviet-Communist philosophy and program of conquest which if unchecked will result in the loss of their independence and the destruction of their free institutions" (29). Ultimately, therefore, noncommunist unity and collective security would be fortified as the nations everywhere rallied behind America's courageous leadership (32–33). "Strength is a more permanent cement than fear" (15).

Prosperity is another cement, and Task Force B maintained that its course of action would best promote it. Prosperity would create a confident environment conducive to investment and trade, and consequently the economies of developing as well as developed nations would expand. At the same time, stabilizing defense costs would allow for more accurate budgeting. A greater reliance on atomic capabilities as both a deterrent and a winning weapon would not reduce defense expenditures. But it would promise the most efficient and effective use of those expenditures, that much more so because no longer would money be wasted fighting inconclusive, peripheral wars (20–21).

Nevertheless, because its alternative "requires the U.S. to maintain for the foreseeable future the military capability to meet the Soviet Union in general war," Task Force B underscored that it would be expensive (3). But America could and should carry the burden. Whatever the short-term dangers to America's financial well-being, they could be controlled. Moreover, "these cannot be weighed [on] the same scale with the grave danger to our national survival," wrote the task force members (20). The "external threat to the very existence of the United States [is] more important than any internal threat to its economic and financial stability" (73). In this realm Task Force B agreed with Task Force A.

Task Force C

So did Task Force C.[26] In fact, it appropriated verbatim Task Force A's economic data and analysis, and from it drew identical conclusions. Its members were "supremely confident," they wrote, "that the United States has the financial and physical capacity to provide for security without damaging social effects" (70). Also as did Task Forces A and B, they rejected the "dual threat" thesis: "[T]here is only one central threat to our security: the combination of 'formidable power and aggressive policy of the Communist world led by the U.S.S.R.'" (11–12).

Task Force C manifested some of the same disadvantages as did Task Force B. It, too, lacked an individual sufficiently committed to and expert about its mandate to assume a dominant role in both conceptualizing and writing the report. More important, to an extent greater than either task force A or B, it could only speculate about the potential benefits and outcome of the course of action it was assigned to advocate. Of the three task forces, C took the longest time to prepare, and the members acknowledged that they held "individual reservations, over details and particulars." Still, the report made explicit that "a general consensus has been reached on the program as a whole" (68).

Task Force C argued that "[m]ere containment is sterile as a continuing policy" because it provided no means for achieving the objective of reducing Soviet power and influence. Further, "Time has been working against us," it said, echoing Dulles. "We have lost ground for a decade." On the Eurasian landmass the "enemy" possessed "a relative preponderance of ready military power," and within a few years the free world's nuclear superiority "will be neutralized largely by decisive [atomic] stocks and delivery capabilities in the hands of the Soviet Union." The resulting mutual vulnerability was inherently unstable—and perilous. "In this conflict one is either winning or losing," it wrote. "There can be no continuing balance, no state of real stability in the face of this [the communist] implacable conspiracy" (10–13).

Task Force C would not go so far as to predict an inevitable general war. But it challenged the view that the Kremlin's concern for its safety and its estimate of the balance of forces would proscribe its accepting "considerable risk" (12). Further, it argued that the Soviets' "mortal hostility, immutable and insatiable, toward the West" would preclude their ever adopting a policy of "less bellicose 'co-existence'" let alone "'true peace'" (237–38, 53). Therefore, the danger of Armageddon would remain as long as the Bolshevik regime survived.

What was more, whereas nuclear deterrence required credibility, the Soviets were likely to perceive America's apparent consent to their post–World War II geopolitical and strategic gains as evidence of fear. "To the Soviet Union," Task Force C maintained, "the greatest provocation is weakness." A "high stakes" game of chicken "must be played boldly" (57, 76).

The logical deduction was that the "[i]mplied acceptance of the status quo" by Task Forces A and B "disqualifies both those alternatives as a means to lasting security and a free world" (10). Lasting security demanded that the United States take measures to weaken "Soviet power and militancy, before the Soviets cross the threshold of ability to inflict critical damage on the U.S." Preventive war was one means, but its consideration was beyond Task Force C's "terms of reference" (80, 83). This left "political action" and "military (short of general war), paramilitary, economic and covert operations" (77). These activities could "separate selected areas [such as Hainan, Albania, Bulgaria, Czechoslovakia, Hungary, and Poland] from the Iron Curtain" and "bring about clear-cut defeats" of communist aggression in places like Indochina and Korea. Forced to shift their efforts to "holding what they already have rather than concentrating on gaining control of additional territories and peoples," the Soviets would be primed for defeat (1–2).

Task Force C acknowledged that its course of action entailed greater risks. But "We are convinced that the only way to end the cold war is to face up to the challenge posed by the Communist conspiracy and devote the necessary effort to the task of winning" (19, 8). The task force was equally convinced that "[t]he way to avoid a hot war is to win the cold war." Unfortunately, in Washington "[c]ounsels of caution have too often prevailed" (70–77).

Because the declassified Task Force C report is heavily sanitized, many details remain obscure. Its basic outline is evident, however. The programs were designed on a region-by-region basis. The precise tactic recommended depended upon the task force's assessment of the particular circumstances. Nonetheless, in virtually all cases it emphasized psychological and clandestine techniques. "[P]*ropaganda and covert operations*," it maintained, "are such an essential part of the 'cold war' being waged against us, that we single them out as functional categories added to the three classic functions of war . . . Political; Military; and Economic." Moreover, although propaganda and covert operations are "but special 'techniques'" of political warfare, their central role in waging a cold war required their distinct treatment (79–80; emphasis in original).

The task force divided its program into short-, mid-, and long-term actions. Success in the short term would allow for greater risk taking in the mid term, and greater still in the long term, until the Soviet menace was completely eradicated (1). Indeed, predicting a domino effect, the task force formulated "a progression of objective-goals which the U.S. will seek in sequence, the culmination of one providing the 'line of departure' for the next" (88). The initial financial cost would be high. Task Force C estimated the budget for its short-term program at $60 billion a year. By 1958, however, the beginning of the mid-term stage, that figure would have declined to below $45 billion. And in the last stage, after "we have won the Cold War," the costs would "be substantially lower" (62).

The first five-year period was the most critical. This was the projected time it would take for the Soviets, if not checked, to achieve the atomic capability to render the free world vulnerable. Moreover, to reverse the tide of the cold war so that it began to run against the East demanded immediate "tactical victories" to create a "climate of victory" in the West (19, 77).

Consequently, the short-term actions prescribed by Task Force C were more aggressive than one might have expected from the sequential risk-taking formula. For example, it proposed taking "every measure to destroy [the PRC] economy" (166) and assisting the Chinese Nationalists in the conduct of "active military operations against Chinese Communists" and the recapture of Hainan (34).

Task Force C advised parallel short-term projects toward virtually every Soviet satellite, client, or target, "overtly and covertly, attack[ing] the Communist apparatus wherever it may be found in the world" (22). The spectrum of specific actions included prosecuting more vigorously any and all current wars (221), the "effective suppression of Communist-inspired guerilla operations" (2), the development of "a world-wide covert apparatus" (4), and the "more virile handling of tactical propaganda" (45).

Task Force C identified a Soviet military withdrawal from Germany as a precondition for "a more aggressive policy toward the Satellites, designed to bring about their liberation from the control of Moscow" (156). Hence the German problem required extraordinary creativity and risk taking. Indeed, although generally opposed to negotiations, it urged that with regard to Germany Eisenhower be willing not only to negotiate but to acquiesce its neutralization (24). As it explained, "a policy accepting a high degree of risk in order to materially reduce Soviet power [in Central Europe] . . . is a risk which might be taken." But to minimize the risk, West Germany's rearmament should be completed prior to unification. U.S. policy makers must be clear, moreover, that "once the Soviet forces were withdrawn we would feel under no obligation to restrict ourselves from giving German neutrality a content which in fact would put that nation securely on the side of the West" (146–47).

As the Soviets were preparing to withdraw, the United States should prepare the groundwork for liberating Eastern Europe. To "keep alive their morale and aspirations for national independence," it should use "all available techniques to reach the populations of the Satellite states." And to "hamper the consolidation of Soviet control" over these satellites, it should "harass and hound every conceivable Communist activity using all available political, legal, financial and economic devices in our possession." Measures intended to tighten the "encirclement" of the Soviet bloc should be taken concurrently (7, 22, 156–64). For example, the Navy should resume its visits to Scandinavian ports in order to "recapture" the Baltic, and other displays of force would be used in the region to provide "visible proof of national interest and influence" (23).

Like Dulles, Task Force C characterized Europe as "politically-weak," having lost its "elan vital, and its leadership" (172). Thus more aggressive behavior would doubtless "produce added strains upon our ties with our Allies" (13). That it would do so, read the report, provided the United States with an additional reason for acting boldly. "Our task is to command respect, not necessarily love and devotion" (6). With each victory, Europe's faith in America's leadership would grow. And so would its confidence (101).

Even so, Task Force C warned, "at best" Europe "will be a continuing brake on the implementation of our courses of action, particularly as we move into the second and more dangerous phase" (101). By this time, Soviet resources would have been severely drained, China would have suffered either a sound diplomatic or military defeat, the Eastern bloc would be in turmoil, Germany would be "ostensibly committed to neither side, although definitely oriented toward the free world," and all Soviet forces would be out of Europe. But communists would still rule the Kremlin, the satellites would "continue their subservience to Moscow" (58–59), and Korea would remain unstable (5). Most significantly, the Soviet Union would have increased its nuclear capabilities, and its troops would be poised on its borders (5).

Even if sometimes dragging along reluctant allies, therefore, the United States must escalate pressure on the Soviet Union and PRC and increase direct although still nonmilitary attacks on the Satellites and communist networks outside the bloc.

Task Force C readily conceded the possibility that the Soviets, desperate, would retaliate by initiating general war. But it insisted that Eisenhower accept this risk so that, after 1965, the United States would finally be in a position to liberate those Satellites which had not already defected to the West and initiate direct pressure against the Soviet Union itself. During this long-term stage, the free world would triumph (4).

Grist for the NSC Mill

The July 16 NSC meeting on Solarium lasted all day. Those in attendance included the JCS, service secretaries, and Planning Board members as well as the NSC's normal participants. After the presentation of the three task force reports Eisenhower commented on them, speaking extemporaneously for about 45 minutes. The president, in Kennan's opinion, "showed his intellectual ascendency over every man in the room."[27] He had "never attended a better or more persuasively presented staff job," Eisenhower said. He ruled out any policy that could not win the support of America's allies, that cost too much, and that accepted a greater risk of general war because of the belief that the United States could survive one. "What would we do with Russia, if we should win a global war?" the president asked when concluding his remarks. He had already provided the answer. The "only thing worse than losing a global war was winning one; . . . there would be no individual freedom after the next global war."[28] Privately he was even more forthright. "Global War as a defense of freedom," he jotted down while listening to the oral reports. "Almost contradiction in terms."[29] As already mentioned, Goodpaster considers that Eisenhower buried any rollback policy by his remarks.

The discussion focused on the overall thrust and budgetary implications of each course of action and, predictably, their most controversial recommendations. It dwelled on Task Force A's advice on German unification and rearmament, Task Force B's emphasis on atomic brinkmanship, and Task Force C's argument that the current international environment made it imperative that the United States move rapidly and aggressively to fracture the communist empire.[30] Dulles expressed his concern with the unilateral character of Task Forces B and C, on the one hand, and the "static" quality of Task Force A, on the other. And none of the reports in his view took adequate account of the anxieties that Germany and Japan still provoked from their neighbors.[31]

The participants reacted most strongly to the task forces' differing assessments of the Soviet threat—especially between Task Forces A and C. The "essential differences" between Task Forces A and C cannot be reconciled," read the official summary of points made during the discussion. Whereas the former argued that over time the inexorable weakening of the Kremlin's power would bring about the retraction of Soviet forces and the moderation of its regime, the latter maintained that "[s]o long as the Soviet Union exists, it will not fall apart, but must and can be shaken apart." And whereas Task Force A was confident that "sufficient deterrents [to Soviet aggression] already exist and are capable of being shaped into a better form," the premise of Task Force C is that the "U.S. cannot continue to live with the Soviet threat."[32]

Yet as the meeting ended, Eisenhower seemed to challenge the thrust of these conclusions. "[M]ore important than the differences between" the presentations, Eisenhower stressed, were their "many similarities." He therefore wanted the three task forces to meet together in order to "agree on certain features of the three presentations as the best features and to bring about a combination of such features into a unified policy."

After Eisenhower left the meeting, the task force members made clear that they were not persuaded. They remained convinced that the reports reflected "fundamental differences which could be compromised into a watered-down position but not really agreed to." Briefed on what was said in his absence, Eisenhower was "very put out". He instructed Cutler "to work out" what he "thought best." Cutler's plan called for the NSC staff to prepare a summary of the reports in consultation with members from each task force. The summary would then be presented to the NSC "with a view toward, a. designating the areas which the Council wishes to have worked on further, and b. directing the Planning Board to prepare recommendations in those areas."[33]

9

Preparing the Basic National Security Strategy

FIRST: We must adapt our foreign policy to a "cold war" strategy that is unified and coherent.

SECOND: In spirit and resolve, we should see in this "cold war" a chance to gain a victory without casualties, to win a contest which can quite literally save peace.[1]

Dwight D. Eisenhower (1952)

The drafting of the new statement of Basic National Security Policy was an extended and contentious process. It took three months for the Planning Board and NSC to complete NSC 162/2. And even after Eisenhower approved it, some issues were not fully resolved, as will be discussed in later chapters.

The Planning Board Mandate

The process began with a July 30 meeting of the NSC to consider instructions to the Planning Board for drafting the strategy paper. In addition to the summaries of the Solarium task force reports that had already been prepared and circulated,[2] Cutler submitted a two-page memorandum of his own, distilling the key points of the reports on one page and setting out a "Proposed New Basic Concept" on the second. The concept consisted of five components, succinctly stated: (1) "capability for a strong retaliatory offensive, a base for mobilization, and continental defense"; (2) creating strong, friendly groupings "centered on Western Europe (including [West] Germany) and on Japan in the Far East"; (3) restricting U.S. foreign aid to such groupings and designated other free nations; (4) defining where Soviet bloc aggression would trigger general war; and (5) taking "selected aggressive actions of a limited scope, involving moderately increased risks of general war, to eliminate Soviet-dominated areas within the free world and to reduce Soviet power in the Satellite periphery." Cutler's paper noted that this strategy "accepts moderately increased risks of general war by taking *some* of the aggressive actions against the Satellites proposed by Task Force 'C'" in order to reduce Soviet power. He estimated, however, that these risks were "less grave at the present time than did Task Force 'A.'" The overall aim of the policy, Cutler made explicit, was to create a "climate of victory . . . while forcing the Soviet bloc on the defensive."[3] Apparently he hoped that the Council would adopt his concept as a directive to the Planning Board.

At the July 30 meeting the Council members commented on several of the specifics of Cutler's paper. Humphrey wanted to be sure that it implied no "big build-up of U.S. military force" and thought that foreign assistance should decline. The president said that while Western Europe, if it united, could make do with less aid, other areas could not. Secretary Dulles said that it was premature to plan a Far Eastern grouping centered on Japan. Several members, including Eisenhower, felt the paper "did not sufficiently emphasize the Middle East."

The Council did not, however, consider Cutler's concept paper as a whole, and it definitely did not adopt it. Indeed, all the members stressed their desire for untrammeled analysis and judgment by the Planning Board in preparing the basic strategy, accenting the need for further study. Secretary Dulles pointed out that "the Council was not agreeing with this paper as policy, but as guidance." And the "President said that was indeed the case." Secretary of Defense Wilson was willing to accept the proposed concept "if it didn't settle anything." General Bradley explicitly warned that the Planning Board "should not be given too much guidance" but should "approach the question with an open mind." Eisenhower agreed that they "should have the broadest possible directive." As now phrased, he felt, Cutler's concept paper "did not give guidance for subsequent work . . . but rather tended to direct and form the policy." He suggested that the paper might better be labeled a "staff exploration based on certain assumptions."[4]

Accordingly, the NSC directed its Planning Board "with the assistance of representatives of the Solarium Task Forces, to draft for Council consideration a new basic national security policy . . . in the light of the above discussion."[5] The intent of this mandate later became an issue between Cutler and the Planning Board.

At the Planning Board meeting the next day, Cutler reported on the NSC discussion and presented a paper subtitled "Points for Consideration in Drafting New Policy." This was his "concept" paper, slightly revised to take account of the specific NSC comments but otherwise the same. His accompanying memorandum seemed to imply that the paper was intended as instructions. After averring that it summarized "the main points of [the NSC] discussion, as general guidlines for drafting a new basic policy," it then added that the president that morning had said "that he thinks these guidelines fairly represent yesterday's discussion."[6]

Apparently sensing that Cutler might present his concept paper as a virtual directive to the Planning Board, Secretary Dulles sent Robert Bowie, his member of the Board, a clarifying memorandum on August 1:

> I have looked over the memorandum dated July 31, 1953, entitled "Points for Consideration [in] Drafting New Policy," attached to Mr. Cutler's memorandum.
> These points, which reflect the main ideas raised at the Council discussion, were approved as general guidelines for the analysis and criticism of the Planning Board. I

do not understand that they represented "decisions" intended to bind the Planning Board.

Accordingly, I think you should feel free, on the basis of your study of the problems, to recommend that some or all of these points should be modified to reflect your judgment as it results from close study of the practical implications of the "guidelines."[7]

Not only did Dulles's memorandum to Bowie accurately reflect the consensus expressed at the NSC meeting of July 30 but, as discussed in chapter 5, it was also congruent with Eisenhower's charge to the Planning Board.[8] As a consequence, the other members of the Planning Board adopted this same approach. But Cutler, as we will see, raised the issue sharply again when the Special Committee submitted its proposed draft on September 18.

Special Solarium Committee of the NSC Planning Board

To prepare an initial working draft for the Planning Board, Cutler named a smaller, ad hoc Special Committee composed of the Board members representing State, Defense, the JCS, and the CIA and chaired by a member of the NSC staff, Deputy Executive Secretary S. Everett Gleason. For the first month it was assisted by a member from each of the Solarium Task Forces.[9]

In addition to the Solarium reports, the initial NSC discussion, and the Cutler memorandum, the Special Committee and the Planning Board had the benefit of various policy studies, debates, and decisions from the first six months of the administration. Among these were the Oppenheimer Report on atomic weapons and disarmament (discussed in chapters 12 and 14); Eisenhower's speech of April 16 on U.S.-Soviet relations following Stalin's death; the May 15 Report to the NSC by the Special Evaluation Subcommittee (Edwards Report) on the Net Capability of the USSR to Inflict Direct Injury on the United States up to July 1, 1953;[10] related materials on continental defense;[11] the intensive review of national security policies in relation to their costs, culminating in NSC 149/2,[12] the Report of the Committee on International Information Activities (Jackson Report),[13] and the various National Intelligence Estimates, especially NIE 90 and NIE 95 on Soviet capabilities and probable courses of action.[14] The State Department Policy Planning Staff also prepared for the Special Committee and the Planning Board studies on "Building Strength in Western Europe" and "Building Strength in Regional Groupings in the Far East."[15] Finally, of course, there were the ongoing NSC discussions on statements of policy on specific countries and issues such as Korea, China, and Germany, which had been prepared in the Planning Board.[16]

On September 3 Cutler conveyed to the Special Committee a directive from the president to include in the draft the JCS proposal for redeploying to the United States forces based abroad (discussed in detail in chapter 12), which he considered a "return to our original thinking" regarding such forces.[17]

The Special Committee labored for six weeks to produce its draft. The various members, especially State, prepared sections that were continually discussed and revised. The committee's draft was distributed to the full Planning Board on September 18.

Forty-two pages long, this draft was organized in two parts. The first, entitled "General Considerations and Conclusions," running to 23 pages, was an analysis of the current situation: the Soviet threat, the position of the United States, the state of the Western coalition and of the less developed areas, and the U.S. capacity to support security costs. This section ended with "Conclusions" regarding the implications for preventing Soviet expansion and reducing the threat.

The second half of the draft succinctly set out the "General Objectives" of U.S. security policy, which were then elaborated by courses of action designed to achieve them. These included measures to maintain the strength of the United States, a vigorous economy, and the alliances; programs related to Western Europe, the Middle East, and East Asia; and actions to prevent Soviet expansion and reduce its power. The committee draft was fully approved by all members except for the section concerning one issue—whether or not "aggressive actions against Soviet-held terrories" should be eschewed. Although agreeing such actions could not substantially reduce the Soviet threat, the Department of Defense and JCS opposed their prohibition, while the State and CIA members supported it.[18]

Two days later Cutler, who until then had entrusted the Special Committee's supervision to Gleason, reacted with a slashing attack on the draft.[19] He conceded that it was "comprehensive and informative and deserves careful reading"; that the "General Considerations reflect a fully developed point of view"; and that the draft covered the issues set out in the "Council's two mandates" (Cutler's "Points for Consideration" memorandum of July 31 and the presidential directive of September 3 on the redeployment of U.S. forces). But he strenuously objected that these issues had been so "watered down and obscured" and "modified and conditioned" that "they do not stand out sharply and clearly for decision."

Consequently, he asked the Special Committee, "as these issues are covered in the paper, are they your individual views or are they the views of your Department heads which they will support before the Council?" In fact, as already indicated, the paper essentially represented the judgment of the Special Committee members, in keeping with their instructions or understanding of their function. Cutler, however, took a different view. "After all," he wrote, "I am responsible to the Council for what is presented. I do not care to have Council members at the meeting publicly disown the views produced by their Special Assistants."

The "great issues" that must be sharpened for decision, he went on to insist, were the same ones he had posed earlier: "(1) the threat to the economy; (2) the emphasis on retaliatory striking air forces; (3) power groupings centered around Germany and Japan; (4) sharp curtailment of future foreign assistance; (5) urgent need for rapid development of our continental defense"; (6) redeployment of forces to the United States in a few years, relying on diplomacy to allay allied concerns; and (7) harassing the Soviet bloc.

The fiscal issue evoked special criticism. The draft, Cutler asserted, "entirely fails to recognize [that] the threat to our economy and liberty" from overspending and prolonged deficits is "co-equal to the threat from external aggression." Thus it was "contrary to Administration policy." He indicated that the Treasury Department (which was not represented on the Special Committee) would submit its views on this matter.

In short, Cutler concluded, "The paper generally may be characterized as not a *new policy* at all. . . . The paper is not a 'niggardly Harriman policy,' but a *more lavish* Harriman policy than ever. Its approval would result in spending more money all over the world." Noting its call for a readiness to negotiate with the Soviet Union on large or small issues, he wrote that the paper "returns to the concept of 'peaceful coexistence'; it is *not* aimed at destruction of Soviet power." Then he added a virtual rebuttal: "Probably in view of the H-bomb this is the only solution, short of initiating aggressive war."

Cutler's critique was in part within his mandate as the president's special assistant for the NSC. Under the system approved by Eisenhower in March, he was intended to manage the policy process to ensure that the Planning Board papers clearly presented contested issues for Council decision, fairly reflecting the divergent views. His criticism of the Special Committee draft on that ground would have to be taken into account by the Planning Board in reviewing the paper, especially with respect to the views of those agencies not represented on the Special Committee.

In two respects, however, Cutler's criticisms were out of order. The special assistant was not intended to be an advocate for particular policies, which his paper certainly seemed to do in its comments on the substance of the committee draft. And second, Cutler's view of the role of the Planning Board was certainly out of line with that of the president. Indeed, Cutler's own NSC plan had stipulated that members of the Planning Board would be expected to "express and stand by their honest views" in preparing policy papers.[20] And Eisenhower had insisted that he wanted Board members, as well as Council members, to advise as individuals and not merely represent their agencies. He had also told the Council that the Planning Board was to contribute to the thinking and analysis of those too busy to do so, and that proposals by NSC members, although always welcome, would be staffed out by the Planning Board before being taken up by the Council.[21]

The NSC Planning Board Revision

The NSC Planning Board devoted the next 10 days to intensive discussion, negotiation, and revision in order to produce its draft of September 30 for consideration by the full Council as NSC 162.[22] Planning Board members such as those from the Department of the Treasury and Office of Defense Mobilization, who had not been on the Special Committee, had the opportunity to present their views on the draft. Moreover, the members of the Special Committee involved their agencies more fully at this stage. For example, Bowie solicited comments from State Department bureaus on the committee draft and the later recasting.[23] In this process the Planning Board adhered to its view of its mandate.

The members of the Planning Board adopted, with only minor editing and additions, the first half of the Special Committee draft ("General Considerations"), which appraised the Soviet threat, its security implications, and the state of the

Western coalition and developing areas. The only exception was the section on the economic threat, which Treasury insisted on redrafting to equate it with the Soviet threat, thus creating dissents ("splits") from the other members.

But in the Planning Board's consideration of the second half of the draft ("Conclusions," "General Objectives," and "Courses of Action"), it quickly became apparent that Cutler's critical reaction had two sources. One was substantive differences. The other, however, was due to the format of the Special Committee's draft. The committee intended its paper to be read as an integrated whole. The courses of action it proposed (paragraphs 31–94), which comprised most of the second half of the paper, were meant to flesh out and supplement the "Conclusions" and "General Objectives." Cutler apparently found this format confusing and lacking in the sharpness or clarity he desired. And in fact it did result in redundancy and did not lend itself well to presenting alternative policy choices for the Council. After discussion, the Planning Board decided to recast completely the format of the second half of the paper. The "Courses of Action" would be eliminated, and their substance greatly condensed and integrated into the "Conclusions" and "General Objectives," which would be combined and retitled "Policy Conclusions."

Accordingly, a revised draft, consolidating these sections in accordance with the new structure, was submitted by Bowie. For example, the "Courses of Action" relating to Western Europe, the Far East, and the Middle East, which were initially eight pages, were sharply compressed into about a page and one-half. This condensation made clearer the consensus on many issues, such as building strength in Western Europe, including West Germany, and in the Far East, especially in Japan, and bolstering stability in the Middle East, or the vital importance of continental defense.

Clearly, Cutler's criticisms also reflected serious conflicts regarding major policies among the key departments. In the Planning Board the main disputes pertained to 1) the economic threat; 2) foreign assistance; 3) reduction of the Soviet threat; and 4) certain defense issues. These differences would have to be decided by the president with the advice of the NSC itself. The task of the Planning Board was to set out as explicitly as possible the alternatives to facilitate the decisions.

The revised version of the paper embodied the substance of the Special Committee draft and was approved by the entire Planning Board except for specific disputed issues. On these, the State member, CIA advisor, and others (depending on the issue) supported the Special Committee positions. To present each split, the proposed alternative policy was printed in a parallel column in the final Planning Board draft submitted to the NSC on September 30.

The competing views on the main disputed issues can be briefly summarized as follows:

1. *Economic threat* (paragraphs 1, 17–27, 32, 39*a* and *b*)
All members agreed that a strong and expanding U.S. economy was essential for the security of the country and the free world over a sustained period. Treasury and the Bureau of the Budget differed from all the others as to the implications of defense spending.

- Treasury: The risk of dangerously weakening the U.S. economy by prolonged deficits or high taxes due to security expenditures was as serious as the Soviet threat and demanded rapid balancing of the budget without raising taxes.
- Non-Treasury: The United States must meet the minimum costs of the policies essential to its security; defense spending at about the current levels will not seriously damage the economy even if higher taxes prove necessary.

2. *Reducing the Soviet Threat* (paragraphs 41 and 43)

All agreed on the analysis of the Soviet threat and much of what the United States had to do to meet it. Among other measures, this included "feasible political, economic, propaganda and covert measures to impose pressures on the USSR." There was, however, a basic split between the State member (and CIA advisor) and the Department of Defense and JCS about the character of such measures and their primary purpose. The split revolved around fundamental questions.

- State and CIA: These measures should be designed primarily to reinforce internal pressures within the Soviet bloc for gradual changes in Soviet aims, which would induce the Soviet leaders to negotiate acceptable agreements for freeing the satellites and for enforceable arms control; but such measures should not include aggressive actions involving force against Soviet bloc territory.
- Department of Defense and JCS: Such measures should include some aggressive actions of the sort proposed by Task Force C in order to coerce Soviet rollback from specific areas of control.

3. *Defense Issues*

The Planning Board draft contained a limited number of divergences regarding defense. Some were minor, such as whether the Soviet Union already had or soon would have the capacity for a crippling atomic strike (paragraphs 3a and 31a). More important was the split regarding redeploying most U.S. forces from abroad in the near term, which had been proposed (somewhat ambiguously) in the JCS August report and, according to Cutler, enthusiastically endorsed by the president (paragraph 37). The Special Committee's draft, however, conditioned any such force withdrawals on compatibility with various political military, and alliance considerations. The September 30 draft made the split more explicit.

- The Planning Board revised this provision to make it even more negative. While conceding that "partial redeployment" from Europe might have some military benefits, it read (paragraph 37b), "Under present conditions, however, any major withdrawal of U.S. forces from Europe or the Far East would be interpreted as a diminution of U.S. interest in the defense of these areas and would seriously undermine the strength and cohesion of the coalition." Hence it merely called for continuous study of the most effective deployment of America's military forces.
- Cutler himself prepared an alternative paragraph that essentially embodied the JCS report. Stressing the advantages of mobility and initiative gained by redeploying and the need to convince the allies of these benefits, it called for an early determination about such redeployment of the bulk of U.S. forces.

4. *Foreign Assistance* (paragraphs 10d and 36): This split mirrored that on the defense budget.

- Treasury proposed that the United States should further curtail economic grant aid and loans to other nations and progressively reduce military aid to Western Europe.
- State, Department of Defense and JCS, and the remaining Planning Board members supported a more flexible approach to military and economic aid to take account of the indigenous needs and capacity of the recipients, relative U.S. interests, and progress in liberalizing trade and access to markets. Military assistance for Western Europe should be continued but reduced as rapidly as the nations could assume the defense burden.

The National Security Council

The NSC, with the president actively participating, took up the Planning Board draft of NSC 162, with its delineated splits, at its meeting on October 7. After vigorous debate among the members, Eisenhower decided most of the major disputed issues, and the Planning Board was directed to prepare a revised draft reflecting these decisions.[24] The revised Planning Board draft (162/1) was considered by the NSC on October 29, amended mainly for clarity, and approved by the president the next day as NSC 162/2.[25]

But while the "Basic National Security Policy" paper (NSC 162/2) was completed, the process of defining the national strategy remained unfinished. As Bowie had pointed out to Secretary Dulles in his briefing memorandum before the October 29 meeting on NSC 162/2, "some of the basic issues discussed at the October 7 meeting [on NSC 162/1] are glossed over rather than clearly decided in the paper." Still, NSC 162/2 provided "a generally satisfactory guide to U.S. policy. Presumably later NSC papers on more specific issues and particular areas will clarify the application of the general policy laid down in this document."[26] On some issues, in fact, the debate continued through 1954.

The next five chapters will discuss the major components of the national strategy, analyzing both their development and substance. In doing so, they will integrate the debate and decisions relating to NSC 162/2 with subsequent papers and actions that clarified or gave more definite content to its general provisions.

PART III

THE STRATEGY

10

The Sino-Soviet Threat

[E]verything points to the fact that Russia is not seeking a general war and will not for a long, long time, if ever. Everything is shifting to economic warfare, to propaganda, and to a sort of peaceful infiltration. Now we must be fully aware of these threats, but we must not sap our strength. . . . [T]his judgment is my own. It is taken after many long, long years of study of this problem.[1]

Dwight D. Eisenhower (1954)

Eisenhower would have conducted a reappraisal of the Sino-Soviet threat even if Stalin had lived. As already discussed, he had formed definite views about the Soviet Union over the years before taking office. Stalin's death in March, however, broadened the range of questions. Would his successors modify Stalin's objectives and methods? How would the growing Soviet nuclear stockpile affect the military threat? How serious were other aspects, such as subversion and political warfare? What were the vulnerabilities of the Soviet bloc? The questions were examined in intelligence estimates, the Jackson Report on psychological warfare, the Solarium exercise, conferences of U.S. ambassadors, reports of Soviet experts (especially Bohlen), and meetings of the NSC Planning Board.[2] In seven months, this process produced the consensus on the threat from the Soviet bloc embodied in NSC 162/2.

The Post-Stalin Regime

At Stalin's funeral Malenkov, Molotov, and Lavrentii Beria had all stressed continuity and extolled "peaceful coexistence." And in mid-March, Malenkov had proclaimed Soviet support for the peaceful resolution of all disputes.[3] How serious this was remained unclear. Eisenhower's April speech on the "Chance for Peace" had, of course, been an initial probe of the new leaders' intentions. As discussed earlier, their reply, while temperate in tone, was not deemed encouraging.

Yet the Kremlin's new leaders clearly were seeking to lower tensions and to appear conciliatory by making small moves. Exit visas were granted to Russian wives of foreigners. The Chinese and North Koreans were encouraged to exchange ill and disabled prisoners of war. The Soviet Union renounced earlier claims on

Turkey and for joint bases on the Straits. It also agreed to Dag Hammarskjold as the successor to Trygve Lie as secretary-general for the UN, and named ambassadors for Greece, Israel, and Yugoslavia.[4]

In the West, these were seen as merely gestures, entailing no real costs or concessions. More substantive was the ending of the stalemate in Korea and completion on July 27 of an armistice, based on the North Korean–Communist Chinese concession that prisoner-of-war repatriation should be voluntary. Dulles and Eisenhower believed that the outcome had been accelerated by hints that delay might result in widening the war.[5]

On the domestic front the new leaders went well beyond gestures. Seeking to bolster the stability and legitimacy of the new regime, they promptly committed themselves to improving the lot of the average citizen in three basic respects:

1) Living standards would be raised by increasing the supply of consumer goods and food. The drive to build heavy industry would be moderated and private peasant plots assisted.
2) Personal security was to be increased, with less arbitrary exercise of police power. An amnesty was declared; some Stalinist victims were rehabilitated; and the so-called "doctors' plot" was branded a fabrication. The secret police were brought under greater control, especially after the arrest of Beria in late June and his subsequent trial and execution.
3) "Collective leadership" was to guard against another Stalin, and the myth of his infallibility was steadily downgraded.[6]

In Eastern Europe the new Soviet leaders also moved to alleviate the harsh Stalinist measures to build socialism rapidly. In East Germany Walter Ulbricht, at the Kremlin's direction, relaxed many of these measures but retained higher workers' norms. The reaction to the higher norms in mid-June was widespread, with spontaneous uprisings in Berlin and elsewhere, which the East German regime could not quell. Thereupon, Soviet tanks and forces crushed the revolt, killing several hundred demonstrators and injuring over a thousand. Communist security forces and officials also suffered substantial casualties. The message was brutally clear: The Soviet Union would hold East Germany at all costs. But the reforms in the satellites continued.[7]

Four months later NIE-99, a national intelligence estimate of the world situation through 1955, concluded that "[d]espite the change in regime in the USSR and the shifts in Soviet foreign and domestic tactics, there has been no change in the USSR's basic hostility to all non-Soviet power. The USSR will continue the cold war against the Free World . . . [and] there is little likelihood of any major Soviet concessions."[8] Ambassador Bohlen agreed; his analysis was more specific. In his view, the new Soviet leaders had two main objectives in foreign policy. One was the strong desire to avoid serious crises or tensions for at least two or three years. This was because, in the first place, they needed a relaxed international environment, free of the fear of war, to carry out their domestic reform programs for the Soviet Union and the satellites. Secondly, detente offered the best prospect of weakening the NATO coalition, and especially of preventing the rearming of West Germany within the North Atlantic alliance.

But as a second objective, according to Bohlen, the Soviets were determined not to give up any of the territories acquired as a result of World War II both for strategic reasons and because of the repercussions of any withdrawal (as from East Germany) on the satellite empire and on the Soviet regime itself.[9] A recent study of this period by a Russian scholar, Vladislav Zubok, based on newly released Soviet documents, bears out this analysis. He concluded, "The Soviet 'peace offensive' did not venture beyond the minimal steps necessary to project the image of the new leadership as strong, but peaceful. It aimed at reducing the likelihood of war, exacerbating contradictions between the United States and its allies, and upsetting plans for West German rearmament."[10]

Accordingly, as depicted in NSC 162/2, the Soviet Union remained hostile to the noncommunist world and intended to consolidate and expand its sphere of control and influence with the ultimate aim of global domination. Stalin's successors would, however, pursue his objectives in a more flexible manner, using "peace gestures" to lull and divide the West and to avoid confrontation during the transition of the new regime. While currently desirous of relaxing tensions and perhaps of settling some specific issues, the new leaders showed no readiness to make significant concessions.[11]

The Soviet Bloc

Moreover, NSC 162/2 concluded, the strength and cohesion of the Soviet bloc had not been significantly weakened by Stalin's death.

The Soviet Union

With respect to the Soviet Union itself, NSC 162/2 summed up the consensus: "The authority of the Soviet regime does not appear to have been impaired by the events since Stalin's death, or be likely to be appreciably weakened during the next few years. The transfer of power may cause some uncertainty in the Soviet and satellite tactics for some time, but will probably not impair the basic economic and military strength of the Soviet bloc." Indeed, that strength was expected to grow steadily.[12]

East European Satellites

The June uprisings in East Germany and other satellite unrest, while quickly suppressed, raised questions about the stability of the Soviet bloc. NSC 162/2 maintained that these events revealed that the Soviets had failed fully to subjugate the satellite peoples or destroy their desire for freedom; that these regimes depended for survival on Soviet forces; and that their own forces were unreliable. Inevitably, this situation would put strains on the new Soviet leaders.[13]

Popular opposition to the imposed regimes would continue, forecast a staff study on the satellite issue. The estimate was based not only on the poor living conditions throughout Eastern Europe but also on the offense to the nationalist and religious sentiments inherent in Soviet rule. But effective resistance would be blocked by

Soviet domination through the Party, secret police, and military. The chance that another leader would emerge and defect, as Josip Tito had in Yugloslavia, was "negligible" (except possibly in Albania). As the East German revolt had shown, there was "every probability that the Soviets would in effect intervene in the face of internal action threatening the overthrow of the Soviet-controlled regimes, except possibly in the case of Albania."[14]

NSC 162/2 stated the conclusion bluntly. "[T]he ability of the USSR to exercise effective control over, and to exploit the resources of the European satellites has not been appreciably reduced and is not likely to be so long as the USSR maintains adequate forces in the area."[15] A JCS proposal to qualify this judgment, which was not adopted, will be discussed in the next chapter.

Communist China

Since 1950 the cold war had expanded in the Far East. There, a staff study in April 1953 concluded, the "central problem" for the United States was "the threat to the U.S. and Free World security resulting from the establishment of control over China by an aggressive and dynamic Communist regime closely aligned with and supported by the Soviet Union."[16] The stalemate in Korea, and the hostilities in Indochina (and the special interest of many Republicans in Asia and Chiang Kaishek) ensured early NSC attention to this region. By April the Planning Board had produced draft reports on the Far East generally as well as on Korea, the Chinese Nationalists, and Japan, and it had reviewed and reaffirmed earlier reports on the Philippines and Southeast Asia. After preliminary discussion, however, the NSC agreed to postpone action until further consideration.[17]

The policy paper specifically on Communist China (NSC 166/1) was prepared by the Planning Board in parallel with NSC 162 and was considered by the NSC at about the same time. The paper was accompanied by a staff study of 10,000 words, analyzing the capabilities and intentions of Communist China and the prospects for the Sino-Soviet alliance as well as the potential for resistance by neighboring Asian and Western nations.[18] The gist of this appraisal, which was detailed and objective, was reflected succinctly in NSC 162/2 and more extensively in NSC 166/1: "The Chinese Communist regime is firmly in control and is unlikely to be shaken in the foreseeable future by domestic forces or rival regimes, short of the occurrence of a major war." Despite potential political pitfalls and economic limits, "for the foreseeable future it is probable that they [the Chinese Communists] will continue to make some progress in developing the economic and political strength of their regime." Their military capabilities, while dependent on Russian assistance, "are sufficient to make invasion of China very costly," and to require major U.S. and Western forces to counter external aggression.[19]

Their external aims were driven, according to NSC 166/1, by nationalist and communist imperatives. They "impel the Chinese Communists toward eventual recapture of the historically Chinese territories which the U.S. and the West now hold or protect; toward eventual expulsion of Western or Western allied forces from adjacent mainland areas; and toward substitution of Chinese Communist influence for that of the West in other areas of the Far East."[20]

The threat to the Far East was greatly enhanced by the Sino-Soviet alliance. This was "based on powerful ties of common ideology and mutual interest" that had not been affected by the death of Stalin. Communist China was not a satellite: there the Soviets had none of the domestic levers in the secret police, military, or Party used to control the East European satellites. China was a junior partner: because it had achieved power on its own, Mao was in a position like Tito. As the Soviets' "only voluntary and genuine ally," it was treated with relative deference.

Both parties benefited substantially from the partnership. The Chinese were heavily dependent on the Soviets for military equipment, capital goods, petroleum, and technical assistance—paid for in cash or goods. Of their total imports in 1952 and 1953, the Soviets had supplied some 53 percent, its satellites some 10 ten, and the West about 28 percent. For the present, China and the Soviet Union shared common aims in Asia. And, for the Soviets, crises like Korea or Indochina diverted Western resources from Europe. While frictions or divergences might develop later, the alliance seemed solidly based.[21]

General War

The growing Soviet nuclear arsenal posed for Eisenhower the same question addressed by NSC 68 in 1950. How would the Soviet nuclear capacity affect its pursuit of its objectives? The key conclusion of NSC 68, it will be recalled, was that 1954, when the Soviets were expected to achieve the atomic capacity to cripple the United States, would be a "year of maximum danger," entailing grave risk of nuclear war.

The question was now more urgent. By mid-1953 the Soviet stockpile had been growing steadily for four years and would continue to do so. It was estimated to reach 335 to 1,000, with yields up to 100 kilotons, by mid-1957, and would also be greatly augmented by H-bombs as a result of their test of August 1953.[22]

The Soviet capacity projected by NSC 68 was rapidly becoming actual. "The USSR," read NSC 162/2, "has sufficient bombs and aircraft, using one-way missions, to inflict serious damage to the United States, especially by surprise attack. The USSR soon may have the capability of dealing a crippling blow to our industrial base and our continuing ability to prosecute a war. Effective defense could reduce the likelihood and intensity of a hostile attack but not eliminate the chance of a crippling blow."[23]

Yet Eisenhower rejected the NSC 68 concept of a "year of maximum danger"; he was convinced that the Soviets could be deterred indefinitely from launching a nuclear attack or risking general war. This conviction was based on his view of Soviet priorities and of the consequences of such a war, views he had held consistently, as has been discussed, since the 1940s. He considered the Soviet leaders to be opportunistic but prudent in their actions. They were rational and calculating—not zealots or adventurers.

Moreover, Eisenhower shared the judgment about Soviet priorities that Bohlen had pressed in the debate over NSC 68. Despite communist hostility and ambitions, Eisenhower had long believed, the Soviet leaders' highest priority was to maintain the regime. They would never risk jeopardizing their security or stability for the sake of expansion.[24] An attack on the United States or its allies would inevitably involve such a risk from retaliation, potential domestic chaos, and satellite unrest. In theory the Soviets might be tempted into attacking if they believed that initial surprise could totally destroy the U.S. capacity for retaliation. But Eisenhower remained satisfied that no Soviet leaders could be confident of orchestrating a surprise attack so perfectly as to avoid substantial risk of retaliation, taking account of failures in weapons and bombers and the necessity for identical timing for striking dispersed targets. Thus the Kremlin leadership, if considering aggression, would weigh not merely relative military strength but also the potential consequences for the stability of the regime of the stresses and strains of such a war and of strategic retaliation.

Hence the Soviets were not likely to initiate general war and would "try to avoid courses of action which in their judgment might involve substantial risk of general war." But there remained the danger of unintended escalation from smaller actions, "especially if seen by one side as an imminent threat to its security."[25] Indeed, NSC 162/2 stated unequivocally that the fear of general war would not deter the Soviets from taking the measures they considered necessary to counter Western actions that they viewed as serious threats to their security. Looking ahead, eventual nuclear plenty for both the United States and Soviet Union "could create a stalemate, with both sides reluctant to initiate general warfare."[26]

NSC 162/2 recognized that the Soviet Union "has and will continue to have large conventional military forces capable of aggression against countries of the free world." Soviet fear of atomic retaliation, however, should still inhibit local aggression, although that "deterrent effect" might "tend" toward being diminished by the growing Soviet atomic capability.[27]

Subversion and Political Warfare

If general war could be avoided, the Jackson Committee foresaw "that the greatest danger of Soviet expansion lies in political warfare and local communist armed action."[28] NSC 162/2 likewise stressed this aspect of the threat: "The USSR will continue to rely heavily on tactics of diversion and subversion to weaken the free world alliances and the will to resist the Soviet power."[29] This conclusion was very much in keeping with Dulles's own appraisal of Soviet strategy: "The verdict of history," he said when defending NSC 162/2 at a subsequent NSC meeting, "was that the Soviet leaders have been rather cautious in exercising their power. They were not reckless, as Hitler was, but they primarily rely not on military force but on the methods of subversion."[30]

Soviet political warfare techniques were diverse and could be adapted to the weaknesses and susceptibilities of their various targets. They included "political and economic pressure, diplomatic action in the UN and elsewhere, propaganda and front activities, the actions of communist parties and communist-party-controlled trade unions outside the Bloc, sabotage, exploitation of subversive and revolutionary movements and of civil wars, and psychological warfare."[31] The Soviets enjoyed advantages in the use of such instruments: central control, experience, tight organization, and freedom from restraints of public opinion or a free press.[32]

To divide the allies, the Soviets could exploit the fear of atomic war and the hope for peace; European dependence on U.S. nuclear capability; distrust as between France and Germany; and other differences in interests. In Asia, Africa, and Latin America, neutralism, nationalism, and anticolonial and anti-Western attitudes offered ready leverage; and weak and unstable societies and governments were subject to manipulation and infiltration by Communist parties, front organizations, and propaganda. Finally, for peoples from less developed countries suffering from extreme poverty, communist ideology and the Soviet Union as a model for progress had great appeal.[33]

Sino-Soviet Vulnerabilities

One of the questions posed by Cutler in early February when starting the review of basic national security policy was whether existing policies "sufficiently weigh or consider the vulnerabilities of the Kremlin regime."[34] In effect, Dulles had made this an issue in the 1952 campaign. Stalin's death gave it even greater urgency. Accordingly, the question had been examined in intelligence estimates, the Solarium exercise, the Jackson Report on political warfare, conferences of U.S. ambassadors, and the NSC Planning Board and NSC. In general the conclusions paralleled those of Kennan in 1948: the Soviet system did have serious vulnerabilities, but they would have effect only in the longer term.[35] Inherent tensions or weaknesses and basic historical forces, it was believed, would ultimately change or undermine the Soviet Union, the satellite empire, and the Sino-Soviet partnership. For some indeterminate period, as already discussed, the system was expected to be able to overcome such forces and to remain solid and intact. But eventually, if expansion was frustrated, they would take their toll. According to NSC 162/2:

> Over time, changes in the outlook and policies of the leadership of the USSR may result from such factors as the slackening of revolutionary zeal, the growth of vested managerial and bureaucratic interests, and popular pressures for consumption goods. Such changes, combined with the growing strength of the Free World and the failure to break its cohesion, and possible aggravation of weaknesses with the Soviet bloc through U.S. or allied action or otherwise, might induce a willingness to negotiate [to end the cold war]. The Soviet leadership might find it desirable and even essential to reach agreements acceptable to the United States and its allies, without necessarily abandoning its basic hostility to the non-Soviet world.[36]

Satellites

The prospects in the satellites were similar, though for different reasons. There, too, as we have seen, Soviet domination was judged to be firmly based by reason of its military presence and penetration of the secret police, the satellite military and parties, and the integration of the economies. In Bohlen's view, "the withdrawal of the Red Army from the satellites was a precondition of liberation."[37]

Yet that reality was not seen as the whole story. Soviet control of the satellites might be intact for an indeterminate period ahead—but not forever. Based on historical experience, there was an equally strong conviction that the "spirit of resistance in Eastern Europe will never die out."[38] The anticommunism of the great majority was deeply rooted. It was "intensified particularly by the loss of personal freedom and a reduced standard of living, as well as by outraged religions and national feelings." Though communist indoctrination of the youth might diminish it somewhat, the nationalist urge, and the yearnings for freedom and a better life, would almost surely outlast and eventually undermine Soviet imperialism. When that might occur could not be predicted. It would depend on the evolution of the Soviet outlook and objectives for expansion and security; the impact of passive and other forms of resistance in the satellites; changing Soviet views of the burdens and benefits of domination; and the success of external efforts to foster change.[39]

The Sino-Soviet Alliance

The vulnerabilities of the Sino-Soviet alliance were radically different from those of the satellites. Like Tito, Mao had not allowed the Soviets to penetrate his secret police, military, or party. As a voluntary partnership based on interests and ideology, the alliance would be in jeopardy only if either side judged that it no longer served its interests and wanted to escape. Still, the factors that now drew them together had the potential of becoming divisive:

- Chinese dependence on the Soviets to supply industrial and military equipment and technical assistance was such a factor. In its impatience to develop its economy and to achieve major power status, the Chinese might well come to demand more than the Soviets were ready to deliver, or disputes could arise over the terms of payment (which the Soviets required in cash or goods).
- The partners differed greatly in their external perspectives. China's concerns were primarily oriented to the neighboring areas of Asia. The Soviet outlook was global, with special interests in Europe and the Middle East and its relations with the United States. In considering actions in the Far East, the Soviets would be concerned with the broader impact as China would not.
- Similarly, with respect to security, and especially risks of nuclear war, the Soviet perspective was bound to differ from China's. A venturesome China might find the Soviets unwilling to support it as it expected (as happened during the Quemoy-Matsu crises in the Taiwan Stait in 1954–1955 and 1958).
- Even in Asia, while both parties might agree on seeking to displace the United States and the Western nations, they might be competing for influence over local Communist parties or within specific states (as in North Korea or Indochina).
- Ideology itself could become a source of friction. Mao fancied himself a creative thinker in Marxist-Leninist doctrine and practice. He had been willing to play second fiddle to the legendary Stalin; he would certainly not be prepared to do so for his successors. Moreover, ideological divergences could develop as Soviet doctrine was adapted to the nuclear era.
- More generally, Soviet leaders were not accustomed to dealing with other states as equals. They recognized the necessity to treat Mao with respect. But as the Chinese became more assertive and more powerful, Soviet tendencies toward dominion or arrogance might come to the fore and create serious frictions.

As this catalog indicates, "the potential difficulties of the Sino-Soviet connection will stem primarily from the internal workings of the partnership and only secondarily from the nature of external pressures or inducements." Outside influences could perhaps create a context for generating or nurturing such tensions.[40] These sober appraisals of the threat from the Soviet bloc and its vulnerabilities, therefore, compelled the administration to examine the alternatives for the strategy of the United States.

11

Strategic Objectives: Rollback?

[Eisenhower] had doubts he said about how much we should poke at the animal through the bars of the cage.[1]

Robert Cutler (1953)

Whether or not the United States should adopt the basic objective of coercing the "rollback" of Soviet power and the ending of the threat to the free world (hereafter simply called "rollback") was inevitably a key issue in preparing the first Eisenhower national security strategy. In the 1952 campaign Dulles had urged a more "positive" and "dynamic" policy than containment for liberating Eastern Europe, albeit limited to peaceful means as Eisenhower insisted.[2] And aggressive rollback had been one alternative examined in the Solarium exercise: Task Force C had laid out a specific course, including use of covert action and limited force, for pursuing it. After Solarium, Cutler's memorandum to the Planning Board on "Points for Consideration" in drafting the new national strategy included "(5) To take selected aggressive actions of a limited scope, involving moderately increased risks of general war . . . to reduce Soviet power in the Satellite periphery."[3]

In essence, supporters of rollback rejected the premises of the containment strategy. In his seminal 1947 "Mr. X" article, Kennan forecast that, if successfully contained, the Soviet threat would eventually wither as the long-term result of internal decay and discord within the Soviet bloc. But that disintegration could take decades. Moreover, it depended on the West maintaining for that period (1) the military and other means to frustrate Soviet expansion and (2) the cohesion and will to use them effectively.

Proponents of rollback questioned whether these conditions would be met, especially when the U.S.S.R. possessed the capacity for a crippling nuclear blow. The Kremlin might then be tempted to launch a surprise strike; or if mutual plenty produced stalemate, that would greatly enhance the Soviet capacity for local aggression and subversion. Further, fear of nuclear war could fatally inhibit and divide the Western coalition. Thus rollback advocates argued that awaiting erosion of the Soviet threat was far too risky. In their view it was vital to coerce or induce retraction or reduction of Soviet power before it achieved nuclear plenty. The most extreme proponents urged preventive war.[4] While NSC 68, as we have seen, eschewed that, it sought "preponderant" power to induce Soviet retraction in some unspecified way.

In practical terms, this issue was decided by NSC 162/2. The JCS prolonged the debate, however, until the end of 1954.

The State/Defense Split

In the drafting of NSC 162 a basic conflict developed in the NSC Planning Board on this critical issue between the State member (supported by the CIA advisor) and the Department of Defense and JCS representatives (supported by the Office of Defense Mobilization and the Foreign Operations Administration). The dispute was *not* about the ultimate goal of U.S. policy: *all* agreed that the objective was "to prevent Soviet aggression and continuing domination of other nations, and to establish an effective control of armaments under proper safeguards; but it is not to dictate the internal political and economic organization of the USSR."[5] Nor was the issue whether the United States "should impose pressures on the Soviet bloc." *All* agreed that it should take "feasible political, economic, propaganda and covert measures designed to create and exploit troublesome problems for the USSR, impair Soviet relations with Communist China, complicate control in the satellites, and retard the growth of the military and economic potential of the Soviet bloc."[6]

The conflict concerned the *nature* of such pressures and their *purpose*. Should the objective be to drive back Soviet power by aggressive measures, including the use of force or the threat of force against the Soviet bloc—such as by attempting to take over Hainan or detach Albania? Or should such pressures avoid force and be designed primarily to foster the long-term process of internal change within the bloc and the resulting change in Soviet external conduct?

State Position

In essence the position of the State member was like Kennan's of 1947. The desired changes in Soviet outlook and purposes would come about only by an extended process of evolution within the Soviet Union and the bloc as a result of a combination of factors over time: (1) frustration of Soviet expansion; (2) "slackening of revolutionary zeal, the growth of vested managerial and bureaucratic interests, and popular pressures for consumption goods"; (3) satellite ferment driven by oppression, nationalism, and desire for freedom; (4) serious frictions straining or fracturing the Sino-Soviet alliance; (5) "the growing strength of the free world and the failure to break its cohesion"; and (6) "possible aggravation of weaknesses within the Soviet bloc through U.S. or allied action or otherwise."[7]

The agreed appraisal of the Soviet threat and its vulnerabilities provided good grounds for expecting such basic changes ultimately to take place. Pending such change, the East-West conflict could be substantially mitigated only by agreements, which both sides considered in their interests, on specific issues like Korea or the

Austrian treaty, and eventually, if possible, for the safeguarded control of armaments, when the Soviets came to recognize, despite their deep-seated hostility, that the arms race and nuclear weapons entailed risks to their own security.[8] Accordingly, actions to impose pressures on the Soviet Union should be designed primarily to foster this process of internal change and to create conditions that would induce Kremlin leaders to be receptive to such acceptable agreements.[9] Such pressures might hasten these processes, but they could not substitute for them.

Therefore, the State member strongly opposed any policy of forceful rollback. To make this explicit, he proposed to include in NSC 162 the provision: "The U.S. should not, however, initiate aggressive actions involving force against Soviet bloc territory."[10] The rationale was based on the relevant national intelligence estimates and agreed appraisals contained in NSC 162. Aggressive actions would be futile, dangerous, divisive, and counterproductive.

Futile because "Limited actions within our capabilities would not materially reduce the Soviet threat even if successful." Paragraph 4 of the strategy draft stated that Soviet control of the satellites would remain intact "so long as the USSR maintains adequate military forces in the area," and that "detachment of any major European satellite . . . does not now appear feasible except by Soviet acquiescence or by war." Moreover, such detachment "would not decisively affect the Soviet military capability either in delivery of weapons of mass destruction or in conventional forces," although it "would be a considerable blow to Soviet prestige and would impair in some degree its conventional capabilities."[11]

Dangerous because such "actions are likely materially to increase the risk of general war." Paragraph 5a of the draft affirmed that while unlikely deliberately to initiate general war, the "Soviets will not, however, be deterred by fear of general war from taking measures they consider necessary to counter Western actions which they view as a serious threat to their security."[12] Forceful actions against bloc territory would surely be so considered.

Divisive because such actions "would place serious strains on the coalition." According to paragraph 14c of NSC 162, Europeans feared U.S. policies toward the Soviets were "too rigid and unyielding," entailing risks that preventive war or liberation might involve them in general war. A policy of rollback would confirm and reinforce those fears. If not overcome such concerns "could imperil the coalition," essential for free world security.[13]

Counterproductive because such actions "might well destroy the chances of agreement with the USSR on the more fundamental aspects of the Soviet threat." The gravest menace to the United States was the growing Soviet nuclear capability. That could be mitigated only by reliable arms control agreements with the Soviet Union. The current chances for such agreements were not encouraging, but might improve over time as the Soviets came to realize "that armament limitation will also serve their own interests and security."[14] The CIA advisor explained the point clearly:

> The Soviets are more likely to become amenable to reason as a result of finding the West strong and united but willing to live with peaceful Russia than they are by an accumulation of minor damage that would not affect their vitals but would tend to reinforce their dogmatic belief in the inevitability of an all-out clash with the capitalist states.[15]

In short, the State Department maintained that the premises of rollback were faulty, its results inconclusive at best, and its risks and potential costs prohibitive.

JCS-Department of Defense Position[16]

The JCS opposed the key elements in the State position and in effect supported rollback. While conceding that the United States should not foreclose the possibility of acceptable settlements, the service chiefs stressed intelligence estimates that Soviet leaders "will almost certainly be unwilling to settle any East-West differences at the cost of major concessions." They would do so only after a radical change in attitudes. The JCS "consider it probable that a basic change in the attitude of the Soviet leaders can be brought about only through our seizure and retention of the initiative in the current cold war."[17] Their suggested revisions and commentary indicated the nature of such an initiative, but without identifying specific actions to be taken.

First, the JCS objected that the draft (paragraph 4b) "appears to foreclose the possibility of detachment of a major European satellite by means short of war." They wished to add "in the near future." Also, in their view the consequences of such a detachment were underestimated by the State Department and CIA; they also recommended NSC 162 assert that it not only would breach the Soviet zone buffer but also "might well initiate a chain reaction leading to a major retraction of the Soviet sphere of influence and control."[18]

Second, the JCS insisted that, short of initiating general war, the Soviet threat could be substantially reduced "only by actions designed to bring about a negotiating attitude in the USSR and its resulting accommodation to the security of the United States and that of the free world." And that result would be fostered "if Soviet stability and influence are reduced." Their reason was that this phrase would indicate "that a weakening of the Soviet structure is a probable prerequisite to the achievement of acceptable negotiated settlements."[19]

Third, and most significant in making clear their position, the JCS urged deletion of the paragraph prohibiting "forceful actions" against the Soviet bloc. Such a policy, they argued,

> is self-defeating and is directly contrary to the positive, dynamic policy required to reduce the Soviet threat before it reaches critical proportions. As the combined strength of the free world increases, and while the United States still retains a substantial margin of [nuclear] superiority over the USSR, a progressively more positive program of action can be adopted without undue risk of general war.[20]

To underscore the urgency of such a program, the JCS stressed paragraph 44 of NSC 162:

> In the face of the developing Soviet threat, the broad aim of U.S. security policies must be to create, *prior to the achievement of mutual atomic plenty*, conditions under which the United States and the free world coalition are prepared to meet the Soviet-Communist threat with resolution and to negotiate for its alleviation under proper safeguards.[21]

This paragraph proposed by the JCS had been included in the draft with little discussion. In the context of the proposed JCS strategy, however, this seemingly simple warning could be interpreted (as we will see the JCS argued during 1954) as virtually setting a deadline for achieving rollback by the "positive" strategy. The effect would be a return to NCS 68's concept of "year of maximum danger."

For the JCS a corollary was that, aside from issues like Korea, negotiations with the Soviet Union, especially for agreements on arms control, were not merely futile; they were contrary to American interests and should not be pursued until the basic Soviet outlook and purposes were changed.

NSC Discussion

The initial debate on the issue in the NSC on October 7 was confused. In presenting the question Cutler seriously muddled the real divergences, misstating especially the State and CIA position (referred to by Cutler as "Side A"). He first asserted that both sides agreed that "short of general war, acceptable negotiated settlements with the USSR are the only means of substantially reducing the Soviet threat."

That was a half-truth, which Cutler subsequently distorted further. Side A (State and CIA), he went on to say, "believed that the best way to induce the Soviets to accept such settlements was for the U.S. to forego [sic] pressures at least against the USSR itself; to attempt to reduce tensions on secondary issues; and to try to convince the Soviet leaders that, if they renounce aggression and domination of other peoples, the United States has no intention of interfering with the internal organization or the territorial integrity of the USSR." In fact, the first clause of Cutler's summary regarding "forgoing" pressures was wrong, and the last clause starting with "to try to convince" was approved by both sides.

"On the other hand," Cutler continued, "Side B [Department of Defense and JCS] believed that the best way of bringing the Soviets to agree to such settlements is to maintain pressures against the USSR which do not involve the grave risk of general war."[22] As explained above, both sides explicitly agreed on seeking to impose pressures—the split was about their nature and purpose. Should they include the use of force against the Soviet bloc—which almost surely *did* risk escalating into large-scale war? Should such pressures aim to coerce the Soviet rollback before it achieved substantial nuclear capacity?

This wholly misleading depiction of the two positions may well have reflected Cutler's own bias expressed in his attack in the Planning Board on the first draft of NSC 162. In any case, it naturally skewed the debate in the NSC. Thus C. D. Jackson suggested erroneously that side A would exclude even Western food relief programs in East Germany, which he had advocated during the July uprising. And Joseph Dodge thought side A proposed "continuous concessions to the USSR." Not surprisingly, the president then asked whether anyone supported Side A. On inquiry by Secretary Dulles Director of the Policy Planning Staff Robert Bowie, who attended only as a silent observer, confirmed that State had supported Side A. But constrained by his status, he left it to Dulles, who had been fully briefed on the actual State position the previous afternoon, to correct Cutler's misrepresentation.[23]

"The President suggested with a smile that this was not the way the Secretary of State usually talked to him about the problem."[24]

Undaunted and aware that the State position had been misstated by Cutler, Secretary Dulles sought to bring the discussion back on course. He argued forcefully that arms control agreements or settlements in Korea or Austria, for example, would have to be mutually acceptable and could not be imposed.[25]

In further discussion of the bases for negotiated settlements, Secretary Dulles strongly insisted that they

> must be mutually acceptable, and what was being proposed [by the JCS] appeared to be reversing this Administration's whole policy—a fact that was all the more dangerous in view of the Soviet possession of the H-bomb. . . . If you subordinate the achievement of mutually agreeable settlements to improving the power position of the United States as against the USSR, you will eliminate all hope of settlements in Korea, Austria, Germany, etc.

At the suggestion of the president, after further discussion it was agreed to drop the JCS version and part of State's language. When the director of the CIA, Secretary Wilson, the JCS, and Foreign Operations Administration (formerly the Mutual Security Administration) Director Stassen urged the omission of the disputed paragraph renouncing forceful actions against the bloc, the president concurred but pointed "out that any proposal involving use of force against such territory, whether overt or covert, would require a prior Council decision."[26]

After discussion of other splits, the NSC referred NSC 162 back to the Planning Board to prepare a revised draft for the Council, "incorporating the agreed amendments."[27] The revised draft was discussed by the NSC on October 29.[28] With regard to pressures on the U.S.S.R., Secretary Dulles expressed the concern within his department over "the absence of the specific inhibition against aggressive action vis-à-vis the Soviet bloc," such as efforts to detach Albania or an assault on Hainan Island. He said, however, that "As long . . . as it is quite clear that no such actions as these would be undertaken without consideration by the National Security Council, he was willing to let the present language . . . stand."[29] With various changes not relevant here, President Eisenhower approved the draft.

Rollback?

What then did NSC 162/2 decide regarding rollback? For over a year thereafter the JCS protested the failure in practice to pursue a more aggressive policy. In arguing for it they contended that option had been kept open in NSC 162/2. And indeed, the express prohibition against "aggressive actions involving force against Soviet bloc territory" had been deleted. In doing so, however, the president had stressed that any such measure would require specific NSC approval; and Dulles had later reiterated this caveat as a prerequisite to accepting the deletion. To support their view, as we shall see, the JCS relied heavily on NSC 162/2's paragraph 45:

> In the face of the developing Soviet threat, the broad aim of U.S. security policies must be to create, prior to the achievement of mutual atomic plenty, conditions under which

the United States and the free world coalition are prepared to meet the Soviet Communist threat with resolution and to negotiate for its alleviation under proper safeguards.[30]

But the JCS interpretation of this paragraph was not shared by others. It had been accepted by the Solarium Committee of the Planning Board without dissent. Most members understood it to be merely a warning that, before atomic plenty, the West must achieve a cohesive coalition (especially by integrating the Federal Republic of Germany firmly into NATO and the Western Community), a suitable strategy, and sufficient forces to maintain deterrence and resist subversive activities. The JCS, however, later insisted that this provision was intended to set a deadline (before mutual atomic plenty—now projected as 1957–1959) for ending the Soviet threat on U.S. terms (shades of NSC 68), which, they said, could be achieved only by aggressive pressure or coercion; that is, some sort of rollback.

Ultimately the question was where the president stood. While agreeing to delete from NSC 162/2 the provision forbidding the use of force against the Soviet bloc, he had explicitly stated that any such action would require NSC consideration and his express approval. Moreover, on various occasions Eisenhower had discussed the issue of preventive war. In fact, in September 1953, shortly before the adoption of NSC 162/2, he had done so in response to a proposal by Dulles based on the secretary's dire forebodings about the danger of the Western coalition's collapse. As will be subsequently discussed, Eisenhower concluded, after an analysis based on Dulles's premises, that if they were carried to their logical ends the United States would be ultimately faced with the alternative of total war or a dictatorial regime. "In such circumstances, we would be forced to consider whether or not our duty to future generations did not require us to *initiate* war at the most propitious moment that we could designate."[31] And in mid-1954 Eisenhower had raised the issue again. If "this were indeed the situation," he stated during an NSC discussion about the fragility of the alliance, "we should perhaps come back to the very grave question: should the United States now get ready to fight the Soviet Union?" The president reminded the NSC that he had "brought up this question more than once at prior Council meetings, and that he had never done so facetiously."[32]

In reality, however, the evidence is very strong that such comments were only abstract musings and that Eisenhower had in fact ruled out preventive war or measures that significantly risked provoking war as serious options. As we have seen, when the Solarium exercise was being organized, the president apparently vetoed examining a fourth alternative based on an ultimatum for a general settlement backed by the threat of preventive war. And he named General Goodpaster to Task Force C to ensure that the study of rollback was objective.[33] As noted earlier Goodpaster was convinced the president had firmly ruled out rollback by the time of Solarium.

Eisenhower believed his reasons for doing so were compelling. He remained profoundly convinced that a general nuclear war would be an unmitigated disaster for all concerned. Conceding that "his imagination as to the horrors of a third world war might be overdeveloped," the president stressed its catastrophic consequences repeatedly at NSC meetings and elsewhere. He doubted "whether any nations as we now know them would continue to exist at the conclusion" of such a nuclear war.[34] "[T]here would be no individual freedom after the next global war"; every free nation involved "would come out of it as a dictatorship."[35] Emphasizing the appalling chaos that would follow the massive destruction, Eisenhower asked: "[W]hat do you do with the world after you have won victory in such a catastrophic war?"[36] In discussing a Planning Board report on war aims, he suggested that the chaos after a global war would be so great as to make such planning futile, concluding that "the main purpose served by this paper was to emphasize how vital it was to avoid a third world war."[37]

Finally, strong statements by Eisenhower in other contexts during 1954 confirm his conviction that no moment could be propitious for initiating general war. In such a war, he commented in March, the United States would be justified in using every available weapon because "we would never enter the war except in retaliation against a heavy Soviet atomic attack."[38] And later that year, on the same issue, he said, "We are *not* going to provoke the war, and that is why we have got to be patient. If war comes, the other side must have started it.[39]

In short, for Eisenhower preventive war or aggressive rollback would be a reckless and self-defeating gamble. The only practical alternative was to make collective security effective for as long as necessary for the erosion of the threat. But for nearly a year the JCS sought to redirect policy in the direction of aggressive rollback. That effort will be discussed after analyzing basic strategy toward Communist China.

Communist China

Since 1950 U.S. policy toward the Soviets' principal ally, the Peoples' Republic of China, had been a critical component of its cold war strategy. Accordingly, the NSC Planning Board had worked on this issue in parallel with the preparation of NSC 162.

It had first addressed the topic in April 1953 in a broader draft report, "United States Policies in the Far East" (NSC 148), supported by a staff study on Communist China. The policy report proposed various forms of pressure on the Peking regime for the purposes of dividing the Sino-Soviet alliance and reorienting China. According to the staff study, basic U.S. objectives should be to end the Chinese threat and ultimately to foster an independent, friendly Chinese government. The most effective route toward this end, the study asserted, was through disrupting the Sino-Soviet alliance and detaching China from the Soviet orbit. Such detachment could occur either by a) defection of the regime from Moscow or b) its overthrow by a regime hostile to Moscow. After analyzing the pros and cons of each course, the staff study argued that a choice between them, despite their apparent inconsistency, was premature: "A policy of increasing pressure on Communist China short of outright U.S. intervention" would promote both courses for a long time to come.[40]

At the meeting on April 8, the NSC was not ready to take long-range decisions. Secretary Dulles "did not feel able at this time to go along with the policy recommendations and implications in the reports." Secretary Wilson concurred. Hence the NSC "deferred action pending further study."[41]

The next day Secretary Dulles, meeting with his State Department advisors, talked of more assertive actions in the Far East: possibly renewing hostilities in Korea to achieve at least a partial victory; expanding programs for Formosa (Taiwan) and Indochina; a threat to Hainan or the long Chinese coastline — "an ideal opportunity for exploiting sea and air power." He was "sure this would place a strain both on China and on Russia." Rather than seeking to induce Mao to follow Tito's lead and defect, Dulles argued, subjecting the Sino-Soviet alliance to increased pressure would "give us the best chance of securing our objectives either with fighting or without fighting." Responding to the suggestion that such a program would cost more money and might require expanding forces, he said, doubtless with the Republican right wing in mind, that "he thought it would be possible to get money for a program of accomplishment."[42]

Seven months passed before the NSC considered the strategy toward China. Meanwhile the actual experience of dealing with the Chinese Communists, Chiang Kai-shek, the European allies, and others regarding the complexities of the Far East in this period moderated Dulles's earlier exuberance. In the interim, while occupied with the Solarium exercise and NSC 162, the Planning Board had also produced parallel papers on Communist China (NSC 166/1 and its Annex) and on the Chinese Nationalists (NSC 146/2 and its Annex).[43]

On November 6 the NSC approved NSC 166/1 virtually as submitted by the Planning Board. At JCS request the NSC inserted, "It would be in the interest of the United States to secure a reorientation of the Chinese Communist regime or its ultimate replacement by a regime which would not be hostile to the United States." But even the JCS conceded that "specific measures which might be effective to this end are not now feasible." And NSC 162/2, adopted a week before, stressed how remote any such prospect was. "The Chinese Communist regime is fully in control and is unlikely to be shaken in the foreseeable future by domestic forces or rival regimes, short of the occurrence of a major war."[44]

In the absence of further aggression or a basic change in the situation, NSC 166/1 explicitly ruled out the use of U.S. armed force for the "overthrow or replacement of the Chinese Communist regime" or in support of an attempt by the Nationalist Chinese regime on Taiwan to do so. Any such course, it stressed, would require a major part of the U.S. forces and of its atomic arsenal; would split the United States–led coalition; and would entail a very high risk of global war involving the Soviet Union. Also rejected were concessions designed to overcome the Chicom regime's basic hostility to the West; they would only sacrifice U.S. security interests without reducing the threat.

Thus the United States must seek to reduce the relative power position of Communist China in Asia by means short of war. These included building up noncommunist Asian countries; deterring and resisting PRC aggression; retarding the growth of Communist power; and impairing Sino-Soviet relations. All feasible political and economic measures, including unconventional and covert, would be used against Communist China for these purposes and to disrupt Sino-Soviet ties.[45]

NSC 166/1 recognized that, while the Sino-Soviet alliance was currently based solidly on communist ideology and community of interests, there were good reasons to expect that basic differences would eventually strain or break their ties. Further, external pressures, while secondary, could, as Dulles had argued, probably foster or hasten this process to some degree. For example, an embargo on trade could retard China's economic growth and enhance its dependence on the Soviet Union and the chances for friction. And political pressures could reduce Communist China's prestige and standing by keeping it out of the UN and other international bodies and by maintaining the Nationalist regime on Taiwan as the "true China."[46]

But pursuing these policies would not be easy. Many of the European allies and of the Asian noncommunist nations favored a more conciliatory course, or at least less stringent restrictions on trade. And the administration itself was split on the trade issue. All recognized, however, that looser restrictions would be strongly opposed in Congress—and not only by the Republican right wing.[47] These issues will be explored in later chapters.

Project Control

Concern about the emerging Soviet capacity for a crippling nuclear attack in a few years, which so troubled the JCS, inevitably spawned various studies of how to deal with it. Of these, one called Project Control was surely the most massive and elaborate. Started in mid-1953 by Colonel Raymond S. Sleeper with priority support of the Air University and the blessing of Air Force headquarters, the project produced a final report in June 1954, supported by some 22 volumes of studies, consultants' reports, and analyses.[48] More important, the report of Project Control was presented to, and discussed with, almost all of the top military officers and civilian officials concerned with national security affairs.

The premise of Project Control was that the United States would enjoy superiority in nuclear weapons and the capacity for their delivery at least until July 1957, and that the Soviets would recognize that fact. Its basic purpose was to develop a strategy to use that superiority (supported by diplomacy, covert action, and other means) to induce or compel the Kremlin to modify its behavior to conform to "terms" for peaceful and secure relations prescribed by the United States. These terms included (among others) lifting the Iron Curtain and freeing the satellites, agreeing to German unity, dissolving the international communist apparatus and the Sino-Soviet alliance, and accepting safeguarded arms control, thereby making aggression infeasible.

Operations to secure acceptance of these terms by Project Control would proceed through three phases as necessary: Persuasion, Pressure, and Administrative. In the Persuasion stage, the United States would "take the initiative" to gain control over Soviet air space and put the Soviet air forces on the defensive by extensive overflights of the Soviet Union and Soviet bloc territory. The United States planes would operate at high altitudes and speed to minimize losses, but some must be expected. "In overflying Russia, we would clearly demonstrate that we have the capability to wipe out Russia and the intent to do so if it becomes necessary. Having demonstrated our *determination*, it is almost axiomatic that Russia would yield reasonable terms and reach lasting solutions with the West."[49] If this confidence in the effectiveness of the "Persuasion" operations, often reiterated in the final report and studies, proved well-founded, there would be no need to pass on to the next phase.

But if the Soviets did not yield, or showed signs of strategic reaction, Project Control would initiate the Pressure stage.[50] This would be a surprise strategic air attack, using targeting intelligence gathered in the first phase, to neutralize the Soviet atomic delivery capacity by initially knocking out air bases and facilities, long-range bombers, atomic submarines, and atomic stockpiles as feasible, assisted by ground, naval, and tactical air forces, especially to preserve allied forces and areas. "Although the possibility of Soviet retaliation will remain to some degree, it can be expected that upon contact with indigenous control groups in the USSR [probably military leaders] proper, acceptable terms might be offered for surrender."[51] If necessary, attacks would be continued, with growing intensity, against defense-related industries and facilities.

The third or Administrative phase would follow surrender and be devoted to policing compliance with the surrender terms, largely by air surveyance to avoid the necessity for occupation.[52]

Starting in May 1954 Colonel Sleeper, who directed the study, gave extensive briefings on Project Control throughout the summer to the top military and civilian officials involved with national security. His first presentation was to a major Air Force conference that included the entire hierarchy of the service ("very favorably impressed"). Then came briefings for the Air Staff (highly inquisitive); RAND Corporation staff (polite interest but also skepticism); CIA Director Dulles ("interesting," but "would absorb a great deal more thought"); the Weapons Systems Evaluation Group ("extremely interesting"); and General Cutler and the NSC staff ("sympathetic . . . but largely non-committal"). At the State Department (Policy Planning Staff, European Bureau, and Deputy Undersecretary Robert Murphy), the reaction to the concept, as described by the briefing record the project staff prepared, was hostile, with the director of policy planning calling it "simply another version of preventive war" and questioning the assumptions regarding Soviet response to overflights and intimidation.

The most sympathetic reception to Project Control came from Admiral Arthur Radford, the JCS chairman. After a first briefing, he arranged to have it repeated for the other service chiefs and their staffs. In the subsequent discussion Radford was recorded as stating "that it was his belief that if the U.S. did not adopt and successfully follow through on a course of action similar to Project Control, that in the period mid-1957–60 there would be either an all-out atomic war or the U.S. would be forced into an agreement which would mean victory for the USSR." He intended to urge the president to receive a briefing and to set up a top level group "to develop, implement, and direct the application of Project Control." There is no record, however, that either the president or Secretary Dulles was briefed on Project Control.[53]

In other contexts, of course, the president and the secretary of state had discussed preventive war in abstract terms. The several times Eisenhower had posed the issue himself, in NSC meetings and in his September 1953 memorandum to Dulles, have already been considered. Moreover, in June 1954 Eisenhower and Dulles had been briefed at an NSC meeting on a memorandum by the JCS's Advance Study Group, "which proposed that the U.S. consider 'deliberately precipitating war with the USSR in the near future' before the Soviet thermonuclear capability became a 'real menace.' Army Chief of Staff Matthew Ridgway denounced this course as 'contrary to every principle upon which our Nation has been founded' and 'abhorrent to the great mass of American people.' The President did not comment himself at this briefing."[54] But the NSC 162/2 update he approved in January 1955 as NSC 5501 explicitly rejected "the concept of preventive war or acts intended to provoke war."[55]

The Review of National Security Policy

When approved on October 30, 1953, NSC 162/2 was expected to cover strategy for several years ahead. The next spring, however, the effort to develop guidelines under NSC 162/2 for the FY 1956 budget brought enhanced concern about two disturbing trends. One was the rapid "growth both in Soviet nuclear capabilities and in the power of nuclear weapons themselves, in the period 1956–59," making total nuclear war so destructive "as to threaten the survival of Western civilization and the Soviet regime." Second, increasing fear of the consequences of nuclear war was making the allies more cautious and reluctant to take decisive action to resist Soviet expansion, as shown by their attitudes toward Indochina, the EDC, and East-West trade.[56]

The guidelines had to take account of these trends. And that exercise prompted a full review of the national security strategy at the end of 1954, which produced a new Basic National Security Policy paper, NSC 5501. Stressing these trends the JCS took the occasion of both the guidelines exercise and the strategy review to renew vigorously their campaign for a more "aggressive" national strategy. They did so, however, only in general terms, refusing to specify any concrete actions for carrying out a "dynamic" strategy.

In March 1954 the Planning Board was directed to draft guidelines under NSC 162/2 for the preparation of the 1956 budget. These were to be based on appraisals, produced by the relevant departments and agencies, of the basic trends for the period 1956–1959. The JCS response on May 21 assessing the military outlook was sobering. They projected that atomic plenty, which both sides could have by 1956–1959, could produce mutual deterrence of general war but lessen the deterrent to peripheral aggression. Then "the Soviets might well elect to pursue their ultimate objective of world domination through a succession of local aggressions, either overt or covert, all of which could not be successfully opposed by the Allies through localized counteraction, without unacceptable commitment of resources." As a result, for the free world "the only alternative to acquiescence" to steady Soviet expansion "would be *a deliberate decision to react with military force against the real source of aggression.*" This situation, they said, served to emphasize the limited time, as recognized in paragraph 45 of NSC 162/2, for establishing satisfactory and enduring arrangements for coexistence.[57]

In June the JCS delivered to the NSC, scheduled to meet the next day, a second memorandum "for consideration in connection with the future application of basic national policy."[58] This laid out "their views concerning certain broader aspects of the situation now confronting the US and its allies, and especially their grounds for strongly opposing negotiations." They warned that the struggle against "the spread of Soviet-Communist domination of peoples and areas has now entered a precarious if not critical stage," marked by "continuing Communist expansion and military growth . . . and divisive strains in the world coalition." If present trends continue, the JCS predicted, in a "relatively short span of years" the Soviet Union will put U.S. security "in such jeopardy as to render it doubtful that any military establishment which our country could continue to support could be relied upon to defend our territory and our institutions in the years ahead." Accordingly, the "threatening course of the cold war . . . makes necessary a reappraisal within the framework of current basic national security policy, of the tactics which have been pursued by the United States in seeking to achieve its objectives."[59]

The JCS concluded that the Soviets would steadfastly pursue world domination and make no concessions "unless and until they have been convinced that failure to achieve lasting solutions of major issues will involve grave risks to the maintenance of their regime." And the Soviet leaders would not be so convinced "until the US and its allies, by means of positive actions, confront the USSR with the risks which might attend such a failure."[60] That must be done, as paragraph 45 of NSC 162/2 warned, before the U.S. atomic capability had been neutralized—by around FY 1959. "The obvious conclusion, therefore, is that if the Western nations hope to reach timely and lasting settlements, they must proceed now to formulate their just demands and then steadfastly to press for their consummation while the United States still holds atomic superiority."[61]

The next day, in a long meeting on the Planning Board draft of "Tentative Guidelines," the NSC discussion ranged widely, if inconclusively. The members discussed the implications of impending nuclear plenty for deterrence strategy, conventional forces, "creeping" communist expansion, allied attitudes and weaknesses, and negotiations and disarmament. In the course of the discussion, Secretary Dulles, referring to the "belief that the United States should take full advantage of its present atomic superiority to exert pressure on the Soviet Union," cautioned that "If we do so, however, very few of our allies will follow us. . . . The tide is clearly running against us in the channel of this 'tough policy'."[62]

After more debate about the situation and the conduct of U.S. policy, the president, "reverting again to the problem of tough policies and soft policies, said he was a pragmatic sort of guy and these labels had meaning to him only when applied to concrete cases."[63] After "further inclusive discussion" at the next meeting, the NSC directed the Planning Board to redraft the paper (NSC 5422) in the light of the Council discussion and additional agency review.[64] As for the JCS memorandum, their official history concluded, "Neither at [the June 24] meeting nor in a subsequent discussion a week later did the [NSC] members show any disposition to accept the JCS viewpoint."[65]

The Planning Board's revised guidelines paper, NSC 5422/1, which came before the NSC on August 5, reflected the earlier discussion by the Council. It therefore did not embody the JCS recommendations for a more positive policy. For this reason the Joint Strategic Survey Committee recommended to the JCS that the paper should be returned to the Planning Board for complete revision. The Joint Chiefs rejected this advice. Instead, they "merely advised" Secretary Wilson that NSC

5422/1 "correctly identified many problems, but that it provided little guidance in meeting them."[66]

Indeed, the only provision relating to rollback appeared in a paragraph regarding Asia. To a sentence calling for efforts to create "a position of strength calculated to block Communist expansion," Defense and the JCS proposed to add "and eventually to contract Communist-controlled areas and power." Secretary Dulles preferred that it be omitted, "because it implied that the rollback would take place only in Asia." He "thought there should be long-range plans for a rollback in the satellites, in Iran, etc., but he wished to emphasize that these plans would have to be very long-range indeed." The president suggested adding a paragraph indicating that "while the time of a significant rollback was far in the future, nevertheless we should watch any opportunities and prepare plans for an earlier contracting of Soviet power." This was done. With a few other minor changes, Eisenhower approved NSC 5422/2 on August 7.[67]

Neither in their June memorandum nor in the NSC meetings did the JCS specify *what* "positive" measures they proposed in order to obtain Soviet compliance with Western demands for retraction from the satellites, or alleviation of the nuclear threat. Nevertheless, despite their lack of success in the guidelines exercise, the JCS would raise the issue of rollback again when revision of NSC 162/2 was taken up by the NSC in November and December.

Revision of NSC 162/2

The guidelines debates had made clear the need for a review of NSC 162/2. The Planning Board started the process in late September 1954. The first step was to request the various departments and agencies to suggest changes in NSC 162/2. The submissions by State and the Department of Defense-JCS showed in general terms the deep cleavages that remained between their views.

State

The State paper reaffirmed existing policy as "generally valid" but in need of clarification and changes in emphasis with regard to three respects.

First, "U.S. policy should focus more effort on meeting the Communists' cold war strategy" by stronger measures to strengthen the political and economic fabric of the free world in order to resist subversion.

Second, "U.S. policy should take full account of the fact that total war would be an incalculable disaster." The primary aim must be to deter any communist armed aggression and avoid the risk of its escalation into general nuclear war. That would require "sufficient flexible military capabilities and firmness of policy." The United States must also forgo provocative actions and be able to conduct limited hostilities that would not inevitably broaden into total war. In basing NATO defense on nuclear weapons, the United States had to recognize its commitment either to keep nuclear-armed forces in Europe or supply such weapons to NATO. At the same time, it should explore whether NATO forces might be designed to avoid exclusive atomic dependence and to give Europeans the sense of choice. Finally, with guided missiles only a few years off, studies should begin of their implications for strategy and alliances.

Third, "Without relaxing its defense posture, the U.S. should be ready, under proper conditions, to negotiate with the Communist powers," both to satisfy world opinion and to explore alleviating or resolving outstanding problems. The aim should be to reduce the Soviet military threat and the risk of total nuclear war by disarmament, or by other means, to reduce areas of tension and conflict. Such efforts would either force "the Communist bloc to substantiate its 'peace offensive,'" or expose its falsity and thereby encourage peaceful trends in the bloc.[68]

The Joint Chiefs-Defense

In their suggestions for the review the JCS again vigorously argued that the East-West struggle was "now in a critical era" and in a few years "will probably reach a decisive state." The communist threat was increasing. Their "objective of achieving world domination, using armed force, if necessary," was unchanged. Their "efforts to infiltrate, subvert, and control non-Communist Governments" continued with augmented means. Their military strength, including "capability for thermonuclear attack, continues to increase."

The JCS were confident that "[t]he non-Communist world, if it takes positive and timely *dynamic* countermeasures, presently has ample resources to meet this situation, with a high chance of maintaining world peace without sacrifice of either vital security interests or fundamental moral principles, or in the event of war being forced upon it, of winning that war without any reasonable doubt." But failure to take these countermeasures could, in a few years, leave the United States isolated, in jeopardy, and with only two choices: "accommodation to Soviet designs or contesting such designs under conditions not favorable to our success."

The problems the United States faced, according to the JCS, stemmed not from NSC 162/2, but rather from its implementation. When adopted it seemed in the JCS's judgment to provide a basis for achieving the broad aim (stated in paragraph 45) of creating acceptable security "conditions" for the free world "prior to the achievement of mutual atomic plenty." That had not been done. While preventive war or acts intended to provoke war were rejected, a wide latitude remained for "more positive measures to be undertaken 'even at the risk of but without deliberately provoking war.'" But the basic objective cannot be achieved "if the US is required to defer to the counsel of the most cautious among our allies or if it is unwilling to undertake certain risks inherent in the adoption of dynamic and positive security measures." Thus the policy of "reactive-type security measures" must be replaced by a "policy of unmistakably positive quality" reflecting the greater urgency of the situations.

As before, the JCS did not suggest any specific methods for implementing paragraph 45 of NSC 162/2. Instead, they recommended that some existing or ad hoc NSC agency with broad membership be charged with defining measures for achieving this purpose. This was just the course that Radford had espoused at the Project Control briefing. The service secretaries and Wilson concurred.[69]

National Security Council

In the NSC discussion of this subject on November 24, Secretary Dulles took sharp issue with the JCS view, indicating the extent to which his views had evolved over the preceding two years. Aside from foreign economic policy and a still immature machinery for covert actions, "our basic policy on the whole was pretty good," he said, "even (speaking sarcastically) if it hasn't got us into war, and he was not sure (again sarcastically) that not getting into war was a bad thing." After reviewing recent events in Asia and Europe, Dulles continued, "[I]t would be hard to argue that our policies are not strong, firm and indicative of a willingness to take risks. But our policy was more or less one which fell short of actually provoking war."

Dulles said that "[i]n one respect only was the United States now facing a general deterioration of its position in the world—namely, the forthcoming achievement of atomic plenty and a nuclear balance of power between the U.S. and the USSR. But how, asked Secretary Dulles, were we to prevent the Soviet Union from achieving such a nuclear balance of power without going to war with the USSR?" Actions on the periphery would not do. In Dulles's judgment, the only place to stop the growth of communist nuclear capabilities was within the Soviet Union—"and this meant action against Russia itself."[70]

Apparently reversing his support for the JCS, Wilson said that he saw "the situation very much as Secretary Dulles did." He ended his remarks by saying, "[W]e must have patience in our effort to defer another world war for long enough to permit the seeds of decay which are inherent in Communism to have their effect."[71]

When Radford was asked by Cutler to suggest some specific actions, he evaded answering. Instead the admiral restated the JCS conviction that once the Soviets attained nuclear balance, "the U.S. could no longer count on the Russians being afraid of starting a general war"; the JCS then "could no longer guarantee a successful outcome"; and that "some time or other the Soviet Union will elect to force the issue." The JCS could not suggest specific courses of action because they would not be exclusively military, but would include diplomatic, political, economic, and propaganda actions. The JCS could, however, "guarantee that if such actions did result either in a limited or a full-scale war, the outcome for the U.S., *prior to Soviet achievement of atomic plenty*, would be successful." In sum, Radford concluded, the Joint Chiefs "feel that if we continue to pursue a policy of simply reacting to Communist initiatives, instead of a policy of forestalling Communist action, we cannot hope for anything but a showdown with the Soviet Communists by 1959 or 1960."[72]

The president said forcefully "that he was completely unable as yet to perceive a fundamental difference in the approach to basic national security policy among the departments, despite whatever the words spelled out." But, he continued, "if our present security policy was as completely futile as Admiral Radford was saying, there would obviously be no need for the Soviet Union to go to war with us; they would achieve their objectives readily enough without resort to war. Where . . . were the real differences between the departments and agencies?" A little later, with "impatience" Eisenhower "asked where and how we got more dynamic."[73]

Responding to Radford and the president, Dulles said that the JCS paper "favored the U.S. taking greater risks for bigger goals." His guess was "that what the military was really advocating was that we should tell the Soviets that they must restore freedom to Czechoslovakia by a certain date 'or else'. Was this correct?" For Dulles, the key question, once again, was "what we can do now to prevent the Soviets from achieving nuclear balance with the United States. . . . The Joint Chiefs' views don't suggest any way of stopping it." When Radford was asked again to respond, he avoided any specific reply, shifting the discussion to Indochina and North Africa to illustrate "the U.S. tendency to defer to the most timid of its allies."[74]

In ending the meeting the president "summarized his view that our national security policies were now well stated." Apparently reflecting his impatience with the failure or refusal of the JCS to flesh out their general criticism of these policies by specifying "where and how" to make them more dynamic, he said "he was tired of abstractions; they got him down." He would consider, nevertheless, Wilson's request to consider the JCS proposal for a high-level group to recommend courses of action to carry out the security policies. He directed the Planning Board to prepare a restatement of basic national security policy in the light of the suggestions and discussion of the NSC.[75]

NSC 5440

The Planning Board draft (designated NSC 5440) basically reflected the State Department strategy with alternate positions shown for some of the key issues. While still deeply hostile and committed to actively extending their power and weakening the West, the Soviets, the draft estimated, would not jeopardize their regime or their control of the bloc in the pursuit of long-term goals for expansion. Specifically, their attainment of the capacity for inflicting crippling damage on the United States "almost certainly would not tempt the Soviets to initiate general war unless convinced they could neutralize, or by initial surprise destroy, U.S. retaliatory power before it could be used." With atomic plenty, they might well increase efforts at local expansion, but not at the risk of even limited nuclear attack.

Thus atomic plenty would probably create a stalemate or mutual deterrence from initiating nuclear war or actions materially increasing the risk of it. The more serious threat was division of the alliance and subversion of developing regions along the periphery.[76] "The U.S. and its allies have no foreseeable prospect of stopping the growth of Soviet nuclear capabilities and of reducing Soviet armed strength—the core of Communist power—except by mutually acceptable agreements with the Soviets or by large-scale military action," which was "not an acceptable course either to the U.S. or its major allies." They "must reject the concept of preventive war or acts intended to provoke war," and make that intention clear by word and conduct.[77]

A central aim of U.S. policy, therefore, must be "to deter Communist use of their military power, by maintaining indefinitely, U.S. and allied" military forces with sufficient strength, flexibility, and mobility to enable them to deal swiftly and severely with communist overt aggression in all its forms and to cope successfully with general war should it develop.[78]

In toto, "U.S. policies must be designed to affect the conduct of the Communist regimes, especially that of the USSR, in ways that . . . lead them to abandon expansionist policies" by (a) deterring aggression; (b) strengthening the stability and cohesion of the free world, and (c) posing alternatives serving mutual interests and exploiting differences within the Soviet system and among the communist regimes. Carrying out this general strategy would require the flexible combination of military, political, economic, propaganda, and covert actions. It "offered the best hope of bringing about at least a prolonged period of armed truce, and ultimately a peaceful resolution of the Soviet bloc-free world conflict and a peaceful and orderly world environment."[79] Accordingly, the United States should be ready to negotiate whenever it clearly appeared that U.S. security interests will be served thereby. State and the JCS split on when that might be. State wished to stress active pursuit of negotiating arms control even though prospects were slim. The JCS continued to assert that negotiations would be futile and hazardous until the U.S.S.R. demonstrated "a basic change of attitude."[80]

JCS Comments

Predictably, the JCS reaction to this draft was highly critical. Essentially, their comments quoted and reaffirmed their earlier memorandum of November 12. They once more stressed paragraph 45 of NSC 162/2, whose stated objective of creating "conditions" for meeting the threat before mutual atomic plenty, the JCS argued, "remains valid." They accordingly emphasized the imperative necessity of replacing the policy of reaction with one of "unmistakably positive quality" that would reflect the greater urgency of the situation and define concretely the "conditions" the United States sought and the actions for achieving them. "None of these recommendations," they said, "appear to have been incorporated in NSC 5440."[81]

The JCS remained convinced that they should be. "[O]ur national strategy," their memorandum read, "should recognize that, until the Communist regimes are convinced that their aggressive and expansionist policies will be met by countermeasures which inherently will threaten the continued existence of their regimes, it will not be feasible to induce a change in their basic attitudes or bring about the abandonment of their present objectives, and that the desired conviction in Communist minds can be brought about only through positive, dynamic and timely action by the United States." And again, without specifying any such actions, the JCS reiterated their earlier recommendation "that an ad hoc or existing NSC agency be charged with formulating a statement of methods of implementing paragraph 45 of NSC 162/2."[82]

NSC Discussion

The NSC meeting on December 21 focused squarely on the JCS views. Secretary Dulles initiated the discussion and immediately addressed the central issue. The record of his comments warrants lengthy quotation. His first words were disarming:

> [Dulles said that] he could not help but have some sympathy for the general view of the Joint Chiefs of Staff in favor of greater dynamism in the American attitude toward the Soviet Union and Communist China. After all, during the course of the 1952 cam-

paign he had himself called for a more dynamic U.S. policy vis-à-vis Communism. However, experience indicated that it was not easy to go very much beyond the point that this Administration had reached in translating a dynamic policy into courses of action, and in any case we had been more dynamic than our predecessors.

But then Dulles directly attacked the JCS position by making explicit and graphic the courses of action implicit in their abstract criticisms and proposals. The memorandum of the NSC meeting continues:

> Secretary Dulles then stated that of course we have ruled out preventive war. In certain quarters it is suggested, however, that while we continue to have atomic superiority over the enemy, we should apply strong and forceful measures to change the basic character of the Soviet system. Secretary Dulles said he assumed that this would call, in effect, for an effort to overthrow the communist regimes in China and in the European satellites and to detach these countries from the USSR.

Then came a searing appraisal. In Dulles's opinion,

> [T]he effort to implement such a course would involve the United States in general war. If it did not, however, and we did succeed in detaching Communist China and the satellites from their alliance with the Soviet Union, this in itself would not actually touch the heart of the problem: Soviet atomic plenty. Even if we split the Soviet bloc, in other words, we would still have to face the terrible problem and threat of an unimpaired nuclear capacity in the USSR itself. Accordingly, Secretary Dulles did not think that this more dynamic and aggressive policy would in fact achieve the desired goal unless it eventuated in a general war which we could win. Moreover, while these more aggressive policies, if successful, might result in the disintegration of the Soviet bloc, they would almost certainly cause the disintegration of the free world bloc, of which we were the leaders, for our allies in the free world would never go along with such courses of action as these. In sum, Secretary Dulles said that he must conclude that this kind of aggressive policy was not in the best interests of the United States.

Then after an extended review of the security situation around the world, Dulles returned to the great concern about the growing Soviet bloc strength. "We need not, however, be too pessimistic. Time might well bring about many changes in the Communist bloc." One could expect "in the future some disintegration of the present monolithic power structure of the Soviet orbit." Nationalism could grow apace in the satellites. Communist China was likely to assert more independence. Such changes would greatly diminish the threat. "In conclusion, therefore, Secretary Dulles said that he felt that our policies were in the main adequate to protect our national security."[83]

The subsequent discussion confirmed the NSC consensus (except for the JCS) on the secretary's view. "Preventive war, said Secretary Humphrey, was obviously out. Moreover, an aggressive course of action to roll back Communism was also out. . . . [W]e would in effect be practicing a policy of coexistence" based on maintaining the balance of power. Hence "we should avoid provocative actions vis-à-vis the USSR," concentrate on areas we are prepared to defend militarily and withdraw elsewhere, such as from India. "Finally," Humphrey concluded, "he was not in the least afraid of coexistence. Our American system was sufficiently strong to undertake such a policy, and in competition with the Soviet Union we would certainly beat them." (As will be discussed later, the president took issue with Humphrey's proposals for withdrawal, especially from South Asia.)[84]

Secretary Wilson also agreed with Dulles, despite his earlier endorsement of the JCS paper. But he favored the term "containment" rather than coexistence. While the Soviet threat had not lessened, the threat of global war had. "Plainly we must live for the time being with Communism. While we ourselves can't do very much externally to destroy it," Wilson went on, he was sure that "ultimately" the Soviet Union "would destroy itself. The same applied in a slightly different way to China."[85]

When Cutler called on Air Force chief General Twining, who was substituting for Admiral Radford, he said "that he had nothing in particular to add to the written comments of the Joint Chiefs of Staff."[86]

Summing up, "[t]he President commented that, as so often, we had come around in a circle and come back to the same place."[87]

The revised national security paper was finally considered by the NSC on January 5, 1955, adopted with minor amendments, and approved by the president on January 7.[88] Despite JCS dissent, there could be no question that the administration's cold war strategy was based on the pursuit of containment.

12

Military Strategy

[The term "New Look"] had a definite place in the parlance of the day; it
had been coined to describe noticeable changes in the style of women's
dresses (not entirely an improvement, some men felt). Thus the tag
"New Look" probably suggested to many minds a picture of a far more
radical change in the composition of our armed forces than was truly the
case.[1]

Dwight D. Eisenhower (1963)

From his experience under Truman as Army chief of staff, as ad hoc chairman of
the JCS, and finally as SACEUR, Eisenhower had formed firm convictions regarding defense strategy, force structure, and budgeting. He had been dismayed by
Truman's inadequate defense spending before Korea, by the interservice feuding,
and by the frenetic across-the-board buildup after the Korean invasion that resulted
in a huge budget deficit and national security spending amounting to 13.8 percent
of the GNP in FY 1953.[2]

In revising Truman's FY 1954 budget, already discussed, Eisenhower applied several of his basic convictions. The pace of the buildup, he insisted, should be designed not to react to a fixed date of peak danger, but for an orderly development of
defense forces capable of being maintained for an indefinite period of cold war—
the long haul. Moreover, the level of defense spending should be sufficient to provide adequate security without damaging the economy, which was an essential
component of long-term security. On the FY 1954 budget he satisfied these criteria
(over the conflicting objections of Humphrey and the JCS) by savings in administration and support forces and deferring advance procurement, without cutting
combat forces. Thus reform of the military strategy was not addressed. That would
be done only during the second half of 1953 in conjunction with the drafting of the
broad national security strategy.

Such a review was called for by more than the change in administration. The era
of nuclear plenty was fast approaching for the United States, and it was not far off
for the Soviet Union. From 1950 to 1952 the U.S. arsenal of atomic warheads grew
from 298 to 832. With the nuclear plant facilities already operational or being built,
that number would rise to 1,161 by the end of 1953 and double that in two years.[3]
Improved design was boosting yields of fission weapons to as much as one-half a

megaton. And the H-bomb, successfully tested in November 1952, would be in production by 1954–1955. Indeed, by then the combined effect would be to raise both numbers and megatonnage astronomically. And smaller weapons would be available for tactical use. While several years behind, the Soviets were steadily accumulating a fission bomb stockpile and had tested a thermonuclear device by August 1953.

Eisenhower's Approach

Eisenhower was convinced that there was need for revision of the strategy both for general war and for local or peripheral conflict.

General War

For the president, the emerging nuclear era had two implications for general war. First, any major nuclear conflict between the United States and the Soviet Union would soon be an unimaginable catastrophe for both sides — virtually suicidal for each society and many others as well. Moreover, he was convinced that even if it started as conventional war, major aggression in Europe would escalate into nuclear war. Consequently, the top priority for military strategy was to deter any such aggression.

His second conclusion was that the current JCS war plans (which had remained basically unchanged since 1949) were unrealistic for the long haul. Under them the immediate response to Soviet aggression in Europe would be an all-out nuclear retaliation by SAC. Eisenhower regarded that course, though dreadful, as inescapable, and the threat of it as the best hope for deterrence.[4] The war plans, however, assumed that, while severely damaged by this blow, the Soviet forces would still be able to overrun most of Western Europe, which would then have to be liberated, virtually by a replay of World War II. To counter this, NATO would have to maintain even larger ground and other forces than agreed in the Lisbon goals, according to the war plans.

This strategy made neither strategic nor economic sense for the period ahead, Eisenhower believed, because it failed to take adequate account of the expanding nuclear arsenals.[5] In his view existing war plans totally underestimated the devastating impact of a SAC nuclear strike and the resulting chaos and paralysis as the arsenals expanded. The notion that the Soviets could then continue a major invasion of Western Europe for months was fanciful. Moreover, as experience had shown, the European NATO members could not develop and maintain force levels on the prescribed scale without excessive strain on their economies and on the coalition.

Above all, based on his conviction as to the priorities of Soviet leaders, Eisenhower was sure NATO forces on the projected scale would not be necessary. Because he was convinced that the Soviet leaders would never jeopardize their regime's survival, he was confident that assuring a U.S. capacity to retaliate massively and manifesting its readiness to do so would deter Soviet initiation of general war or actions likely to bring it on. "Our estimates of the enemy's capabilities always tend to overlook what the United States was capable of doing to the enemy," he said.[6] Strategic planners should "turn themselves into Russians" and try "to figure out what the Russians were thinking with regard to what the United States could do to them. They must be scared as hell."[7]

Conventional Forces in NATO

According to Eisenhower's analysis, NATO conventional forces could be reduced well below the Lisbon goals. Such forces would nevertheless still be needed to complement the SAC offensive, to compel the Soviets to mobilize if planning aggression, and thereby provide advance warning, and to reassure the Europeans that they would not be overrun by a surprise attack before the SAC offensive could take effect.[8] JCS chairman Bradley revealed the reasons: "There is presently no means other than the use of atomic weapons which will enable the West to overcome the Soviet superiority in conventional armed forces." Bradley was confident that Europe could be retaken if it was lost, as called for by OFFTACKLE. He added, however, that in this circumstance "the people we now know would be gone."[9]

U.S. forces were an essential component as a gage of America's commitment to Europe's security—and its survival. "[W]e certainly cannot depend solely, or perhaps even primarily on atomic weapons if we continue to regard Europe as our first line of defense," Eisenhower said at one of his first meetings of the NSC.[10] Nuclear weapons "may—in the long run—bring about some fundamental changes that will tend to outmode what we are now trying to do," he wrote in March to William Draper, the permanent U.S. representative to the North Atlantic Council (NAC). But for the present, he continued, "I am quite sure" that "a different defense policy could not lessen the need" for the "military units that we are now striving to produce in Western Europe."[11]

NATO forces adequate for these purposes would also require the German contribution that was to be provided according to the European Defense Community Treaty (the EDC), which was pending ratification and will be discussed in the next chapter. Because no European state would be satisfied with a strategy that assumed its occupation and liberation, the forward strategy of meeting a Soviet advance at the Rhine was the "only politically acceptable NATO plan."[12] And the forward strategy depended on the integration of a minimum of eight infantry and four armored German divisions planned to be built up over the next several years.[13] In short, wrote Livingston Merchant, Dulles's assistant secretary for European affairs, without a German contribution Western forces in Europe "can never rise to an acceptable level. . . . Neutralism and appeasement are at the end of this logical road."[14]

The Far East

The Far East posed different and in some ways more complex challenges for the United States. The war in Korea had forced the United States to deploy substantial forces to the region and ended Truman's indecision regarding the defense of Taiwan.[15] And two principal U.S. regional allies, the National Chinese and South Koreans, appeared too eager to raise and deploy their armies. In fact, because Chiang Kai-shek and Singman Rhee seemed to view war as a means to pursue nationalist agendas, Washington planners feared becoming "stuck" in a "kind of flypaper."[16]

The Korean War's severe drain on U.S. conventional capabilities was a major factor in Eisenhower's insistence on terminating the hostilities. Yet, as he emphasized repeatedly, the North Korean attack provided an object lesson in the price for failing to make clear free world resolve to potential aggressors. Thus U.S. forces would need to remain deployed in the region even after an armistice was concluded. They would be required both to secure the peace and constrain Chiang Kai-shek and Singman Rhee. As in Europe, they were also essential to reassure indigenous populations that the United States intended to protect them from being overrun and occupied. And as in Europe, a U.S. presence was necessary to encourage allies to build up their forces to provide ballast against Sino-Soviet intimidation. Conditions in Asia made any equivalent of NATO or the proposed European Defense Community out of the question.[17]

Recognizing Japanese discomfort with the U.S. nuclear shield as the sole deterrent, Washington encouraged Tokyo to develop its own conventional forces. The Pentagon calculated that a Japanese National Safety Force of 10 divisions, or 325,000 troops, could repel an invasion by 500,000 Soviet-Chinese troops. Citing political and constitutional constraints, the Shigeru Yoshida government balked at these figures. Japan's financial constraints, moreover, required that it expand resources for military programs gradually. Hence under the best circumstances the United States would have to make up for the shortfalls for at least three years.[18]

Local Conflict

Local aggression, especially by Soviet proxies, was widely seen as a growing danger. How to cope with it, however, was baffling. Eisenhower had supported the U.S. defense against the Korean invasion, but the lesson he drew from the experience there was that the United States should avoid committing its ground troops in such conflicts. Instead, it should assist exposed countries to develop indigenous defense forces — "to build redoubts throughout the free world," as he put it — and back them up with U.S. air and naval support in case of aggression. Whether tactical atomic weapons might be used effectively in such hostilities was uncertain and debatable. And while Dulles's idea of enhancing the deterrent against such aggression by the threat not to confine the response to the point of attack but to target other assets of the aggressor had appeal, it posed inherent problems as well.[19]

A New JCS

To assure a fresh approach to the strategic issues, free from past commitments, Eisenhower decided to appoint a new slate of service chiefs and JCS chairman, to take office in August when the terms of most incumbents were to expire.[20] This would serve a political purpose as well by placating the Republicans. The party's right wing, especially Senator Taft, had castigated Chairman Bradley in particular for subordinating the Far East to Europe, and for "politicizing" the JCS for the benefit of the Democrats. Taft's angry reaction to Eisenhower's FY 1954 budget prompted the president to advance the time for announcing the new slate. In May, after meeting with the Senate majority leader and submitting legislation to reorganize the Department of Defense to enhance civilian control and augment the JCS chairman's authority, Eisenhower announced his nominations.[21]

To replace Bradley, Eisenhower appointed Admiral William Arthur Radford. A fiscal conservative with impeccable credentials as an Asia-firster and on record as an air and naval power enthusiast, Radford doubtless would appeal to the Taft wing of the GOP. Moreover, as vice chief of naval operations during the 1949 "Revolt of the Admirals," Radford had distinguished himself as "a ruthless partisan and outstanding bureaucratic infighter." Although these attributes had frustrated Eisenhower's efforts as ad hoc JCS Chairman to forge unity among the services and cobble together a defense budget agreement, he had been impressed by Radford's intelligence, dedication, tenacity, and courage to speak his mind.[22]

Concurrently he nominated Air Force General Nathan F. Twining to succeed Hoyt Vandenberg, and General Matthew B. Ridgway to succeed Army Chief of Staff General J. Lawton Collins. Ridgway seemed an especially appropriate choice, both militarily and politically. He had served with distinction in both Asia and Europe, taking over from MacArthur the command of the UN forces in Korea and then following Eisenhower as NATO's SACEUR. The president chose Admiral Robert B. Carney to replace Admiral William M. Fechteler as chief of naval operations, but he left General Lemuel C. Shepherd, Jr., as commandant of the Marine Corps.[23]

Eisenhower's revision of national defense strategy would develop through several channels. The new JCS would begin to make its contribution by preparing for the president a report in midyear. At the same time a program for continental defense was developed through the NSC and approved in September. Many of the strategic issues were thrashed out and settled in preparing NSC 162/2, approved by Eisenhower at the end of October. And during October and November, the JCS worked out JCS 2101/113, its recommendations for budgets and force structures through FY 1957. As the official JCS history confirms, when Eisenhower approved JCS 2101/113 in December, "the administration's new look at the entire defense picture was complete."[24]

Continental Defense

While the new JCS and the Solarium exercise were being organized, the NSC took up the problem of continental defense for the United States, and especially for protection of the SAC retaliatory capacity—what one State Department staffer labeled the "Achilles heel of our national security."[25] As discussed in chapter 1, the Truman administration, although aware of the concern, had taken no practical measures to provide such protection. At the very end of his tenure, however, Truman did recognize the need for action in the form of recommendations for the next administration. Indeed, on his final day in office, it will be recalled, Truman had appointed an NSC subcommittee, chaired by Lt. General Idwal H. Edwards, to prepare a net assessment of the capacity of the Soviets to damage the United States by nuclear war.

Moreover, NSC 141, submitted on January 19, 1953, had urged the new administration to allocate "large additional resources to continental defense."[26] And in its
report, which awaited Eisenhower when he took office, Robert Oppenheimer's
Panel of Consultants on Disarmament, appointed by Acheson, seconded this view.
"There are some students, we know, and some high officers of the government, who
do not believe that there can ever be any worthwhile defense against atomic attack,"
the panel acknowledged. But "[w]e ourselves believe that there is urgent need for
a greatly increased effort in this area." This increased effort would do more than
minimize the possiblity of the Soviets scoring a "knock-out blow," the report
stressed. It would also "dissuade Soviet leaders from attempting any catastrophic attack" in the first place.[27]

Eisenhower had long subscribed to this premise, and, as was evident in both
NSC 149/2 and 153/3, he unhesitatingly embraced this dimension of the Oppenheimer report.[28] Further, even as the Solarium task forces were preparing their reports, a Continental Defense Committee within the NSC Planning Board began to
address the deficiencies identified in NSC 140/1, the net assessment that the Edwards Committee submitted in May.[29]

The ultimate result was NSC 159/4, which Eisenhower signed in September.[30]
It stipulated that "[i]n any program of national security, our offensive capability
must be maintained not only for gaining our war objectives, but for its marked deterrent value in protecting our homeland." Because of Soviet capabilities, a defense system "approaching invulnerablity is probably unattainable." Nevertheless,
a "reasonably effective defense system can and must be attained." Toward this end
NSC 159/4 recommended a series of costly measures. Eisenhower approved them
after uncharacteristically little debate.[31] And NSC 162/2 reaffirmed that "in the
face of Soviet atomic power, defense of the continental United States becomes
vital to effective security: to protect our striking force, our mobilization base, and
our people."[32]

The "Fresh View" of the New JCS

In publicly announcing the new JCS slate, the president warned against expecting
them to propose any abrupt or radical changes in strategy. "The great facts that affect a so-called strategic situation and plans do not change rapidly," he explained.
"No strategic plans suitable for the United States can be greatly different from any
other, as long as it is based upon these facts." But Eisenhower stressed that there
could be differences in methods and means. He promised, moreover, that there
would be "a new approach, a study that is made without any real chains fastening to
the past."[33]

Accordingly in mid-July, about a month before the new JCS members took office, the president met with them to initiate the study.[34] Elaborating on a memorandum he had sent to Secretary Wilson two weeks earlier, the president directed
the service chiefs to provide him with a written summary of their individual and
collective views on current strategic concepts and implementing plans, the roles
and missions of each service, the composition and readiness of present forces, the

effectiveness of military assistance programs, and the implications of new weapons and weapons systems.[35]

Eisenhower did not want a detailed staff study. "What I am seeking," he explained, is a "fresh view" that would provide "interim guidance to aid the Council in developing policies for the most effective employment of available national resources to insure the defense of our country for the long pull which may lie ahead." The president did not impose any budgetary, material, or personnel limitations. He did, however, instruct the service chiefs to take into account NSC 149/2, to solicit the advice of the Treasury Department and BOB, and to tour the "great atomic energy plants" before presenting him with their report.[36]

Following a visit to the military installations and a three-day conference with top military and civilian officials at the Marine Corps base at Quantico, Virginia, the JCS-designees spent August 6–8 sequestered aboard the Navy yacht *U.S.S. Sequoia*. By the morning of the last "long and difficult" day Radford had in hand a typed report, signed by each chief, which he submitted immediately to Wilson.[37]

The report dealt summarily with some of the questions posed by the president. It commended the military plans and their implementation since June 1950 as "sound and adequate"—having averted a general war—and endorsed existing service roles and missions. It foresaw no new weapons to enhance overall military power, "except perhaps in the atomic field." And it pleaded too little time to permit examining force composition. On the question of military assistance, the report merely stated that the United States "should be more discriminating in extending any form of our aid or protection, and should require an appropriate contribution or concession in return."[38]

While asserting explicitly that security "includes the stability and durability of our economy," the report also insisted that any across-the board cut in the military budget would reduce security almost equally. It held out no hope for a quick budgetary fix; existing forces were inadequate to meet existing commitments, and even adopting the course to be recommended, if feasible, would involve at least two years of budget deficits, with the amount of savings uncertain.

Militarily, the report reaffirmed the primacy of nuclear retaliation for security: "[T]he most critical factors . . . are air defense of our Continental U.S. vitals and our ability to retaliate swiftly and powerfully in the event we are attacked." Thus these air defenses needed substantial bolstering. This conclusion was in keeping with policy statements Eisenhower had already approved.

The report made two substantive recommendations. The first was that the new administration should formulate and, when authorized by the president, announce "a clear, positive policy with respect to the use of atomic weapons." While implied, the content of this policy was not further specified or developed.

The second recommendation was developed at some length. Its premise was that U.S. military forces were gravely "over-extended." The cause was that we "continue to place our major emphasis in the military field on peripheral deployments overseas, to the neglect of our vitals in the Continental United States." As a result, "[o]ur freedom of action is seriously curtailed, the exercise of initiative severely limited," and readiness dangerously degraded.

"Of the broad courses of action examined," the JCS concluded, "only one, in our opinion, offers reasonable promise of improving our general security position. The course we have in mind would reverse our present strategic policy." The report explained: "It would place in first priority the essential military protection of our continental U.S. vitals and the capability of delivering swift and powerful retaliatory blows. Military commitments overseas—that is to say, peripheral military commitments—would cease to have first claim on our resources."

The JCS-designates recognized that this course "would involve a change in basic foreign policy of fundamental and far-reaching implications." It would risk damaging repercussions on the part of allies, adversaries, the public, and Congress, if not carefully prepared and implemented with delicate diplomacy and public education. Meanwhile, the JCS advised that it should be kept secret. Accordingly, they recommended only that Eisenhower direct the NSC to "examine, as a matter of priority, the effects on the national interests of the adoption of [this] course of action."

Even though the president himself was vacationing in Denver at the "Summer White House," Cutler put the JCS report on the agenda for the NSC's meeting on August 27.[39] The discussion revealed the deep divisions among the JCS and within the Council. Radford vigorously advocated adopting what soon came to be called the "new concept." He downplayed the impact of the redeployment, explaining that the plan envisioned the United States continuing to deploy the naval and air forces that constituted the primary deterrent. Indeed, from his perspective what was critical in the report was its explicit recommendation of a "clear, positive policy with respect to the use of atomic weapons." Made credible by the presence of U.S. air and naval capabilities, the administration should announce that in the event of a major conflict these forces would "use atomic weapons both in the tactical and in the strategic realm." As Radford "saw it, we had been spending vast sums on the manufacture of these weapons and at the same time were holding back on their use." It was "high time," he concluded, that the United States "clarified" its position.[40]

Among the new JCS only the Air Force's Twining, who was on record as criticizing America's timidity in exploiting its nuclear superiority, agreed with him.[41] Indeed, the JCS chairman feared that Chief of Naval Operations Carney and Army Chief of Staff Ridgway would preemptorily "kick over the traces" of the new concept.[42] They came close. Carney warned that air and naval forces alone "could never constitute an effective deterrent to enemy ground attack." He stressed that budgetary limitations had driven the new concept and that under closer scrutiny it might prove "unacceptable."[43]

Ridgway went further, all but disavowing the new concept in its entirety. MacArthur's successor in Korea, Ridgway had been intimately involved in discussions over the possible use of atomic weapons in that war.[44] Moreover, having just served as SACEUR, he was all too aware of the potential impact on NATO and the prospects for a European Defense Community should the United States adopt the redeployment proposal.

In addition, just before returning to Washington, Ridgway had submitted to NATO's Standing Group his study of "NATO strategy assuming the use of atomic weapons." This report concluded that providing the Alliance forces with a tactical atomic capability would not reduce the forces needed for defending Europe. To the contrary, it would entail air and ground force levels greater than the Lisbon goals.[45] But if NATO followed his recommendations for "timely actions" to correct its manpower deficiencies, the report predicted that "this command could be made capable, within the next two to three years, of effectively defending Western Europe against a full scale Soviet attack."[46]

Ridgway therefore forcefully expressed his objections to the "new concept." He pointed out that the JCS report of August had maintained unequivocally that "the advent of new weapons or tactics" could not substitute for conventional forces, and that it "merely recommended a careful examination of the concept it set forth." For his part, Ridgway "would not possibly subscribe to any theory that you can prevent war through the deterrent effect of any single military arm." He likewise "desired to make it crystal clear that he did not subscribe to the withdrawal of our forces stationed overseas." All four chiefs agreed, however, that the United States was now overextended.[47]

The members of the NSC also took opposing sides. Humphrey was delighted: The "report was terrific. He could not be more impressed," he said. "What with the hydrogen bomb, people are demanding a genuine reappraisal of our national security position." The United States "could not go on as we have been going another year." Dulles spoke for most of the members, however, in expressing serious reservations. The secretary of state sympathized with Radford's desire to place greater reliance on U.S. nuclear superiority. He feared the likely effect, however, of a redeployment of U.S. forces on America's allies. To "take any measures which destroyed the unity of the free world," he said, "would not be a real economy in the long run. The 'art of the thing' is to reshape our policy and program in such fashion that we can still maintain enough free world cohesion to provide for a common pooling of resources."[48]

After extended discussion of the proposals, the NSC agreed only to recommend to Eisenhower that he authorize Dulles "to explore, from the point of view of foreign policy, the possibility of adopting the concept set forth in this report."[49] Several days later Cutler flew to Denver to brief the president on the report and the debate in the NSC.[50] Radical as it was, the JCS's redeployment proposal was congruent with Eisenhower's preconceptions. Like his civilian advisors, however, he had grave doubts about the timing and impact on allies.

The president, therefore, agreed without hesitation that the State Department should investigate "whether and how the concept could be worked out." But he instructed Cutler to amend the NSC meeting's record of action to include the words, "This concept is a crystallized and clarified statement of this Administration's understanding of our national security objectives since World War II," stressing that it was not new. Pacing up and down the room Eisenhower added, although not for the official record, that "[f]rom the beginning, people who really studied foreign and military problems have considered that the stationing of American troops abroad was a temporary expedient," to foster allied confidence and strength. He also directed Cutler to have the NSC Planning Board address this issue in its preparation of NSC 162.[51]

Cutler's visit was followed immediately by one from Dulles. The secretary reviewed his concerns about the potentially adverse reaction of America's allies to a redeployment of U.S. troops. He and Eisenhower then discussed his idea for seeking detente with the Soviet Union by a "spectacular" offer for mutual withdrawal of Soviet and U.S. forces from Europe and arms control, as will be described in the next chapter.[52] Dulles reported to the NSC on September 9 that Eisenhower shared his opinion that to avoid jeopardizing "our whole security position overseas," any withdrawal of U.S. troops would have to be "very carefully handled."[53]

The Framework of Military Strategy

The basic concepts of the military strategy were worked out in the course of preparing NSC 162/2. The force structure, which gave the concepts specific content, was settled in November and December in the context of DOD/JCS planning for the budget and force levels to be achieved by FY 1957.

The various elements of the strategy were discussed and defined by stages in the debates and decisions in the Planning Board meetings, which produced its September 30 draft of NSC 162 and its revision of October 19, and in the NSC meetings of October 7, 13, and 29. In the interest of clarity and coherence, we will trace separately the development of each of the main components as it evolved through this process.

The "Long Haul" and "Great Equation"

The basic premise was that strategy and forces must be designed and developed for an extended period of cold war—the "long haul." For reasons already discussed the administration rejected the notion that the Soviet threat would peak at some specific time. It assumed that deterrence of general war was feasible and a prime objective. The aim was to keep spending for national security on a scale that could be sustained indefinitely without impairing the vitality of the economy. This was what Eisenhower called the "Great Equation."

The relation between spending for security and the impact on the economy once again pitted the Treasury Department (Humphrey) and the Bureau of the Budget (Dodge) against virtually all the other NSC participants in drafting NSC 162. Thus the Planning Board draft contained a number of splits pertaining to this issue. Essentially, all agreed that a sound, robust economy was an essential foundation for maintaining an adequate defense posture over the long term: the Planning Board draft explicitly so stated at several points. But Treasury and the Bureau of the Budget insisted that the paper should begin by equating the danger of weakening the economy by sustained deficits or high taxes for defense spending with the Soviet threat.[54]

At the October 7 meeting of the NSC Humphrey and Dodge argued vigorously in support of this position. In Humphrey's words, "If we mean to face this Soviet threat over a long time, we must spend less than we are now spending and do less than we are now doing." Secretaries Dulles and Wilson took strong exception.

"[W]e certainly couldn't throw the common defense system out the window be-cause we had to balance the budget," said Dulles. Balancing the budget was not "an absolute." Indeed, Wilson argued, the United States could "spend more money on defense . . . without radically changing the American way of life." Humphrey in-sisted that "no one wanted to balance the budget at the sacrifice of the national se-curity." But he was equally insistent that there could be no higher priority than keeping defense spending at the essential minimum: "The military ought to be so damned dollar conscious that it hurts."[55]

After Cutler lamented that "the meeting of the National Security Council was degenerating into a debating society," Eisenhower intervened. The president sug-gested that NSC 162 begin with a section already included later in the Planning Board draft. It read:

> *Basic Problems of National Security*
> 30.   a.   To meet the Soviet threat to U.S. security.
>   b.   In doing so, to avoid seriously weakening the U.S. economy or undermining
>   our fundamental values and institutions.[56]

This formula summed up rather subtly Eisenhower's position. The "In doing so" clause gave priority to security. Other provisions of NSC 162/2 made this explicit. Soviet hostility, military power, and means of subversion constituted "the primary threat to the security, free institutions, and fundamental values of the United States." And a later section, after warning against impairing the economy, went on: "The United States must, however, meet the necessary costs of the policies essential for its security." Yet such costs "should be kept to the minimum consistent with car-rying out these policies." The paper also reaffirmed in several contexts the need for "a sound, strong and growing economy" as the foundation to "support over the long pull a satisfactory posture of defense," and counseled that national security expendi-tures "must be carefully scrutinized with a view to measuring their impact on the national economy." But the provisions Dulles objected to as giving priority to bal-ancing the budget and branding taxes as "repressive" were deleted.[57]

Treasury's pressure for austerity in defense spending nonetheless continued. For example, at the first NSC meeting on the defense budget for FY 1955, on October 13, when the Department of Defense projected a small increase over 1954, Humphrey predicted dire consequences if the FY 1955 budget was not in balance: "[T]he Ameri-can economy will go to hell and the Republican Party will lose the next election." Dodge, for the Bureau of the Budget, deplored that the tentative defense budget was only slightly less than the Truman projection for FY 1955. In rebuttal, Wilson insisted on the need to reassure the public regarding the Soviet hydrogen bomb and conti-nental defense. And Dulles added that budget cuts in foreign assistance would be the "worst kind of economy." Agreeing, the president "said that if he could be convinced that we need all this money he was prepared to fight for it everywhere and with all the energy he could summon up," but "he did not want to scare people to death and did want our military posture to be calculated on a long-term basis." And, as he closed the meeting, Eisenhower again directed the JCS to compute force levels "on a genuine austerity basis, pointing out that he did not want cuts in combat strength, but rather in the support forces and other such personnel."[58]

Strategic Retaliatory Capacity

As under Truman, for Eisenhower the U.S. "capability to inflict massive retaliatory damage by offensive strategic striking power" was to provide the primary deterrent, and, if necessary, the initial counter to a Soviet attack on the United States and NATO. And effective continental defense was essential to safeguard this capability, as already provided by NSC 159/4, approved on September 25. These had been called "the most critical [military] factors" for U.S. security in the JCS August report.[59]

Yet agreement did not extend to the implications for other forces. The JCS, and especially Ridgway and Carney, were anxious to put the SAC primacy in perspective. Their initial comments on the Planning Board draft of September 30 urged that the provision for the retaliatory strike force be introduced by the words "A *strong military posture to include*" that capability, and the NSC concurred.[60] When the Planning Board, in revising NSC 162 for the next NSC meeting, changed "to include" to read "with emphasis on," the JCS vigorously objected. In the NSC meeting, however, Eisenhower preferred "emphasize . . . because it provided some sense of priority for our military planning. Certainly we do not want to build up equally all types and varieties of military strength."[61]

Admiral Carney insisted that such a change, which was "bound to affect the character and composition of our forces," was premature "as long as our present commitments remained unchanged." The JCS version, he said, recognized that "the armed forces [also] had very important defensive jobs to do" that required "a reasonable balance of military capabilities." In approving the change to "with emphasis on," Eisenhower was revealing in his explanation: "After all, deterring war was even more important than winning a war. No deterrent to war could compare in importance with this retaliatory striking power. Why don't we therefore say what we mean to emphasize." And when Cutler suggested noting a JCS dissent, the president responded "with considerable warmth" that he would not "tolerate" that; the service chiefs "were, after all, his advisors; he made the decisions." Later, he continued, if they found it did not serve our best interests, "he fully expected them to come and tell him so," and he could reconsider. Secretary Dulles added that any shift toward more emphasis would take two or three years, and would not be done with "undue haste," though a decision now was needed. Eisenhower remarked that Dulles had expressed his own views better than he had.[62]

Collective Security

While SAC was indispensable, so, too, was collective security, and especially NATO. On this, NSC 162 was categorical: "The United States cannot . . . meet its defense needs, even at exorbitant cost, without the support of allies." Overseas bases would be essential for effective SAC operations for many years, and indefinitely for general war. Loss to the Soviet bloc of the major industrialized states, isolating the United States, would gravely jeopardize its ability to win a general war or "to maintain an adequate defense without undermining its fundamental institutions." In sum, the U.S. alliances were "a direct and essential contribution to the maintenance of its own freedom and security."[63]

The allies, in turn, were dependent on the United States especially for the nuclear deterrent, but also for aid. Thus they must be convinced that U.S. policy would serve mutual interests for security. As NSC 162 stressed, however, the coalition was subject to many serious stresses and weaknesses.[64] Accordingly, as will be developed in the next chapter, maintaining cooperation and cohesion was a constant preoccupation of Eisenhower and Dulles.

Nonstrategic Forces

The scale and role of forces other than SAC—mainly Army and Navy—were central to the effort to reduce total defense forces. The "emphasis" NSC 162/2 placed on strategic nuclear forces did not entail any increase in force goals for the U.S. Air Force. As a matter of fact, the target under Eisenhower was set for 138 wings, compared to 143 under Truman. What it did entail was some shrinkage of both Army and Navy forces.

NSC 162 called for maintaining "U.S. and allied forces in readiness to move rapidly initially to counter aggression by Soviet bloc forces and to hold vital areas and lines of communication."[65] Their role was perceived as most relevant with respect to Western Europe for the "forward strategy" of NATO. There, NSC 162 recognized, the NATO buildup under Truman would enable its existing forces to make Soviet aggression "costly" but not prevent the overrunning of Western Europe. Moreover, even with planned German forces, current rates of European spending and U.S. aid would not produce NATO forces able to prevent initial loss of a "considerable portion" of the continent. "Therefore, since U.S. Military Assistance must eventually be reduced, it is essential that the Western European states, including West Germany, build and maintain maximum feasible defensive strength." Even so, the "major deterrent" to Soviet aggression there was "the manifest determination of the United States to use its atomic capability and massive retaliatory striking power if the area is attacked."[66]

This provision evoked no discussion until the October 29 NSC session, when the JCS suggested a merely stylistic change to underscore that NATO's force levels must continue to increase. Humphrey strongly objected to urging the allies to spend more on defense, when their economies were already strained. The president, however, approved the revised paragraph.[67]

What kinds and amounts of military forces were required to cope with peripheral conflict posed a very different and difficult problem. The protracted hostilities in Korea, which had been so costly in men, materiel, and public support, had had a sobering impact. Dulles had repeatedly expressed his deep concern that the Soviets could nibble the United States and its allies to death by such proxy actions around its immense perimeter. For Eisenhower, the lesson of Korea was that U.S. forces should not become bogged down again on the periphery in ground warfare. And the burden of the JCS "fresh look" of August was to downgrade the claim of "peripheral military commitments" on U.S. resources in order to correct America's "over-extension." While the JCS memorandum proposed *redeployment* of U.S. forces from overseas, the new chiefs also advocated being "more discriminatory [sic] in extending any form of our aid or protection," which seemed to suggest greater selectivity in committing force in such areas.[68]

The Planning Board draft of NSC 162 provided that "the forces required to counter local aggressions must be supplied largely by our allies and cannot be furnished by the United States."[69] The JCS immediately requested deletion of "and cannot be furnished by the United States." The chiefs first justified the request on the basis that "United States naval and air forces might be made available to support allied forces in countering local aggressions."[70] Later, they asserted that this clause was "inexact since the United States can and may have to furnish ground forces despite our desire to avoid doing so (i.e., as in Korea)."[71]

With the NSC's concurrence Eisenhower approved this change. But the JCS effort to obtain general authority for the use of atomic weapons in local hostilities generated one of the most critical debates. And the question of how much conventional capability the United States required, primarily for limited war, remained a contentious issue until Eisenhower left office.

Redeployment

The August 27 meeting on the JCS August report had revealed the diversity of views within the JCS, and among the NSC members, regarding redeployment of overseas forces. All seemed aware, as stressed by Dulles, Ridgway, and C. D. Jackson, that such redeployment could undermine NATO if executed without convincing the allies that it was not a retreat to Fortress America or abandonment of their defense. Consequently, to reiterate, the NSC had merely recommended that the secretary of state should "explore, from the point of view of foreign policy, the possibility of adopting the concept."[72] Eisenhower, it will be recalled, had emphasized to Cutler at his Denver briefing that the "concept" was merely a return to the original intent that the stationing of U.S. troops in Europe should be "a temporary expedient" to reassure and protect the allies. And he directed that this concept "could and should be included" in the Basic National Security Paper.[73]

In drafting NSC 162, the entire Planning Board (including the JCS advisor, Air Force Major General John K. Gerhart) agreed on a provision stating that while a "partial redeployment . . . might" have benefits for continental defense, mobile reserves, and sharing defense burdens, "under present conditions, however, any major withdrawal of U.S. forces from Europe or the Far East would be interpreted as a diminution of U.S. interest in the defense of these areas and would seriously undermine the strength and cohesion of the coalition." The inescapable conclusion, therefore, was that "[c]ontinued study of our strategic concepts would determine the most effective deployment of our military forces."[74]

Unsatisfied with this unanimous provision, Cutler added an alternative version (Side B) based on the JCS August report. It stated (a) As now deployed, U.S. armed forces were overextended, "depriving us of mobility and initiative"; (b) "Our diplomacy must concentrate upon clarifying for our allies . . . that the best defense . . . rests on the mobility of U.S. forces centrally based; upon our political commitment to strike back hard directly against any aggressor who attacks such allies";

and upon their own security efforts. Finally, (c) the NSC should decide whether, "with the understanding of our allies," America should start soon and carry out during the next few years the redeployment to the United States of the bulk of its forces (except from the Far East, where significant forces would be required until the war conditions there were settled).[75]

When this issue was discussed in the NSC on October 7, the president at once remarked that the phrase "with the understanding of our Allies" was critical in the Cutler alternative. When Radford stated that the JCS, with minor qualifications, endorsed this version, Dulles, while conceding that their position "seemed sound," interjected that he "felt obliged to say" that "the redeployment could bring about the complete collapse of our coalition in Europe" unless done "under cover of another and larger [constructive] operation." (Apparently Dulles had in mind his "spectacular" effort for U.S.-Soviet mutual withdrawals and arms control agreements, which he had discussed with Eisenhower in early September and, as will be analyzed in the next chapter, was then developing.) The "redeployment simply could not be done as a separate and distinct move." Accordingly, the secretary wanted to retain paragraph *b* of the Planning Board version, which stressed the grave damage to the coalition of withdrawal under present conditions. When Humphrey took issue, Eisenhower reminded him that the loss of Europe would "hopelessly upset" the world balance of power "against us." Further, "that Western Europe not fall to the Communists was a *sine qua non*." The U.S. "divisions in Europe had done marvels in restoring Europe's faith in itself."[76]

Ultimately Cutler proposed a compromise provision drawing on both versions. Paragraph *a* would be from his side B (pertaining to lack of mobility and initiative). Next would come paragraph *b* from the Planning Board version (withdrawal would undermine the coalition). Finally, paragraph *c* would be the second paragraph of his version (the requisite diplomacy to seek to persuade the allies that redeployment would improve defense). The Council accepted this proposal. Cutler's paragraph about actual withdrawal would therefore be omitted, but it was understood, he said, that the NSC was "sympathetic . . . under certain conditions."[77]

On his return from a trip to London two weeks later, Dulles wrote a strong memorandum to the president on the subject. The press, he commented, was asking about rumored plans for force withdrawals from Europe. Having been entrusted with handling this issue, he had concluded "with Admiral Radford, that nothing of this sort could be done at this time without great injury to NATO and the prospects of EDC." The French were fearful of rearming the Germans unless the United States and Britain "keep troops in Europe substantially as at present." Therefore, any rumors about "our thinking of pulling troops out of Europe must be denied."[78]

In the final NSC meeting on NSC 162 on October 29, Humphrey pressed one more time for early redeployment. The administration's goal, he said "with some heat," was to arrive at "a thorough-going revision of our whole military strategy. If we did not propose . . . a real change in our military posture," he went on, "the whole purpose and objective of our deliberations was lost." He was again strongly rebuffed by Eisenhower and Dulles, who both stressed the political contribution of U.S. forces in Europe.[79]

Thus, as approved on October 30, NSC 162/2 contained the October 7 version of paragraph 38, warning of the serious dangers of any redeployment "under present conditions."[80]

The Use of Nuclear Weapons

As its second recommendation, the JCS August report had called for adopting "a clear, positive policy with respect to the use of atomic weapons."[81] Unlike the redeployment issue, this recommendation did not initially evoke much commentary. In general terms it had, after all, been a central feature of the Eisenhower campaign. In short order, however, the effort to prescribe such a policy with any degree of specificity proved extremely contentious.

The Planning Board draft of NSC 162 had provided for the use of atomic weapons "whenever they are required by the national security"; and for seeking "understanding and approval of this decision by friendly governments and people." In their October 6 commentary on the draft, the JCS wanted to state instead that nuclear weapons "shall be held available for use by U.S. forces in the same manner as other munitions. This policy should be announced at an early date."[82]

When the issue arose at the NSC meeting on October 7, Eisenhower suggested at once that securing allied approval and understanding must be made a precondition for using atomic weapons; "nothing would upset the whole world" as much as an announcement at this time of an American decision to use them. When Wilson and Radford insisted that the Department of Defense must know whether or not to plan on their use, the "President replied that after all, he had to make the ultimate decision, and if their use was dictated by the interests of U.S. security, he would certainly decide to use them." As for war plans, the JCS should "count on making use of special [nuclear] weapons in the event of a general war. *They should not, however, plan to make use of them in minor affairs.*" There were certain places "where you would not be able to use these weapons," the president went on to explain. "If, however, we actually got into a global war, we would certainly use the weapons." And stressing again his desire for allied understanding and approval, he added, "We need . . . to be able to hit the Soviets, if necessary, from any point on the compass." At this point General Ridgway volunteered that Churchill and West German Chancellor Konrad Adenauer had recently assured him in strict confidence of their approval of such use from their territory.[83]

A week later, in the NSC meeting on the preliminary FY 1955 defense budget, Wilson pointed out that the JCS had not been able to plan force reductions because there had been no change in the estimate of the Soviet threat or U.S. security policy, and no clear decision on the use of atomic weapons. Eisenhower replied that even so, savings could be made by seeking "a respectable posture of defense" (explaining "We cannot hope for a perfect defense"); by more careful timing of procurement for the long haul; and by austere paring of support forces. To get manpower down to 3 million from 3.5 million, he "did not wish to see this cut made in combat units," but everywhere else in the Department of Defense.[84]

The vigorous discussion that ensued revealed that positions, if anything, had become more entrenched over the past several months. When questioned, Radford conceded that the budget estimates did not reflect the recent discussion of the use of atomic weapons. Moreover, after Cutler reread the provision from NSC 162, which Eisenhower approved, Radford responded simply that the JCS regarded the provision as "insufficient guidance to enable them to effect any real change."[85]

Eisenhower reiterated his disagreement: the "only war that the United States was really scared of was a war initiated by the enemy against us," he underscored. "In this contingency we could always use atomic weapons from our own bases," although their use from foreign bases might be more uncertain.[86] (At a subsequent meeting Eisenhower's language was more graphic: the atomic response to an attack would be "a force so terrible that one simply could not be meticulous as to the methods by which the force was brought to bear.")[87] Then, after Cutler suggested that Radford provide a "clear text" on the use of atomic weapons for the policy statement, Eisenhower answered emphatically "no . . . we could not do better than the present language."[88]

Humphrey intervened to insist that it was "absolutely essential" to all but abolish any restrictions on atomic weapons. "Only their use on a broad scale could really . . . cut the costs of the military budget." Radford concurred. He made clear that in the military's judgment, "unless we could use these weapons in a blanket way, no possibility existed of significantly changing the present composition of our armed forces."[89]

The Planning Board revised the draft in light of the debate in time for the October 29 meeting of the NSC. The key sentence on atomic weapons of what was now NSC 162/1 read: "In the event of hostilities, the United States will consider nuclear weapons to be as available for use as other munitions."[90] In his briefing memorandum to Secretary Dulles, Robert Bowie, the State Department's director of policy planning and representative on the NSC Planning Board, described this sentence as "for planning purposes" and raised the question "whether in order to avoid any implication of change" reference should not be made to the "established procedure that nuclear weapons should be used only by decision of the president."[91]

The JCS's evaluation of NSC 162/1 made no mention of the sentence, thus implying it was acceptable. And at the October 29 NSC meeting, it was not discussed. Hence the version, as revised, was included as paragraph 39b in the statement of basic national security policy Eisenhower approved as NSC 162/2 on October 30. As would soon become evident, however, a fundamental difference of opinion remained as to the meaning of this paragraph.[92] Consequently, it would become a subject of sharp dispute between the Departments of State and Defense in December during the planning of force levels for FY 1957.

Strategy and Force Composition

While NSC 162/2 set the concepts and criteria for the future military strategy, they still had to be applied to planning the actual size and composition of the armed forces. Reshaping existing forces would be carried out over several years to achieve the new size and structure by FY 1957.

In the preliminary FY 1955 defense budget estimates considered by the NSC in mid-October, discussed above, the JCS presented total requests of $43 billion, with small increases for each service. This was slightly more than the revised FY 1954 budget, and $3 billion more than the target set for FY 1955 by NSC 149/1. Wilson and the JCS had insisted that a lower budget was not feasible until the issues of redeployment and use of nuclear weapons were decided. No decisions were taken; the president directed Wilson and the JCS to rework this budget and the longer range planning, urging them to shrink support forces, not combat units, in seeking austerity.[93]

Several days later, on October 16, Wilson issued a directive to the JCS in order to facilitate force planning for the long haul. After summarizing the "salient factors" of NSC 162/2, he requested the service chiefs by December 1 to submit their recommendations on three matters. First was an outline of military strategy designed to implement NSC 162/2. Second, the size and composition of the armed forces for FY 1955, 1956, and 1957, starting from the forces planned for the end of FY 1954. This would take account of (1) "feasible annual spending and new appropriations," guided by the Treasury Department and the Bureau of the Budget; (2) military personnel of 2.5 to 3 million men; (3) adequate continental air defense; (4) maintaining readiness and modernization, and mobilization potential; and (5) the assumption that nuclear weapons "will be used in military operations . . . whenever it is of military advantage to do so."

Third, feasible U.S. politico-military action "in modifying existing commitments or to enhance implementation of the strategy."[94]

The JCS at once appointed an ad hoc committee, headed by Lt. General F. F. Everest and including two officers from each service, to prepare a reply. The committee made its report to the JCS promptly on November 30, focusing on steady-state levels for FY 1957.

On strategy they fleshed out NSC 162/2. Massive retaliatory capacity would be emphasized as a major deterrent to and critical response in general war, and would be safeguarded by an adequate continental defense system. To form a ready, mobile strategic reserve, U.S. forces would be withdrawn from Korea, and from Japan as its indigenous forces developed. Air and naval forces, armed with nuclear weapons, would remain in the Far East. The Army committee members resisted any reduction in forces stationed in Europe until justified by political conditions; the other members wanted to limit such divisions to three by 1957 while educating the allies on the merits of the new strategy and persuading them to expand their own ground forces. In any case, a maximum of six Army divisions would be available for overseas deployment. Foreign aid should be used to encourage allied force expansion; creation of German and Japanese forces should be expedited.

Tactical atomic support would be provided for U.S. and allied forces in general war and in local aggression whenever militarily advantageous. Control would be maintained over essential sea and air lines of communication. Finally, the armed forces would be kept qualitatively superior, and an adequate mobilization base preserved for general war.

The Everest Committee was unable to agree on a proposal for force composition. Using Treasury/Budget Bureau estimates, they projected that $33.8 billion would be available for military expenditures in FY 1957 (not including atomic energy or mutual security assistance). The figure adopted by the committee for military manpower was 2.75 million, the midpoint of Wilson's suggested range. Treating both guidelines as imposed ceilings, the Army member protested that they entailed undue risks; the other service representatives considered the risks acceptable.

In attempting to allocate the total among the services, however, the committee diverged, with members tending to favor their respective services in the distribution. The range was relatively narrow, however, and all would allow the Air Force to increase its force levels while reducing those of the other services.

On receiving the committee report, the JCS accepted the recommended strategy. But initially, each of the Joint Chiefs backed the force composition proposed by the members of his service. After extensive discussion, however, all the JCS accepted the substance of the report. They were able to agree on the FY 1957 force levels by raising the manpower total to 2.815 million, which was sufficient to allocate service strengths only 3 to 6 percent below those proposed by the service members of the committee.

The formal JCS decision on their response to the Wilson directive (JCS 2101/113) was approved on December 10.[95] As to force composition, it recommended the following figures to be achieved by FY 1957:

Service	Personnel (thousands)	Force Levels	Cost (millons)
Army	1,000	14 divisions	$7,387
Navy	650	1,000 ships	8,790 with Marines
Marines	190	3 divisions	
Air Force	975	137 wings	14,100
Not Allocated by Service			2,635
			$32,912

Clearly, this involved a major reshaping of the armed forces over the next three and one-half years. Total manpower would drop by nearly 600,000. The Army would decrease nearly a third, the Navy about 15 percent, and the Marine Corps about 20 percent, whereas the Air Force would grow by over 60,000. Of the projected FY 1957 defense spending, the Army would receive about 22.3 percent, the Navy-Marine Corps, 26.6 percent, and the Air Force about 43 percent.[96]

Responding to Wilson's third item—feasible politico-military actions to facilitate the strategy—the JCS listed the use of foreign aid to shape allied military forces, expediting German and Japanese defense contributions, and educating NATO allies on the strategy.

In sending JCS 2101/113 to Secretary Wilson, the JCS said that their recommendations were based on the assumption that tensions and threat remained about the same; any material change in the threat "would require complete new studies and estimates."[97]

Although all the JCS approved JCS 2101/113, their individual perspectives and attitudes toward it were very different, as their later statements and congressional testimony revealed. Radford and Twining fully supported the strategy and force structure, and the reliance on nuclear weapons. They also agreed that the JCS should take account of economic vitality as a component of security over the long haul. In contrast, Ridgway believed that economic aspects should be left to the top civilian officials. He continued to oppose "overemphasis" on strategic airpower and to reject the notion that atomic weapons justified manpower cuts; he later testified to Congress that the FY 1957 force levels were dictated by "fixed manpower and dollar ceilings."[98] Carney shared most of Ridgway's reservations, especially concerning strategic air power and the effect of nuclear weapons on manpower, but he was more temperate in expressing his criticisms.[99]

On December 16 Radford presented the proposed strategy and force structure of FY 1957 to the NSC, and Acting Secretary of Defense Roger Keyes submitted a revised defense budget for FY 1955 requesting materially lower spending than in 1954 as a step toward the FY 1957 targets. The NSC and the president approved both the programs of JCS 2101/113 and the proposed FY 1955 budget. Presented to Congress on January 7, 1954, the FY 1955 budget estimated $37.475 in total defense expenditures.[100]

This action brought formal closure to Eisenhower's fresh look at the military strategy and force levels. But one loose end remained.

Control of the Use of Nuclear Weapons

Secretary Wilson's directive of October 16 to the JCS for a new strategy "assumed" that nuclear weapons would be used "whenever it is of military advantage to do so." Presumably, this assumption was based on his interpretation of paragraph 39b in NSC 162/2, which stipulated that the United States would "consider nuclear weapons as available for use as other munitions."[101] It was also in keeping with Radford's strong desires, and was a key premise of the JCS strategy outlined in JCS 2101/113.

While the JCS was developing its force projections, however, a sharp dispute arose in the NSC Special Committee on Atomic Energy (composed of representatives of State, Budget Bureau, and the AEC) over the interpretation of this paragraph 39b. The Department of Defense argued at a meeting on December 1 that it must be "construed" as a "firm and clear decision that nuclear weapons" would be used for both strategic and tactical purposes. Otherwise, the "fundamental thesis of the policy paper [NSC 162/2] may well be vitiated." Further, the JCS would face the "almost impossible" task of planning and preparing forces on two different bases: assuming their use and their nonuse.[102]

The State Department and AEC immediately objected, insisting that the provision was not such a blanket advance authorization for use. In their view, the requirement for presidential approval was inherent in paragraph 39b. When Cutler briefed Eisenhower on this dispute the next day, the president stated that the military should make plans based on "full availability" of the use of nuclear weapons, but they should, despite the difficulty, distinguish between tactical and strategic use.[103]

This led to a meeting between Eisenhower and the Special Committee on December 22. Undersecretary Walter Bedell Smith presented a memorandum setting out State's opinion that paragraph 39b did not predelegate to the military the authority to use atomic weapons "in the event of *any* hostilities." AEC chairman Lewis Strauss fully concurred. The NSC designed the paragraph, he maintained, "to give effect to the concept that nuclear weapons ought to be considered within the arsenal of normal military equipment," not that "they would be so generally available that their use could be arbitrarily decided upon by a local commander."[104]

The president approved the State memorandum in toto and had it issued by NSC executive secretary James Lay on January 4, 1954, as his official interpretation of paragraph 39*b* of NSC 162/2:

1. "The purpose of the paragraph is primarily to permit the military to make plans on the basis of the availability of nuclear weapons."
2. "The paragraph is not a decision in advance that atomic weapons will in fact be used in the event of *any* hostilities." In certain cases that would be "automatic" from the start, such as "if there were an atomic attack on the United States or Western Europe."
3. "Many situations, however, will involve political questions of the gravest importance which cannot be precisely foreseen." In the event of "limited hostilities," for example, "it will be essential to consider whether immediate use of atomic weapons by the United States would increase the danger of their strategic use by the enemy, lose the support of allies, expose them to devastation, or widen the hostilities."
4. "The President should be in a position to consider such issues and make his decision as each case arises, in the light of the circumstances existing at the time. This is inherent in his role as Commander-in-Chief."
5. "This position does not unduly enhance the uncertainty for planning purposes." The president always has to decide the "nature and scope" of U.S. military action, which "will inevitably involve questions of the manner and extent of use of atomic weapons in any such hostilities. These questions are so intimately bound up with political and other factors that they cannot be governed by hard and fast rules adopted in the abstract."
6. "This interpretation does not prejudice our basic strategy of relying on retaliatory atomic power as the principal deterrent to Soviet aggression, or our military planning based on its prospective use. The use of atomic weapons for such retaliatory purposes is not in doubt."[105]

Public Presentation

Although this statement surely disappointed Radford, the JCS chairman loyally launched the administration's "public information program designed to introduce and explain our new national security policies" in a speech to the National Press Club on December 14, 1953. Military strategy was "new" in but two respects, he said: it was the product of the recently appointed JCS, and its premise was the long-haul approach as opposed to year of maximum danger. Near the end of the speech Radford did stress the strategy's "emphasis" on "modern air power." But at the same time, he was careful to interject that the JCS continued to adhere to the concept of balanced forces and placed a premium on "mobile, combat forces in readiness" in order that the United States was prepared for local conflicts as well as general war.[106]

Following Radford, Dulles arranged to deliver and have broadcast over television and radio a "major address" to the Council of Foreign Relations on January 12, 1954.[107] As was customary, the secretary of state sent the draft text to Eisenhower for comments. The president marked it up extensively, focusing primarily on the section that explained the administration's emphasis on atomic weapons. He suggested several additions. One was a sentence that read, "The basic decision [of the administration] was to depend primarily upon a capacity to retaliate, instantly, by means and at places of our choosing." Eisenhower also advised Dulles to say that this decision would allow the JCS to "shape our military establishment to fit what is our policy, instead of having to be ready to meet the enemy's many choices. That permits of [sic] a selection of military means instead of a multiplication of means." Finally, Eisenhower revised the following Dulles sentence by adding the underscored words: "The way to deter aggression is *for the free community* to be willing and able to respond *vigorously* and at places with means of its own choosing." The final text of Dulles's speech, "The Evolution of Foreign Policy," incorporated verbatim the president's suggestions.[108]

Reaction to Dulles's remarks was rapid, intense, and largely critical.[109] While the speech had dealt with the various dimensions of the strategy, its central message for many observers was conveyed by the sentences drafted by Eisenhower, especially "The basic decision was to depend primarily upon a great capacity to retaliate, instantly, by means and at places of our choosing." That was widely understood to mean that strategic nuclear retaliation was to be the panacea for deterring and combatting all forms of aggression.

The problem arose because several different thoughts had been crammed into a single short sentence. "Instant" massive retaliation was intended to deter and respond to a major Soviet surprise attack—U.S. strategy since 1948. But "by means and at places of our choosing" pertained to lesser, local aggressions; and as Eisenhower had ruled only a week before, even tactical nuclear weapons might not be used at all, and in any case, only after a deliberate decision by him.

To counter the adverse reaction, within two days Dulles arranged for the influential journal *Foreign Affairs* to publish an article by him to clarify the policy. Its editor, Hamilton Fish Armstrong, identified some of the questions he hoped Dulles would address in the article.[110] They included: What was "the precise meaning" of the statement, "The way to deter aggression is for the free community to be willing and able to respond vigorously at places and with means of its own choosing"? And "who is to decide whether or not there is to be a 'response' in a particular case"? If the answer was the United States alone, was not this policy akin to the kind of isolationism associated more closely with the Republican Party's Taft wing? Would U.S. help in the event that local aggression actually occurred "take the form of atomic attacks on the Soviet Union itself"? And "Are we placing all reliance on the threat of retaliation, with the aim of deterring aggression, for the reason that we cannot in fact count on our ability to reply to actual aggression effectively?" Finally, will the NATO allies defect out of fear that "our reliance on retaliation will in the end lead to our abandoning them"?[111]

While busy preparing for and attending the Berlin conference, Dulles, with active assistance from the Policy Planning Staff, completed the manuscript prior to the February 25 deadline for publication in the April issue.[112] In order to smooth "out a few points which had led to some misconception," he told the president, "particularly in relation to 'massive retaliatory power'" he extensively revised those sections of his January 12 speech. He also followed Armstrong's advice and retitled the article "Strategy for Security and Peace."[113]

The article sought to provide a balanced and coherent explanation of Dulles's and Eisenhower's conception of the New Look.[114] The administration had decided, Dulles wrote, on a strategy that placed "primary reliance" on the "combining of two concepts, namely the creation of power on a community basis and the use of that power so as to deter aggression by making it costly to an aggressor." In short, he placed massive retaliatory power in the context of "community" power, as one major component. "The cornerstone of security for the free nations must be a collective system of defense. . . . No single nation can develop for itself defense power of adequate scope and flexibility," the article continued. "Without the cooperation of allies, we would not even be in a position to retaliate massively."[115]

Dulles explained that the various regional pacts and the United Nations were based on the concept of collective security. In principle, each member state should contribute to the collective defense "in accordance with its capabilities and facilities." NATO had gone furthest "in organizing joint forces and facilities as part of the integrated security system."[116]

The article asked: What was the best collective strategy "for maximum protection at minimum cost? The heart of the problem was how to deter attack." It was the belief of the administration, Dulles stressed, "that a potential aggressor must not be left in any doubt that he would be certain to suffer damage outweighing any possible gains from aggression." The free world cannot match "Communist forces, man for man and tank for tank, at every point where they might attack." It therefore must develop a strategy "based on its own special assets, . . . especially air and naval power and atomic weapons," both strategic and tactical.

That strategy must recognize that "to deter aggression, it is important to have the flexibility and the facilities which make various responses available" so that the free world would not "put itself in the position where the only response open to it is general war." This flexibility required "a system in which local defensive strength is reinforced by more mobile deterrent power." This would afford the free world the "means," Dulles said, for "responding effectively on a selective basis when it chooses." Of course, "[t]he method of doing so will vary according to the character of the various areas."[117]

Western Europe, with its vital industrial power, was a special case. It was therefore particularly fortunate, Dulles wrote, that with U.S. strategic support, their "military tradition," and the "large military potential" inherent in the European Defense Community, the allies would be able to create "an adequate defense of the Continent."[118]

Dulles made clear that peripheral areas of less strategic importance presented a different problem. The administration held that these regions should have sufficient military strength to "maintain order against subversion and to resist other forms of indirect aggression and minor satellite aggression." Beyond that "A would-be aggressor will hestitate to commit aggression," Dulles argued, "if he knows in advance that he thereby not only exposes those particular forces which he chooses to use for his aggression," but also that "he can and will be made to suffer for his aggression more than he can possibly gain by it." It only made sense, therefore, that in the world's periphery above all, "the main reliance must be on the power of the free world to retaliate with great force by mobile means at places of its own choice."[119]

Dulles quickly added that this "does not mean turning every local war into a world war. It does not mean that if there is a Communist attack somewhere in Asia, atom or hydrogen bombs will necessarily be dropped on the great industrial centers of China or Russia." All that was certain, Dulles wrote, was that "the free world must maintain the collective means and be willing to use them in the way that most effectively makes aggression too risky and expensive to be tempting." The Eisenhower program, accordingly, "will retain a wide variety in the means and scope of responding to aggression." If the "potential of massive attack [is] always kept in a state of instant readiness," however, there should not be any aggression that required a response. The New Look promised peace, as well as security.[120]

13

Strengthening the
Noncommunist World

So we are persuaded by necessity and by belief that the strength of all
free peoples lies in unity; their danger, in discord. To produce this unity,
to meet the challenge of our time, destiny has laid upon our country the
responsibility of the free world's leadership.[1]

Dwight D. Eisenhower (1953)

For Eisenhower's national strategy, the strength and cohesion of the noncommunist world were just as vital as was the military component. Indeed, the support
of the allies was essential for deterrence and defense. Peace and security over the
long haul required cooperation among the industrialized nations and with developing ones, especially in the Middle East and Asia, for many purposes. Even if, as
NSC 162/2 anticipated, major Soviet aggression was deterred, "[t]he USSR will continue to rely heavily on tactics of division and subversion to weaken the free world
alliances and will to resist Soviet power" and to increase its influence in the less-de-
veloped nations. These were dimensions of the communist threat that were "likely
to continue indefinitely and grow in intensity." Unless the noncommunist nations
achieved economic progress, overcame political instability, elevated their confidence and morale, and nurtured their sense of interdependence and common purpose, the Soviets would be able to exploit their fears, hopes, divergences, neutralism, and nationalism.[2] A stable and prosperous West would likewise act as a magnet
for peoples trapped behind the Iron and Bamboo Curtains, thereby transforming
Soviet assets into liabilities. Finally, it would alleviate sources of conflict and war
that had disrupted global relations throughout the twentieth century.

"United States policies must, therefore, be designed," NSC 162/2 stressed, "to retain the cooperation of our allies, to seek to win the friendship and cooperation of
the presently uncommitted areas of the world, and thereby to strengthen the cohesion of the free world." More generally, the task was to "create and sustain the hope
and confidence of the free world in the ability of its basic ideas and institutions not
merely to oppose the communist threat, but to provide a way of life superior to
Communism."[3] Eight years earlier at London's Guildhall General Eisenhower had
expressed his conviction that this task could and must be achieved. "No petty differ-

ences in the world of trade, traditions or national pride should ever blind us to iden-
tities in priceless values. . . . [W]hen this truth has permeated to the remotest
hamlet and heart of all peoples," he continued, "then indeed may we beat our
swords to plowshares and all nations can enjoy the fruitfulness of the earth."[4]

The strategy as outlined in NSC 162/2 dealt separately with the two aspects of the
task: first, maintaining the cohesion of the "coalition" (all the states actively associated with the United States in the defense of the free world by treaty, regional alliance, or otherwise);[5] and second, increasing cooperation with the uncommitted
areas. In each case NSC 162/2 detailed the formidable obstacles to realizing the
goal and the policies for attempting to overcome them. On this component of the
strategy there was general agreement both in the Planning Board and the NSC,
with serious divergences limited mainly to foreign assistance and redeploying U.S.
forces, as already discussed. In drafting it the Planning Board drew substantially on
two studies prepared for its use by the State Department's Policy Planning Staff:
"Building Strength in Western Europe" and "Building Strength in Regional Groupings in the Far East."

Bolstering the Coalition

Within the coalition Western Europe and the North Atlantic Alliance were the
most important components, not merely for security but also for peace and prosperity. Yet as stated in NSC 162/2 many factors weakened Atlantic and European cohesion and impeded enhancing Europe's strength. Foremost among them were the
state of East-West trade; the relative defense burdens and levels of U.S. economic
assistance; political instability, as was most pronounced in France and Italy; colonialism; fear of general war; and the desire for detente and negotiations with the Soviet Union.

Exacerbating these factors, moreover, many Europeans criticized "U.S. attitudes
toward the Soviet Union as too rigid and unyielding and, at the same time, as unstable, holding risks ranging from preventive war and 'liberation' to withdrawal into
isolation." As a result "allied opinion, especially in Europe, has become less willing
to follow U.S. leadership."[6] So serious were the problems that the status report on
U.S. national security programs at mid-1953 concluded that internal support for the
coalition was declining and that "the unity of the coalition headed by the United
States is less solid now than in January 1953."[7]

Dulles, as we have seen, had frequently expressed his concern about the frailty
of the Atlantic alliance. That had been his theme in conversations on the *Helena* in
December 1952, during the debate over the April speech following Stalin's death,
and most dramatically, in the talks prompting the Solarium exercise. His pessimism
came to a head in early September just after the Soviet test of a thermonuclear device and the JCS proposed its new concept. Meeting with Eisenhower in Denver,
Dulles presented him with a memorandum calling for "urgent reconsideration" of
"our collective security policies" and discussed it with him.

The memorandum forecast a truly cataclysmic crisis for U.S. security. "The
NATO concept was losing its grip," the secretary said, due to the growth of Soviet

nuclear capability, allied doubts about strategic deterrence and the U.S. guarantee, and budgetary pressures. In this context, the "peace offensive" by the new Kremlin leaders was producing "wishful thinking" about the Soviet threat, "neutralism," and defense cuts. The allies would interpret U.S. plans for changes in the defense budget and strategy, including the greater emphasis on continental defense and strategic mobility, as "final proof of an isolationist trend" and the adoption of the "Fortress America" concept. Dulles's conclusion: "I doubt that any eloquence or reasoning on our part would prevent disintegration and deterioration of our position, with growing isolation through the reaction of our present allies." With the collapse of the alliance, "the balance of world power, military and economic, would doubtless shift rapidly to our great disadvantage. . . . [E]xpenditures would have to mount very sharply."

As a countermeasure to "be explored," Dulles proposed that Eisenhower "make a spectacular effort to relax world tensions" globally on the basis of U.S. and Soviet mutual force withdrawals from Western Europe and the satellites, leaving the latter free but friendly to the Soviet Union (like Finland), buttressed by international control of nuclear weapons and missiles. The secretary estimated that the "present is a propitious time" for his proposal "because we will be speaking from strength rather than weakness." The communists had recently suffered a "major reversal" in Iran with the coup and in Germany with the election, the "full impact of Soviet advances in non-conventional weapons has not yet been felt in Europe and Japan," and an agreement to end the war in Korea had been concluded "in an atmosphere of our willingness to enlarge the war unless the armistice was accepted."[8]

On his return from Denver Dulles reported to his director of the Policy Planning Staff, Robert Bowie, that the president had been "entirely sympathetic" and agreed that "we must bring things to a head." He assigned Bowie the task of developing the proposal.[9] Bowie's subsequent efforts became involved in preparing the president's "Atoms for Peace" speech in December, discussed in the next chapter. Eisenhower's written response of September 8, which was probing and subtle and the product of several drafts, suggests that Dulles did not fully understand the president's reaction to the concept.[10]

Eisenhower wrote that he was in "emphatic agreement that renewed efforts should be made to relax world tensions on a global basis." But while thus encouraging Dulles to develop the proposal, he warned it must not be put forth prematurely. First, it would be "indispensable" to educate the public, both at home and abroad, about the "fundamentals" of the situation and the rationale for the proposal, especially the significance of the hydrogen bomb and atom bomb. Otherwise we will "drift aimlessly, probably to our own eventual destruction." Second, planning any real revision of policies "will first require intensive study by the ablest group of individuals we can possibly assemble."

But the president did not stop there. As he often did when analyzing possible policies, he pursued the premises to their logical conclusion to test their consequences and validity.[11] (Solarium was an organized application of this method.) He realized that the Soviets were unlikely to accept the Dulles proposal. After all, the largely similar program he set out in the April "Chance for Peace" speech had evoked no positive response. If the Kremlin did reject this new initiative and the administration accepted Dulles's predictions about the collapse of the Western alliance, the crucial question for Eisenhower was: What followed? One would have to assume from the Soviet refusal to "make any honest effort toward international [arms] control" that they could be "contemplating their aggressive use." The costly effort to maintain an effective deterrent indefinitely without allies "would either drive us to war—or into some form of dictatorial government." To the president, this scenario led to the inescapable conclusion that the United States would have to consider initiating a preventive war.

But evidence already presented indicates that Eisenhower did not consider preventive war a viable option. Instead, he was actually challenging the premises that underlay Dulles's memorandum. Eisenhower did not share Dulles's fatalism about NATO. From his service as SACEUR, he was fully aware of its tensions and weaknesses. But he also knew at first hand the strong desire of European leaders and publics for continuance of the U.S. nuclear umbrella despite their ambivalence about U.S. reliability. And he had faith that their respect for the United States and affinity for its values was a cohesive bond. On several occasions in the NSC when the collapse of NATO had been predicted, the president had used the same stark method to shock the debate back to reality.

What was necessary, in Eisenhower's judgment, was to strengthen the coalition for the long haul by reducing strains and stresses, bolstering confidence, and fostering economic progress. Time was on the side of the West, he was certain, so long as it made effective use of it. If "your memorandum proves nothing else," Eisenhower concluded somewhat cryptically to Dulles, "it proves that we must get our thinking on these vast problems organized and coordinated so that as a first step all in responsible positions can have confidence that our conclusions are essentially correct."

The effort to develop Dulles's proposal, examined in the next chapter, persuaded him to abandon it and to turn his attention to bolstering the coalition, especially with the European allies.[12] During his tenure as secretary, he devoted a major part of his time, energy, and travel to conferences, smaller meetings, and consultations for this purpose. His special concern was to keep West Germany firmly tied to the West in order both to co-opt its population and resources and to safeguard against its again becoming a threat or a loose cannon.[13] FRG chancellor Konrad Adenauer and his governing Christian Democratic Union were equally convinced that this course best served German interests. But the opposing Social Democrats vigorously castigated this policy for subordinating the goal of reunification, to which the party gave top priority. Suspicious by nature, Adenauer repeatedly needed reassurance that German interest would not be sacrificed during crises or any talks with the Soviets, which Dulles provided. Over time the two men developed a friendship and trust that each considered invaluable.[14]

European Integration

In seeking to solidify the coalition, the Eisenhower strategy promoted the concept of a European Community and sought to alleviate many of the sources of tension and friction. The "building of an integrated European Community," NSC 162/2 accordingly stated, was essential to "achieve a stronger Europe."[15] By reconciling West Germany with France and its other neighbors within a supranational regime, a European Community would open the way for the full revival of Germany and for the cooperation within Europe essential for economic progress, stability, and security. France had initiated the European Coal and Steel Community (ECSC) in May 1950 as a first step toward unity, and Adenauer had responded enthusiastically. Two years later, with the active support of the Truman administration, the ECSC had been ratified and was operating with six continental members but without Britain.[16] Meanwhile, after NATO decided in September 1950 to rearm West Germany, France reluctantly proposed the creation of the European Defense Community (EDC) with integrated military forces in order to avoid the formation of German national forces, which the Pentagon favored.

Both Eisenhower and Dulles strongly supported European integration and the EDC. Dulles had done so from the start. "A genuine union of interest between Germany and France is an enormous insurance for a peaceful future," he wrote shortly after the French initiative in 1950. "Catastrophic" was his adjective later for the consequences of EDC's defeat.[17] The allies "must match Soviet unity . . . with equal unity," the secretary of state told NATO's council in 1953. "If France and Germany cannot be woven together in a European fabric of mutual understanding and common endeavor," there could "be no real strength in Europe," he insisted. Indeed, "The history of the past two hundred years in Europe showed that Western Europe would tear itself to pieces unless the Franco-German problem were resolved." If only for this reason, "our policy with respect to Europe" must not "involve a choice between France *or* Germany. It is based on France *and* Germany."[18]

As NATO's first supreme commander, Eisenhower had initially had misgivings about creating an integrated European force.[19] But by June 1951, after meeting with Jean Monnet, the fount for the French proposals, Eisenhower had changed his appraisal. What was involved, he concluded, was primarily "a political rather than a military problem." Or, as he explained to General Alfred Gruenther, the "real issue was relations between peoples."[20] Several weeks later, in addressing the English-Speaking Union in London, Eisenhower made an eloquent plea for the establishment of a "workable European federation." Through federation, he predicted, the peoples of Europe would "produce miracles for the common good" by realizing their full potential in material well-being, ending their distrust and suspicion, and securing their future.[21]

From then on as SACEUR Eisenhower provided staff advice and assistance in helping the negotiators to shape a practical military structure. And as president he stressed the broader benefits of EDC. "Well, if we could get EDC over, we could feel we'd made real progress," he told his legislative leaders. "This whole picture would be different—Europe would be a bastion of strength instead of a cesspool of weakness. By golly, if we could get this done and beat down all those national jealousies, we could feel we'd done the greatest things since Charlemagne."[22]

Indeed, if adopted the EDC did offer many advantages. Militarily, it would provide 12 German divisions for helping to meet the critical NATO goals for ground forces in the most politically feasible way in light of French, German, and

British attitudes.[23] Further, an integrated European Army seemed the best guarantee against a resurgent and remilitarized Germany ever again threatening the West by either aggression or currying Moscow's favor in order, in Eisenhower's words, to "blackmail" the NATO powers.[24] It would also be another "major step in the long-range program of European integration" and in eroding the distrust and enmity in relations between France and Germany.[25] Moreover, it could energize efforts to develop a European Political Community, which was already being discussed.[26] And domestically, the creation of the EDC would be the best response to those in Congress, particularly Republicans, who sought to curtail aid to Europe to an extent far beyond what Eisenhower considered prudent by claiming that the United States must stop wasting its resources on "vague and illusory promises of European unity."[27]

Despite its many benefits, however, the prospects for EDC adoption were uncertain. With Adenauer's reelection in September, West Germany was sure to ratify the treaty and was probably prepared to meet French conditions regarding access to the coal and steel resources of the Saar Basin; and approval by the other parties, except for France, seemed assured. French leaders, however, kept putting off submitting the treaty to the Assembly for a vote and raising new conditions aside from access to the Saar. Meanwhile, overall support for the treaty steadily eroded. Stalin's death nurtured a climate of detente and doubts about the need to rearm Germany. The hostilities in Indochina were a constant drain on French forces. And the British refusal to join the EDC left many French leaders uneasy about being left alone with a rearmed Germany.[28]

In fact, the British attitude toward European integration was decidedly unhelpful, to the dismay of Eisenhower and Dulles.[29] Reluctant to adjust to its declining status, British leaders still viewed Europe from a traditional balance of power perspective. Moreover, they strove continually to set Britain apart from America's allies on the continent in order to affirm their special relationship.[30]

For this, Eisenhower and Dulles held Winston Churchill particularly culpable. "Frankly, I believe that, subconsciously, my great friend is trying to re-live the days of his greatest glory" during World War II, wrote Eisenhower in his diary not long after Churchill had regained the prime ministership. "He is struggling hard to bring about a recognition of specially close ties between America and Britain. . . . To my mind, he simply will not think in terms of today."[31]

Churchill's meetings with Eisenhower and Dulles just before the inauguration reinforced this assessment. "He indicated that he would like to settle major questions arising by sitting around a table with General Eisenhower," Dulles commented afterward. The president was more expansive in his diary. "He has fixed in his mind a certain international relationship" in which "Britain and the British Commonwealth are not to be treated just as other nations would be treated by the United States," the January 6, 1953, entry read. "[S]o far as I can see, he has developed an almost childlike faith that all of the answers are to be found merely in British-American partnership."[32] The answers to Europe's peace and security, however, NSC 162/2 made clear, demanded multilateral cooperation and, ultimately, integration.

Accordingly, after the French Assembly rejected the EDC treaty in August 1954, the administration was not satisfied with the incorporation of West Germany into NATO the next year. It continued to support the European Coal and Steel Community, and for the purpose of promoting European integration, assisted its six members in relaunching the process with the formation of Euratom and the Common Market in 1957.

Shoring Up the Atlantic Alliance

The administration recognized that the indigenous forces that weakened and divided America's European allies were impervious to quick-fix solutions. Overcoming them would require patience, empathy, and skilled diplomacy, primarily from the United States as the leader.[33] A "constant concern of [American] leadership," Eisenhower insisted, must be to ensure that "differing national attitudes and policies . . . do not become such bitter issues between NATO nations that we tend to fall apart."[34] He was acutely aware of how difficult this task would be. "Our allies must be genuinely convinced that our strategy is one of collective security," read NSC 162/2. "The alliance must be rooted in a strong sense of community of interest and firm confidence in the steadfastness and wisdom of U.S. leadership."[35]

That confidence had been shaken by what the Europeans had heard about the "New Look" in the early months. To begin with "many Europeans distrusted the Republican party . . . for the past isolationist tendencies of certain of its leaders" and doubted that the United States "had sufficient experience in foreign affairs to offer wise and farsighted leadership." Such doubts, maintained NSC 162/2, "materially impair cooperation and, if not overcome, could impair the coalition."[36] And at the NATO Council meeting in April 1953, the stress by Dulles (accompanied by Humphrey) on fiscal constraint evoked widespread trepidation that the United States "refuses to accept a genuine partnership in NATO" and might reassess its commitment to Europe's recovery and defense.[37] Before the meeting ambassador to France Douglas Dillon had warned that some Europeans would view such an emphasis and proposals for increased cost-sharing as a "return to isolationism, feeling that withdrawal first of general economic aid and then of special defense aid will be followed by withdrawal of troops." Assistant Secretary of Defense for International Affairs Frank Nash seconded Dillon. "You can well imagine," he wrote Secretary Wilson, "that many Europeans will be quick to misinterpret, through fear or suspicion, indications that the U.S. is weakening its defense efforts."[38]

The Europeans were indeed disturbed by perceived indications of a waning of the United States's commitment to Europe's defense, such as the failure, caused largely by its debate over conventional force levels, to provide on schedule the precise data required for NATO's 1953 Annual Review. Other indications included, the NSC Planning Board reported, "such things as our advocacy of a shift in emphasis from a rapid build-up to a long-term NATO program, our acquiescence without serious protest to cutbacks in the defense programs of our NATO allies, cutbacks in our own defense programs, and delays in certain basic decisions in Washington." The combined result was a "sense of depression and concern" within the NATO Council. "I believe that many influential Europeans believe that we have lost confidence, if not interest in Europe and its defensibility if war should come," said Dulles. The Department of Defense's Office of North Atlantic Treaty Affairs was more alarmist still. "[U]nless something is done rapidly to indicate that the U.S. has not cut back seriously in NATO, either in force commitments or financial support," wrote Colonel Harrison Gerhardt to Nash in August, the "NATO structure will unravel at the seams."[39]

NSC 162/2 addressed this concern by proscribing the redeployment of U.S. forces or significant reduction of assistance to Europe under "present conditions." It stressed that "the presence of U.S. forces in Western Europe makes a contribution other than military to the strength and cohesion of the free world coalition."[40] As the Policy Planning Staff paper on which this judgment was premised explained, "Even in the absence of a judgment that Western Europe can be rendered defensible [against Soviet attack], the U.S. should not abandon the objective of creating a force which, in a continuing cold war, will enhance European confidence."[41]

Fear of Atomic War

"It is generally believed," reported the chiefs of U.S. missions to Europe, "that American impatience and implacable hostility to Communism might result in hasty and ill-considered action and . . . might set up a chain reaction leading to military conflict."[42] NSC 162/2 was more pointed. "Many Europeans fear that American policies may involve Europe in general war."[43] For his part, Secretary Dulles went even further, saying that, more than a few of America's allies believe that "some important influences in the U.S. indeed favor a general war."[44]

Dulles explained the dilemma bluntly: whereas the administration "regarded atomic weapons as one of the great new sources of defensive strength, many of our allies regarded the atomic capability as the gateway to annihilation."[45] As a consequence, in the estimate of his Policy Planning Staff, "European susceptibility to Soviet placatory gestures and 'peace' moves will compel European governments to urge the U.S. to explore all possible avenues to a peaceful settlement of the cold war, even at the price of compromises which might, in U.S. opinion, approach appeasement."[46]

So strong and widespread was the European opposition to going beyond a conventional defense of Korea that when in a February 1953 NSC meeting Eisenhower raised the question of using tactical atomic weapons in the Kaesong area, Bradley cautioned that it was "unwise to broach the subject" with the allies.[47] Eisenhower accepted Bradley's counsel and "ruled against" any discussion of military plans with the British or French.[48] "[W]e could not blind ourselves to the effects such a move [dropping a 'couple of atomic weapons in Korea'] would have on our allies, which would be very serious," he explained in March.[49] "We, more than any other people," the president subsequently said, "have accepted the atomic age in which we now live. Many European peoples are lagging far behind us and think of themselves as the defenseless targets of atomic warfare."[50]

Hence even as NSC 162/2 stipulated that in "the event of hostilities, the United States will consider nuclear weapons to be as available for use as other munitions," the same paragraph stressed the necessity for the United States to "seek, as and when feasible, the *understanding* and approval of this policy by free nations."[51] These allied concerns required, in addition, evidence of the administration's willingness to negotiate arms limitation and control, the subject of the next chapter.

Mutual Assistance

The mutual assistance program split Eisenhower's party and the NSC. For Republicans impatient to balance the budget, such as Humphrey and Dodge in the cabinet and Daniel Reed and John Taber in Congress, cutting economic assistance to Europe was, in the president's words, "a natural," but in his opinion it was also "pennywise and pound-foolish." At stake was not simply NATO's military capability, or even the financial well-being of the continent, although both would suffer. What concerned Eisenhower most of all was the potential to "damage irreparably" the progress toward allied unity and confidence in Washington that "we have been trying so laboriously to build up." Echoing Eisenhower, both Dulles and Mutual Security administrator Harold Stassen warned that a radical reduction of aid to Europe would be a "very bad psychological move" as well as a "serious material blow." The less economic assistance the U.S. extended, the greater the Europeans' misgivings about a return to American isolationism.[52]

Despite the objections of Humphrey and Dodge, Eisenhower insisted that aid to Europe remain integral to his national security policy. In the drafting of NSC 162, when Treasury and Bureau of the Budget sought to specify flatly that U.S. assistance to "the regional grouping in Western Europe" would be "[p]rogressively lessened," Eisenhower "with some warmth" commented that he would "never agree" to this categorical statement. Hence NSC 162/2 provided that the United States "must continue to assist in creating and maintaining mutually agreed European forces, but should reduce such assistance "as rapidly as the United States security interests permit."[53]

Moreover, to counter the widespread perception that such assistance was a "giveaway," Eisenhower instructed his representatives to avoid using the term "foreign aid" and instead to present economic assistance as a cost-effective means immediately to "buy security" and gradually to reduce the U.S. defense budget and expand *its* economy. He also assured that mutual security funds would be managed more carefully and distributed more selectively.[54] Congress still forced the president to accept a smaller allocation for FY 1954 than his budget proposed.[55]

Trade Not Aid

The concept of "trade not aid" was central to Eisenhower's initial foreign economic policy. He strongly favored liberalized trade and believed that, coupled with foreign private investment, it would make possible tempering and ultimately ending government assistance while fostering global growth.[56] He believed just as strongly that the United States had to lead the fight against the centrifugal force of economic nationalism. Challenging protectionist sentiment in Congress, he requested a three-year extension of the Reciprocal Trade Agreements Act in his first State of the Union address.[57] "[S]timulating international trade" as the basis for "healthy growth" was a core component of NSC 162/2.[58]

Many in Congress, however, especially Republicans, were opposed to lowering tariffs and other barriers. In May, therefore, Eisenhower requested Congress to create a bipartisan Commission on Foreign Economic Policy. By August it was approved. Eisenhower appointed Clarence Randall, head of the Inland Steel Company and liberal trade proponent, as chairman, and mostly free trade enthusiasts as members; the representatives from Congress included both supporters and opponents.[59] The commission completed its work in January 1954, with the minority filing a separate report. Essentially, the majority report supported the concept of freer trade and private investment in place of foreign aid. While endorsing the continued ban on exports to Communist China and North Korea and strategic goods to the Soviet bloc, it approved exports of peaceful goods behind the Iron Curtain. It said almost nothing about Third World problems.[60]

In March Eisenhower sent a special message to Congress requesting approval of most of the Randall Report recommendations, including tariff reductions, fostering private foreign investment, and ending grant assistance as soon as possible. Because of splits within his own party, the president had to settle for a one-year extension of the Reciprocal Trade Act. But he successfully resisted Humphrey's effort to curtail even further development loans by the Export-Import Bank.[61]

These policies prevailed for several years, but by 1954–1955 they had begun to evolve toward more public assistance for development in the Third World. As will be discussed in the concluding chapter, this was one policy area where by the end of Eisenhower's tenure radical change had occurred, due largely to the president's own initiative.

East-West Trade

Eisenhower inherited from Truman a system of tight controls on East-West trade initiated by NSC 104/2 in 1951 and concerted with the European allies through the Paris-based Coordinating Committee (COCOM). Many Europeans felt the broad scope of the restrictions disregarded their views and needs. As a consequence, at the president's instigation the NSC during one of its first meetings directed the Planning Board to prepare an assessment of the controls.[62]

The Planning Board submitted its report (NSC 152) in May 1953. "With respect to our allies, the economic problems posed by [East-West] trade restrictions are greater for Western Europe than they are for the United States," it read. "Many [NATO] countries have been distressed about U.S. measures to increase the severity of trade controls against the Soviet Bloc." NSC 152 then continued: "The fear of a downturn in economic activity and the fear of a protectionist commercial policy on the part of the United States heighten the pressures in Western Europe for more rather than less trade with the Bloc." Moreover, the Battle Act, which made economic assistance contingent on European compliance and had been in force since 1951, evoked the image of an American bully. The Planning Board surveyed alternatives ranging from intensifying the current program of controls to abandoning it entirely, weighing the pros and cons of each without indicating a preference.

The NSC must recognize, it nevertheless wrote unequivocally, that "certain aspects of the present program area are a source of constant irritation in our international relations."[63]

Eisenhower strongly favored the selective relaxation of controls on East-West trade. He "simply could not agree with the general philosophy underlying NSC 104/2," the president stated when the Council first took up the matter. The "real basis for policy should be who gets the best of the trade." In terms of nonstrategic materiel, a carefully designed program of more liberal trade with the communists would produce a net advantage for the West, Eisenhower predicted. It would also promote discord within the Eastern bloc by making the communist states "depend and depend and depend on us" so that "when Moscow wants them to hurt us or do this or that . . . they have to say, we can't afford to."[64]

Most importantly, it would promote cohesion, strength, and support for the United States within the Western bloc. "If we continue to pressure our European allies to the point which we seemed prepared to do under this [the current] policy," Eisenhower warned the NSC, "we might very well confront a situation of virtual isolation." The "standard of living in most countries of Europe" was "too damned low," the president said. To "keep these nations on our side in the struggle with the Soviet Union," the United States must demonstrate its commitment to raising it. "We must recognize the fact that many of these nations live on trade, and we cannot adopt a policy which compels them to remain 'cold and hungry.'" The United States had to recognize as well that Europe's perception of America's empathy, and trust in American leadership of the alliance, hung in the balance.[65]

Many NSC members, Secretary Dulles included, still resisted reducing significantly the existing list of controls, especially those on trade with Communist China.[66] Loath to impose his views on his advisors, Eisenhower approved a compromise statement of policy, NSC 152/2. "Our economic defense program must be framed and administered with full recognition of the fact that the economic defense system of the free world is part of the larger system of military and political alliance," it stipulated. "Accordingly, in determining the measures which the United States should adopt and those to be urged on other nations, the impact upon the existing international system of economic defense as a whole, and upon the free world military and political alliances, must be taken into account."[67]

But NSC 152/2 did not indicate what, if any, different measures the United States should adopt. Without providing any specifics, it only recommended giving "greater weight in determining U.S. actions to the impact of the control system on the economic, political and financial situation of our allies and to their views and intentions," and to "consulting with the other principal free world nations before entering into new major economic defense programs." Moreover, the United States would encourage the allies to develop alternative markets and sources of supply so as to reduce their interest in East-West trade, and oppose any relaxation of trade with the Communist Chinese whatsoever. As for NSC 162/2, it included the controls on exports to the Soviet bloc among the specific "sources of irritation" within the coalition, but limited its prescriptions to "consider[ing] a modification" of policies.[68]

Eisenhower's perspective, however, was reflected in the implementation of NSC

162/2. The administration notified the allies that it would entertain proposals to modify the export control program, which served to spur COCOM negotiations. Another spur was the Randall Commission report, which supported "more trade in peaceful goods between Western Europe and the Soviet bloc." By the middle of 1954 COCOM had reached an agreement to reduce radically the restrictions on East-West trade.[69]

Colonialism

Colonialism was both a source of discord within the alliance and an impediment to cooperation with the developed nations. The administration would not accommodate its NATO partners' efforts to retain or regain their imperial status. To "be in the position of negatively resisting inevitable and proper change in the world," in Washington's view, would be incompatible with promoting political stability and economic progress within the newly emergent nations, and with establishing the durable relationships with them that the security and political economy of the free world required.[70]

NSC 162/2 explained the reason: in addition to the "vast manpower" of the less developed regions, "their essential raw materials and their potential for growth are such that their absorption within the Soviet system would greatly, perhaps decisively, alter the world balance of power to our detriment." Conversely, "their orderly development into more stable and responsible nations, able and willing to participate in the defense of the free world, can increasingly add to its strength."[71]

Heading NSC 162/2's inventory of factors that inhibited the Third World's alignment with the West and exacerbated its vulnerability to communist propaganda and subversion were "racial feelings, anti-colonialism, [and] rising nationalism."[72] These feelings endangered security in both the core and periphery. On the one hand, Moscow could exploit the troubles the European states were experiencing to exacerbate dissension among the NATO partners and sap their individual and aggregate resources. On the other hand, the heavy-handedness of the colonial powers militated against building firm ties with the Third World. "By reason of their colonial experience," advised State's Policy Planning Staff, "these countries are apt to distrust Western motives almost as much as they distrust those of the Communists. They are ultrasensitive to policies or attitudes which seem to them to partake of colonialism or reflect on their sovereignty."[73]

Thus the issue of colonialism worried Eisenhower immensely. In much of the Third World, he entered in his diary after meeting with Churchill just before taking office, "immediate independence would result in suffering for people and even anarchy." Yet "Nationalism is on the march," he went on, and "Moscow leads many misguided people to believe that they can count on communist help to achieve and sustain nationalistic ambitions." As a consequence, the "Western powers must not appear before the world as a combination of forces to compel adherence to the status quo." To the contrary, "we must convince dependent peoples that their only hope of [attaining and] maintaining independence . . . is through cooperation with the free world."[74]

Eisenhower believed that it would be "far better" for the United States and its European allies "to proceed independently toward the solution of knotty [colonial] problems" while seeking to concert before making separate proposals.[75] The difficulty of achieving even this level of cooperation was among his chief frustrations. The administration's differences with France over Indochina, even while assisting its struggle, were a prominent example of such difficulties.[76] Far more divisive was the Suez Canal crisis of 1956, which was illustrative of what Eisenhower described as Britain's "rather old-fashioned, paternalistic approach" toward its colonies and traditional spheres of influence.[77]

When, as in the Iranian case (discussed later), the president perceived—or misperceived—the threat of an imminent communist takeover, he put aside his qualms about British motives and approved Project AJAX, which was, in essence, a London-initiated covert operation to oust the regime of Dr. Mohammed Mossadegh. Yet this operation to support London's goals was the exception; as a rule Eisenhower deemed Britain's imperial behavior inimical to free world interests.[78] After one dispute he exploded: "Churchill will be satisfied with nothing less than a statement from me that Cyprus is his own little private island. I am not going to give him that statement at any time. . . . We just can't side with [the] colonial aspirations of Great Britain."[79]

U.S. efforts to foster mutually acceptable solutions to such disputes, NSC 162/2 conceded, "tend to leave both sides dissatisfied and to create friction within the alliance." Thus the "colonial issue weakened our European allies" and produced "ferment which weakens the whole free world." What this meant, in practice, was that the United States would seek to "encourage orderly settlements" on a case-by-case basis.[80]

Beyond Europe

NSC 162/2 acknowledged that resentment against the West was not the only obstacle to developing noncommunist strength, stability, and support outside of Europe. Many Third World nations were "so preoccupied with other pressing problems" that they were "presently unwilling to align themselves actively with the United States and its allies." These problems included the "popular demand for rapid social and economic progress," "over-population," and "the breakdown of static social patterns." Compounding these were mutual suspicions, the "general unreliability of the governments," and the "volatility of their political life."[81]

NSC 162/2 dedicated a single subparagraph to large portions of the less developed world. Most of Africa was still colonized; Latin America came under the Monroe Doctrine, Rio Pact, and Organization of American States; and liberal trade and private investment seemed the most efficient means to promote economic growth.[82] For these areas basic national security policy, therefore, required only that, on the one hand, the United States furnish to them "limited" military aid and technical and economic assistance "according to the calculated advantage of such aid to the U.S. world position," and, on the other hand, that it "counter any threat of a party or individuals directly or indirectly responsible to Soviet control to achieve dominant power."[83]

But in the vital areas of the Far and Middle East, basic security policy required building new centers of free world strength. Toward this end, Eisenhower, complaining that he "was very weary of hearing our efforts to assist other nations described as the real cause of our unbalanced budget," overruled Treasury and the Bureau of the Budget and continued economic assistance to both areas.[84] But the regional dynamics of each posed a more formidable challenge. In Asia and the Middle East, the United States confronted forces of weakness and division more diffuse than they were in Europe even as they were more intractable.

The Far East

Coping with the "altered structure of power" produced by the Chinese Communist regime and the Sino-Soviet alliance constituted the "primary problem of U.S. foreign policy in the Far East."[85] NSC 162/2 characterized Mao's regime as solidly in control, and the Sino-Soviet alliance, while subject to strain or breakup over the long term, "appears to be firmly established and adds strategic territory and vast reserves of military manpower to the Soviet bloc."[86]

The People's Republic of China's Communist government recognized "that in specific locales and world contests," wrote the NSC staff study, its goal of seizing political control of other Asian countries "involves risks and costs that the regime is not able to assume. Without abandoning the ultimate aim, its policies are therefore often directed at intermediate goals of an economic, political, or security nature." These goals included "neutralizing sources of Western support in Asian countries, preventing the rise of stable, firmly anti-Communist governments wherever possible, encouraging 'neutralism,' and perverting to Communist purposes Asian strivings for independence, progress, and peace."[87]

Both to frustrate these immediate communist efforts and to build strength in Asia for the long haul, America's principal objective, read the NSC Planning Board's first policy statement draft on the Far East, must be the evolution of "stable and self-sustaining non-communist governments, friendly to the United States, acting in accordance with the purposes and principles of the United Nations Charter, and having the will and ability to maintain internal security, to withstand communist influence, and to prevent aggression."[88]

The first step toward this goal, stressed NSC 162/2, had to be Japan's revival.[89] Japan's "developed industry," coupled with the "relatively advanced technical training" and the "aptitudes of its population," made it the "most important prize" in the Far East, the "one Asiatic power" capable of stimulating the economies of the others.[90]

But it was also capable of becoming the Soviets' "workshop of war," and in 1953 Japan remained economically and politically unstable. This condition could grow worse after the cessation of hostilities in Korea brought to an end the windfall that the Japanese derived from U.S. wartime procurement.[91] Moreover, combined with the popular fear that alignment with the West could draw Japan into a military conflict, its feeble economy provided sustenance for neutralists and communists, and the administration had much less confidence in Prime Minister Shigeru Yoshida than in Adenauer.[92] America may have "licked" the wrong country in World

War II, remarked a disconsolate George Humphrey at an early NSC meeting. "[Y]ou don't mean that," Eisenhower said, but he conceded that America may have licked the Japanese "too thoroughly."[93]

Hence regardless of budgetary constraints and congressional opposition, the United States had "to undertake a substantial economic aid program to Japan." But direct U.S. assistance was at best a palliative. Japanese commerce was foundering because of its traditional partners' political complexions, historical memories, and meager means of payment. In addition, its "natural trading area of South and Southeast Asia" appeared to be hostage to the communist-led insurrection in Indochina.[94] America's own policies, moreover, blocked Japan from trading with the Chinese mainland, and constraining its efforts to find alternative channels were competition from Europe and Japan's dollar deficit.[95]

Thus although military measures to prevent the Indochina domino from falling were necessary to provide regional strength and security, they would be insufficient unless Japanese commerce expanded. Without "adequate trade the Japanese were bound to suffer economic strangulation which would result in their almost certainly turning to the Communist side," explained Dulles.[96] Indeed, his Policy Planning Staff advised that administration support for an "increase of Japanese trade with the Communist mainland . . . may be unavoidable." (The administration relaxed most restrictions on Japanese trade with the PRC by 1958.)[97] More generally, Japan had to be integrated into an interdependent and "friendly system of Far Eastern countries" that extended to India.[98]

In this regard, pro-Western Asian states in the Far East proved as much of an obstacle to U.S. policies as did neutrals and communists. Throughout Asia and the Pacific, nations that identified with the free world expressed their trepidation that a revived Japan meant an aggressive Japan. They resisted U.S. appeals to negotiate commercial treaties with their former enemy let alone to sanction its rearmament.[99] Eisenhower's emissaries repeatedly sought to reassure its neighbors and warned of the regional repercussions of an economically vulnerable and military defenseless Japan. In certain cases these arguments made matters worse. Led by the Nationalist Chinese and South Koreans, Far Eastern leaders accused the United States of seeking "the restoration of Japan's lost colonial empire" and expending resources on Japan to which they were more entitled.[100] "[O]f course Japan eventually would become the power center of the Far East," commented Dulles in late July. But, he told the NSC, "For some time yet we must deal individually with Far Eastern countries and not alienate them by pushing Japan out in front."[101]

Hence it was clear to U.S. policy makers that Japan's weakness and isolation were both a cause and a consequence of "the conflicting purposes of the various Asian nations with regard to collective action."[102] Instead of uniting to defend against the Sino-Soviet threat and to further mutual economic growth, the noncommunist states in the Far East remained atomized by a "welter of variant, opposing, and emotionally supported views." As a result, there existed "little common ground" on which "shared aspirations" could "develop into collaborative arrangements." It was vital, therefore, that the United States "encourage the countries of this area to resolve their differences and overcome other obstacles to cooperation."[103]

The administration explicitly identified the Taipei and Seoul regimes as obstacles to cooperation. For obvious reasons each could contribute valuably to regional security and development, and on this basis each warranted continued U.S. aid. Yet the attitude of both toward Japan was but one among many issues on which they refused to "play ball" with their neighbors or the United States. Chiang Kai-shek and Singman Rhee felt that their irredentist agendas took precedence over U.S. efforts to create in Asia an environment conducive to generating security and interdependence. From their perspective war, not stability, best served their national interests.[104]

For the near term, then, the administration could count on neither the Japanese, Nationalist Chinese, nor South Koreans to provide the leadership necessary to build strength and cohesion in the Far East. At the region's other extremity, Nehru's commitment to nonalignment disqualified India, and Indonesia "followed the Indian lead."[105] U.S. leadership could help, but only up to a point. The reaction of the peoples of Asia and the Pacific to the ANZUS treaty indicated a "widespread suspicion" that the pact "represented either a revival of 'western imperialism' or an instrument of 'white supremacy.'"[106] British demands for membership in ANZUS (the defense pact between Australia, New Zealand, and the United States), moreover, and in any future regional associations, magnified these suspicions.[107] The more conspicuous and formal the role the United States played in collective ventures, the more difficult it would be to refuse Britain's participation, and for that matter that of France and the Netherlands. U.S. relations with both Asia and Europe would suffer. The "irritations engendered by such pressures," agreed the State and Defense Departments, "would militate against the growth of the general spirit of cooperation" in Asia and the Pacific.[108]

NSC 162/2 acknowledged that the United States could not solve the Far East's "basic problems." Until "more comprehensive and regional arrangements become feasible," therefore, "strength must be built on existing bilateral and multilateral security arrangements." But by playing "second fiddle," the United States could encourage and nurture the emergence of indigenous leaders with the potential to "invigorate and unify non-Communist Asian forces."[109] More generally, through "[c]onstructive political and other measures, not related solely to anticommunism," it could promote regional cohesion and development and "persuade uncommitted countries that their best interests lie in greater cooperation and stronger affiliations with the rest of the free world."[110]

The Middle East

Next to East and Southeast Asia, the Middle East, so rich in oil and so vital to America's strategic planning, was the peripheral area of greatest concern to the administration. Because indigenous Communist parties were weaker there, and the Soviets lacked an ally remotely akin to the PRC, the threat of a direct military attack was much less severe than in Asia. Yet the Middle East lacked a nation with a skilled workforce and infrastructure that approached Japan's, nor was there a military force comparable to that of Nationalist China or South Korea. Further, the Middle East's endemic political and economic immaturity, combined with the virulent Arab-Israeli hostility and rivalries among the Arab states themselves, presented obstacles to regional cooperation and mutual development even more imposing than those in the Far East.[111]

Along with a program of economic assistance targeted toward the strongest and weakest nations, the administration, as an admittedly tentative step toward promoting strength and cohesion, initially encouraged the creation of a Middle Eastern Defense Organization (MEDO). The concept of a security pact among the United States, Britain, France, Turkey, and the Arab states had evolved during Truman's final year in office after the collapse of an earlier plan to establish a Middle Eastern Command (MEC) linked to NATO.[112] Washington predicted little in the way of military dividends to result from MEDO. Its responsibility would be confined to planning, coordination, and liaison; no members would permanently contribute forces. But by institutionalizing a relationship beween the United States, Europe, and the indigenous regimes, MEDO would lay the groundwork for future economic and political as well as military cooperation.

Yet the same factors that attracted the Eisenhower administration to the MEDO boded ill for its realization. What it promised, above all, was a means to lessen if not overcome the British legacy in the Middle East while at the same time providing a mutually acceptable formula by which London and Washington could share military and political responsibilities. The difficulty of realizing this promise was demonstrated, however, by Britain's protracted negotiations with Egypt over Cairo-Suez Canal base rights. The tensions with Egypt doomed the MEC; contributed to the overthrow of King Farouk by Muhammed Naguib, Gamal Abdul Nasser, and the Free Officers associates; and generated demands by Egyptian nationalists to terminate the Anglo-Egyptian Treaty of 1936.[113]

Complicating matters further, as Egyptian participation in MEDO became less likely, Pakistan's eagerness to take part in joint planning and contribute much needed ground troops became more tempting. Dulles returned from a spring 1953 tour of the Middle East and South Asia persuaded that Pakistan was the "one country" with the "moral courage to do its part in resisting communism." In his view, it deserved U.S. military support. Moreover, the secretary of state was convinced that Karachi would be a "cooperative member of any defense scheme that may emerge in [the] Middle East." In fact, to Dulles a regional alliance comprised of Pakistan and the northern tier states—Turkey, Iraq, and Iran—seemed more feasible than one centered around Egypt.[114]

While the military benefits of Pakistani participation in a collective Middle Eastern security regime were attractive, Eisenhower had to weigh them against the inevitable political fallout. Just the rumor that the Truman administration planned to offer Karachi membership in MEDO had been sufficient to evoke indignation in New Delhi and further undermine U.S. efforts to walk the South Asian tightrope. Jawaharlal Nehru interpreted any sign of the United States embracing Pakistan militarily as a threat to India's delicate position in Kashmir and anathema to his objective of keeping the subcontinent neutral in the cold war. The prospect of alienating Nehru to the point that India might withdraw from the Commonwealth would seriously dampen British enthusiasm for participating in any Middle Eastern consortium, regardless of its form.[115]

So daunting were these problems that NSC 162/2 conceded that "[i]n the Middle East, a strong regional grouping is not now feasible." Until one was, rather than pursue the MEDO "the United States should build on Turkey, Pakistan, and, if possible, Iran."[116] Eisenhower was caught in a quandary. Unlike advisors like Humphrey, who in the interest of economy recommended that the United States write off India, the president insisted that the free world could not afford to lose "a population of 350 million." The administration had to weigh the benefits, especially the potential benefits, as well as the costs of its policies and programs, including those toward neutrals. Pragmatism, not ideology or orthodoxy, must be its guide.[117]

The president was therefore adamant that India, despite its nonalignment, remain a recipient of U.S. aid. Yet he could not allow New Delhi, notwithstanding its importance to free world interests, to veto measures designed to promote regional strength. Hence Eisenhower agreed to extend military assistance to Pakistan even as he fretted about India's reaction to his doing so.[118] The Mutual Defense Assistance Agreement signed in May 1954, which Eisenhower later confessed to have been a "terrible error," and the subsequent Baghdad Pact among Pakistan, Turkey, Iraq, and Great Britain, represented, above all, the administration's capitulation to noncommunist weakness and disarray in the Middle East.[119]

Covert Operations and Psychological Warfare

Even as the Middle East's cacophony of priorities and symphony of anticolonial resentment militated against regional cooperation and pro-Western alliance formation, they invited communist propaganda and subversion. "[Soviet] Bloc political warfare capabilities will depend to a large degree not only upon the situation within the Bloc but also upon the success with which the non-Communist world meets the challenges to its stability which would exist even if there were no Communist threat," estimated the CIA.[120] The situation in Iran was testimony to this peril. "[T]here is increasing danger that relations between Iran and the West will deteriorate to such an extent," wrote Bradley early in the Eisenhower administration, "that Iran will fall into the Soviet orbit through the acquisition of power by the Tudeh [i.e., Iran's Communist] party."[121]

From the time he took office, Eisenhower sought to improve the covert and paramilitary capabilities of the United States to counter this very kind of threat. It was in part for this reason that he appointed Foster Dulles's brother, Allen, as director of the CIA.[122] More significantly, he asked Lt. General James Doolittle to chair a committee to evaluate the agency's past performance. "If the United States is to survive," it reported, "long-standing American concepts of 'fair play' must be reconsidered." The Doolittle Committee recommended that the CIA "learn to subvert, sabotage and destroy our enemies by more clever, more sophisticated and more effective methods than those used against us."[123]

Eisenhower agreed. Nevertheless, he "was much more constrained" than Truman when it came to sanctioning high-risk operations where the Soviets' vital interests were engaged.[124] Indeed, virtually concurrent with authorizing AJAX, Eisenhower rejected proposals to distribute arms to the East German rioters in June 1953, insisting that the United States confine its response to broadcasting praise for the insurgents' courage and compassion for their plight and orchestrating a modest food relief program. Eisenhower feared that the new Kremlin leaders might overreact to more ambitious projects. He feared no less that an overreaction by anxiety-ridden Western Europe would further divide the Alliance.[125] As illustrated by his reply to C.D. Jackson's suggestion in the aftermath of the June East German uprising that the administration seek "at once" to implement certain "bits and pieces" of Solarium Task Force C's recommended covert actions for "detaching Satellite X," the president's caution outweighed his sympathy. He instructed the Planning Board merely to study the matter.[126]

But Eisenhower actively embraced covert actions in regions like the Middle East, where the risk of triggering a general war was negligible and few political constraints applied. CIA director Allen Dulles was both more adventurous than his predecessor, Bedell Smith, and better insurance against poor coordination with the State Department. Iran became Dulles's first test, and he succeeded fully. By August 1953 the CIA had routed the Tudeh party, forced the resignation of Prime Minister Mohammed Mossadegh, and returned Shah Mohammad Reza Pahlavi to the Peacock Throne.[127]

The NSC did not predicate general policy toward the Middle East on the anticipation of many Irans, however. According to U.S. intelligence, the Tudeh party was atypically well organized. Further, while the success of Operation AJAX reinforced the administration's confidence that a Third World cancer as overtly malignant as it perceived Mossadegh to be could be isolated and surgically removed, a confidence buttressed by the ouster of Guatemala's Jacobo Arbenz in 1954,[128] it also reinforced the estimate that the Soviet rulers would "conclude that the area can be effectively denied to the West without being brought under direct Communist control and without forcing the USSR *prematurely* to accept full responsibility for supporting Communist regimes in the area." Moscow could therefore be expected to confine its efforts to encouraging "extremism of many kinds" in order to promote instability and accelerate the decline of Western influence.[129]

NSC 162/2 made clear that as a counter the United States should "assist in achieving stability" by extending military, economic, and technical assistance. But this assistance would have to be "limited" to what America could afford and the Middle Eastern nations could absorb. And what held true for the Middle East applied throughout the periphery. Therefore, NSC 162/2 placed a premium on U.S. propaganda and psychological warfare. These "political actions" would serve, on the one hand, to "discredit Soviet prestige and ideology as effective instruments of Soviet power." On the other hand, they "are needed to persuade uncommitted countries that their best interests lie in greater cooperation and stronger affiliations with the rest of the free world."[130]

The interest of Eisenhower and Dulles in psychological warfare, already discussed, led to the early establishment of the Jackson Committee on International Information Activities, which had recommended that the Psychological Strategy Board be replaced by the Operations Coordinating Board. Even before the Jackson Committee completed its examination, Allen Dulles reported that "propaganda and psychological warfare programs have developed to an unprecedented degree." Two of the primary instruments were Radio Free Europe and Radio Liberty, which unlike the Voice of America were wholly subsidized by the CIA.[131]

Similar to covert operations, the focus of much of Eisenhower's psychological warfare was on nations and regions beyond the direct control of Moscow and Peking. But unlike covert operations, the reason had less to do with Eisenhower's concern over the possible consequences than with his acknowledgment of limited capabilities. "Our national psychological effort is at greatest disadvantage in the USSR and Communist China," read the report Eisenhower received from the Psychological Strategy Board the day after he took office. "U.S. psychological actions, within the limits of the world power position, are slowly but steadily improving, but they remain inadequate for taking immediately effective psychological action contributing to a retraction of the Kremlin's power and influence."[132] The testimony presented to the Jackson Committee was equally unequivocal. "[O]ur capabilities to affect the satellites or the USSR are limited and are steadily *decreasing*," said the CIA's Robert Lounsbury. "Miracles might happen," added R. W. Tufts of the Department of State, "but it is unwise to count on them."[133]

The administration did not believe that psychological warfare would produce a miracle in the Middle East either. "Notwithstanding its efforts to serve as moderator and mediator," the United States, in the minds of many of the region's nationalists, was tainted by its association with their former masters, whose imperious attitudes and behavior continued to grate on indigenous sensibilities, and by its support for Israel.[134] Still, broadcasts, the distribution of literature, and comparable programs could "combat, particularly in the Near and Middle East . . . extremist tendencies threatening the undermining of the cohesion and stability of the free world and withdrawals of governments and peoples into neutralism." More positively, Eisenhower intended his psychological strategy for the Middle East to "strengthen Western influence" by "establishing a new relationship with these states which will recognize their desire to achieve status and respect for their sovereign equality."[135] That was Eisenhower's goal throughout the developing world.

14

Reducing the Nuclear Danger: Arms Control

Of the various presidential tasks to which I early determined to devote my energies, none transcended in importance that of trying to devise practical and acceptable means to lighten the burdens of armaments and to lessen the likelihood of war.[1]

Dwight D. Eisenhower (1965)

The effort to constrain the arms race and to reduce the risk of war was a major component of Eisenhower's strategy. His commitment to this aim was rooted in some of his strongest convictions. For him, as we have stressed, nuclear weapons were a curse: they posed an unprecedented direct threat to the U.S. society and economy, and he seemed haunted by the specter of a global nuclear holocaust. In various meetings, he reiterated the view "that he could perceive no final answer to the problem of nuclear warfare if both sides simply went ahead making bigger and better nuclear weapons."[2] As he repeatedly said, he would gladly have abolished them if that had been feasible with certainty.[3] Because it was not, deterrence of their use was essential. But the inevitable arms competition entailed its own dangers as well as the waste of enormous resources. And the fear of nuclear war imposed severe strains on the allied cohesion required for containment.

Eisenhower's earlier concerns had been greatly reinforced by two Atomic Energy Commission briefings he received as president-elect in November 1952 to bring him up to date. They had impressed on him the increasing tempo of weapons tests; the startling improvements in weapons design and destructive power; and most of all, the recent successful test of an American thermonuclear device in the Pacific.[4] Then the following August came the Soviet test of its own thermonuclear device.

Eisenhower was preoccupied with these forebodings and with what could be done to mitigate them from the beginning to the end of his tenure. In his inaugural he said, "We stand ready to engage with any and all others in joint efforts to remove the causes of mutual fear and distrust among nations so as to make possible drastic reductions in armaments."[5] Indeed, nearly a year earlier, while SACEUR, he had expressed the hope that after the NATO buildup the Soviet leaders "may finally be willing to participate seriously in disarmament negotiations."[6] After swearing in Lewis L. Strauss as AEC chairman in July 1953, Eisenhower told him, "Lewis, let us be clear about *this*: my chief concern and your first assignment is to find some new approach to the *dis*arming of atomic energy."[7] And finally, in his memoirs, he wrote that "the little success in making progress in global disarmament or in reducing the bitterness of the East-West struggle" was "my greatest disappointment on leaving the White House."[8]

Oppenheimer Panel

The daunting difficulties Eisenhower would face in making any progress were made manifest by two reports awaiting the president on taking office. One was a progress report on NSC 112 ("Formulation of a United States Position with Respect to the Regulation, Limitation, and Balanced Reduction of Armed Forces and Armaments," approved on January 19, 1951) submitted by Truman's secretaries of state and defense that reviewed the 1952 activities of the UN Disarmament Commission that was charged with developing treaties for comprehensive disarmament, including outlawing nuclear weapons, and means for verification and safeguards. In essence, the report stated that the United States had provided the commission working papers on various relevant topics, but that the Soviets had responded merely with propaganda.[9]

Far more significant was a long report on disarmament completed in mid-January after eight months of study by a distinguished panel of consultants appointed by Secretary Acheson.[10] The panel members were Robert Oppenheimer (chair), Vannevar Bush, John S. Dickey, Allen W. Dulles, and Joseph E. Johnson. As indicated by its title—"Armaments and American Policy"—their report considered the subject in a wide context.

In its analysis the report contrasted the stalemate on arms regulations with the unprecedented menace of the nuclear arms race. The Soviets, it asserted, had not negotiated seriously on arms regulation since 1946, but had merely engaged in propaganda for reasons of basic hostility, distrust, and secrecy. And serious Western interest had flagged as a result of frustration and the focus on rearming.

The panel summed up its conclusion in "three general propositions which are hard to reconcile with one another."

"First, no regulation of armaments, however limited, has ever proved feasible except as part of a genuine political settlement." The experience of the 1920s and 1930s with arms limitation in the Pacific and Europe seemed to indicate that effective arms control depended on resolving the major political problems as a prerequisite.

"Second, . . . even if peaceful coexistence is possible . . . it certainly seems unlikely to involve anything that could be called a general settlement for some time to come." The cold war conflict was too deep-seated for "any genuine large-scale political settlement . . . within the present generation." Thus the only recourse "was to maintain armed strength adequate to deter and, if attacked, defeat the Soviets."[11]

But "the argument cannot safely be ended there." To do so would ignore the vital third proposition: "[U]nless the contest in atomic armaments is in some way moderated, our whole society will come increasingly into a period of the gravest kind."[12]

The atomic arms race posed a unique danger in three respects: 1) "unprecedented destructive power is accumulating, probably on both sides, at a quite phenomenal rate"; 2) the effect is to put "the heart" of both the Soviet Union and the United States "into the front line of any major military contest"; and 3) the United States "is heavily committed to a swift and almost unlimited use of atomic retaliation in the event of major Soviet aggression."[13]

Together, these three features created compelling reasons for wishing "to find some way to get these weapons under control."[14] Regrettably, however, the panel could suggest no way to launch serious negotiations for that purpose or to overcome the obstacles of Soviet secrecy, their lack of a sense of mutual advantage from disarmament, and the level of suspicion and tension.[15]

Yet despite their pessimism about the desperate dilemma, they refused to abandon all hope. Even negotiation, which then seemed so remote and unlikely, "may become feasible in the reasonably near future." After all, the "dangers of the arms race are at least as great for the Soviet Union as they are for the United States, and the passage of time may well increase the pressure on the Kremlin for serious consideration of alternatives to the present policy."[16]

Accordingly, the five specific recommendations of the panel did not include disarmament proposals. They were to gradually discontinue participation in the UN Disarmament Committee as futile; to expand direct contacts with the Soviet Union if only to minimize the chances of miscalculation or to detect any shift in Soviet attitudes that might occur when Stalin died, or from the impact of the arms race, or from the growing potential for mutual annihilation; to intensify greatly the building of continental defense; to involve allies more closely in nuclear planning; and, finally, to adopt greater official candor in informing the public of the nuclear predicament in order to sustain trust and support.[17]

On arms regulation the panel limited itself to general advice proffered in an annex. Developing "detailed blueprints" was premature and undesirable. Moreover, any future proposals should be judged against the existing dangerous situation and "not against some arbitrary vision of a world of total peace and harmony." More specifically, the panel offered three general guidelines: seek to curtail the reciprocal capacity for devastating surprise attack; seek methods of verification that minimize direct intrusion; and ensure that nuclear reductions do not destabilize the security balance.[18]

Eisenhower's Reaction

The president found the analysis of the Oppenheimer Report largely congenial with his own thinking about the nuclear danger. At one of the first NSC meetings, on February 18, 1953, he asked the other members of the Council whether they had read the report (which had been distributed) "and said that he expected all to do so and to be thoroughly familiar with the conclusions and recommendations." The memorandum of the NSC discussion recorded the president himself as expressing "a high opinion of the report," although he was doubtful about its advice to disengage from UN discussions about disarmament. To do so, he remarked, might be "bad psychologically."[19]

The NSC discussed the Oppenheimer Report and the Progress Report on NSC 112 briefly at its meetings on February 18 and 25. Consistent with the president's views, the Council agreed not to disengage from UN discussions of disarmament, as the panel suggested, but to take a "temporizing position" in the forthcoming UN General Assembly while exploring "the possibility of a new U.S. proposal" by its September session.[20] On the panel's proposal for greater "candor" with the public about the implications of eventual nuclear plenty, the president was "unconvinced." Nevertheless, he agreed to refer the report to the NSC Senior Staff (the precursor to the Planning Board) for a study of carrying out all of its recommendations.[21]

The death of Stalin on March 5 opened up the possibility of a radical change by his successors, especially in the field of the atomic danger. Would the new leaders be more aware of the dangers of nuclear plenty and of the common interest in minimizing the risks and burdens, or more flexible in their approach to safeguards and controls? In his "Chance for Peace" speech, Eisenhower took a much broader approach. The agenda it laid out, as we have seen, was a comprehensive program for ending the cold war, starting with the settling of major political issues as a prelude to tackling the radical reduction and control of armaments.

When that sweeping initiative proved sterile, Eisenhower adopted a very modest, long-term strategy for making gradual progress by small steps. Its premise was that the Soviet leaders would pursue their expansionist purposes, but that even so the Soviet Union actually would share a common interest with the West in avoiding suicidal nuclear catastrophe. Hence the task was both to convince the Soviet leaders of the need to cooperate to minimize the nuclear danger and burden and to devise adequate methods of verification that they might accept. He recognized that the criterion of verification should not be absolute certainty of detecting evasion, but should be to assure that the risks of violation of the specific restraints were less than those of unconstrained arms competition. This strategy presupposed that limited joint measures might gradually erode distrust and the Soviet obsession with secrecy, and open the way for more significant restraints. The early steps would be judged more by their contribution to getting the process started than by the degree of arms control achieved.[22]

Eisenhower explained his approach in a letter to his brother and closest confidant, Milton, about his "Atoms for Peace" speech:

> It grew out of my original basic idea that as long as the more extensive Baruch plan had been rejected by the Soviets—and in the absence of any new idea we found everything to be on dead center that involved the effort to do anything with atomic energy aside from making bombs —that possibly a gradual approach would open up new possibilities, new lines of study, and bring some hope to replace fear in the world.[23]

In his approach Eisenhower received almost no help from his top advisors. As he himself recalled, for many months "disarmament was a subject of varying, and often sharply opposing, views among departments and agencies of the United States government and outside them."[24] The issue arose during the first two years in four different contexts: (1) fixing the U.S. course for meetings of the UN General Assembly and its Disarmament Commission; (2) drafting the basic national security paper (NSC 162); (3) preparing the "Candor" speech ("Atoms for Peace"); and (4) the work of the Special Committee charged with reviewing U.S. disarmament policy. Most of these strands of policy-making proceeded more or less in parallel and involved the same top officials. Our effort to trace their course will reveal the diversity of views regarding the feasibility and desirability of arms regulation and appropriate U.S. policy. As will become apparent, none of his principal advisors shared the president's convictions or commitment in this period. Active support came mainly from State's Policy Planning Staff and a few midlevel officials in the State Department and the AEC, and their efforts achieved little success in overcoming top-level resistance, though gradually Secretary Dulles began to modify his "traditional" views. At an NSC meeting in May 1954 Eisenhower, frustrated by the attitudes of its members, said that he "believed it was wrong for the United States merely to take a negative view of this terrible problem. We must try to find some positive answer, and to do so would require more imaginative thinking than was going on at the present in this Government."[25] Indeed, it was the president himself who dictated the disarmament portion of the "Chance for Peace" speech and who had originated the "atomic pool" idea of "Atoms for Peace." And the later "Open Skies" proposal at the 1955 Summit had come to him from an unofficial panel.[26]

U.S. Position in UN Disarmament Commission

Dulles's original plan to pursue merely a "temporizing" or "delaying" tactic in the UN disarmament discussions was somewhat complicated by the death of Stalin.[27] The policy guidance adopted in mid-May for the U.S. activities in the Disarmament Commission still called for no new initiatives; for primarily exploring and probing the Soviet position; and for reiterating earlier concepts concerning safeguarded disarmament. The "peace offensive" of Stalin's successors had included some changes in earlier Soviet positions designed to make them appear nearer to Western proposals, but it was unclear whether these were serious moves or merely more skillful propaganda or tactical gestures intended to split the West. In either case, they meant that the United States could not rely solely on past Soviet intransigence to discredit them. The basic U.S. position, it was decided, should be that taken by President Eisenhower's "Chance for Peace" speech: settlements of major political issues were necessary to create the trust needed for proceeding with arms reduction. In case Soviet concessions or other pressures required more, the United States should be ready with new studies, such as on the control organ, or even to elaborate on its disarmament program for safeguarded balanced reductions and atomic control based on the UN plan, unless modified by the pending U.S. studies and review of disarmament policy.[28]

Thereafter the NSC Planning Board on September 1 submitted a report on the possibility of a new U.S. disarmament proposal for the UN General Assembly as requested by the NSC in February. In essence the report reiterated the substance of the May guidance: no progress was likely; major political settlements were preconditions; serious negotiations on disarmament were likely to progress only bilaterally or multilaterally outside the UN; and previous U.S. principles and concepts remained valid. Because the Soviet "peace offensive" and its August test of a hydrogen bomb or device had heightened allied interest in arms control, however, the United States should show its abiding desire for comprehensive and safeguarded disarmament by proposing a UN resolution affirming the principles from the "Chance for Peace" speech. Appended was an analysis of the advantages and disadvantages of the various possible disarmament proposals, concluding against submitting any of them.[29]

The NSC approved the recommendations of the report, with one exception. The UN (Baruch) Plan should not be reaffirmed, because it was outmoded. The technical inability to account for past production of fissionable materials made the plan inherently unworkable. For the present, the United States should merely say that its past proposals had been designed to conform to principles it still espoused.

But the NSC recognized that the United States now had no viable disarmament plan. It needed a thorough review of its disarmament policy, which had not been seriously examined since the adoption of NSC 112 in July 1951. Accordingly, the NSC requested the president to designate the secretaries of state and defense and the AEC chairman as a special committee to undertake such a review and report "as a matter of urgency . . . with particular reference to international control of atomic energy."[30] The work of the Special Committee will be discussed after considering how this issue was handled in drafting NSC 162/2 and in preparing the "Atoms for Peace" speech.

Negotiation in Basic National Security Strategy

In the drafting of the basic national security strategy, the role of negotiation in reducing the Soviet threat and the nuclear danger emerged as an extremely contentious issue that was debated through 1954 and even beyond. The JCS (except for General Ridgway) vigorously pressed their fixed negative view. Eisenhower's other advisors were less clear or were inconsistent.

The reason for the divergent views was not that anyone expected that a general agreement on comprehensive disarmament could be achieved anytime soon. On the contrary, as already discussed, six months after Stalin's death policy makers and the CIA concurred in the conviction that his successors were firmly committed to his expansionist policies despite their conciliatory "gestures" and more moderate style.

Thus with no dissent NSC 162/2 recognized "that the prospects for acceptable negotiated settlements are not encouraging. There is no evidence that the [new] Soviet leadership is prepared to modify its basic attitudes and accept any permanent settlement with the United States, although it may be prepared for a *modus vivendi* on certain issues." Control of atomic and other major weapons, which would require adequate and enforceable safeguards, including international inspection and supervision, would be extremely difficult for either side to accept under existing conditions of suspicion and distrust. The prospects might, however, be improved by resolving conflicts or by the eventual Soviet realization that armaments limitation would serve their own interests and security. "The United States," paragraph 14 of NSC 162/2 continued, "should promptly determine what it would accept as an adequate system of armament control which would effectively remove or reduce the Soviet atomic and military threat."[31]

Even the Defense Department and JCS did not object to providing that the "United States must also keep open the possibility of negotiating with the USSR and Communist China, acceptable and enforceable agreements, whether limited to individual issues now outstanding or involving a general settlement of major issues, including control of armaments." The Soviet willingness to reach agreements might be enhanced over time if the West increased its strength and cohesion and maintained a sufficient retaliatory deterrent, or "if for any reason Soviet stability and influence are reduced."[32]

In the drafting of NSC 162/2 the split in the Planning Board on this issue between the JCS and State and others was precisely about under what conditions or for what purposes serious negotiations should be pursued. State's Planning Board member contended that, although a general settlement would require a basic change in Soviet objectives and policies, it might be possible while the cold war continued to reach agreements settling some issues or mitigating the nuclear danger. But as its draft paragraph stated, any such reduction of the Soviet threat could be attained "only through settlements which both the United States and the USSR find it in their interest to accept."[33]

The JCS adamantly opposed *any* negotiations until the Soviet Union radically changed its basic purposes and attitudes (i.e., as a result of the success of containment or rollback). Until then any negotiation would be contrary to U.S. interests and security. As expressed in their draft of the split paragraph: "Short of initiating general war, substantial reduction of the Soviet threat over a longer period of time can be accomplished only by actions designed to bring about a negotiating attitude in the USSR and its resulting accommodation to the security of the United States and that of the free world."[34]

The NSC took up the issue at its meeting on October 7. Divorced from the underlying debate in the Planning Board, the text of the split in the draft of NSC 162 was too elliptical to make entirely clear the real divergences, and it was further clouded by Cutler's misleading presentation already discussed. Dulles, however, who had been fully briefed as usual the afternoon before, understood the issue and attacked the JCS position forcefully. He strongly asserted that the United States could not impose agreement for the reduction of armaments on the Soviet Union. The same applied to negotiations concerning Korea or Austria. Later he "warned again that in his view we could not reduce tensions with the USSR if in each case we expected to gain all the advantage and the Soviets none. Such settlements, he repeated, must be mutually acceptable." At the president's suggestion, both of the proposed alternatives were deleted, leaving only the remaining provisions on "keeping open the possibility of negotiations" and the factors that might enhance it.[35]

The JCS and Department of Defense were still primarily concerned with blocking serious negotiations on nuclear disarmament or arms control. So the following April, when guidelines were being developed for implementing NSC 162/2 and the Special Committee was considering disarmament policy, the JCS mounted a special study on "Negotiations with the Soviet Bloc" and submitted their report to the NSC and Special Committee through the Defense Department in June. The report elaborated and justified their earlier position. Convinced that the East-West struggle had "entered a precarious if not critical stage," the JCS briefly reviewed Soviet tactics and methods for expansion, including the use of negotiation. In this context, they concluded that "Soviet bad faith, evasion, and outright violation would render any disarmament agreement sterile, except as a means to advance Soviet objectives." Moreover, "the Iron Curtain would make a mockery of any inspection system which might be devised." The Soviets would not "make substantive concessions in the course of international negotiations, even on a *quid pro quo* basis, unless and until they have been convinced that failure to achieve lasting solutions of major issues will entail grave risks to the maintenance of their regime." (Hence the urgent necessity for a "positive" Western policy before nuclear plenty, as already discussed.) Until then negotiations will be "not only fruitless but hazardous" due to allied "irresolution" and the slippery-slope danger. Consequently, until the requisite change in basic Soviet attitude, the United States should refrain from negotiations "on the subjects of disarmament, atomic energy, or any other of the world issues."[36]

Shortly thereafter, the NSC considered NSC 5422 (the guidelines for NSC 162/2 submitted by the Planning Board on June 14). On disarmament, the paper again contained split positions. The JCS proposed that the topic not be treated pending the review by the Special Committee and also questioned whether any safe system was feasible in view of the uncertainties about past nuclear production and Soviet secrecy. The alternative (State) position urged exploring fully the possibility of a practical arms limitation, especially of safeguards less risky than no limitation and effective nuclear disarmament without conventional disarmament.[37]

At the NSC meeting on the paper, Eisenhower said that the two sides of this split were not in substantive conflict. The JCS doubts were not incompatible with the position "that the United States [should] continue to reexamine its position on disarmament and especially to determine whether safeguards could be devised entailing less risk for U.S. security than no limitation of armaments. No one in his right mind," Eisenhower continued, "would disagree that we should continue to examine this question." As to accepting nuclear disarmament without conventional, he repeated that he would gladly do so if that could be "sure and enforceable," but he added that appeared impossible "in the foreseeable future."[38] Thus the substance of both sides of the split was combined in the Guidelines (NSC 5422/2) as approved on August 7, 1954.[39] Yet Eisenhower's comment left no doubt about his determination to seek negotiations.

During the fall the Planning Board prepared a new version of the basic national security paper to integrate and update both NSC 162/2 and the guidelines for its implementation (NSC 5422/2). With respect to negotiation with the U.S.S.R., the new draft essentially reproduced the prior positions of State and the JCS. Both accepted that "[t]he U.S. should be ready to negotiate with the USSR whenever it clearly appears that the US security interests will be served thereby"; and that the United States should advance constructive proposals "to put the Soviets on the defensive and win public support on both sides of the Iron Curtain." Then came the split: the JCS side opposing any negotiations until there occurred "a basic change in Soviet attitude" (to be induced, according to their memo of comments, by positive measures "which inherently will threaten the continued existence of their regime");[40] the State side espousing active negotiations for settling specific issues, for seeking to reduce tensions, and for mitigating the Soviet threat (as by safeguarded limitation of armaments).[41] In their "detailed" comments, however, the JCS proposed to substitute, as the essential precondition for negotiations with the Soviets, "demonstrated good faith."[42]

When the NSC considered the draft on December 21, Cutler asked for specific Council guidance regarding negotiation. Dulles at once proposed confining the paragraph to the two agreed sentences quoted above, dropping both alternatives of the split. The president thought that proposal sufficient; "we should negotiate whenever and wherever it looks profitable." That, he had already said, "could really only be dealt with on a case-by-case basis." The JCS argument that entering negotiations "would cause the free world to let down its military guard seemed to be based on the assumption that the State Department was incapable of distinguishing fraudulent from honest changes in the Soviet attitude." Moreover, Eisenhower stressed that "we cannot hope to get continued support of public opinion in the free world if we always say 'no' to any suggestions that we negotiate with the Soviets." After further discussion, it was decided to adopt only the first sentence of the paragraph expressing American readiness to negotiate "whenever it clearly apppears that U.S. security interests would be served thereby."[43]

Thus the paper provided no real guidance regarding arms limitation except to endorse its active pursuit and to reject the rigid JCS restriction on negotiation. Any more specific proposals or direction were left to the Special Committee that was reviewing NSC 112 at the same time.

"Atoms for Peace"

The report of the NSC Planning Board on the Oppenheimer Panel (NSC 151), endorsing the recommendation for greater "candor" regarding the nuclear predicament, was considered by the NSC on May 27 with Bush and Oppenheimer attending. Some concern was expressed about merely frightening the public; the president commented that the "emphasis should be on vigilance and sobriety, not on panic." Before deciding to proceed, Eisenhower said, he wanted to see a draft of a speech, which he asked C. D. Jackson to prepare.[44]

Achieving an acceptable speech took six months. According to Jackson, "Many drafts of Candor [were written from late May] through September—[but] none were satisfactory because they either told too much or too little and were uniformly dull." After a moratorium pending new ideas, Jackson polled top officials by letter on September 25 as to whether to proceed with a speech, despite the "absolute rash" of press and radio coverage of the subject.[45]

In the light of their replies Jackson wrote a briefing memorandum on October 2 for the president in preparation for a meeting the next day. "The need for a frank speech on the atomic age and Continental Defense is, if anything, greater than ever." But, Jackson went on, "It must besides contain a tremendous lift for the world — for the hopes of men everywhere." It must be a package meeting "three requirements Foster Dulles has in mind": (1) contain fresh proposals acceptable to the Russians if they wish coexistence; (2) not jeopardize the West if accepted; and (3) make clear, if rejected, that the "moral blame for the armaments race, and possibly war, is clearly on the Russians" and "that we must all prepare for the worst." Secretary Dulles, he suggested, should be charged with producing such a "package." In a burst of hyperpole Jackson added, "This can not only be the most important pronouncement ever made by any President of the United States, it could also save mankind."[46]

The "package" idea was apparently derived from Dulles's proposal for a "spectacular effort" for global detente, outlined in his memorandum of September 6 and discussed the next day with the president, as already described.[47] Clearly, however, Jackson's billing for it entered the realm of fantasy. No speech, no matter how inspired, could hope to resolve the cold war at a stroke. And the package itself posed formidable problems.

At a breakfast meeting on October 3, attended by Secretary Dulles, Jackson, Strauss, Radford, Stassen, and Allen Dulles (as well as Emmet Hughes and John Eisenhower), the president approved the suggested course and asked Secretary Dulles to prepare a draft for the second half of the "Candor" speech. Dulles assigned the task to Robert Bowie, director of State's Policy Planning Staff and its Planning Board member. Despite grave personal doubts about the enterprise, Bowie, working with Dulles, labored to produce a draft speech based on the secretary's "concepts," suitable for delivery at the UN, and seeking to meet the criteria enumerated by Jackson.[48]

The speech, of course, *also* had to be consistent with the basis for a secure peace set out in Eisenhower's "Chance for Peace" speech in April. His speech had not, however, indicated what concessions the United States might be prepared to offer in return for those requested from the Soviet Union. As a prelude to possible negotiation, the package could not afford to be too precise or detailed. Within these constraints the draft attempted to suggest the sorts of accommodations that could be discussed if the Soviets wished to reach a general settlement. Thus in arms control the United States would be ready to make major nuclear reductions, its field of advantage, if accompanied by conventional reductions and controls, such that the aggregate balance of forces would remain unchanged, if buttressed by safeguards to ensure compliance. Under these conditions the United States would be prepared to accept limitations of its forces and facilities located outside its borders in return for a Soviet withdrawal from Eastern Europe and freeing of the satellites, which could, however, remain "friendly" to the Soviet Union and would not be allied with the West. The West would, however, insist that a unified Germany be allowed to be a member of the European Defense Community as the most reliable means of ensuring future peace and security within Western Europe and safeguarding against a revival of German militarism and aggression. Furthermore, to ensure that Soviet security was not prejudiced, measures could be worked out for a demilitarized zone in the area of East Germany and Austria, and for mutual nonaggression pacts. "In Asia, the outstanding issues should be settled on similar principles, starting with the creation of a unified Korea and restoration of stable peace in Southeast Asia." The whole program would require safeguards of various kinds, including inspections and enforcing compliance with arms control agreements. A special UN agency might be organized for these functions.[49]

In presenting the draft to the Planning Board on October 14, Bowie outlined some of the complications inherent in the effort. He first stressed that it was not intended as propaganda but as a "serious proposal which the Russians might accept. It contains the maximum concessions consistent with U.S. security interests." While addressed to the Soviet leaders, it also sought to explain the U.S. position to the American people and the allies.

He went on to suggest some dilemmas and concerns. Was a speech the best "way to initiate serious negotiations with the U.S.S.R.?" The State Department would prefer quiet talks. Were the objectives of explaining America's position to the U.S. public and our allies while testing Soviet intentions concerning a settlement feasible in a single speech?

"The speech is purposefully vague and does not put all our cards on the table," Bowie said. "The objective is to make it as a 'come on' to the Russians, but not give away one's negotiating hand." Moreover, the draft was intentionally fuzzy "regarding Asia because of the Congressional political dynamite" involved in these issues. The president, however, had found the draft to be clear when Secretary Dulles had read it to him.

The parts of the package, Bowie stressed, were interdependent. Until nuclear weapons were controlled, the United States could not withdraw its forces and abandon its bases. Further, "there is no prospect of any improvement" in U.S.-Soviet relations without disarmament. The objective was not to abolish nuclear weapons but to reduce and control them.

Most of the other Planning Board members and Cutler vigorously criticized the draft. Some focused on ambiguities but doubted it was in America's interest to be more specific. The Defense Department and JCS members denounced any disarmament proposal as impractical and unwise; it was likely to be interpreted and exploited by the Kremlin as a sign of defeatism and fear of the growing Soviet nuclear capacity. Any offer of force withdrawals would "blow up NATO." The proposal as a whole, they said, would be twisted and exploited by the Soviets. Several days later, Cutler sent Dulles and Eisenhower memoranda summarizing the reactions of the Planning Board and himself.[50]

Meanwhile, the secretary, who had been attending a foreign ministers meeting in London, had talked to Walter Hallstein, the West German secretary of state for foreign affairs, and Herve Alphand, the French ambassador to NATO.[51] They allayed some of the profound pessimism underlying his September 6 memorandum. On his return, he wrote Eisenhower that he had reconsidered the views expressed in his September 6 memorandum and now concluded "that we ought not seriously

to seek discussion with the the Soviets until decisions have been taken on E.D.C."
Premature discussions would be used by the Soviets to disrupt Western defense
plans and paralyze progress on the E.D.C. "There may be a fair chance of some settlement with the Russians," Dulles thought, "if we have a firm foundation in Western Europe—but not before." Accordingly, the far-reaching proposals of the State
Department draft "should be held back until after the first of the year."

Moreover, the "cogent comments" of the Planning Board on that draft

> compel me to conclude that it is probably a mistake to try to make serious proposals by
> means of a public speech. The specific and simple terms desirable for a speech are not
> a good basis for beginning negotiations. Either they seem to give away too much of
> one's case or else they seem to be merely propaganda, which would be likely to pro-
> voke only a propaganda response. . . . [W]hen the time comes, the approach should
> be primarly private.[52]

Thereupon, still seeking an ending for the "Candor" speech, Jackson turned to
an idea suggested by the president himself in early September. While vacationing
in Denver, Eisenhower "began to search" for some initiative on the "atomic problem" that would sidestep "Russian intransigence" on inspection. "One day [he] hit
upon" the following proposal, which he asked Jackson and Strauss to consider:

> Suppose the United States and the Soviets were each to turn over to the United
> Nations, for peaceful use, X kilograms of fissionable material.
> The amount X could be fixed at a figure which we could handle from our stock-
> pile, but which it would be difficult for the Soviets to match.[53]

AEC chairman Strauss's initial reaction was tepid: "The proposal is novel and
might have value for propaganda purposes," he wrote Eisenhower. But "[i]t has
doubtful value as a practical move." It was risky and might favor the Soviets. The
United States knew too little about the relative size of the two stockpiles and their
rates of expansion; and the nature of the hydrogen bomb made the size of the stockpile of fissionable material less important. Still, the "proposal ought to be carefully
explored."[54]

When Eisenhower insisted on further study, Strauss developed a more elaborate
plan based on the idea of a nuclear materials "bank." His proposal, which he discussed with Secretary Dulles on October 31, called for both sides to stop the mining
and refining of uranium and the production of plutonium and to transfer increments of existing nuclear material to an international agency for storage in a secure
location and physical state to be available for peaceful uses. The inspection required for this scheme, he felt, would be much less onerous and more feasible than
for direct control of nuclear weapons, which might come later.[55] This plan greatly
appealed to Jackson, and he incorporated it into his next draft for the "Candor"
speech. Strong objections came at once from the JCS, who adamantly opposed any
such partial measure of arms control as stopping the production of fissile materials.
Accordingly, those provision were deleted.[56] The speech was shown to the British
and French at the Bermuda meeting in early December and delivered at the UN
on December 8. In its final form this portion of the speech proclaimed: "The
United States, heeding the suggestion of the General Assembly of the United

Nations, is instantly prepared to meet privately with such other countries as may be 'principally involved' to seek 'an acceptable solution' to the atomic armaments race which overshadows not only peace but the very life of the world."[57] The United States, he said, would "carry into these private or diplomatic talks a new conception," namely: "The Governments principally involved, to the extent permitted by elementary prudence, to begin now and continue to make joint contributions from their stockpiles of normal uranium and fissionable materials to an International Atomic Energy Agency."

Conceding that initial contributions would be small, Eisenhower stressed his rationale for the proposal. It "has the great virtue that it can be undertaken without the irritations and mutual suspicions incident to any attempt to set up a completely acceptable system of world-wide inspection and control." Among the benefits he perceived was to "open up a new channel for peaceful discussion, and initiate at least a new approach to the many difficult problems that must be solved" in order "to make positive progress toward peace."[58]

The speech was generally well received around the world. The Soviet response, however, while accepting talks, was negative on the grounds that the proposal failed to limit the use of nuclear weapons or the arms race. Eisenhower confided his own appraisal of the speech to his diary. He recognized that this proposal was extremely modest — "the tiniest of starts," was how he described it. Still, it served some useful purposes. It might get the Soviet Union working with the United States on some aspect of the nuclear field, and if successful, might lead to something more consequential. The avoidance of inspection might induce their participation. If they refused, there would still be some propaganda benefits. And finally, as the Oppenheimer Panel had advised, he had described the nuclear predicament, and the size and strength of atomic capabilities, as an argument for peaceful negotiation rather than a contributor to the "atmosphere of truculence, defiance, and threat." And he concluded, "Underlying all of this, of course, is the clear conviction that as of now the world is racing toward catastrophe — that something must be done to put a brake on the movement." Speeches, while not a brake, may encourage people to "devise ways and means by which the possible disaster of the future can be avoided."[59]

How to implement the president's speech promptly provoked intense dispute within the government, reflecting basic divergences regarding disarmament. Eisenhower had made two proposals: (1) private talks "to seek 'an acceptable solution' to the atomic armaments race," and (2) the creation of an atomic materials pool under an international agency. What was the relation of the two? What was required by the first? After all, Bohlen, as instructed by Dulles, had explicitly told Molotov that the "chief purpose of [the] speech was specifically to state U.S. willingness to talk privately on [the] whole atomic armaments problem with [the] Soviet government and others interested" and that it was "a sincere and serious offer by the President."[60] In a December 28 meeting Bowie, who had been named to head the State Working Party on the speech, interpreted this to imply a serious effort to explore what might be done toward atomic arms control "without reference to total disarmament, including conventional weapons." Frank Nash, representing Defense, vigorously opposed this view, contending that this would reverse all past disarmament and current defense planning. Jackson reported this clash to the president, who suggested that Secretaries Dulles and Wilson, Strauss, and Jackson meet with him on this matter.[61]

Before the meeting took place Dulles, after a preliminary session with Eisenhower, met with the other top advisors to concert their views. They readily agreed that in discussions with the Soviets the United States should concentrate on the president's atomic pool proposal and merely listen to the Soviets on nuclear disarmament, which they viewed as wholly impractical without the ending of the Iron Curtain and other basic changes in Soviet policy.[62] In his meeting with the group Eisenhower reiterated his readiness to abolish nuclear weapons separately if fully reliable safeguards were feasible, but he recognized that was impossible under existing conditions. Consequently, the president approved the consensus that the United States would listen to any Soviet proposals for control or abolition of nuclear weapons but would not "be drawn into" any negotiations on this subject, and would press for entirely separate negotiations on the peaceful use of atomic energy.[63]

Three years of tortuous negotiations were required for the foundation of the International Atomic Energy Agency in mid-1957.

The Special Committee: A New Disarmament Policy?

The Special Committee (secretaries of state and defense and AEC chairman) appointed in mid-September 1953 to review disarmament policy had been asked to make their report "as a matter of urgency." Yet five months later the committee had apparently not met and had submitted no report. Indeed, there is no record that it followed up on Strauss's October plan for a production cutoff and pool of atomic materials.[64] All work going on in State's Policy Planning Staff or the Defense Department's staffs was self-initiated. In consequence, at an NSC meeting on February 11, 1954, after an oral report by Cutler, the president requested the Special Committee to "expedite" its review and report.[65]

Two months later, citing "the lack of progress to date" by the Special Committee, Secretary Wilson advised Secretary Dulles of his appointment of Major General Herbert B. Loper to head a Department of Defense working group and suggested that he meet with State Department and AEC counterparts promptly to initiate the study.[66]

At their first meeting on April 14, they formed a working group composed of Bowie (State), Loper (Defense), and John Hall (AEC).[67] This started an intensive process of studies and debate, first within the working group and the NSC Planning Board, and ultimately among the principals, that went on for some nine months.

Meanwhile, the Special Committee itself was called on to advise the NSC regarding a proposal for the suspension of nuclear tests submitted to the UN Disarmament Committee by India in early April. That initiative had been provoked by the contamination of Japanese fishermen by radioactive fallout from a U.S. thermonuclear test in the Marshall Islands on March 26. The event had created a widespread reaction in Japan, Britain, and elsewhere, "driving our allies away from us," Dulles said.[68]

The issue of whether the United States should agree to such a test moratorium was thrashed out in three NSC sessions. At the first on May 6 Strauss, Radford, and Wilson were strongly opposed. Dulles, leaving aside the technical aspect, was favorably inclined because of the propaganda advantages in calming fear and opposition to nuclear weapons in allied and other public opinion. Dulles, Wilson, and Strauss, with CIA assistance, were asked to report on the "desirability of an international moratorium."[69]

The opponents elaborated their objections. Conforming to NSC 112, a JCS memorandum, supported by Defense, opposed any restriction on atomic weapons or tests separate from a "comprehensive program" for restricting "all armed forces and all armaments."[70] Strauss emphasized the risks of Soviet evasion, the uncertainty of policing any ceiling, and the potential loss of valuable technical advances or even the U.S. lead. At the NSC meeting on March 27 it became evident that Dulles was growing uneasy about possible Soviet exploitation of a conditional U.S. acceptance and developing serious questions regarding effective policing. The president, however, "reiterated" his "despair" at looking ahead "to a future which contained nothing but more and more bombs."[71]

By the NSC meeting on June 23 Dulles had come full circle. His draft report essentially adopted the objections of the Defense Department and Strauss, as well as his own doubts about the net propaganda value of accepting a supension. It recommended that "the United States not agree to a testing moratorium."[72] The president "thoroughly agreed" with this conclusion, though adding "at this time" to the formal decision at the suggestion of Allen Dulles. He "would strongly challenge," however, the committee's premise that the United States should "oppose abolition of atomic weapons except as part of a general disarmament program." Eisenhower said once again that he would be the first to endorse such abolition, "regardless of any general disarmament," if he knew any "really fool-proof system to ensure abolition."[73]

During the summer and fall work on the broader review of NSC 112 and general disarmament was proceeding in the Working Group of the Special Committee and the three agencies. The task was addressed in two phases. In the first months each member prepared a draft study of disarmament from the perspective of his agency, but without obtaining agency clearance. In addition, two background studies were jointly approved.[74] Then, as the studies became available, they were discussed in the Working Group and the NSC Planning Board in order to identify agreements and differences and the implications for U.S. policy.

On October 18, the Planning Board considered the report of General Loper of the Defense Department. The sharp clash between the views of the State and Defense members of the working group quickly became apparent. The conclusions of the Defense report ("A Review of the United States Policy on the Regulation, Limitation, and Balanced Reduction of Armed Forces and Armaments," dated August 27, 1954) were stark and explicit: no disarmament agreement was in the U.S. interest. This was because any agreement depended on the "good faith" of the Soviets, which could not be relied on; and the technical inability to account fully for past production of fissionable material would allow nuclear weapons to be concealed. Thus the abolition of nuclear weapons was no longer feasible. More broadly, it was impossible to balance factors of war potential as a basis for making reductions. Finally, complete inspection would so upset the "whole way of life" of a party as to be unacceptable. Still, public opinion required the United States to continue to deal with disarmament.[75]

While not yet ready to submit concrete proposals, the State member suggested that "a somewhat different approach" could lead to quite different conclusions. The criterion for a disarmament system or measure, Bowie said, was "What is the alternative?" The alternative is the growth in capabilities of the U.S. and U.S.S.R. for mutual annihilation. While tending to deter war, that condition "would also produce tensions which might eventually increase the risk of war. Disarmament proposals must be measured against this risk, rather than against some ideal standard [of security]."[76]

Bowie agreed that comprehensive disarmament or abolition of nuclear weapons was now impractical. Instead, he urged, the focus should be on seeking partial or limited measures to mitigate the nuclear danger and lead to further steps. Might a cutoff of production of fissionable material slow the nuclear arms competition? Would balanced reductions of arms be feasible and beneficial? Concealed weapons, Bowie said, are a threat only if they can be used in warfare: could that capability be constrained through control of the means of delivery? Conceivably, he said later, the Soviets might be willing to make such agreements to reduce the nuclear risks to themselves, without abandoning their ambitions for expansion. After further debate, the Planning Board agreed to resume discussion in six weeks on the basis of a report showing agreements and disagreements to be prepared by the Working Group.[77]

The Working Group met on November 17 for this purpose. Bowie had provided the State Department draft on November 9, outlining its approach and the basic elements of a disarmament program. On November 2 the AEC had made its response to certain questions submitted by the State Department in April. The AEC report confirmed that the inability to account for past production or to detect concealed nuclear materials made the UN plan for abolition of nuclear weapons impractical. But a cutoff of fissionable materials and reducing nuclear stockpiles, as suggested by State, was feasible, although with some risks.[78] The Working Group also agreed that current military trends, especially nuclear, were not favorable to the United States and that any disarmament must be effectively safeguarded from the start, proceed by stages, "including both nuclear and conventional aspects," and be enforced by "self-help in case of violations."[79]

But the basic State-Defense split remained undiminished. The State member reaffirmed an approach based on proceeding step-by-step by partial, safeguarded measures, and working out successive steps by building on experience and confidence gained from the preceding stage. And the Defense member again rejected *any* disarmament plan as disadvantageous and dangerous, and especially anything less than a comprehensive, detailed and enforceable program covering both atomic and conventional arms and forces.[80]

To resolve the issue, Cutler scheduled an NSC meeting in January 1955 (later deferred until February 10). To assist the Special Committee in its meeting, the Planning Board prepared a memorandum identifying the principal issues and the

respective positions of State and Defense on the basis of their reports.[81] The memorandum catalogued item by item the conflicting views already described. Cutler
sent the memorandum to the Special Committee members on December 10. The
next day, Wilson wrote to Dulles and Strauss that the studies and meetings of the
Working Group had made apparent "a major and probably irreconcilable divergence in basic concepts and principles and in the application of principles between
the State and Defense working groups." A formal Defense paper consistent with
JCS views was, he wrote, now being reviewed by the top civilian officials and would
soon be ready. He suggested the Special Committee meet soon to prepare an
agreed position or separate views for the NSC meeting on January 6. Dulles called
a meeting for January 4.[82]

On December 29, Dulles held a State Department session to decide on his position for the Special Committee and NSC meetings. The discussion was somewhat
confused. The secretary questioned whether nuclear weapons could be eliminated
without reducing Soviet conventional superiority, but thought that was too complex
to be feasible. Yet, as the president stressed, only nuclear weapons threatened
America's industrial potential. When told "that Defense believed any form of disarmament was contrary to U.S. interests because of distrust of the Soviets," he commented "that there was little difference between his views and those of the Defense
Department, since he believed it would be impossible to insure absolutely that a
disarmament program would be in our security interests." But then he added that
"it came down to the question of the kind of risks we were willing to assume, and he
believed that the real issue was how to maintain intact our industrial potential."[83]

Bowie argued for starting a "little segment" such as cessation of nuclear fuel production, which would only require "simpler" safeguards, in order to gain experience. Others objected that while this would be in the U.S. interest, the Soviets
would probably reject it, as would the British.[84]

In concluding, the secretary said he "believed that this was the kind of a problem
which fundamentally could not be solved by controls or limiting weapons."[85]

At this point, Robert Murphy, the deputy undersecretary of state, presented a
memorandum, initiated by Bowie and concurred in by all the interested bureaus,
proposing that the secretary ask the NSC to recommend that the United States continue efforts to achieve safeguarded disarmament and that the president promptly
appoint an "outstanding person" for this purpose. The secretary agreed that this
would be advisable and said he would consider it.[86]

The Special Committee held meetings in early January, and a month later, before the NSC finally took up the disarmament issue on February 10. The meetings
were marked by some movement in Dulles's thinking and by an eventual conclusion that some other procedure was needed to deal with disarmament policy in
view of its complexity and the divergent approaches.[87]

The Defense position, however, remained unchanged: opposition to any disarmament plan for all the reasons already discussed. A major one was that an effective
"proof against evasions or violations" would necessitate control and inspection so
extensive as to require the Soviets to radically change "their political and strategic
orientation." But in that case they would be ready to resolve the major political issues, which would be far less complex to achieve than disarmament and which

would lead to that "almost as a matter of course." In the January meeting Secretary Dulles confessed his ambivalence. First, he doubted "the U.S. could work out any disarmament agreement plan with a powerful nation which we did not trust and which we believed had most ambitious goals." But second, "we had to keep trying to work out agreement on such a plan," if only in response to public opinion and to hold onto the allies. But "he was not optimistic."[88]

When Bowie again urged trying a limited measure such as stopping nuclear production to test the feasibility of an inspection system, Dulles was negative. "He thought it was much easier for the Soviets to reach agreement with us in other areas than in the armaments field." Strauss took issue with this view. In fact, he saw the Soviets as too "psychologically committed" to political issues like maintaining the Comintern or the German question to make concessions. But if the United States "put the right kind of psychological pressure on the Soviets, there "might be a new inducement in the armaments field."[89]

The January 4 meeting ended inconclusively. Secretary Dulles asked what the Special Committee could propose to the NSC. Bowie suggested naming "a qualified man of national prestige to take the lead in reviewing the problem." Strauss asked whether the committee might suggest basic principles rather than a detailed plan. Wilson and Dulles seemed to concur, relying on working groups to develop a detailed plan. Then, said Dulles, bringing in a new top-level man could be considered.[90]

In opening the Special Committee meeting on February 9, Secretary Dulles suggested the committee prepare for the NSC discussion the next day a list of issues on disarmament requiring decisions by the president. For example, should the United States continue to insist that nuclear limitations be linked to conventional reduction? Another question was "[W]ere we prepared to proceed in a disarmament program on the basis of working out each stage at a time, entering upon the first stage without necessarily having developed and agreed upon the later stages, and proceeding in developing the latest stages from the experience derived through carrying out each proceeding stage?"[91] This question provoked a lively discussion of partial measures for most of the meeting, which indicated some evolution in Dulles's thinking. Defense strongly objected to proceeding step-by-step or separating nuclear and conventional aspects: this approach would raise dangers for U.S. security. Strauss was afraid that if an initial stage was based on stopping production of nuclear fuels, the United States might never be able to restart or regain its present impetus in weapons production if the plan broke down.[92]

Surprisingly, Dulles countered that "Atoms for Peace" embodied the concept of a limited first step. While a limited approach in disarmament involved more complicated problems, "this should be dealt with concretely and not as an abstract issue, in order to see whether the specific limited approach . . . would be in U.S. interests." The only practical measure of a limited nature the United States had actually confronted, he said, was the Indian proposal for a moratorium on nuclear weapons tests. He recalled that the NSC carefully considered that "on the merits" and rejected it not because it "failed to cover the waterfront but because it was not practical. Therefore, in fact we had another precedent for examining a limited approach to disarmament which did not cover all aspects of this complex question."[93]

Deputy Secretary of Defense Robert Anderson volunteered that if he had written the Defense paper, he "would have placed greater emphasis on the need to see if there was any possibility of developing a successful proposal in the disarmament field." Strauss, stressing the need for more study, suggested that the Special Committee should perhaps be made permanent. Bowie again urged instead that the review be continued under the direction of an "individual of outstanding qualifications" because the members of the Special Committee could not devote adequate time or attention to the subject. Anderson, Secretary Dulles, and Allen Dulles supported this idea. The director should be full-time, they agreed, with access to the president and cabinet members, and assisted by staff from the concerned agencies. Cutler agreed to draft a statment of the issues, drawing on the State and Defense papers, for NSC consideration the next day.[94]

At the NSC meeting on February 10 Cutler distributed a list of five questions for discussion. Before Secretary Dulles could begin the president intervened to express his great interest in the first question about naming an outstanding person to concentrate on disarmament. In his view, "we greatly needed such a man." Eisenhower explained, "Certainly disarmament was a subject with which some one exceptional brain ought to occupy himself exclusively. This was one of the most important fields in the entire government."[95]

Again, Dulles expressed a more open and flexible approach. Arms control, he said, "was as urgent and as difficult as any problem which society faced today." History might suggest it was insoluble, because arms limitation was a product "of mutual trust among nations rather than . . . a producer of mutual trust." Yet "there were now a number of new factors." Of these nuclear weapons "were of transcendent importance." Secondly, he went on, "the risks of not doing something in this field of disarmament were far greater than they had ever been before in history. . . . In any event, we must accept the working hypothesis that a solution of this terrible problem *can* be found."[96]

The president recalled his repeated statements of his readiness to abolish nuclear weapons without regard to conventional reductions if a really foolproof system of safeguards was feasible. But now, he said, he was convinced that no foolproof system could be devised and therefore was compelled to revert to a linkage of nuclear and conventional control.

Secretary Dulles commented on the view of many people "that until you can get an absolutely fool-proof system of disarmament you should not seriously take any steps" in that direction. He "pointed out that if no steps at all were taken and we continued in our present situation, we also ran very grave risks." Agreeing with Dulles, Wilson said "we could never afford to give up the effort" to solve the problem of disarmament."[97]

Eisenhower was anxious to find the right man promptly, and to assure that he had full access to information, support from the agencies concerned, and consultants.

As for the upcoming UN disarmament meeting, which Lodge said would once more be mainly "propaganda-making," it was decided that the United States would continue to support its current positions, including the UN plan, with some update for existing stockpiles, but to "avoid materially prejudicing the possible introduction of later proposals."[98]

On March 19, 1955, President Eisenhower announced the appointment of Foreign Operations Administrator Harold L. Stassen as his special assistant, with cabinet rank, to develop studies and recommendations on disarmament. The Departments of State and Defense and the AEC had proposed various candidates. None had suggested Stassen.[99] Ultimately, Eisenhower's choice failed to provide him the support he wanted.

While Eisenhower's appointment of Stassen had been prompted by his frustration with the earlier procedures, the debates and disagreements had brought out important concepts and premises that helped to clarify both the objectives and modalities of future successes. The most fundamental of these were the following:

1) Blueprints for total and complete disarmament (including the UN's Baruch Plan) were an impractical mirage and a distraction from serious efforts.
2) Atomic weapons created a common interest even between adversaries with other conflictive aims.
3) For the indefinite future, realistic objectives for arms control were to reduce the risks of nuclear war; to moderate the arms competition and the spread of nuclear weapons; and to reinforce deterrence.
4) In pursuing these aims, the most hopeful means were partial measures, such as controls of testing, fuel production, and delivery systems.
5) Verification, though essential to arms control, could never be foolproof or perfect. Its adequacy should be judged by its capacity for detecting any significant violation and providing warning in time for other parties to counter it or take compensating action before their security was jeopardized.
6) The test of any arms control system is whether the risks under it (including possible evasion) are less than those without it.

These concepts would be further developed in the later years of the administration with the assistance of the Science Advisors and would largely shape efforts for arms control thereafter.

PART IV

EPILOGUE

15

The Eisenhower Legacy

Eisenhower, before, during and after his Presidency, put the pursuit of peace at the top of his agenda, and at the top of his agenda for peace he put nuclear danger.[1]

McGeorge Bundy (1988)

The decade of the 1950s was a formative period for U.S. security policy, when the strategic context of the cold war was transformed by the coming of mutual nuclear plenty. Truman's last three years in office were preoccupied with this prospect and its implications, and Eisenhower's entire tenure with adjusting to its emergence under new Soviet leaders.

The Challenge

The response of President Truman to the prospective Soviet nuclear capacity, as embodied in NSC 68, was a major reappraisal of the Soviet threat, U.S. objectives to counter it, and appropriate means of pursuing them. Its growing nuclear capability, NSC 68 argued, would embolden the Soviet Union to take much greater risks in executing its expansionist "design"; by 1954 (later 1953) its capacity for a crippling surprise nuclear attack was expected to make that a year of peak danger. To counter this threat the U.S. objective had to be to achieve before that time preponderant power through a massive U.S. and NATO military buildup, especially in conventional forces; the purpose was not only to deter or defeat Soviet aggression but also to induce retraction or "rollback" of Soviet power and a basic change in the Soviet system. The analysis of NSC 68 seemed to be vindicated by the Korean invasion.

Although that aggression was thwarted, the results of two and one-half years of strenuous effort under Truman fell far short of the objectives of NSC 68, leaving a legacy of disarray in policy and programs. U.S. defense spending had indeed more than tripled, and U.S. forces doubled. While the U.S. nuclear arsenal was still far superior to the Soviets', the conventional forces of the United States and NATO remained well below the goals projected for a secure Europe. Thus SAC would have to provide the backbone of deterrence and defense indefinitely. No rollback of

Soviet power or control had been achieved or was in prospect. Furthermore, defense spending was imposing unacceptable economic and political strains on the European NATO members and large budgetary deficits in the United States. Serious divergences were developing regarding NATO strategy. Widespread discontent in the United States had severely undermined public support for Truman and his foreign policy. In essence, the strategy of NSC 68 proved to be a false start.

The challenge for Eisenhower was to develop a coherent cold war strategy based on feasible objectives and security programs with better balance between ends and means. Because "[c]rises will continue to be," Eisenhower said in his Farewell Address, "there is a recurring temptation to feel that some spectacular and costly action could become the miraculous solution to all current difficulties." Both the government and public must resist giving in to it, he warned. "[E]ach proposal must be weighed in the light of a broader consideration: the need to maintain balance in and among national programs. . . . Good judgment seeks balance and progress; lack of it eventually finds imbalance and frustration."[2]

Eisenhower also had to restore domestic and allied confidence and support for the U.S. role and for NATO, and to do so under conditions that were bound to be uncertain and unsettled. First, the nuclear context was rapidly becoming far more ominous. With the growing output from Truman's huge expansion of nuclear facilities, the U.S. stockpile would reach over 1,700 weapons by 1954 and more than double that number by 1956. Fission weapons were being made 25 times more powerful than those used on Japan. The U.S. hydrogen bomb, which was tested in October 1952 and would enter the stockpile in 1954, had the yield of 15 megatons—enough to destroy New York and scatter deadly fallout over an area more than 50 miles wide and 250 miles long. The Soviet nuclear arsenal, while much smaller, was growing rapidly; the Soviet test of August 1953 indicated they would be only a year or so behind in having the hydrogen bomb.[3]

Second, Stalin's death just after Eisenhower took office meant the West would face an unfamiliar and untested Soviet leadership. Who would emerge as leader(s)? After how much feuding? And with what aims? Third, with the fall of China, the Korean War, and the Indochina conflict, the cold war had spread beyond Europe and become global.

Fourth, keeping the NATO alliance vigorous and intact was becoming more difficult. The sources of strain were varied. The ending of the Korean war, the death of Stalin, and the "peace offensive" of his successors sharply reduced the European fear of Soviet attack, which had already begun to decline during 1952. Parochial or separate national interests were less constrained by the priority for security cooperation. That, plus domestic recovery, made the Europeans more restive about U.S. leadership. In addition, European dependence on the U.S. nuclear umbrella was a source of conflicting anxieties, especially as the Soviet arsenal and U.S. vulnerability grew. Inevitably, any effort to adapt NATO's strategy to changing conditions was unsettling. And finally, the progressive breakup of the colonial empires was spawning many unstable new states, which seemed to offer tempting targets for communist subversion.

Broadly, these were the conditions that would prevail until the end of the cold war.

Eisenhower's Enduring Contribution

President Eisenhower came to office with unusually well-formed and informed views on the Soviet threat, U.S. objectives, and suitable means for pursuing them. Yet in developing his national security policy, he conducted a more extensive and systematic review of these issues than any other president, using expert committees, consultants, the Solarium exercise, and the NSC process. The basic elements of the resulting strategy, although modified in detail, continued to govern Eisenhower's security policy throughout his tenure. And in our view, its central concepts served as enduring guides for the later stages of the cold war. Among these concepts, the following are especially significant.

The Imperative of Preventing Nuclear Holocaust

Eisenhower's conviction that major nuclear war would be a suicidal catastrophe, and a global disaster, was the bedrock of his strategy. He eloquently told President Singman Rhee of Korea in July 1954, "Atomic war will destroy civilization. It will destroy our cities. There will be millions of people dead. War today is unthinkable with the weapons which we have at our command. If the Kremlin and Washington ever lock up in a war, the results are too horrible to contemplate. I can't even imagine them."[4]

In March 1954 following the Bikini hydrogen bomb test, Eisenhower wrote Churchill that finding ways of lessening or if possible ending the nuclear danger had been "my principal preoccupation throughout the last year." As he often said, he would gladly have abolished nuclear weapons if that had been feasible.[5] Because it was not, even as the United States continued its efforts to block further Soviet expansion it had to give top priority to preventing the occurrence of nuclear war. Thus deterrence of nuclear war was the foundation for peace and security.

The Feasibility of Deterrence

Eisenhower was confident that deterring nuclear war was feasible despite, or even because of, the horrendous nuclear capacity each side would have. His confidence was based on his assessment of the priorities of the Soviet leaders. He did not accept the view of NSC 68 that they were so dedicated to achieving the "Kremlin design" for world domination, and so ruthless, that they would use any means for that purpose and would take substantial risks in doing so. Like Bohlen, Eisenhower believed that view totally misjudged their priorities. He did not doubt their commitment to extending Soviet influence and control. But he had long been convinced that their overriding goal was to preserve their personal power and the Soviet regime: they would do nothing for expansion that would jeopardize or risk that primary aim. As he put it in a 1954 television talk, "The very fact that those men, by their own design, are in the Kremlin, means that they love power. . . . Whenever they start a war, they are taking the great risk of losing that power. . . . And those men in the politburo know that."[6]

For Eisenhower, this was the key to deterrence of a major nuclear war. Soviet leaders would not engage in aggressive action that they believed entailed the risk of retaliation endangering the regime. Hence they must be left in no doubt about this risk. Thus, contrary to partisan allegations of bomber and missile "gaps," Eisenhower expanded the U.S. nuclear stockpile and delivery capabilities during his administration to the extent he felt necessary to impress and deter the Soviets.[7] (In fact, his failure to constrain the momentum of weapons building generated by Truman's vast expansion of facilities resulted in some 18,000 nuclear weapons by 1961. And SAC's targeting plans projected such extreme "overkill" that Eisenhower was "[s]hocked and angered" when ultimately briefed about them.)[8]

Further, Eisenhower sought to reinforce this deterrent by stressing the menace of nuclear war through speeches such as "Atoms for Peace," remarks at press conferences, and informal talks with the Kremlin leaders, as at the 1955 Geneva Summit. We now know that Khrushchev understood the consequences of nuclear war by September 1953. And just after the U.S. hydrogen bomb test in March 1954, Soviet atomic scientists conveyed to the political leaders their grim assessment of nuclear war: explosion of about a hundred large hydrogen bombs would "create on the whole globe conditions impossible for life." They concluded "that over the human race there hangs the threat of an end of all life on the earth."[9] For the next year Soviet leaders debated this challenge to communist doctrine: whether both sides or only the capitalists would perish in such a war. Returning from the Geneva Summit, however, Eisenhower reported on television that "there seems to be a growing realization by all that nuclear warfare, pursued to the ultimate, could be practically race suicide."[10]

The Necessity of a Secure Second Strike

To fortify the deterrent, Soviet leaders had to be convinced that the U.S. capacity to retaliate could not be knocked out by a decisive surprise nuclear attack. Thus it was essential to assure that sufficient retaliatory capacity would survive such an attack to be able to impose unacceptable damage by a second strike. This requirement, which the Truman administration had neglected until its last months, was a high priority for Eisenhower. Initially, he had launched an extensive program for early warning and continental defense. But this system, while useful against bombers, would not be effective against ballistic missiles, which were expected to be developed within five to seven years. Accordingly, in 1954 Eisenhower appointed the Technological Capabilities Panel, headed by James R. Killian, to report on "Meeting Surprise Attack." The panel made several extremely important proposals for this purpose in its report: for accelerating the development of ballistic missiles; for building the U-2 spy plane for better intelligence on Soviet armaments; and for the Polaris submarine missile system.[11] Virtually invulnerable, the Polaris system would assure the existence of a secure second strike capacity for the rest of the cold war. The resultant "large, secure, and redundant strategic nuclear triad"—the Polaris, ballistic missiles, and the B-52 bomber—made coordinating a disarming surprise attack impractical.[12]

The Rejection of Coerced Rollback

Eisenhower rejected the objective of coercing rollback of Soviet power and control espoused by NSC 68. Because it would seriously increase the risk of global war, he did not consider it a conceivable choice. Yet he was confident that, if major war could be prevented and the Western coalition maintained, retraction of Soviet power and control would eventually occur as a result of waning ideology, internal ferment, and decay. The role of the West, he said, would be to help sustain resistance to Soviet control there until it "can be gradually weakened and loosened *from within*."[13] This was a return to the orginal containment concept.

Nonetheless, this issue was actively debated during the making of the president's first strategy. Rollback was one of the alternatives explored in the Solarium exercise, but as attested to by General Andrew Goodpaster, Eisenhower's purpose was to put the option to rest. NSC 162/2 did embody Eisenhower's attitude. As we have seen, however, the JCS continued for several years to press for the NSC 68 objective of inducing retraction of Soviet power and control by "positive" and "dynamic" measures before the U.S.S.R. achieved a sufficient nuclear capacity for surprise attack. The State Department and others, in the Planning Board and the NSC itself, opposed and asked in vain for specifics. It was Dulles, as we saw, who finally summed up the opposing consensus that such a course would be ineffective, risk provoking general war, and divide the alliance.

Defense Forces for the Long Haul

In Eisenhower's view the cold war and containment would extend over many years—if major war could be prevented. There would be no year of peak danger as foreseen by NSC 68. Thus military forces must be designed to maximize deterrence and to be maintained over the "long haul." Accordingly, the level of defense spending by the United States and NATO must be compatible with healthy economies and be politically supportable indefinitely. Eisenhower's experience as SACEUR convinced him that the Europeans would not or could not sustain forces approaching the projected NATO goals; Truman's "Testament" (NSC 141) had reached much the same conclusion as his tenure ended.[14]

Moreover, in Eisenhower's judgment such high force levels were militarily unnecessary. They were based on the assumption that after an all-out SAC retaliatory strike, the Soviet forces would still be able to overrun Europe unless opposed by comparable NATO ground forces. Although the JCS did not formally abandon this World War II "paradigm" until 1955, Eisenhower essentially buried it in 1953.[15] He was certain that with the huge increase in numbers and yields of nuclear weapons, a massive nuclear exchange would leave both sides too crippled for active, protracted hostilities. In this respect, his analysis was similar to the 1952 British Global Strategy paper (although direct influence has not been shown). In his view, NATO would still need enough ground forces to hold the line against an initial ground attack, but not for extended hostilities. Politically, forces on the ground served to reassure the NATO allies as to forward defense, and the U.S. divisions also were a gage of the U.S. commitment to Europe's defense.

The outcry of critics against "massive retaliation" ignored the past reality, at least as concerned Europe. NATO's dependence on nuclear weapons and SAC in the "New Look" was in fact no greater than what Eisenhower had inherited from Truman. As its deterrent to general war, NSC 135/3, approved in late 1952, called for the United States to "[d]evelop and maintain, under all foreseeable conditions, the capacity to inflict massive damage on the Soviet war-making capacity." And this dependence would have continued indefinitely according to NSC 141.[16] In reducing NATO conventional force goals Eisenhower had simply acted on the conclusion that any major attack would begin or rapidly become nuclear, and would be so devastating in the first phase as to make a replay of World War II thereafter unthinkable.[17] Stressing nuclear retaliation reinforced the primary aim of deterrence.

More limited conflicts on the periphery were another matter entirely. Eisenhower never expected "massive retaliation" to be appropriate for them, except to keep them from escalating. Indeed, he had warned the JCS that, unlike in general war, they would not be able to count on using nuclear weapons in such hostilities unless authorized by him at the time.

But the Korean experience had convinced him that the United States should not become engaged with its ground forces in local conflicts except under extraordinary circumstances. Instead, the United States must 1) build up indigenous forces; 2) support them with mobile U.S. air and naval forces; and 3) enhance their deterrent effect by threatening to respond against an aggressor by means (i.e., possibly tactical nuclear weapons) and at places of America's own choosing (i.e., at vulnerable targets other than the point of attack—but that did *not* necessarily mean Moscow or Peking).

During the decade of the 1950s, however, the strategic environment was radically changed by two developments. Both sides achieved "nuclear plenty," or virtual "parity." And both developed ballistic missiles with intercontinental range. The consequences were unsettling. The United States and SAC became much more vulnerable to surprise attack with almost no warning. Yet a SAC strike to knock out Soviet strategic missiles, whether preemptive or retaliatory, would be more difficult to execute due to an inability to locate or target them if they were dispersed, mobile, or concealed. How would parity affect Soviet behavior? Would the Soviets be more tempted to exploit their conventional superiority in Europe, relying on mutual nuclear stalemate? Or would they become more prone to limited aggression on the periphery? And how might this condition affect the United States and NATO, and confidence in the U.S. nuclear umbrella?

These and related questions produced an intense debate on the implications for military strategy inside the U.S. government, in NATO, and among outside experts for the remainder of Eisenhower's tenure (and well beyond). Reactions ran a wide gamut. The Air Force and General Nathan Twining, Radford's successor as JCS chair, continued to defend traditional targeting and strategy, identifying more and more targets and justifying expanded capabilities. General Maxwell Taylor, who replaced Ridgway in 1955, insisted on the necessity for much larger forces for limited wars, with greater mobility and with tactical nuclear weapons for use as appropriate. Chief of Naval Operations Admiral Arleigh Burke, stressing the security of the Polaris system, which would become available by mid-1960, urged consideration of a "finite" deterrence strategy, allowing sharp reduction in strategic forces and expansion of those for limited hostilities.

Even Secretary Dulles, deeply troubled by the divisive effects on NATO of the doubts and uncertainty, argued during 1958 at several meetings with defense officials and others that the United States must move beyond undue reliance on massive retaliation; that the United States would have to develop a doctrine—and forces to support it—to meet less than all-out threats. At first Dulles focused on developing tactical nuclear weapons; later on conventional capabilities, as advocated then by Gerard Smith, director of the Policy Planning Staff, and initially by Bowie, his predecessor.[18] And as NATO's supreme commander, General Lauris Norstad developed the concept of a "pause" before a nuclear response in case of a less than all-out attack and sought a force of 28–30 divisions to reinforce it.

Eisenhower, however, refused to modify his basic strategy or the force composition significantly despite the new conditions. He remained convinced that its underlying premises were still valid. For fear of endangering their regime, in the president's estimate, Soviet leaders regardless of the changes would be deterred from initiating general war, nuclear or conventional, or taking other actions that might lead to such a war. But Eisenhower did approve measures to improve the security of the second-strike capability (including greater readiness, airborne alert, and fail-safe launching procedures) and to accelerate development of the intercontinental missiles and Polaris system. As for local or limited war, he adhered to his view that the United States should not provide major ground forces, which should be furnished indigenously or by others. The U.S. role was to supplement and support these by its mobile naval and air capabilities, using tactical nuclear weapons as appropriate.

The Centrality of Noncommunist Cooperation

The vitality and cohesion of the noncommunist nations were prime concerns in the Eisenhower strategy. Cooperation among allies and with the developing nations was essential for security in the cold war. But it was also indispensable for their political and economic well-being in an interdependent world. Nurturing such relations was a constant preoccupation of Dulles as well as Eisenhower. Their concern reflected their firm conviction that the broader purpose of foreign and security policy was to preserve and advance international conditions favorable to economic and social progress.

Allies

The revival and strengthening of the European nations (and Japan) had, of course, been a major aim of U.S. policy under Truman. The European Recovery Program, NATO, and the European Coal and Steel Community had been milestones along this course. Eisenhower and Dulles strongly supported these measures, as well as the pending European Defense Community. Both were particularly concerned with integrating West Germany as well as Japan into the Western system.

Having spent eighteen months as SACEUR, Eisenhower fully understood the European attitudes and concerns at first hand, and had worked with many of the leaders, both in that capacity and earlier in World War II. He and Dulles put heavy stress on consulting with the NATO partners, through the NATO Council of Deputies, regular meetings of the foreign ministers, and frequent bilateral, tripartite, and larger meetings, especially with Britain, France, and the Federal Republic of Germany. Dulles traveled extensively for this purpose throughout his tenure.

In making policy decisions, Eisenhower was consistently sensitive to the political and other concerns of the Europeans. For example, despite his original view that deployment of U.S. forces to Europe should be temporary, he rejected JCS advice to bring most back to the United States, recognizing their political contribution to reassurance and stability, as strongly urged by Dulles. Similarly, he sympathized with the European desire for relaxing restrictions on nonmilitary trade with the Soviet bloc. And he and Dulles actively supported the European Community as a means of reconciling France and Germany, integrating the FRG into the Western system, and restoring Europe's role in world affairs.

Eisenhower also sought ways to enable the allies to participate in the nuclear deterrent, including espousal at the end of his tenure of a multilateral seaborne nuclear force.[19] And when a split with the allies did occur, as with Britain and France over the Suez invasion, he worked hard to reknit relations as quickly as possible. The continued viability of NATO despite the diverse strains of the 1950s was largely due to the confidence that Eisenhower enjoyed among the European members and his and Dulles's constant attention to the alliance.

In the Far East, Eisenhower had less success with U.S. allies. Nationalist Chinese and South Korean irredentism exacerbated regional discord and volatility. Progress was made in linking a reviving Japan to the West. But despite the benefits in trade, assistance, and protection, many Japanese resisted the close ties, as evidenced by the mass protests against the ratification of a Japan-American mutual defense treaty, which forced the cancellation of Eisenhower's visit his last year in office. No longer, however, was the Far East perceived as the stepchild of U.S. policy. And in important respects, the basis was laid for improving bilateral and multilateral relations in the future.

Expanded Assistance for the Developing Countries

The 1950s were marked by growing concern with the less developed regions outside of Europe. The tide of nationalism in Asia, Africa, and the Middle East was undermining European colonialism and influence, and generating disputes like those of Britain with Iran over oil and with Egypt over the Suez base and canal. The emerging nations were generally poor and underdeveloped, with leaders generally lacking experience in governing and often anti-Western.

Eisenhower in principle sympathized with the aspirations of these new nations, and understood the importance of their achieving stability and "self-dependence," and the difficulties of their doing so.[20] Further, he frequently stressed that in an interdependent world many of the less developed countries were major sources of the raw materials and fuels essential to the Western economies. And he repeatedly expressed his fear that their weak societies might be readily susceptible to Soviet infiltration or subversion. NSC 162/2 had made clear that "[c]onstructive policies, *not related solely to anti-communisism,* are needed to persuade uncommitted countries that their best interests lie in greater cooperation and stronger affiliations with the rest of the free world." Accordingly, the United States "should assist in stimulating . . . the healthy growth of underdeveloped areas."[21]

The priority of this objective and the programs for pursuing it increased radically in the course of the Eisenhower administration, due largely to his own initiative.[22] During the first two years or so, help for the less developed countries was governed largely by the principle "trade not aid": by fostering free trade (the Trade Agreements Act) and private investment, with some loans by the Export-Import Bank, primarily to stimulate agricultural exports, as indicated by the enactment in 1954 of the Agricultural Trade and Assistance Act (PL 480). It was during this period as well that the "successful" CIA operations in Iran and Guatemala generated undue confidence that covert action could effectively contain indigenous unrest.

The administration's approach subsequently matured. By 1956 the U.S. policy of "trade not aid" was manifestly inadequate for fostering development, ferment was rising in many of the former colonies, and the campaign of the Soviet leaders to woo the Third World and the nonaligned nations with visits and generous promises of economic assistance was in full swing. Especially after the CIA's ill-fated 1957–58 project in Indonesia demonstrated the limitations of covert operations,[23] Eisenhower and Dulles, deeply concerned by the Soviet "economic offensive," became convinced of the urgent necessity for greatly expanding the U.S. program for public economic assistance to the developing nations.

Consequently, for the rest of his tenure the president gave this objective high priority and devoted much of his energy and attention to it. In this effort, with the active help of Dulles, his successor Christian Herter, and Deputy Undersecretary of State for Economic Affairs C. Douglas Dillon, and supported by the Policy Planning Staff, he overrode the opposition of Humphrey and like-minded "trade not aid" ideologues in the administration.

In his Second Inaugural Address Eisenhower spoke eloquently on the necessity of assistance to the "one-third of all mankind" in their "historic struggle for . . . freedom from grinding poverty." He said that extending such assistance was not only the right thing to do but was also essential both for the United States's own prosperity and well-being and to safeguard against this huge part of the globe's population falling under Soviet influence.[24] As Stephen Ambrose has written, "Over the next four years, Eisenhower would try every form of persuasion at his command to demonstrate to his countrymen the importance of the Third World to the United States. It was one of the most frustrating experiences of his life."[25] Foreign aid remained unpopular and was in fact actively opposed by many in the Congress, including key committee chairmen. Repeatedly it reduced his requested appropriations and curtailed other initiatives, such as the United States Development Loan Fund.

But the president persisted, and the riots that endangered Vice President Richard Nixon in 1958 when he toured Peru and Venezuela undercut his opponents. By the time Eisenhower left office he had succeeded in putting in place the main components, both national and multilateral, of the development programs pursued by his successors. For the international institutions, he obtained increased funding for the International Bank for Reconstruction and Development (IBRD or World Bank) and for the International Monetary Fund (IMF) to enhance their capacity for development financing. The Inter-American Development Bank (IADB) was formed as the first regional bank. The International Development Authority (IDA) was created to provide development loans on "soft" terms (low-interest, long-term). Finally, he included in his last budget, after a late-1959 trip to South Asia, support for the Indus River Project under IBRD auspices; and after a 1960 trip to Latin America, Eisenhower proposed a Social Development Fund under the IADB.

In the United States the most significant innovation for foreign aid was the establishment of the Development Loan Fund (DLF), based on a study of the Policy Planning Staff, which was intended to provide long-term soft loans.[26] But Eisenhower's greatest contribution was his sustained efforts to increase the appropriations for development. In this struggle Congress continued regularly to object to the size of the president's requests for foreign aid, and just as regularly reduced them. Still, funding substantially increased from year to year.

Based on his intensive examination of Eisenhower's efforts, Burton Kaufman concluded, "Subsequent administrations merely built on the legacies that Eisenhower left them." He was "critically important" in starting major public financing for development in the Third World. In doing so, the president reoriented assistance programs from military to economic assistance, and from Europe to the developing world, and he began to move to a more regional emphasis, as in Latin American and South Asia. Indeed, as Kaufman argues, the basis for Kennedy's Alliance for Progress program "can be traced to the 1960 Act of Bogota for broad economic social and economic reforms endorsed by the Eisenhower administration." His administration helped to expand the role of multinational agencies (IDA, IBRD, and IMF), as discussed above. And the creation of the Development Loan Fund served to focus assistance on economic development as a specific goal, and to emphasize the need for longer term perspectives. And Eisenhower "was personally responsible for the directions taken by his administration."[27]

Priority for Realistic Arms Control

Eisenhower's profound concern about nuclear catastrophe led him to seek ways to reduce the nuclear danger and constrain arms competition throughout his tenure. He strongly believed that despite their intense rivalry and distrust, the Soviet Union and the United States shared a common interest in avoiding a nuclear cataclysm and in mitigating the risk of its occurrence through miscalculation or accident. He knew that the grandiose schemes for total and general disarmament were not feasible or serious but mere propaganda exercises. Instead, he sought to make modest breakthroughs toward practical restraints (which were later called "arms control") in the hope that they could be expanded over time.

As we have seen, Eisenhower left office deeply disappointed by his lack of success. The principal obstacle was the fact that the Soviet leaders were not yet ready for such agreements. Until 1963, Khrushchev seemed to think that nuclear weapons, however disastrous if used, could still be exploited as "blackmail" for political advantage, as he showed in the Berlin and Cuban crises. And the Soviet obsession with secrecy was a barrier to verification.[28]

But Eisenhower's own advisors also posed an obstacle. Despite the president's personal commitment to arms control, he lacked the requisite staff support, especially in his first five years in office. The JCS were adamantly opposed, and so was chairman of the AEC Strauss. Dulles was for some time skeptical of any progress, although he favored negotiations to satisfy public opinion and later became more supportive; Bowie, head of State's Policy Planning Staff, shared the president's outlook and sought to promote initiatives, but he was not able to break through cabinet-level blockage. Harold Stassen, as Eisenhower's special assistant for disarmament, was ineffective. Not until Eisenhower named a science advisor (first James Killian, then George Kistiakowsky), assisted by a Science Advisory Committee, did he have adequate help from competent experts who embraced his purposes. With their assistance, and that of Gerard Smith, Bowie's successor, Eisenhower's initiatives on a nuclear test ban and surprise attack led to the first serious negotiations and discussion on arms control, although agreements were achieved only by his successors. (Smith headed the U.S. delegation to the SALT I negotiations.)[29]

Despite his lack of success, Eisenhower made an invaluable contribution to eventual arms control and laid the basis for future concrete results.

First, his efforts legitimated serious efforts for arms agreements with the Soviets even while the cold war rivalry continued. As the Oppenheimer Panel underscored, no genuine negotiations had taken place from the Baruch Plan in 1946 to 1953. NSC 68 had insisted that such negotiations would not be feasible or desirable until basic changes occurred in the Soviet system and purposes. Eisenhower rejected this premise. In his view, the unprecedented nuclear danger made equitable arms control a shared interest, despite ongoing rivalry and distrust, although they impeded agreement. In pursuing detente and deterrence in tandem, he anticipated the NATO Harmel Report of 1967.[30]

Second, Eisenhower recognized that the only way to make progress under existing conditions was by partial measures for arms control (like a test ban) that could reduce the nuclear danger or constrain the arms competition, even though both sides remained heavily armed. Comprehensive programs for total disarmament, such as had long been futilely proposed, were not only impractical but an obstacle to achieving such limited positive results. This critical shift opened the way to major future steps.

Third, and most basic, in appraising any arms control measure the proper criterion, Eisenhower stressed, was the *relative* risks and benefits of adopting it compared with not doing so. While any arms control measure involved risks of violation, it was essential to realize that the status quo also entailed grave dangers. The appropriate question was whether on balance a particular agreement would improve the situation.

Finally, Eisenhower understood that while verification was an essential safeguard against violation, no system could be perfect or foolproof. The proper test was the probability of its providing warning of any militarily significant violation in time for effective countermeasures. And the risk of discovery (and the possible consequences) was itself a form of deterrence of violations. Further, of course, in choosing among possible constraints, the feasibility of verification would be one criterion. The development of satellite photography and electronic eavesdropping (later called "national technical means") facilitated verification by less obtrusive methods.

This approach of Eisenhower's to arms control marked a sharp break with the past and provided the foundation for the arms control measures agreed to during the following decades of the cold war.

In toto, this Eisenhower strategic legacy, in our view, justifies the conclusion that it set the basic lines for implementing the containment concept that underlay the course of the West for the three decades until the collapse of the Soviet empire. This is not to imply that the Eisenhower policies and programs were without flaws. Like those of his successers they inevitably rested on fallible judgments regarding external conditions; the conduct of allies, opponnents, and others; and the impact of U.S. actions, which could well prove mistaken.[31] While the NSC process and oval Office practice might mitigate this risk, they could not remove it. Furthermore, one must not argue that the New Look led linearly to the Kremlin's demise. The Soviet collapse and the peaceful resolution of the cold war was ultimately due to the bankruptcy of the system and the recognition by the new leaders of that reality and the necessity for basic reform. Western containment, nevertheless, provided the indispensable external context for producing that outcome.

The credit for initiating the original containment concept, moreover, clearly belongs to Truman and his associates, especially from 1947 to 1950. Yet effective containment depended on the ability of the United States and its allies to adapt the concept to radically changed conditions and to implement it indefinitely. Eisenhower's strategy reshaped the implementation to be compatible with the new context and to be sustainable for the long term. Recognizing his critical contribution does not derogate from that of either his predecessors or his successors.

Policy-Making Legacy

Although our primary focus has been on the legacy of Eisenhower's policies for the course of the cold war, our analysis of the process by which the president developed those policies has broader relevance. As in the years this book addresses, the United States again confronts the challenge of formulating a strategy and policies suitable for novel conditions of uncertainty and rapid change. Eisenhower's policy-process offers lessons that could be valuable in meeting this challenge.

Eisenhower took office convinced that process and product were inseparable and interdependent, and that the failure to recognize this symbiosis was a major source of the Truman policy disarray. Eisenhower believed that careful and integrated planning, systematic exposure to diverse points of view and the broadest range of available information, methodical review, and effective teamwork and coordination were essential for making policies that best serve the national interest. He knew that this process could not guarantee sound policies, but he never doubted that without such planning, exposure, review, and teamwork, the potential for policies that poorly serve those interests increases dramatically.

No modern president began his tenure with greater experience and firmer convictions than Dwight D. Eisenhower. Yet no modern president was more sensitive to his need for help, and thus placed a higher premium on marshaling expert advice and encouraging candid debate prior to making his decisions. And there are no indications that at any time Dulles, Humphrey, Bradley and then Radford, or any other participant, statutory member of the NSC or not, muted his expressions of opinion or manifested any of the other "consensus-seeking" pathologies commonly associated with "groupthink."[32]

That they did not was in large part a function of the NSC system that Eisenhower instituted. He began by appointing a special assistant to the president on national security affairs who was not to be a policy advisor but the manager of the NSC system. Thus, Robert Cutler (and his successors) effectively if imperfectly promoted multiple advocacy by playing a role that closely approximated Alexander George's model "custodian manager."[33] He chaired the NSC Planning Board, which was central to the system; Eisenhower insisted that issues come to the NSC through the Planning Board. Its deliberations and papers were the means for drawing on the expertise of the national security agencies, clarifying areas of agreement, and defining alternative views on disputed issues.

The distribution, in advance of NSC meetings, of Planning Board and other papers, coupled with intelligence estimates, all but ensured informed and heated NSC debate. These debates played a vital educational role for the president, and even more so for those he depended on to offer him options and to mobilize the resources essential to implementation. Eisenhower was able to exploit bureaucratic competition even as he urged his advisors to transcend parochial perspectives. His advisors freely vented their views but loyally supported his decisions.

The Solarium exercise was an elaborate exemplar of Eisenhower's method, even though it was unique. The purpose was to staff out and rigorously examine three suggested approaches to national strategy. It was not intended to resolve issues but to initiate the process of designing a long-range strategy that would allow tactical flexibility yet coherent and consistent pursuit.

As a consequence, the ultimate influence of the detailed task force reports appears to have been mainly the discussions they generated. Each team presented its analysis and recommendations at a meeting attended by officials responsible for both formulating and executing policy. There, and at a subsequent NSC meeting, they were discussed and then referred by the Council to the Planning Board, with the direction to prepare a draft national strategy paper, using the Solarium reports as it saw fit. In their deliberations the Planning Board members integrated the fruits of the Solarium exercise with myriad other available policy papers and commission reports, and supplementary studies and analyses from their respective bureaucracies.

From the totality of these resources the Planning Board produced a draft statement of national security policy at the end of September 1953 containing a number of disputed alternatives. The NSC discussed NSC 162 for another month. Eisenhower decided disputes incrementally, and the Planning Board incorporated his decisions into revised statements. He did not achieve unanimity among his advisors; he never expected to. But he did expect that before he approved NSC 162/2, he would receive the broadest range of informed advice and assurance of support in public they could offer. He did.

Yet in the final analysis, Eisenhower's own leadership was at least as important, if not more so, to the productive arguments that occurred in the NSC as were the mechanics. He displayed an uncanny ability to enter directly and forcefully into a debate without squelching it. And he took pains to foster dissent. For instance, during the 1954 review of NSC 162/2, when General Matthew Ridgway criticized the policy's heavy reliance on the capacity for atomic retaliation, the president objected immediately. But in response to suggestions from members of the NSC that the Army chief of staff was simply defending his service's institutional interests at the expense of those of the nation as a whole, Eisenhower expressed his confidence in the general and urged his advisors to do "justice to General Ridgway's views." By doing so the president, despite his own disagreement, not only fostered their consideration but also encouraged Ridgway to continue to speak his mind.[34]

In most respects the fundamental elements of Eisenhower's national strategy so closely paralleled his prepresidential views that one could argue that he would have adopted similar policies without the Solarium exercise, the numerous commissions, panels of consultants, staff studies, Planning Board papers, and even the vigorous NSC debates. In certain instances, moreover, such as the "Chance for Peace" speech following Stalin's death, the outcomes resulted largely from Eisenhower's personal initiative, not from the formal NSC structure.

Nevertheless, there can be no question that Eisenhower found the NSC process valuable. Throughout his two terms he regularly devoted two to three hours each week to presiding over the NSC meetings, except when he was out of town. They brought Eisenhower's thinking into sharper focus by forcing him to weigh it against a range of alternatives that were presented and defended by individuals whose opinions the president took seriously and whose exposure to requisite information and expertise he assured. These individuals, in turn, were educated about the problems in the same way as was Eisenhower.

The consequences were reflected not only in coherent long-range planning that integrated both advice and information, but also in the more informal decision making in the Oval Office during emergencies and crises, when advisors were prepared to make informed recommendations on short notice. They could do so within the context of a wide range of well-deliberated security policies, which had involved analyses of U.S. interests and of the concerns and actions of major foreign governments, friendly and hostile. Likewise, the president in dealing with the daily flow of recommendations and reports had the benefit of this deeper, more inclusive perspective in making specific decisions. The participants also came to understand and respect the process, the president and his views, and each other. Hence, once Eisenhower made his decision, he could count on a united administration when seeking congressional, public, and international support.

Yet while Eisenhower's policy-making procedures were effective for his own administration, they did not outlast his terms in office. In the view of John Kennedy and Lyndon Johnson, whose experience before the presidency was in Congress, the

NSC process seemed too rigid and cumbersome. Favoring informal and ad hoc meetings with individual advisors or small groups, they relied little on the NSC and disbanded much of Eisenhower's architecture. Richard Nixon, while ostensibly committed to its revival, perverted the entire system to serve his own and Henry Kissinger's penchant for secrecy and deviousness, even with key advisors. And since then the huge expansion of the NSC staff into a small State Department has seriously confused the lines of responsibility and authority among the State Department, NSC, Department of Defense, and Oval Office.

But future presidents would do well to consider the Eisenhower system in their effort to shape a new order for relative peace and prosperity in a complex world of interdependence and instability.

Notes

Key to Sources and Abbreviations

These sources are referred to by the following abbreviations. Although some collections and series will be abbreviated, folder titles will not and will be denoted by quotation marks. To conserve space further, unless essential to provide context, documents are identified only by page numbers. For this same purpose, the notes substitute for a bibliograhy. We apologize for the inconvenience. Fuller notes and a select bibliography can be found on Richard Immerman's home page on the Web page for the Department of History at Temple University. The current URL address is http://www.temple.edu/histdept/immerman.html.

AE   Eisenhower, Dwight D., *At Ease: Stories I Tell to Friends*, Garden City, New York, 1967.

AJKP   Arthur J. Krock Papers, Seeley G. Mudd Library, Princeton University, Princeton, New Jersey.

AWD   Ann Whitman Diary—in AWF.

AWDP   Allen W. Dulles Papers, Mudd Library.

AWF   Dwight D. Eisenhower as President of the United States, 1953–1961 (Ann Whitman File), Dwight D. Eisenhower Library, Abilene, Kansas.

AWR   Arthur W. Radford Collection, Hoover Institution on War, Revolution, and Peace, Stanford, California.

BBP   Bernard Baruch Papers, Mudd Library.

CDJP   C. D. Jackson Papers, Eisenhower Library.

CDJR   C. D. Jackson Records, Eisenhower Library.

CE   Eisenhower, Dwight D., *Crusade in Europe*, Garden City, New York, 1948.

C–EC   Boyle, Peter G., ed., *The Churchill-Eisenhower Correspondence*, 1953–1955, Chapel Hill, North Carolina, 1990.

CIA   U.S. Central Intelligence Agency, Records, RG 263, National Archives.

CRP   Clarence Randall Papers, Mudd Library.

CS   Chronological Series—in DPEL.

DDEPP   Dwight D. Eisenhower Pre-Presidential Papers, 1916–1952, Eisenhower Library.
DH   *Diplomatic History.*
DLP   David Lawrence Papers, Mudd Library.
DPEL   John Foster Dulles Papers, 1951–59, Eisenhower Library.
DPP   John Foster Dulles Papers, 1888–1959, Mudd Library.
DSB   *Department of State Bulletin.*
ED   Ferrell, Robert H., ed., *The Eisenhower Diaries,* New York, 1981.
EDS   Eisenhower Diary Series—in AWF.
EJHP   Emmet J. Hughes Papers, Mudd Library.
EP   Chandler, Alfred D., Jr., and Louis Galambos, Jr., eds., *The Papers of Dwight D. Eisenhower,* Baltimore, Maryland, 1970– .
FR   *Foreign Relations of the United States,* followed by year and volume number.
GCMS   General Correspondence and Memoranda Series—in DPEL.
HD   Ferrell, Robert H., ed., *The Diary of James C. Hagerty: Eisenhower in Mid-Course, 1954–1955,* Bloomington, Indiana, 1983.
HJCS 4 Poole, Walter, *The Joint Chiefs of Staff and National Policy, 1950–52,* vol. 4 of *History of the Joint Chiefs of Staff* (Wilmington, Delaware, 1979).
HJCS 5 Watson, Robert, *The Joint Chiefs of Staff and National Policy, 1953–54,* vol. 5 of *History of the Joint Chiefs of Staff* (Washington, 1986).
JCS   U.S. Department of Defense, Records of the Joint Chiefs of Staff, RG 218, National Archives.
JFDOH   John Foster Dulles Oral History Project, Mudd Library.
LM   Eisenhower, John S. D., ed., *Letters to Mamie,* New York, 1978.
MC   Eisenhower, Dwight D., *The White House Years: Mandate for Change, 1953–1956,* Garden City, New York, 1963.
NSCPB   U.S. National Security Council, Records of the Planning Board, RG 273, National Archives.
NSCS   National Security Council Series—in AWF.
NYT   *New York Times.*
OSD   U.S. Department of Defense, Office of the Secretary of Defense Central Decimal File, RG 330, National Archives.
PC   Final Report and Supporting Documents Pertaining to "Project Control: The Concept of Control by Air and Other Means," Air War College, Air University, Maxwell Air Force Base, Alabama.
PCIIA   President's Committee on International Information Activities (Jackson Committee) Records, Eisenhower Library.
PJ   Eisenhower, Dwight D., *Peace with Justice: Selected Addresses of Dwight D. Eisenhower,* New York, 1961.
PP–E   *Public Papers of the Presidents of the United States: Dwight D. Eisenhower, 1953–1960/61,* Washington, D.C., 1958–1961.
PP–T   *Public Papers of the Presidents of the United States: Harry S. Truman, 1945–1952/53,* Washington, D.C., 1961–1966.
SBP   Stephen Benedict Papers, Eisenhower Library.
S/P   U.S. Department of State, Policy Planning Staff Files, RG 59, National Archives.
S/S–NSC U.S. Department of State, Secretary of State–National Security Council Files, RG 59, National Archives.

WHC   White House Central (Confidential) File, Dwight D. Eisenhower
        Library, Abilene, Kansas.
WHMS   White House Memoranda Series — in DPEL.
WHONSC   White House Office of the National Security Council Staff, Eisenhower
        Library.
WHONSCS   White House Office, National Security Council Staff Papers, Eisenhower
        Library.
WHOSANSA   White House Office of the Special Assistant for National Security Affairs
        Records, Eisenhower Library.
WHOSS   White House Office of the Staff Secretary, Eisenhower Library.

Introduction

1. Quoted in Emmet John Hughes, *The Ordeal of Power: A Political Memoir of the Eisenhower Years* (New York, 1963), 251 (emphasis in original).

2. Richard H. Immerman, "Confessions of an Eisenhower Revisionist: An Agonizing Reappraisal," *DH* 14 (Summer 1990): 319–42; Stephen G. Rabe, "Eisenhower Revisionism: A Decade of Scholarship," *DH* 17 (Winter 1993): 97–115.

3. David L. Porter, "American Historians Rate Our Presidents," in *The Rating Game in American Politics*, ed. William Pederson and Ann McLaurin (New York, 1987), 13–37.

4. See, for example, Robert A. Divine, *Eisenhower and the Cold War* (New York, 1981).

5. Bowie, who attended the NSC meetings as an observer and then heard Gleason's Planning Board briefings, attests to the accuracy of the accounts.

1   The Truman Legacy

1. Paul Nitze, "A Project for Further Analysis and Study of Certain Factors Affecting Our Foreign Policy and Our National Defense Policy," September 15, 1954, Consultants' Papers (Tab L), PC.

2. We discuss his motivations in detail in chapter 4.

3. Stephen E. Ambrose, *Eisenhower*, vol. 1: *Soldier, General of the Army, President-Elect, 1890–1952* (New York, 1983), 498–99; *AE*, 370–72.

4. *ED*, 209–13, 176–77, 180–83.

5. See for example, John Lewis Gaddis, *Strategies of Containment: A Critical Appraisal of Postwar United States National Policy* (New York, 1982), 25–53; Melvyn P. Leffler, *A Preponderance of Power: National Security, the Truman Administration, and the Cold War* (Stanford, 1991), 255–320.

6. *FR, 1948*, 1:589.

7. Ibid., 609, 614, 662–69.

8. Ibid., 662–69.

9. Our account of this period draws on Samuel R. Williamson, Jr., and Steven L. Rearden, *The Origins of U.S. Nuclear Strategy, 1945–1953* (New York, 1993), especially chapter 5; Townsend Hoopes and Douglas Brinkley, *Driven Patriot: The Life and Times of James Forrestal* (New York, 1992), chapters 27, 29, and 30; David A. Rosenberg, "The Origins of Overkill: Nuclear Weapons and American Strategy, 1945–1960," *International Security* 7 (Spring 1983): 12–21.

10. Quoted in David McCullough, *Truman* (New York, 1992), 649–50.

11. Williamson and Rearden, *Origins of Nuclear Strategy*, 90.

12. *FR, 1948*, 1:624–28.

13. Hoopes and Brinkley, *Driven Patriot*, 406–7.

14. Williamson and Rearden, *Origins of Nuclear Strategy*, 94–96.

15. *ED*, 154–58.

16. Williamson and Rearden, *Origins of Nuclear Strategy*, 108.

17. Ibid., 102–4; Rosenberg, "Origins of Overkill," 19–21.

18. Thomas Etzold and John Lewis Gaddis, eds., *Containment: Documents on American Policy and Strategy* (New York, 1978), 360–64.

19. *HJCS* 4, 163–64; Williamson and Rearden, *Origins of Nuclear Strategy*, 124. WSEG was a technical advisory body for the JCS. Truman was briefed on the WSEG report shortly before his hydrogen bomb decision, but he did not receive the Harmon report.

20. *HJCS* 4, 161–62.

21. See *ED*, 154–57, for accounts of the bitter service infighting over the strategic nuclear mission, and Truman's agreement with Eisenhower, including "to support strongest possible air force."

22. Ibid., 159.

23. Williamson and Rearden, *Origins of Nuclear Strategy*, 108–11.

24. McCullough, *Truman*, 111–26; Williamson and Rearden, *Origins of Nuclear Strategy*, 125–26.

25. *FR*, 1950, 1:141–42, 22–44; Dean Acheson, *Present at the Creation* (New York, 1969), 344–49.

26. *FR*, 1950, 1:235–92, 234–35; Acheson, *Present at the Creation*, 373–74; *HJCS* 4, 32.

27. *FR*, 1950, 1:400.

28. Ibid., 287–92.

29. See Ernest R. May, ed., *American Cold War Strategy: Interpreting NSC 68* (Boston, 1993).

30. Paul Nitze with Ann M. Smith and Steven L. Rearden, *From Hiroshima to Glasnost: At the Center of Decision—A Memoir* (New York, 1989), 97.

31. George Kennan, "Is War with Russia Inevitable? Five Solid Arguments for Peace," *Reader's Digest* 56 (March 1950): 1–9; Acheson, *Present at the Creation*, 371–77.

32. Mr. "X" [George Kennan], "The Sources of Soviet Conduct," *Foreign Affairs* 25 (July 1947): 566–82; *FR*, 1948, 1:662–69, 615–24; Kennan, "Is War with Russia Inevitable?" 1–9.

33. *FR*, 1950, 1:238, 262–63.

34. Ibid., 246, 237–38.

35. Ibid., 145.

36. Ibid., 287–88, 263–64, 266–67.

37. Ibid., 251–52, 263–67.

38. Ibid., 221–25.

39. *FR*, 1948, 1:667–68.

40. *FR*, 1950, 1:289.

41. Ibid., 263–64, 266–67.

42. Ibid., 241–42.

43. Ibid., 284.

44. Ibid.

45. Ibid., 282, 291, 253.

46. Acheson, quoted in Leffler, *Preponderance of Power*, 488.

47. *FR*, 1950, 1:282, 284, 287, 248 (our emphasis).

48. Ibid., 284. See also *FR*, 1952–54, 2:67–68. Interestingly, while NSC 68 occasionally refers to "rollback" and "retraction," it often uses the more anodyne term "the objectives," and Nitze generally adopted the same practice.

49. *FR*, 1950, 1:253.

50. Ibid., 281–82.
51. Ibid., 267.
52. Ibid., 244, 253, 285.
53. Ibid., 269–76; 291.
54. Ibid., 271.
55. Ibid., 291, 273–74.
56. *HJCS* 4, 67; *FR*, 1950, 7:1308.
57. *FR*, 1950, 1:467–74; *HJCS* 4, 66–71.
58. For statistics see the table on p. 75 of *HJCS* 4.
59. *PP–T*, 746–47.
60. *HJCS* 4, 83.
61. Ibid., 88–89.
62. *FR*, 1951, 1:127–57; *HJCS* 4, 91–93.
63. *FR*, 1951, 1:147; *HJCS* 4, 82–86.
64. *HJCS* 4, 94–101, 170–74.
65. Rosenberg, "Origins of Overkill," 22; *HJCS* 4, 145.
66. Rosenberg, "Origins of Overkill," 23.
67. Ibid.
68. *Nuclear Weapons Databook*, vol. 1, 15; *HJCS* 4, 167.
69. *HJCS* 4, 213, 218–19.
70. Robert Wampler, *Ambiguous Legacy: The United States, Great Britain, and the Formulation of NATO Strategy, 1948–1957* (Ph.D. dissertation, Harvard University, 1991), 30.
71. *HJCS* 4, 307–8.
72. Ibid., 241–47; Acheson, *Present at the Creation*, 559–60.
73. *HJCS* 4, 267, 275–79, 289–93. SACEUR estimated Soviet D-day forces at 134 divisions, rising to 320 by D + 30.
74. Wampler, *Ambiguous Legacy*, 267.
75. Acheson, *Present at the Creation*, 426.
76. *HJCS* 4, 109.
77. Ibid.; Williamson and Rearden, *Origins of Nuclear Strategy*, 148–49.
78. *HJCS* 4, 109–113.
79. Raymond L. Garthoff, "Assessing the Adversary: Estimates by the Eisenhower Administration of Soviet Intentions and Capabilities," *Brookings Occasional Papers* (1991), 16; Harry Rositzke, *The CIA's Secret Operations: Espionage, Counterespionage and Covert Action* (New York, 1977), 168–72.
80. *FR*, 1951, 1:88–89, 101–3.
81. Ibid., 221–25, 106–8, 163–66, 170–72, 177–78, 166–69, 169–70, 172–75, 180–81.
82. Ibid., 165.
83. Ibid., 181.
84. Ibid., 172–75.
85. Ibid., 177–78 (emphasis in original).
86. Ibid., 181.
87. Acheson, *Present at the Creation*, 752–53 (note to p.375).
88. *FR*, 1951, 1:234–35, 235–36, 237–38.
89. *FR*, 1952–54, 2:142–50, 209–31.
90. *FR*, 1951, 1:234–35, 235–36.
91. *FR*, 1952–54, 2:18–20.
92. Ibid., 60–68; In May Harry Schwartz, executive secretary to the PPS, had written a memorandum to Bohlen, arguing that even with atomic weapons, the Soviets could not conceivably knock out all the U.S. bases by a surprise blow, and that in view of the Soviet con-

cern for security of the regime the inevitable prospect of retaliation would deter any deliberate general war against the U.S., ibid., 12–17.

93. Ibid., 2:58–68.

94. Ibid., 68–73, 87–88, 80–86, 73–78, 89–113.

95. Ibid., 119–23, 136–39, 142–56.

96. Ibid., 147.

97. Ibid., 210.

98. Ibid.

99. Ibid., 89–94, 87, and compare with Acheson's comments at the September 3, 1952, NSC meeting, ibid., 119.

100. See ibid., 12–17.

101. Ibid., 145–47 (our emphasis).

102. Ibid., 144–45.

103. Ibid., 144 (our emphasis).

104. Ibid., 147–48, 155.

105. Leffler, *Preponderance of Power*, 490–91; John Ranelagh, *The Agency: The Rise and Decline of the CIA from Wild Bill Donovan to Bill Casey* (New York, 1986), 219–20.

106. *FR*, 1952–54, 2:187–88.

107. Ibid., 93.

108. Ibid., 229.

109. Ibid., 205.

110. *PP–T*, 1200–201.

111. *FR*, 1952–54, 2:901.

112. Ibid., 893.

113. Ibid., 146–50.

114. *HJCS* 4, 125–26.

115. *FR*, 1952–54, 222, 213–14.

116. Ibid., 211–22.

117. *HJCS* 4, 199. See also Wampler, *Ambiguous Legacy*, chapter 6.

118. Wampler, *Ambiguous Legacy*, 378–82; *HJCS* 4, 299.

119. Wampler, *Ambiguous Legacy*, 270–73; *HJCS* 4, 299, 326–27.

120. Wampler, *Ambiguous Legacy*, 276.

121. Ibid., 298–323.

122. Ibid., 340–42.

123. "Defense Policy and Global Strategy," Report by the British Chiefs of Staff, D(52)26, June 17, 1952, reprinted in Alan MacMillan and John Baylis, "A Reassessment of the British Global Strategy Paper of 1952," *Nuclear History Program Occasional Paper* 8 (1994), 19–63.

124. Ibid.

125. *HJCS* 4, 309.

126. Wampler treats this whole episode in detail in *Ambiguous Legacy*, 340–54.

127. *HJCS* 4, 304–6; Wampler, *Ambiguous Legacy*, 418.

128. Wampler, *Ambiguous Legacy*, 437; Poole, *HJCS* 4, 310.

129. Acheson, *Present at the Creation*, 707–9.

130. *FR*, 1952–54, 2:202–4.

131. Ibid., 211.

132. *FR*, 1950, 1:283.

133. *FR*, 1952–54, 2:167–68.

134. Ibid., 152.

135. Ibid., 114–17, 141–42.

136. Ibid., 120–23.

137. Ibid., 138–40.

138. Ibid., 164–65.

139. Ibid., 182–84. See also ibid., 142n.3. Whether the paper was submitted to the president is not clear.

140. Ibid., 205–7.

141. Ibid., 211, 213–14.

2   The Prepresidential Eisenhower

1. *ED*, 225.

2. Robert R. Jervis, *Perception and Misperception in International Relations* (Princeton, 1976); Richard H. Immerman, "Psychology," *Journal of American History* 77 (June 1990): 169–80.

3. The most detailed account of this phase of Eisenhower's career is Ambrose, *Eisenhower*, vol 1. Unless indicated otherwise, we draw on this biography.

4. *AE*, 213.

5. *LM*, 38 (emphasis in original). For similar assessments, *EP*, 1:617, 2:795.

6. *ED*, 137–38.

7. Thomas G. Paterson and Robert J. McMahon, eds. *The Origins of the Cold War* (3rd. ed., Lexington, 1991).

8. Walter Isaacson and Evan Thomas, *The Wise Men. Six Friends and the World They Made: Acheson, Bohlen, Harriman, Kennan, Lovett, McCloy* (New York, 1986).

9. *EP*, 11:1312, 8:1609.

10. Ibid., 12: 659–60.

11. *ED*, 210.

12. *EP*, 12:488.

13. U.S. Cong., Senate, *Hearings Before the Committee on Foreign Relations and the Committee on Armed Services on S. Con. Res. 8*, 82nd Cong., 1st Sess. (Washington, 1951), 2. See also U.S. Cong., House, *Hearings Before the Committee on Armed Services on Universal Military Training*, 80th Cong., 2nd Sess. (Washington, 1948), 986.

14. The term "Great Equation" was popularized by Charles J. V. Murphy in "The Eisenhower Shift: Part I," *Fortune*, January 1956, 87.

15. *EP* 8:1596.

16. Ibid., 13:963.

17. *ED*, 210.

18. Ibid., 143–44.

19. *CE*, 476. On Eisenhower's consistent advocacy of military preparedness in the aftermath of World War II see also his statements in U.S. Cong., House, *Hearings Before the Select Committee on Postwar Military Policy*, 79th Cong., 1st Sess. (Washington, 1945), 487–88; and U.S. Cong., House, *Hearings Before the Committee on Military Affairs on H.R. 5682*, 79th Cong., 2nd Sess. (Washington, 1946), 2–15; U.S. Cong., House, *Hearings Before the Committee on Armed Services on Universal Military Training*, 80th Cong., 2nd Sess. (Washington, 1948), 986–1013; U.S. Cong., Senate, *Hearings Before the Preparedness Subcommittee of the Committee on Armed Services on S. 1*, 82nd Cong., 1st Sess. (Washington, 1951), 1186–1204.

20. *EP*, 13:896 (emphasis in original).

21. *ED*, 142.

22. *EP* 9:1852, 10:563; *ED*, 156–57.

23. *ED*, 211–12, 200–201.

24. Ibid., 157–58.

25. *Hearings Before the Senate Committees on Foreign Relations and Armed Services,* 19.

26. Daniel Yergin, *Shattered Peace: The Origins of the Cold War* (rev. ed., New York, 1990), 42–68.

27. *ED,* 160; *EP,* 13:1098. For Eisenhower's earlier belief that a "'live and let live' type of agreement [with the Soviets] could be achieved and honestly kept," see *CE,* 475; *EP,* 6:314–15.

28. *EP,* 7:619; *LM,* 65; *EP,* 6:257, 7:591–92; *CE,* 470–74.

29. Eisenhower to David Lawrence, March 14, 1952, "Eisenhower, Dwight D.," DLP. In 1947 Eisenhower expressed the fear that his relationship with Zhukov contributed to the marshal's "eclipse." *EP,* 8:1530–31. After Stalin's death the Kremlin resurrected Zhukov as defense minister. At the 1955 Geneva summit the former comrades–in–arms lunched at the president's villa. Memorandum of conversation, July 20, 1955, "Strictly Confidential U–Z (2)," GCMS.

30. Entry for March 17, 1953, "Hughes Diary Notes 1953," EJHP. A slightly different version of Eisenhower's quote appears in Emmet John Hughes, *The Ordeal of Power: A Political Memoir of the Eisenhower Years* (New York, 1975), 107. For an earlier instance of Eisenhower's recalling this conversation to support his image of Stalin, see *EP,* 9:2021–22.

31. *CE,* 469.

32. Eisenhower to Field Marshal the Viscount Montgomery of Alamein, May 2, 1956, "Montgomery (NATO), 1953–56 (3)," Name Series, AWF; *Hearings Before the Senate Committees on Foreign Relations and Armed Services,* 25; *FR, 1951,* 3:456; *EP,* 13:867.

33. Eisenhower's markup of "A National Strategy for the Soviet Union," address by Rear Admiral L. C. Stevens, January 25, 1951, is located in "Harriman, W. Averell (4)," DDEPP. In addition to the quote on pp. 20–21, the underscorings and marginalia on pp. 27 and 32 are particularly revealing. Eisenhower wrote in his diary, "Some days ago I read a remarkable paper on Soviets, by an Admiral Stevens. I think I'll put it in the back of this book [he did not] *because,* with minor exceptions, it represents my beliefs exactly." *ED,* 189 (emphasis in original). Stevens served on the JCS staff after a three-year stint as naval attaché in Moscow, a period that coincided with Bedell Smith's tenure as ambassador.

34. On Eisenhower's faith in his ability to calculate what he called the "personal equation," see Fred I. Greenstein, *The Hidden-Hand Presidency: Eisenhower as Leader* (New York, 1982), 25–30.

35. *EP,* 12:488–89 (emphasis in original).

36. Ibid., 12:868, 8:1609.

37. *ED,* 137, 201; *FR, 1950,* 3:450; *EP,* 12:488–89.

38. Eisenhower to David Lawrence, March 14, 1952, "Eisenhower, Dwight D.," Correspondence, DLP.

39. *EP,* 11:1488.

40. *EP,* 13:1125–26. On "imperial overstretch" see Paul Kennedy, *The Rise and Fall of the Great Powers: Economic Change and Military Conflict from 1500 to 2000* (New York, 1987).

41. *EP,* 7:1196–97. Although the agent for the nuclear revolution was the hydrogen bomb, it was anticipated by theorists such as Brodie. See Bernard Brodie et al., *The Absolute Weapon: Atomic Power and World Order* (New York, 1946). See also Robert Jervis, *The Meaning of the Nuclear Revolution: Statecraft and the Prospect of Armageddon* (Ithaca, 1989). Eisenhower highlighted the sentence in the manuscript of Brodie's "Military Policy and the Atomic Bomb" that read, "Whether or not the ideas presented above are entirely valid, they may perhaps stimulate those to whom our military security is entrusted to a more rigorous and better informed kind of analysis which will reach sounder conclusions." His marked-up copy can be found in "Atomic Weapons and Energy (2)," DDEPP.

42. Eisenhower address, October 8, 1952, "September 26, 1952," Speech Series, AWF.

43. *AE*, 186.

44. *EP*, 2:1250.

45. *MC*, 312–13; quoted in Gar Alperovitz, *Atomic Diplomacy: Hiroshima and Potsdam—The Use of the Atomic Bomb and the American Confrontation with Soviet Power* (rev. ed., New York, 1985), 1, 14. For evidence that challenges the assertion that at the time Eisenhower opposed Truman's decision to use the bomb, see Barton J. Bernstein, "Ike and Hiroshima: Did He Oppose It?" *Journal of Strategic Studies* 10 (September 1987): 337–79.

46. Eisenhower address, October 8, 1952; Eisenhower address, May 16, 1950, *NYT*, May 17, 1950; *EP*, 11:1374, 13:1126.

47. Eisenhower, "World Peace—A Balance," March 23, 1950, in *PJ*, 18; Arthur Krock private memo, January 5, 1951, "Eisenhower, Dwight D.," Correspondence—Selected, AJKP. Eisenhower held to this estimate of Soviet intentions consistently. See *EP*, 7:1106–7n.3; *NYT*, February 6, 1948; *EP*, 9:2217n.2, 13:867, 1230, 1263.

48. Krock private memo, January 5, 1951, AJKP; Eisenhower address to the American Legion Convention in New York, August 25, 1952, "July 12, 1952—September 14, 1952," Speech Series, AWF.

49. *FR*, 1951, 3:456; *EP*, 8:1308, 11:1184–85, 13:867, 1125 (emphasis in original); *ED*, 213. On the loose and not–so–loose talk of preventive war, and planning for such an option, see Marc Trachtenberg, "A 'Wasting Asset': American Strategy and the Shifting Nuclear Balance," *International Security* 13 (Winter 1988/89): 5–49; Tami Davis Biddle, "Handling the Soviet Threat: Project Control and the Debate on American Strategy in the Early Cold War Years," *Journal of Strategic Studies* (September 1989): 273–302; Russell D. Buhite and Wm. Christopher Hamel, "War for Peace: The Question of an American Preventive War against the Soviet Union, 1945–1955," *Diplomatic History* 14 (Summer 1990): 367–84. On the security dilemma see Robert R. Jervis, "Cooperation under the Security Dilemma," *World Politics* 30 (January 1978): 167–214.

50. *EP*, 10:564.

51. Ibid., 563–64.

52. *FR*, 1951, 3:457; *EP*, 13:867; *Hearings Before the House Committee on Armed Services*, 987; *CE*, 477.

53. Printed in Harold Stassen and Marshall Houts, *Eisenhower: Turning the World Toward Peace* (St. Paul, 1990), 357–61.

54. *FR*, 1951, 3:450.

55. *ED*, 206; *EP*, 9:2218–19, 13:1099–1101, 12:398 (emphasis in original).

56. *Hearings Before the Senate Committees on Foreign Relations and Armed Services*, 3–7; *FR*, 1951, 3:450.

57. Gunter Bischof and Stephen E. Ambrose, eds., *Eisenhower: A Centenary Assessment* (Baton Rouge, 1995), 64–83.

58. *EP*, 12:98, 8:1567–68. As will be seen, Eisenhower retained these views but determined that for political reasons, U.S. troops would have to remain overseas indefinitely.

59. *ED*, 143; *EP*, 12:224–25.

60. This pervasive geopolitical perspective and Eisenhower's acceptance of it is developed best in Leffler, *Preponderance of Power*.

61. *EP*, 13:1098–1103.

62. *ED*, 13–15.

63. Ibid., 222–24.

64. Ibid.; *EP*, 12:224–25, 6:403–4, 12:1148. For Eisenhower's prepresidential efforts to improve these capabilities, see *EP*, 8:1763–64; Eisenhower to John Foster Dulles, November 26, 1952, "Confidential—Memos and Letters (3)," Subject Series, DPEL.

65. On Wisner, see Evan Thomas, *The Very Best Men: Four Who Dared: The Early Years of the CIA* (New York, 1995).

66. *EP*, 10:428; "The Pursuit of Liberty," an address by John Foster Dulles, December 13, 1949, "Liberation—1949," DPP. Eisenhower's sponsorship of the National Committee for a Free Europe can be traced in "Clubs and Associations, National Committee for a Free Europe Correspondence," Subject File, DDEPP.

67. For the spectrum of categories for organizing the presidency, see Richard Tanner Johnson, *Managing the White House: An Intimate Study of the Presidency* (New York, 1974).

68. *ED*, 209–13, 176–77, 180–81, 182–83.

69. Eisenhower address, October 8, 1952. Indicative of the importance Eisenhower attached to this principle, excerpts from this speech were circulated among national security planners during the administration's first months. Barklie Henry to William H. Jackson and enclosure, March 16, 1953, "Misc. File Material—A–F (3)," PCIIA; Elmer B. Staats memorandum for the Professional Staff, OCB, September 29, 1953, "Budget-Federal (1)," Special Assistant Series, Subject Subseries, WHOSANSA.

70. Greenstein, *Hidden-Hand Presidency*, 133.

71. Quoted in Stephen E. Ambrose, *D-Day, June 6, 1944: The Climactic Battle of World War II* (New York, 1994), 61.

72. *EP*, 9:2250.

3   The Presecretarial Dulles

1. *ED*, 237.

2. Eisenhower interview, JFDOH.

3. Richard H. Immerman, ed., *John Foster Dulles and the Diplomacy of the Cold War* (Princeton, 1990), 9; Immerman, "Eisenhower and Dulles: Who Made the Decisions?" *Political Psychology* 1 (Autumn 1979): 21–38.

4. The best examination of Dulles's early years is Ronald W. Pruessen, *John Foster Dulles: The Road to Power* (New York, 1982).

5. See, for example, *FR*, 1952–54, 7:829.

6. John Foster Dulles, *War, Peace and Change* (New York, 1939). "The thoughts herein expressed are the result of much thinking and study since the Paris Peace Conference of 1919," Dulles began his book (ix).

7. Dulles to William E. Borah, April 3, 1939, "Borah, William E.—1939," DPP.

8. Leonard Mosely, *Dulles: A Biography of Eleanor, Allen, and John Foster Dulles and Their Family Network* (New York, 1978), 89–100. For Dulles's references to Germany as a more dynamic country than Britain and France, and his perspective on the Munich conference, see *War, Peace and Change*, 68, 91–92, 97, 146–48, 154–55, 162.

9. "A Christian Message on World Order from the International Round Table of Christian Leaders," July 1943, "Church Activities—1943," DPP. See also memorandum of conference with the president, March 26, 1943, "Federal Council of the Churches of Christ in America—Commission to Study the Bases of a Just and Durable Peace—1943," ibid.

10. Mark G. Toulouse, *The Transformation of Dulles: From Prophet of Realism to Priest of Nationalism* (Macon, Georgia, 1985), 10.

11. Louis L. Gerson, *John Foster Dulles* (New York, 1967), 25.

12. Pruessen, *Dulles*, 221–37.

13. Dulles to Henry P. Van Dusen, March 29, 1939, "Van Dusen, Henry P.—1939," DPP. The dean of Union Theological Seminary, Van Dusen was a longtime friend and frequent collaborator of Dulles with whom he regularly corresponded about ethics and religion.

14. Dulles to Clark M. Eichelberger, October 25, 1943, "Eichelberger, Clark M.—1943," DPP.

15. Dulles's *War, Peace and Change* represented the culmination of a series of his writ-

ings articulating his views on the deteriorating Versailles system, especially, "The Road to Peace," *Atlantic Monthly* 156 (October 1935): 492–99, and "The Problem of Peace in a Dynamic World," *Religion in Life* 6 (Spring 1937): 191–207; and his March 19, 1936, Stafford Little Foundation address at Princeton University, "Peaceful Change within the Society of Nations," located in the file by the same title, DPP.

16. Dulles, *War, Peace and Change*, passim.

17. Dulles to the Right Honorable Viscount Astor, February 18, 1943, "Astor, Waldorf—1943," DPP; Dulles to Arthur Hays Sulzberger, October 21, 1943, "Sulzberger, Arthur Hays—1943," ibid.

18. Dulles to Astor, February 18, 1943; Dulles address, "The Balance of Power," March 10, 1950, "Soviet Union and Communist Party," DPP; Dulles redraft of Federal Council of the Churches of Christ in America statement on "Soviet-U.S. Tension," "Federal Council of the Churches of Christ in America,—1946," ibid.; Dulles address, "Foreign Policy—Ideals, Not Deals," February 10, 1947, "Re: Church Activities—1947," ibid.; Dulles address, "The Christian Citizen in a Changing World," August 22, 1948, "Soviet Union and Communist Party—1948," ibid.; Dulles address, "For a Spiritual Offensive: An Appeal for a Dynamic Foreign Policy Under the Moral Law," *Princeton Alumni Weekly*, March 7, 1952, 11–12; Dulles, *War or Peace* (New York, 1950), 16, 233–41, 262.

19. Memorandum to Dewey, "General Observations"; "Foreign Policy—Ideals, Not Deals"; speech enclosed with JFD to Thomas E. Dewey; "The Defense of Freedom"; untitled top secret memorandum, May 18, 1950, "China, People's Republic of—1950," DPP; "U.S. and Russia Could Agree but for Communist Party's Crusade: An Interview with John Foster Dulles," *U.S. News & World Report*, January 21, 1949, 33.

20. Dulles address, "American Tradition," March 11, 1948, "Re Church Activities—1948," DPP.

21. "U.S. and Russia Could Agree but for Communist Party's Crusade," 35; Dulles to Vandenberg, September 12, 1946, "Vandenberg, Arthur H.—1946," DPP; Dulles address, "Appraisal of United States' Foreign Policy," February 5, 1945, "Re Speech by JFD, February 5, 1945," ibid.

22. Dulles, *War or Peace*, 236; "Foreign Policy–Ideals, Not Deals."

23. Council of Foreign Relations, "Digest of Discussion, Marshall Plan Group," February 2, 1948, "Marshall Plan—1948," ibid; Dulles address, "Christian Responsibility for Peace," May 4, 1948, "Re: Church Activities—1948," ibid.

24. "Foreign Policy–Ideals, Not Deals"; Dulles, *War or Peace*, 233–41.

25. Dulles did not mention the Soviet Union in *War, Peace and Change*.

26. Dulles to Astor, February 18, 1943; Dulles to Sulzberger, October 21, 1943; Pruessen, *Dulles*, 270.

27. Dulles to Sulzberger, October 21, 1943; Dulles to John C. Higgins, December 4, 1945, "Higgins, John C.—1945," DPP; Dulles to Carle C. Conway, December 15, 1943, "Conway, Carle C.—1943," ibid.; Dulles to Henry Luce, September 29, 1943, "Luce, Henry R.—1943," ibid.; Dulles to Laird Bell, March 27, 1945, "Bell, Laird—1945," ibid.; Dulles to Edward C. Carter, January 22, 1947, "Nehru, Jawaharlal—1947," ibid. For Toynbee's influence on Dulles, see Pruessen, *Dulles*, 306–7,

28. Dulles to Henry P. Van Dusen, November 17, 1941, "Van Dusen, Henry P.—1941," ibid.; Dulles to Lionel Curtis, September 19, 1944, "Curtis, Lionel—1944," ibid.; Dulles to Astor, February 18, 1943.

29. Dulles believed that the Soviet Union warranted special considerations in Eastern Europe and reacted enthusiastically to the Yalta conference. See Dulles to Raymond L. Buell, February 13, 1945, "Federal Council of Churches—1945," ibid.; Dulles, "A Personal Appraisal of the Crimea Conference," February 26, 1945, "Re: Yalta Conference—1945," ibid.

30. Extract from notes dictated in advance of meeting of Commission on a Just and Durable Peace. November 8, 1947, "Byrnes, James F.—1945," ibid.

31. Dulles to Higgins, December 4, 1945. On atomic diplomacy see J. Samuel Walker, "The Decision to Use the Bomb: A Historiographical Update," *DH* 14 (Winter 1990): 97–114; "Hiroshima in History and Memory: A Symposium," *DH* 19 (Spring 1995): 197–365. Dulles's logic illustrates the psychological "inherent bad faith model" scholars have used to explain his perceptions of the Soviets once he became secretary of state. See Ole R. Hosti, "Cognitive Dynamics and Images of the Enemy: Dulles and Russia," in David J. Finlay, et al., *Enemies in Politics* (Chicago, 1967), 25–96; Deborah Welch Larson, "Crisis Prevention and the Austrian State Treaty," *International Organization* 41 (Winter 1987): 27–60.

32. Dulles, "What I've Learned About the Russians," *Collier's*, March 12, 1949, 25, 57; Dulles to The Right Honorable Hector McNeil, M.P., May 3, 1948, "Soviet Union and the Communist Party—1948," DPP. On p. 7 of the "Know Your Enemy" chapter of *War or Peace*, Dulles argued that *Problems of Leninism* was a more authoritative "guide to [Bolshevik] action" than the writings of Marx, Engles, or Lenin.

33. Dulles to Alice Hill Byrne, September 12, 1946, "Soviet Union and the Communist Party—1946," DPP.

34. Dulles, "Thoughts on Soviet Foreign Policy," *Life* 20 (June 3, 1946), 112ff; and June 10, 1946, 118ff.

35. Dulles to William Kostka, September 27, 1946, "Re: *Look* Magazine Forum—1946," DPP; Dulles address to Philadelphia Foreign Policy Association, March 1, 1946, "Foreign Policy Association—1946," ibid.

36. "Thoughts on Soviet Foreign Policy" (part 1), 113–18, 123; Dulles address, "The United Nations—Its Challenge to America," February 22, 1946, "Speech by Dulles, February 22, 1946," DPP; address to Philadelphia Foreign Policy Association.

37. Dulles, "What I've Learned About the Russians"; minutes of Council of Foreign Ministers meeting, June 6, 1947, "Council of Foreign Ministers meetings—1947," DPP.

38. Dulles, "Why Russia Cries 'War,'" *Talks* 13 (January 1948).

39. "U.S. and Russia Could Agree but for Communist Party's Crusade," 33–34; "The Christian Citizen in a Changing World"; Dulles address, "Our International Responsibilities," June 4, 1950, "Speech by Dulles, June 4, 1950," DPP; Dulles address, "Not War, Not Peace," January 17, 1948, "Council of Foreign Ministers—1948," ibid.

40. Dulles to A. J. Muste, June 17, 1946, "Muste, A. J.—1946," ibid.; "Improving Relations with Russia: An Interview with John Foster Dulles," *U.S. News & World Report*, July 8, 1949, 31; "The Balance of Power"; "The Strategy of Soviet Communism." Dulles and Federal Council of Churches president Bishop G. Bromley Oxnam did issue a statement immediately following the destruction of Hiroshima and Nagasaki expressing concern over the impact of atomic weapons on the future conduct of international relations. See statement for publication in morning papers, August 10, 1945, "Atomic Weapons—1945," DPP.

41. "The Defense of Freedom"; "Christian Responsibility for Peace"; "American Tradition"; "Our International Responsibilities." This view of war contrasts sharply with Dulles's pre–cold war belief that at times war had "been of benefit to mankind and the only way in which that benefit could have been achieved." See Dulles to Clark M. Eichelberger, October 25, 1943, "Eichelberger, Clark M.," DPP.

42. "Christian Responsibility for Peace."

43. Ibid.

44. Dulles to Arthur Vandenberg, September 28, 1948, "Italy—1948," DPP.

45. Dulles, "Europe and the Atlantic Pact," *Philadelphia Evening Bulletin Forum*, March 23, 1949.

46. "Thoughts on Soviet Foreign Policy" (part 2), 119; Dulles redraft of Federal Council of Churches statement; "Our International Responsibilities."

47. Pruessen, *Dulles*, 454; quoted in Harry S. Truman, *Memoirs: Years of Trial and Hope* (Garden City, New York, 1956), 336; Department of State press release, May 29, 1951, "Soviet Union and the Communist Party—1951," DPP.

48. Speech draft enclosed with Dulles to Dewey; memorandum to Dewey re: Foreign Policy, "General Observations," October 26, 1948, "Dewey, Thomas E.—1948," ibid.; "For a Spiritual Offensive"; Dulles statement before the Foreign Relations Committee of the United States Senate, May 4, 1949, "North Atlantic Pact—1949," DPP.

49. "The Defense of Freedom"; "Christian Responsibility for Peace"; "American Tradition"; "Our International Responsibilities."

50. Dulles to James P. Pope, April 28, 1942; "Our International Responsibilities"; "American Tradition"; "Foreign Policy–Ideals, Not Deals"; speech draft enclosed with Dulles to Dewey.

51. "The Defense of Freedom;" "Christian Responsibility for Peace"; "Our International Responsibilities".

52. "Notes on Foreign Policy," June 29, 1949, "Ferguson, Homer—1949," DPP; "U.S. and Russia Could Agree but for Communist Party's Crusade," 33–34; memorandum of conversation with Lovett, August 28, 1948, "Lovett, Robert A.—1948," DPP.

53. Jean Smith, *Lucius D. Clay: An American Life* (New York, 1990), 416–18.

54. The ECSC was formed in 1951; France killed the EDC in 1954.

55. Dulles untitled secret memorandum, March 7, 1947, "Germany—1947," DPP; Dulles to Charles Edmundson, May 20, 1947, "Edmundson, Charles—1947," ibid.; minutes of CFM meeting, June 6, 1947, "Council of Foreign Ministers Meeting—1947," ibid.; Dulles to Vandenberg, September 12, 1946, "Vandenberg, Arthur H.—1946," ibid; Dulles to Vandenberg, July 21, 1947, "Vandenberg, Arthur H.—1947," ibid.; "Item C," copy of memo of secret meeting at Blair House between [George] Marshall, [Robert] Lovett, Vandenberg, and Dulles, April 27, 1948, "Vandenberg, Arthur H.—1948," ibid.; Dulles memorandum to Allen Dulles, January 19, 1950, "Dulles, Allen W.—1950," ibid.; Dulles to Jean Monnet, May 23, 1950, "Monnet, Jean—1950," ibid.

56. "Improving Relations with Russia," 31–33; Dulles statement before the SFRC; transcript of CBS "Capitol Cloakroom," June 29, 1949, "Berlin—1949," DPP; "What I've Learned About the Russians," 25, 57.

57. Dulles, *War or Peace*, 242.

58. Dulles address, "The Strategy of Soviet Communism," March 14, 1950, "Soviet Union and Communist Party—1950," DPP; "Our International Responsibilities."

59. Dulles statement before the SFRC.

60. Dulles, *War or Peace*, 75–76; Council of Foreign Relations Study Group Digest of Discussion, October 23, 1950, "Japan and Japanese Peace Treaty—1950," DPP; Dulles address, "Strategy for the Pacific," March 14, 1951, "Speech by Dulles, March 14, 1951," ibid.; Dulles address, "The Free East and the Free West," December 2, 1951, Department of State press release, November 29, 1951, "Soviet Union and the Communist Party—1951," ibid.; Dulles to Chester Bowles, March 10, 1952, "Bowles, Chester—1952," ibid.; Dulles address to World Affairs Council of Seattle, September 18, 1952, "Containment Policy—1952," ibid.

61. "To Save Humanity from the Abyss," *New York Times Magazine*, July 30, 1950; Dulles memorandum to Pierre Crevesse, October 27, 1950, "Japan: Japanese Peace Treaty—1950," DPP; Dulles top secret memorandum, May 18, 1950, "China, People's Republic of—1950," ibid.; memorandum of conversation with Dean Acheson, Frank Pace, and others of the State Department, July 1, 1950, "Acheson, Dean—1950," ibid; Dulles address, "Where Are We?"

December 29, 1950, "Soviet Union and the Communist Party—1950," ibid.; Dulles to Ferdinand Mayer, November 9, 1950, "Mayer, Ferdinand L.—1950," ibid.

62. "Where Are We?" Dulles address, "Can We Stop Russian Imperialism?" November 27, 1951, "Speech: November 27, 1951," DPP.

63. Conventional critiques are represented by Hans Morgenthau, "The Dulles Doctrine: 'Instant Retaliation,'" *New Republic*, March 29, 1954," 10–14; William W. Kaufmann, "The Requirements of Deterrence," in Kaufmann, ed., *Military Policy and National Security* (Princeton, 1956), 12–38, and Henry Kissinger, *Nuclear Weapons and Foreign Policy* (New York, 1957).

64. Dulles to Mayer, November 9, 1950; Transcript of "Meet the Press," "Speech [Interview] by Dulles, February 10, 1952," DPP; Dulles to Thomas K. Philips, February 1, 1952, "Containment Policy—1952," ibid. On manipulating risk see in particular Thomas Schelling, *Arms and Influence* (New Haven, 1966). John Gaddis explores Dulles's "wedge theory" in *The Long Peace: Inquiries into the History of the Cold War* (New York, 1987), 147–94.

65. Memorandum to Dewey, "General Observations" (emphasis in original); Dulles to Eustace Seligman, January 9, 1951, "Seligman, Eustace—1951," DPP; State Department press release re: Dulles address, May 30, 1951, "Soviet Union and the Communist Party—1951," ibid.

66. Dulles address, "The United Nations—Its Challenge to America," February 22, 1946, "Speech by Dulles, September 22, 1946," DPP; Dulles to Kennan, October 2, 1952, "Kennan, George F.—1952," ibid. In this letter Dulles referred to a speech he delivered on September 26, 1952. It is located in "Republican Presidential Campaign—1952," ibid. For Kennan's reply, see Kennan to Dulles, October 22, 1952, and enclosed "observations" dated August 18, 1952, "Kennan, George F.—1952," ibid.

67. Dulles to William G. Coxhead, June 4, 1947, "Federal Council of the Churches of Christ: Commission for the Study of a Just and Durable Peace—1947," DPP; "The Defense of Freedom"; "Strategy of Soviet Communism"; Dulles, *War or Peace*, 242–52; Dulles letter to the editors of *The Commonweal*, September 5, 1952, "Containment Policy—1952," DPP.

68. Untitled and unsigned State Department document, December 4, 1952, Subject Series, "State Department—Personnel," DPP.

69. Dulles to Herter, December 22, 1948, "Herter, Christian—1948," ibid.

4 Campaigning for Security with Solvency

1. *EP*, 13:1254.

2. *ED*, 189, 195. See also, Herbert S. Parmet, *Eisenhower and the American Crusades* (New York, 1972), 45–149; Robert Divine, *Foreign Policy and Presidential Elections, 1952–1960* (New York, 1974), 3–85; Chester J. Pach, Jr., and Elmo Richardson, *The Presidency of Dwight D. Eisenhower* (Lawrence, Kansas, 1991), 20–27.

3. *ED*, 240, 269. The best biography of Taft remains James T. Patterson, *Mr. Republican: A Biography of Robert A. Taft* (Boston, 1972).

4. Taft in fact did not fully subscribe to the "Fortress America" concept advocated by those Republicans who rallied behind former President Hoover. See Robert A. Taft, *A Foreign Policy for Americans* (Garden City, New York, 1951).

5. *AE*, 371–72; Eisenhower interview, Columbia Oral History Collection, Columbia University, New York.

6. Parmet, *Eisenhower*, 39, 59, 99–101.

7. Eisenhower address in Philadelphia, September 4, 1952, *NYT*, September 5, 1952. Prior to the official opening of the campaign, on August 25 Eisenhower had spoken at the Ameri-

can Legion Convention in New York City also concerning foreign policy. See also Eisenhower's comments immediately following his nomination, *NYT*, August 12, 1952.

8. On this analogy see Piers Brendon, *Ike: His Life & Times* (New York, 1986), 220–21.

9. Duane Tananbaum, *The Bricker Amendment Controversy: A Test of Eisenhower's Political Leadership* (Ithaca, 1988). Domestically, Truman's decision in April 1952 to seize control of the steel industry on the basis of his power as commander in chief provided further impetus for the Bricker amendment.

10. *EP*, 13:1255.

11. A corps of wordsmiths led by *Time-Life* veterans Emmet J. Hughes and C. D. Jackson drafted most of Eisenhower's addresses, but the final speeches were very much his own.

12. See, for example, Eisenhower's address in Flint, Michigan, October 1, 1952, *NYT*, October 2, 1952. As Eisenhower underscored, moreover, Michigan was the home state of the godfather of Republican support for NATO, Arthur Vandenberg.

13. "What Men and Platforms Say," *NYT*, July 27, 1952; Eisenhower address in Philadelphia; Eisenhower foreign policy statement issued on October 4, 1952, ibid., October 5, 1952.

14. Eisenhower address in Flint, Michigan.

15. U.S. Cong., Senate, Committee on Foreign Relations, *Nomination of John Foster Dulles, Secretary of State-Designate: Hearing Before the Committee on Foreign Relations*, 83rd Cong., 1st Sess., January 15, 1953, 8.

16. Divine, *Foreign Policy and Presidential Elections*, 29–36.

17. Parmet, *Eisenhower*, 103.

18. Eisenhower, *MC*, 41.

19. Divine, *Foreign Policy and Presidential Elections*, 64; David M. Oshinky, *A Conspiracy So Immense: The World of Joe McCarthy* (New York, 1983), 234–38.

20. SCFR, *Hearing on Dulles Nomination*, 15–17.

21. For evidence that Eisenhower had reason to be concerned, see Norman A. Graebner, *The New Isolationism: A Study in Politics and Foreign Policy since 1950* (New York, 1956).

22. *EP*, 13:1254.

23. Dulles, "A Policy of Boldness," *Life*, May 19, 1952, 146+. Read in draft by Eisenhower and key party leaders, this article was central to the Republican campaign and was reflected in the foreign policy planks of the GOP platform, much of which Dulles wrote.

24. Dulles to Walter Millis and enclosure, May 23, 1952, "Millis, Walter—1952," DPP; Dulles, "Policy of Boldness," 151.

25. *EP*, 13:1179.

26. Dulles to Eisenhower, April 25, 1952, "Dulles, John Foster," DDEPP.

27. Dulles, "Policy of Boldness," 152. See also the draft "Foreign Policy Memorandum by John Foster Dulles, 4/11/52 Corrected to 5/1/52, "Dulles, John Foster, 1952," Selected Correspondence and Related Material, AWDP.

28. *EP*, 13:1254–55; C. L. Sulzberger, *A Long Row of Candles: Memoirs and Diaries, 1934–1954* (New York, 1969), 770; 1952 Republican Platform, *National Party Platforms, 1840–1956*, compiled by Kirk H. Porter and Donald Bruce Johnson (Urbana, IL, 1956), 499.

29. For example, see Eisenhower address at Baltimore, Maryland, September 25, 1952, "Sept. 15, 1952 — Sept. 25, 1952," Speech Series, AWF.

30. Quoted in Emmet John Hughes, *The Ordeal of Power: A Political Memoir of the Eisenhower Years* (New York, 1975), 28.

31. Eisenhower address in Baltimore, Maryland.

32. Dulles, "Policy of Boldness," 160, 157.

33. Dulles to Walter Millis and enclosure, May 23, 1952.

34. Athan G. Theoharis, *The Yalta Myths: An Issue in U.S. Politics, 1945–1955* (Columbia, Missouri, 1970).

35. Eisenhower address to the American Legion Convention in New York, August 25, 1952, "July 12, 1952—September 14, 1952," Speech Series, AWF.

36. *National Party Platforms*, 497–99.

37. Harold Callender, "Europe Is Puzzled by G.O.P. Platform," *NYT*, July 18, 1952.

38. Parmet, *Eisenhower*, 124–25. For evidence that Dulles learned his lesson, see SCFR, *Hearing on Dulles Nomination*, 5–6.

39. Eisenhower address to the American Legion (our emphasis); Eisenhower address in Philadelphia.

40. Eisenhower address in San Franciso, California, October 8, 1952, "September 26, 1952," Speech Series, AWF.

41. Ibid.

42. Ibid.

43. W. H. Lawrence, "Eisenhower for Korean War but Says Blunders Led to It," *NYT*, August 22, 192; Burton I. Kaufman, *The Korean War: Challenges in Crisis, Credibility, and Command* (New York, 1986), 301–2.

44. Eisenhower address in Detroit, October 14, 1952, *NYT*, October 25, 1952.

45. Eisenhower address in Baltimore; Eisenhower address in San Francisco.

46. Dean Acheson, "Crisis in Asia: An Examination of United States Policy," January 12, 1950, *DSB* 22 (January 16, 1950), 111–17.

47. Eisenhower address in Philadelphia; Eisenhower address at the New York City Waldorf Astoria Hotel, October 16, 1952, *NYT*, October 17, 1952; Eisenhower address in San Francisco.

48. Eisenhower address in San Francisco. See also Eisenhower address in Champaign, Illinois, October 2, 1952, *NYT*, October 3, 1952.

49. Eisenhower address in Detroit.

50. Ibid.

51. Ibid.

52. Marquis Childs, *Eisenhower: Captive Hero* (New York, 1958), 159; Rosemary Foot, *The Wrong War: American Policy and the Dimensions of the Korean Conflict, 1950–1953* (Ithaca, 1985), 194; *EP*, 12:1251.

53. Eisenhower address in San Francisco; Eisenhower address in Baltimore.

54. Eisenhower address in San Francisco.

55. Eisenhower address in Baltimore.

56. Eisenhower address in San Francisco.

57. Eisenhower address in Baltimore.

58. Gary W. Reichard, *Politics as Usual: The Age of Truman and Eisenhower* (New York, 1988), 82.

59. Ibid.

5 Organizing For National Security

1. *FR*, 2:631.

2. *MC*, 114.

3. Eisenhower, "The Central Role of the President in the Conduct of Security Affairs," in Amos A. Jordon, ed., *Issues of National Security in the 1970s: Essays Presented to Colonel George A. Lincoln on his Sixtieth Birthday* (New York, 1967), 207.

4. Ibid., 87.

5. *ED*, 237.

6. *MC*, 94–95; Arthur W. Radford, *From Pearl Harbor to Vietnam: The Memoirs of Admiral Arthur W. Radford*, ed. Stephen Jurika (Stanford, 1980), 302–5.

7. For the complete list of those who traveled with Eisenhower on the *Helena*, see Guest Quarters Commencing 8 December 1952, "Special Draft: Ending War in Korea," EJHP.

8. *MC*, 96; Radford, *From Pearl Harbor*, 305.

9. Other than a few handwritten notes in Dulles's files, the only other written source on the *Helena* talks is "Reminiscences of Vice Admiral Means Johnston, Jr., Concerning Eisenhower's Visit to Iwo Jima, Korea, U.S.S. *Helena*, and Honolulu, Early December 1952," located in "A Brief Resume of the Life and Experiences of Arthur W. Radford, Admiral, United States Navy (Ret.)," February 4, 1966, Arthur W. Radford Collection, Hoover Institution on War, Revolution and Peace, Stanford, California, on which Radford based his memoir.

10. Summary of J.F.D. remarks at meeting with Eisenhower, Wilson, Brownell, Bradley, and Radford, Kaneohe, Hawaii, December 11, 1952, Subject Series, "S.S. Helena Notes," DPP (emphasis in original).

11. Notes, December 4, 1953, "Bermuda—President's Notes December 1953 (1)," International Series, AWF.

12. Radford to David Lawrence, "Radford, Arthur," Correspondence, DLP; Handwritten notes, February 2, 1953, "C–2 (2), February 25 and March 6, 1953," Cabinet Series, WHOSS.

13. Quoted in Fred I. Greenstein, *The Hidden-Hand Presidency: Eisenhower as Leader* (New York, 1982) 108.

14. See, for example, W. Y. Elliott memorandum for Mr. Arthur S. Flemming, December 23, 1952, "NSC—Organization and Functions [1949–1953] (1)," NSC Series, Administrative Subseries, WHOSANSA; Milton S. Eisenhower to Robert Cutler, "NSC—Organization and Functions [1949–1953] (2)," ibid. PACGO was not formally established until January 29, 1953.

15. Neil MacNeil and Harold W. Metz, *The Hoover Report, 1953–1955* (New York, 1966).

16. Untitled document, December 4, 1952, "State Department—Personnel," Subject Series, DPP. See also *The Hoover Commission Report on Organization of the Executive Branch of the Government* (New York, 1949), 155–56.

17. Eisenhower address in Baltimore, Maryland, September 25, 1952, "Sept. 15, 1952–Sept. 25, 1952," Speech Series, AWF.

18. Robert Cutler, *No Time for Rest* (Boston, 1966), 275–92. For an example of Cutler's contribution to a campaign speech on the NSC, see his comments on the foreign policy speech for San Francisco, 10/6/52, "October 8, 1952, San Francisco, California," SBP.

19. Proceedings of the cabinet meetings, January 12–13, 1953, "Cabinet Meeting January 12–13, 1953," Cabinet Series, AWF.

20. Ibid.

21. Enclosed with Cutler to Eisenhower, December 27, 1952, "Cutler, Robert A., 1952–54 (5)," Administration Series, AWF.

22. Marshall testimony, NSC Study, February 19, 1953, "NSC—Organization and Functions [1949–1953] (5)," NSC Series, Administrative Subseries, WHOSANSA.

23. The following discussion of the NSC organization is derived from ibid.; W. Barton Leach to Robert Cutler, January 19, 1953, "NSC—Organization and Functions [1949–1953] (3)," ibid.; W. Leach, "Observations on the NSC," February 3, 1953, ibid.; Charles E. Bohlen testimony, NSC Study, January 31, 1953, ibid.; James S. Lay, Jr., "Suggestions for Further Strengthening of the National Security Council," January 19, 1953, "NSC—Organization and Functions [1949–1953] (2)," ibid.; Notes of Study Group Conference, February 13, 1953, "NSC—Organization and Functions [1949–1953] (4)," ibid.; George A. Morgan to Cutler, February 16, 1953, ibid; Notes of Study Group Conference, February 17, 1953, "NSC—Organization and Functions [1949–1953] (5)," ibid.; Paul H. Nitze memorandum to Cutler, February 17, 1953, ibid.; William Bundy to the assistant deputy director/Intelligence, March 2, 1953, "NSC—Organization and Functions [1949–1953] (6)," ibid.

24. Both the JCS chair and director of the CIA attended the NSC regularly as advisors, and each meeting began with an oral briefing by the DCI. Cutler arranged special procedures for Eisenhower to receive personal briefings from his staff secretary.

25. During the campaign Eisenhower proposed calling upon "civilians of the highest capacity, integrity and dedication to public service" to inject "fresh point(s) of views" into the NSC deliberations. Eisenhower address in Baltimore, Maryland.

26. Cutler, *No Time for Rest*, 296.

27. Elliott memorandum to Flemming, December 23, 1952 (emphasis in original).

28. Eisenhower quoted in Notes of Study Group Conference, 13 February 1953; Cutler Report to the President, "Operations of National Security Council, January 1953–April 1955," "April 1955 (1)," Special Assistant series, WHOSANSA.

29. *FR*, 1952–54, 2:245–57.

30. *FR*, 1951–54, 2:257–58.

31. The following account of the NSC's operation is derived from Townsend Hoopes's memorandum to Robert Blum, n.d., "JC Numbered Documents (7)," PCIIA; *FR*, 1952–54, 2:245–57; Cutler Report to the President, April 1, 1956; Cutler statement before the Senate Appropriations Committee in support of the appropriation requested by the NSC for FY 1954, n.d., "Budget—NSC—Previous Years (1)," NSC Series, Administrative Subseries, WHOSANSA; Anna Kasten Nelson, "The 'Top of Policy Hill': President Eisenhower and the National Security Council," *DH* 7 (Fall 1983): 307–26.

32. Eisenhower, "The Central Role of the President in the Conduct of Security Affairs," in Amos A. Jordon, Jr., ed., *Issues in National Security in the 1970s* (New York, 1967), 214; *ED*, 379–80.

33. Robert R. Bowie, "The President and the Executive Branch," in Joseph S. Nye, Jr., ed., *The Making of America's Soviet Policy* (New Haven, 1984), 73.

34. *FR*, 1952–54, 2:251.

35. Robert Cutler, "The National Security Council under President Eisenhower," testimony to the Subcommittee on National Policy Machinery, in Henry M. Jackson, ed., *The National Security Council: Jackson Subcommittee Papers on Policy-Making at the Presidential Level*, New York, 1965), 112.

36. *FR*, 1952–54, 2:249 (emphasis in original).

37. The chairman of the National Security Resources Board, the predecessor to the ODM, was also a statutory member. Ultimately the administration transferred the NSRB statutory membership to ODM.

38. Eisenhower, "The Central Role of the President," 217.

39. Richard M. Nixon, *Six Crises* (New York, 1962), 158–59.

40. Fred I. Greenstein and Richard H. Immerman, "What Did Eisenhower Tell Kennedy about Indochina? The Politics of Misperception," *The Journal of American History* 79 (September 1992): 568–87.

41. Memorandum of NSC meeting, March 19, 1953, "137th meeting of the NSC," NSC Series, AWF.

42. Eisenhower to Robert Bowie, April 8, 1953 (our possession).

43. Brief notes on Planning Board meeting, May 6, 1953, CJCS 334 (NSC) 1953, RG 218.

44. As on the NSC, the JCS and CIA had advisory representation on the Planning Board. Until its abolition, so did the Psychological Strategy Board. On occasions when deemed appropriate by either Cutler or Joseph Dodge, a representative of the Bureau of the Budget also attended Planning Board meetings.

45. On the NSC organization as approved by Eisenhower, see Cutler's Report to the President, April 1, 1955; and his "National Security Council," 111–39.

46. James S. Lay, Jr., "Concept of the National Security Council and Its Advisory and

Subordinate Groups," October 15, 1953, "President's Papers 1953 (3)," Special Assistant Series, Presidential Subseries, WHOSANSA.

47. Memorandum of NSC meeting, March 19, 1953.

48. Ibid.; Robert Cutler memorandum for Robert Bowie with copy for General John Gerhart, September 25, 1953, "Cutler's Memos—1953 (5)," Executive Secretary's Subject File Series, WHONSC.

49. Entry for March 1, 1954, Clarence Randall Journals, volume 1, "Washington After the Commission," CRP.

50. *FR, 1952–54*, 2:253.

51. *FR, 1958–60*, 3:58, 61 (emphasis in original).

52. Informal notes of Jackson Committee meeting, March 28, 1953, "Special Assistant (Cutler) memoranda, 1953 (1)," Executive Secretary's Subject File Series, WHONSC (emphasis in original); statement of NSC progress reports attached to James S. Lay, Jr., memorandum for the NSC, September 9, 1953, CCS 334 NSC (9–25–47), sec. 12, JCS; PCIIA report, May 21, 1953, "Correspondence File M (8)," PCIIA.

53. Elmer B. Staats memorandum for the professional staff, OCB, September 29, 1954, "Budget—Federal (1) [October 1953–September 1954]," Special Assistant Series, Subject Subseries, WHOSANSA.

54. Proceedings of cabinet meetings, January 12–13, 1953; Eisenhower to James S. Lay, Jr., January 24, 1953, "President's Papers 1953 (9)," Special Assistant Series, Presidential Subseries, WHOSANSA. In addition to William Jackson, its members included Cutler, C. D. Jackson, Sigurd Larmon, Gordon Gray, Roger Keyes, Barklie McKee Henry, and John C. Hughes. The executive secretary was Abbott Washburn.

55. So named because of the chair, William Jackson, not, as frequently believed, C. D. Jackson, who served on it as the State Department representative. The formal name of the Jackson Committee was the President's Committee on International Information Activities.

56. Ten Points concerning the functionalization [sic] of "Cold War" psychological activities, "Miscellaneous File Material—A–F (3)," PCIIA.

57. Barklie Henry report of interview of Sir Frederick S. Bartlett, March 9, 1953, "Correspondence File C—Restricted," ibid.

58. Robert Blum memorandum for Townsend Hoopes, March 31, 1953, "Miscellaneous File Material—M–P (5)," ibid.; Blum memorandum for William H. Jackson, April 13, 1953, ibid.; W. F. Millikan and W. W. Rostow, "Organization of the Government for the Conduct of Political Warfare," "Miscellaneous File Material—A–F (2)," ibid.

59. See especially the Elliott memorandum for Flemming, December 23, 1952; Lay, "Suggestions for Further Strengthening of the National Security Council," January 19, 1953; notes of Study Group Conference, February 13, 1952; notes of Study Group Conference, February 17, 1953.

60. Townsend Hoopes memorandum to William H. Jackson, "Miscellaneous File Material—M–P (5)"; PCIIA report, May 21, 1953.

61. Karl G. Harr, Jr., "Eisenhower's Approach to National Security Decisionmaking," in Kenneth W. Thompson, *The Eisenhower Presidency: Eleven Intimate Perspectives on Dwight D. Eisenhower* (Lanham, Maryland, 1984), 93.

62. *FR*, 2:1854–55.

63. Ibid., 1855–57; Statement on NSC Progress reports attached to James S. Lay, Jr., memorandum for the NSC, September 9, 1953, CCS 334 NSC (9–25–47), sec. 12, JCS. The OCB assumed responsibility for these progress reports in 1954.

64. *FR*, 2:1795–1867.

65. *FR*, 2:1877–78; press release, July 8, 1953, "Time, Inc. File: Jackson Report," CDJP.

66. Robert Blum memorandum for William H. Jackson, April 13, 1953, "Miscellaneous File Material—M-P (5)," PCIIA; Cutler memorandum for Elmer B. Staats, March 3, 1954, "Chronological—Richard L. Hall 1954 [March] (4)," NSC Series, Administrative Subseries, WHOSANSA.

67. Vincent H. Everding [National War College], "The Formulation and Management of United States National Policy, June 1, 1956," "E—General (2)," Special Assistant Series, Subject Subseries, WHOSANSA; William Jackson memorandum for Eisenhower, December 31, 1956, "Jackson, William (1)," Administration Series, AWF; Dwight D. Eisenhower, *The White House Years: Waging Peace, 1956–1961* (Garden City, New York, 1965), 634.

6 How Much Is Enough?

1. U.S. Cong., Senate, *Hearings Before the Committee on Foreign Relations and the Committee on Armed Services on S. Con. Res. 8*, 82nd Cong., 1st Sess. (Washington, 1951), 2.

2. *FR, 1952–54*, 2:223–30.

3. Ibid.

4. Ibid., 230–31.

5. U.S. Cong., House, *Hearings Before the Committee on Armed Services on Universal Military Training*, 80th Cong., 2nd Sess. (Washington, 1948), 986.

6. *PP-E*, 1953, 1–8.

7. Charles J. V. Murphy, "The Eisenhower Shift: Part 1," *Fortune*, January 1956, 87.

8. Quoted in Emmet John Hughes, *The Ordeal of Power: A Political Memoir of the Eisenhower Years* (New York, 1975) 28.

9. Cabinet notes, March 20, 1953, "C-3 (1), March 20, 1953," Cabinet Series, WHOSS; Department of Defense directive, July 26, 1954, attached to Charles E. Wilson to David Lawrence, January 19, 1956, "Wilson, Charles E.," Correspondence, DLP; Arthur W. Radford memorandum to JCS, September 12, 1955, and attached John K. Gerhard memorandum to Radford, August 10, 1955, CJCS 334 National Security Council (12 September 1955), JCS; HJCS 5, 15–16; E. Bruce Geelhoed, *Charles E. Wilson and the Controversy at the Pentagon, 1953 to 1957* (Detroit, 1979), 156.

10. *ED*, 237.

11. *PP-E*, 1953, 15–17.

12. *FR, 1952–54*, 2:469.

13. HJCS 5, 60.

14. J. K. Gerhart memorandum for Omar Bradley, January 30, 1953, CCS 381 U.S. (1-31-50), sec. 23, JCS; Frank C. Nash memorandum, February 4, 1953, CD 381 (General) 1953, OSD.

15. The NSC had actually met a week earlier so that Cutler could announce Eisenhower's intention to devote the February 11 meeting to a discussion of existing national security policy. Record of Actions by the NSC, February 4, 1953, "Records of Action NSC 1953 (1)," NSC Series, AWF.

16. *FR, 1952–54*, 2:236–37.

17. Ibid.

18. HJCS 5, 2–3. On February 10 NSC Executive Secretary James Lay distributed to the NSC members a draft of NSC 142 that included all its sections except the "Military Program." Lay Note to the NSC, February 10, 1953, "NSC 142–Status of US National Security Programs (1)," Status of Projects Subseries, NSC Series, WHOSANSA.

19. Joint Strategic Plans Committee (JSPC) 851/76, January 31, 1953, CCS 381 U.S. (1-31-50), sec. 23, RG 218; JSPC 851/81, February 16, 1953, CCS 370 (8-19-45), sec. 39, ibid.

20. Chief of Naval Operations memo to the Joint Chiefs of Staff, February 10, 1953, CCS 381 U.S. (1–31–50), sec. 24, RG 218.

21. JSPC 851/76; JSPC 851/81.

22. Memorandum of NSC discussion on February 18, 1953, February 19, 1953, "132nd Meeting of the NSC," NSC Series, AWF.

23. Ibid.; Dodge to Humphrey, February 13, 1953, "President's Meeting with Civilian Consultants, March 31, 1953," NSC Series, Subject Subseries, WHOSANSA; Humphrey to Dodge, February 16, 1953, ibid.

24. Memorandum of NSC discussion, February 18, 1953.

25. Ibid.

26. HJCS 5, 5–6; memorandum of NSC discussion, February 25, 1953, February 26, 1953, "134th Meeting of the NSC," NSC Series, AWF.

27. Eisenhower address in Baltimore, Maryland, September 25, 1952, "Sept. 15, 1952–Sept. 25, 1952," Speech Series, AWF.

28. Memorandum of NSC discussion, February 25, 1953.

29. Anderson was a partner in the law firm of Baker, Botts, Andres & Parish; Black, president of Pacific Gas & Electric; Cowles, publisher of the Minneapolis *Star & Tribune*; Holman, president of Standard Oil of New Jersey; Mallott, president of Cornell University; Robertson, president of the Brotherhood of Railroad Firemen and Enginemen; Thomas, president of Monsanto Chemical.

30. Memorandum of discussion at the NSC meeting of March 4, 1953, March 5, 1953, "135th meeting of the NSC," NSC Series, AWF.

31. Ibid. Dodge proposed that virtually the entire remainder of the savings could be found in the mutual security program.

32. Ibid.; draft [for presentation to congressional leaders], June 5, 1953, "Legislative Program and Congressional Relations June 1953–June 1957 (2)," NSC Series, Subject Subseries, WHOSANSA.

33. Lay Note to the NSC on Status of United States Programs for National Security as of December 31, 1952, March 6, 1953, and NSC 142, n.d., both in "NSC 142–Status of US National Security Programs (1)," Status of Projects Subseries, NSC Series, WHOSANSA.

34. Ibid.

35. JSPC 851/84, March 16, 1953, CCS 370(8–19–45), sec. 40, RG 218; Omar N. Bradley memorandum for the secretary of defense, March 19, 1953, CD 111 (1954) 1953, OSD; HJCS 5, 6.

36. Ibid.

37. Memorandum of the discussion at the NSC meeting of March 18, 1953, March 19, 1953, "137th NSC Meeting," NSC Series, AWF.

38. FR, 1952–54, 2:258–64.

39. Ibid.; draft [for presentation to congressional leaders], June 5, 1953.

40. W. J. McNeill memorandum for Secretary Wilson and attachments, n.d., CD 111 (1954) 1953, OSD.

41. Discussion outline, meeting of NSC and civilian consultants, March 31, 1953, "President's Meeting with civilian consultants, March 31, 1953 (10)," NSC Series, Subject Subseries, WHOSANSA.

42. Memorandum on the use of Civilian Consultants, March 2, 1953, "Consultants—NSC [February–March 1953] (1)," NSC Series, Administrative Subseries, WHOSANSA; Cutler notes for briefing of NSC consultants, March 11, 1953, ibid.; memorandum on the subject of consultants to the National Security Council, March 2, 1953, CCS 334 NSC (9–25–47), sec. 9, RG 218.

43. Outline, third draft, March 25, 1953, "Consultants—NSC [February–March 1953]

(1)," NSC Series, Administrative Subseries, WHOSANSA; "Defense Spending and the National Budget: Views of the Consultants to the National Security Council," March 31, 1953, "Documents Pertaining to the March 31, 1953 Meeting," NSC Series, AWF. The following summary draws on these documents and *FR*, 1952–54, 2:264–81.

44. Memorandum of discussion of the NSC meeting, March 31, 1953.

45. For the procedure the administration adopted, see Bureau of the Budget Memorandum, "Financial Data for NSC Purposes," June 12, 1953, 334 NSC (9–25–47), sec. 10, RG 218; Cutler memorandum "Preparation and Use of Financial Data in Connection with NSC Procedures," July 7, 1953, July 7, 1953, 334 NSC (9–25–47), sec. 11, ibid.; "Preparation and Use of Financial Data in Connection with National Security Council Procedures," July 23, 1953, CCS 381 U.S. (1–31–50), sec. 27, ibid.

46. On March 11 and 23 the White House issued public statements announcing the names and purpose of the Panel of Civilian Consultants. *PP–E*, 1953, 120–22.

47. NSC 149, April 3, 1953, Lot 61 D167, S/S–NSC; *FR*, 1952–54, 2:281–87.

48. Ibid.

49. New obligational authority for the military would be kept to $36 billion.

50. NSC 149.

51. *FR*, 1952–54, 2:287–90.

52. Now NSC 149/1.

53. *HJCS* 5, 7–9, 60–63; *FR*, 1952–54, 2:291–302.

54. *FR*, 1952–54, 2:291–302.

55. *HJCS* 5, 60–63.

56. *HJCS* 5, 3–9; *FR*, 1952–54, 2:291–316.

57. Eisenhower remarks to congressional leaders, April 30/53 revision—final, "Cutler, Robert," CDJR (emphasis in original); notes on Legislative Leadership meeting, April 30, 1953, "April 30, 1953 Meeting," Legislative Leaders Series, AWF.

58. Notes on Legislative Leaders meeting, April 30, 1953.

59. Fred I. Greenstein, *The Hidden-Hand Presidency: Eisenhower as Leader* (New York, 1982), 70–72.

60. Notes on Legislative Leaders meeting, April 30, 1953.

61. *HJCS*, 5, 60–63, Tables 9–10, 85–86, and 205–9; Iwan W. Morgan, *Eisenhower Versus "The Spenders": The Eisenhower Administration, the Democrats, and the Budget, 1953–1960* (New York, 1990), 49–53.

7   A Chance for Peace?

1. *MC*, 144.

2. Handwritten notes of cabinet meeting, March 6, 1953, "C–2 (2)," Cabinet Series, WHOSS; entry for Tuesday, May 12, [1953], "Hughes Diary Notes 1953," EJHP. At the end of 1952 the Psychological Strategy Board had begun a "Program of Psychological Preparation for Stalin's Passing from Power." *FR*, 1952–54, 8:1059–60.

3. Allen Dulles, typewritten notes on Stalin's death, n.d., "Central Intelligence Agency 1954," AWDP; *FR*, 1952–54, 8:1083–90. It should be noted that only at the end of February had Eisenhower nominated Bohlen for the post of ambassador to the Soviet Union, and the opposition of rightwing Republicans delayed his confirmation for a month.

4. Immediately prior to the meeting Eisenhower had met with Allen Dulles, C. D. Jackson, and press secretary James Hagerty to prepare a statement to the Soviet people. *FR*, 1952–54, 8:1085.

5. *FR*, 1952–54, 2:1091–95.

6. Evidently State's Office of Intelligence Research drafted its estimate immediately after

learning of Stalin's illness. Dulles certainly would have been briefed on its conclusions prior to the NSC meeting. Ibid., 1086–90.

7. *FR, 1952–54*, 2:1091–95.

8. Ibid.

9. Ibid., 1173–83; Walt Whitman Rostow, *Europe After Stalin: Eisenhower's Three Decisions of March 11, 1953* (Austin, 1982), 35–60, 133–35 (Rostow quotes Eisenhower's question to Jackson on p. 41).

10. *FR, 1952–54*, 8:1173–83; Jackson to Dulles, March 10, 1953, "Time Inc. File—Stalin's Death: Speech Text and Comments—Full Evolution," CDJP.

11. "Draft for NSC: Proposed Plan for Psychological Warfare Offensive," March 1953, ibid.; Jackson to Dulles, March 10, 1953.

12. Ultimately entitled *The Dynamics of Soviet Society* and published in 1953.

13. *FR, 1952–54*, 8:1075–77; entry for March 6, 1953, "Diary Notes 1953," EJHP.

14. Rostow, *Europe After Stalin*, 84–90.

15. Entry for March 9, 1953, "Diary Notes 1953," EJHP.

16. *FR, 1952–54*, 8:1100–1113.

17. *FR, 1952–54*, 8:1111–13.

18. Jackson to Dulles, March 10, 1953.

19. Samuel Lubell, *The Future of American Politics* (Garden City, New York, 1952).

20. Sam Lubell memorandum to Baruch, March 7, 1953, attached to Baruch to Eisenhower, March 7, 1953, "Eisenhower, D. D. 1953," Selected Correspondence 1946–65, 1953 D-H, BBP.

21. In a follow-up memorandum, Lubell acknowledged that his proposal would require "a virtual review of our whole system of intelligence as regards Russia." Lubell memorandum to Baruch, March 14, 1953, ibid.

22. Lubell memorandum to Baruch, March 7; Eisenhower to Baruch, March 10, 1953, "Eisenhower Diary December 1952–July 1953 (2)," Eisenhower Diary Series, AWF; Eisenhower memorandum to the secretary of state, Dr. Gabriel Hauge, Mr. Emmet Hughes, Mr. C. D. Jackson, March 11, 1953, "White House Correspondence 1953 (5)," WHMS, DP-Eisenhower.

23. *FR, 1952–54*, 8:1117–25. Unless otherwise noted, this is the source for our review of the NSC meeting.

24. The Intelligence Advisory Committee comprised the intelligence organizations of the State Department, individual military services, and the JCS, as well as the CIA.

25. SE-39, March 10, 1953, CD 092 (Poland-SEASIA), OSD. Actually drafted on March 6, the foreword emphasized that SE-39 was a provisional estimate.

26. On the 1952 note as an important precedent for Dulles, see John Van Oudenaren, *Detente in Europe: The Soviet Union and the West since 1953* (Durham, 1991), 25–26.

27. *C-EC*, 32.

28. *FR, 1952–54*, 8:1180.

29. Ibid, 1181.

30. For a comparison of the two drafts, see Rostow, *Europe After Stalin*, 84–93; entry for March 13, 1953, "Diary Notes 1953," EMJP.

31. Malenkov quoted in Stephen E. Ambrose, *Eisenhower: The President* (New York, 1984), 91. See also *FR, 1952–54*, 8:1105–6, 1130–32; James G. Richter, "Perpetuating the Cold War: Domestic Sources of International Patterns of Behavior," *Political Science Quarterly* 107 (Summer 1992): 281–82.

32. "Soviet Lures and Pressures since Stalin's Death, March 5 to 25, 1953," "Stalin's Death—Soviet Lures and Pressures Since," CDJR. For the argument that Malenkov was sincere, see Richter, "Perpetuating the Cold War." As we will see, Eisenhower was less willing to rule out this possibility than others.

33. Nitze to Dulles, April 2, 1953, "The President's Speech April 1953 (1)," Draft Correspondence and Speech Series, DP-Eisenhower.

34. Dulles memorandum of a conversation with the president, March 16, 1953, "March 1–March 17, 1953," CS, DPEL.

35. Entry for March 16, 1953, "Diary Notes 1953," EJHP; handwritten "Notes from a Political Diary, 1952 [sic]," ibid.; Emmet John Hughes, *The Ordeal of Power: A Political Memoir of the Eisenhower Years* (New York, 1975), 103–05 (all emphases in originals). Hughes notes in his personal diary that he rechecked all his quotes and is confident that "they are as faithful as anything but a tape-recording."

36. Hughes, *Ordeal of Power*, 107; entry for March 17, 1953, "Diary Notes 1953," EJHP. Complaining afterward of Eisenhower's "kind of Boy Scout, PTA approach to the Russians," after this March 17 meeting Jackson retreated into the background. Ibid.

37. Entry for March 17, 1953, Hughes Diary.

38. Dulles telephone conversation with Hughes, March 16, 1953, "March 1–March 17, 1953 [telephone calls]," CS, DPEL; handwritten "Notes from a Political Diary, 1952 [sic]"; entry for March 17, 1953, Hughes Diary.

39. Dulles telephone conversation with Hughes, March 16, 1953; FR, 1952–54, 8:1133–34; Paul H. Nitze memorandum to Dulles and attachments, March 20, 1953, "The President's Speech April 1953 (3)," Draft Correspondence and Speech Series, DPEL; Nitze to Dulles, April 2, 1953, "The President's Speech April 1953 (1)," ibid.

40. Entries for March 28 and April 3, 1953, "Diary Notes 1953," EJHP.

41. Nitze to Dulles, April 2, 1953.

42. C–EC, 31; Steven Fish, "After Stalin's Death: The Anglo-American Debate Over a New Cold War," DH 10 (Fall 1986): 333–55.

43. C–EC, 36–38. Regardless of U.S. objections, as will be discussed, in May Churchill proposed a four-power summit.

44. Memorandum of NSC discussion [April 8, 1953], April 16, 1954, "NSC Meeting, April 8, 1953," NSCS, AWF; entries for April 6, 8, and 9, 1953, "Diary Notes 1953," EJHP.

45. C–EC, 37–38; entries for April 6 and 8, 1953, "Diary Notes 1953," EJHP.

46. Entries for April 6, 7, 9, and 10, 1953, ibid.; Hughes memorandum for the president, April 8, 1953, "Eisenhower, Dwight 1953," EJHP.

47. Dulles memorandum for Hughes, April 10, 1953, "April 1–April 30, 1953 (3)," CS, DPEL.

48. Entry for April 11, 1953, "Diary Notes 1953," EJHP; C–EC, 41–45.

49. Entry for April 11, 1953, "Diary Notes 1953," EJHP.

50. Entries for April 11 and 12, 1953, ibid.

51. Ibid; C–EC, 43.

52. Entries for April 12–16, "Diary Notes 1953," EJHP. Eisenhower did drop occasional phrases near the end of his speech.

53. Minnich Notes on Foreign Policy Speech, June 4, 1953, "Miscellaneous—F, January 1953–July 1958," L. Arthur Minnich Series, WHOSS.

54. FR, 1952–54, 8:1147–55. The following discussion of the speech derives from this source.

55. Minnich notes on foreign policy speech; "Foreign Radio Reactions to President Eisenhower's 16 April Speech Before the American Society of Newspaper Editors," April 16–17, 1953, "CIA Foreign Broadcast Information, January–April 1953," NSC Series—Briefing Notes, WHOSANSA; "Foreign Radio Reaction to President' Eisenhower's Speech of 16 April Before the American Society of Newspaper Editors," n.d., ibid.

56. The initial outline for and successive drafts of the speech indicate a progressively

more belligerent, even hostile tone. See the material in "Speech: April 18, 1953," Speech, Statements, Etc. Series, DPP.

57. Our source for Dulles's speech is Rostow, *Europe After Stalin*, 122–31.

58. The secretary's rule was never to make a public address without the president's approval.

59. Sam Lubell, "Russian Reply to Eisenhower, April 29, 1953, "Lubell, Samuel 1953," Selected Correspondence 1946–65, 1953 I–M, BBP; memorandum to Baruch from Lubell, July 3, 1953, ibid; Kennan to Allen Dulles, April 25, 1953, "Kennan, George," CDJP.

60. *FR, 1952–54*, 8:1162–66.

61. Ibid.; *FR, 1952–54*, 8:1168–69.

62. John Lewis Gaddis, *Strategies of Containment: A Critical Appraisal of Postwar United States National Policy* (New York, 1982), 163.

63. C–EC, 47.

64. "If you could only trust that bastard Malenkov," Eisenhower commented a day after his speech. Entry for April 17, 1953, "Hughes Diary Notes," EJHP.

65. Jackson to Dulles, April 16, 1953, "Jackson, C. D.," Selected Correspondence and Related Material, DPP; memorandum for the chairman, Psychological Strategy Board, April 28, 1953, "OCB—Misc. Memos (3)," CDJR; William A. Korn memorandum, "Some Thoughts on President's Speech of April 16," May 1, 1953, "Russia—Stalin's Death and Reaction and Results of President's Speech of April 16, 1953 (5)," Subject Series, WHC; memorandum for the chairman, Psychological Strategy Board, June 8, 1953, ibid.

66. Vladislav M. Zubok, "Soviet Intelligence and the Cold War: The 'Small' Committee of Information, 1952–53," *DH* 19 (Summer 1995): 457–61; Vladislav M. Zubok and Constantine Pleshakov, *Inside the Kremlin's Cold War: From Stalin to Khrushchev* (Cambridge, Massachusetts, 1996), 156–57; James G. Richter, *Khrushchev's Double Bind: International Pressures and Domestic Coalition Politics* (Baltimore, 1994), 30–52.

67. Memorandum of NSC discussion, April 8, 1953, April 9, 1953, "139th meeting of the NSC," NSCS, AWF; memorandum of NSC discussion, April 28, 1953, April 29, 1953, "141st meeting of the NSC," ibid.

8 The Solarium Exercise

1. Memorandum of conversation [probably by Cutler], "Solarium Project," May 8, 1953, lot 66D148, S/S–NSC.

2. Record of meeting of the NSC Planning Board, May 1, 1953, CCS 334 NSC (9–25–47), sec. 10, JCS; Bowie memorandum to Dulles, June 8, 1953, Lot 61 D167, S/P; *FR, 1952–54*, 2:373–77, 379–86.

3. As our discussion will demonstrate, the hitherto sole primary source for this gathering, Cutler's memoir, is not altogether reliable. Robert Cutler, *No Time For Rest* (Boston, 1966), 307–9.

4. Memorandum of conversation [probably by Cutler], May 8, 1953. The following discussion derives from this memorandum.

5. Clearly the concept came from Eisenhower, not Smith, as Cutler asserted in his memoir. Cutler, *No Time For Rest*, 308.

6. Memorandum of NSC meeting, May 13, 1953, May 14, 1953, "144th NSC Meeting," NSCS, AWF; NSC Tentative Agenda for Future Meetings, May 27, 1953, 334NSC (9–25–47), sec.10, JCS.

7. *FR, 1952–54*, 2:323–28; Cutler memorandum for Smith, May 15, 1953, lot 66D148, S/S–NSC.

8. Memorandum of NSC discussion, May 13, 1953.

9. Cutler memorandum for the record, May 9, 1953; *FR*, 1952–54, 2:399–400, 412.

10. Summaries prepared by the NSC Staff of Project Solarium presentations and Written Reports, n.d., *FR*, 1952–54, 2:416; "A Report to the National Security Council by Task Force 'C' of Project Solarium," July 16, 1953, "Project Solarium—Report by Task Force 'C' (1–10)," NSCS, Subject Subseries, WHOSANSA.

11. Robert Amory, Jr., memorandum for Smith, Allen Dulles, and Cutler, "Project 'Solarium,'" July 8, 1953, lot 66D148, S/S–NSC.

12. Alternative D's premise and mission can be inferred from Amory's attaching it to the memorandum in which he refers to it. SE-46, 8 July 1953, attached to Amory memorandum for Smith, Dulles, and Cutler, July 8, 1953.

13. Personnel Recommendations for Task Forces, May 18, 1953, lot 66D148, S/S–NSC.

14. Cutler memorandum for the acting secretary of state, "Solarium Project," May 11, 1953, ibid; *FR*, 1952–54 2:325–26, 395–96; Personnel Recommendations for Task Forces, May 18, 1953.

15. "Project Solarium: A Collective Oral History with General Andrew J. Goodpaster, Robert R. Bowie, and Ambassador George F. Kennan," February 27, 1988, Princeton University, Princeton, New Jersey; Andrew J. Goodpaster, "Organizing the White House," in Kenneth W. Thompson, ed., *The Eisenhower Presidency: Eleven Intimate Perspectives of Dwight D. Eisenhower* (Lanham, Maryland, 1984), 71.

16. Dulles telephone conversation with Gen. Cutler, June 1, 1953, "June 1953 [telephone calls]," CS, DPEL.

17. *FR*, 1952–54 2:325–26; Personnel Recommendations for Task Forces, May 18, 1953; Dulles telephone conversation with Cutler, June 1, 1953; Kennan to Cutler, May 25, 1953, "Kennan, George," Subject Series, DPP; Cutler to Kennan, May 26, 1953, ibid.

18. For Eisenhower's respect for Kennan, see in particular *DDEP*, 11:721.

19. *FR*, 1952–54, 2:360–64.

20. At this session Task Force C conceded it had fallen behind "in getting things on paper." Ibid., 388–93.

21. For a list of the attendees, see ibid., 394–96.

22. We refer to the original reports, not the summaries published in *FR*, 1952–54, 2:399–434. These summaries, however, contain quotes from the discussion at the NSC meeting.

23. See the preface to "A Report to the National Security Council by Task Force 'A' of Project Solarium," July 16, 1953, "Project Solarium—Report by Task Force 'A' (3–7)," NSC Series, Subject Subseries, WHOSANSA. Unless otherwise noted, the following analysis of the task force arguments and recommendations derives from the most recently declassified respective reports. Page references appear in the text.

24. Project Solarium Collective Oral History; *FR*, 1952–54, 2:400. The Doolittle Panel's terms of references obscured distinctions between NSC 20/4 and subsequent basic policy statements.

25. "Project Solarium—A Report to the National Security Council by Task Force 'B' of Project Solarium," July 16, 1953, "Project Solarium, Report by Task Force 'B' (1–5)," NSCS, Subject Subseries, WHOSANSA.

26. Report of Task Force "C".

27. Goodpaster, "Organizing the White House," 65. See also George F. Kennan, *Memoirs: 1950–1963* (New York, 1972), 186.

28. *FR*, 1952–54, 2:397.

29. Eisenhower diary, n.d., "Diary December 1952–July 1953 (1)," Diary Series, AWF.

30. Although no memorandum of this meeting's discussion can be found at either the

Eisenhower Library or the National Archives, NSC executive secretary James Lay enclosed a summary of the discussion along with summaries of the task forces' presentations and reports prepared by the NSC staff. *FR, 1952–54*, 2:399. See also notes 21 and 22.

31. Dulles handwritten notes [on Solarium], n.d.,"General Foreign Policy Matters," Box 8, WHMS, DPEL; Robert Bowie handwritten notes from NSC meeting, July 1953, lot 64D S63, S/P files.

32. *FR, 1952–54*, 2:432–34.

33. *FR, 1952–54*, 2:396, 398.

9 Preparing the Basic National Security Strategy

1. Eisenhower address in San Francisco, California, October 8, 1952, "September 26, 1952," Speech Series, Whitman File.

2. *FR, 1952–54*, 2:399–434.

3. [Cutler], "Summary of Basic Concepts of Task Forces," July 30, 1953, "Project Solarium (1)," NSCS, Subject Subseries, WHOSANSA.

4. *FR, 1952–54*, 2:435–40.

5. Ibid., 440.

6. Cutler memorandum, "Points for Consideration in Drafting New Policy," July 31, 1953, "Cutler memos — 1953 (4)," Executive Secretary's Subject File Series, WHONSC.

7. Dulles memorandum to Bowie, August 1, 1953, Lot 64 D63, S/P. In our possession, this document was released to Bowie.

8. *FR, 1952–54*, 2:535.

9. Cutler memorandum for special committee of the Planning Board, July 31, 1953, "Cutler memos — 1953 (4)," WHONSC.

10. *FR, 1952–54*, 2:328–349, 355–59, 367–70.

11. Ibid., 465–66n.2.

12. Ibid., 305–16.

13. Ibid., 1796–1874.

14. NIE 90, August 18, 1953, CIA; NIE 95, September 25, 1953, ibid.

15. "Building Strength in Western Europe," September 18, 1953, NSC 162, sec. 4, NSCPB; "Building Strength in Regional Groupings in the Far East," September 18, 1953, ibid.

16. These materials will be discussed as relevant in subsequent chapters.

17. *FR, 1952–54*, 2:455–57.

18. Draft statement of basic national security policy prepared by the special committee of the NSC Planning Board, NSC 162, sec. 3, NSCPB.

19. Cutler, "Overall Comment on Policy Paper, Sept. 18/53, of Solarium Special Committee," September 20, 1953, "Cutler's Memos — 1953 (5)," WHONSC. Until otherwise indicated, the following paragraphs derive from this source. All emphases are in the original text.

20. *FR, 1952–54*, 2:254.

21. Ibid., 535.

22. Ibid., 489–91. As printed in the *Foreign Relations* series, the typewritten notes appended to NSC 162 reproduce the text of Robert Bowie's briefing memorandum to Dulles. Until indicated otherwise, the following discussion derives from this source, supplemented by Bowie's recollections.

23. Ibid., 463–64. The Solarium reports had been sent to the main State Department bureaus on August 12 with a brief explanation of the project and request for cooperation as needed. Ibid., 441–42.

24. Ibid., 514–34.

25. NSC 162/1, Lot 61 D167, S/S-NSC; *FR*, 1952-54, 2:565-76; ibid., 577-97.
26. Ibid., 565-67.

10   The Sino-Soviet Threat

1. *HD*, 134.
2. Intelligence reports included SE-36 (March 5, 1953), *FR*, 1952-54, 8:1096-98; SE-39 (March 12, 1953), ibid., 1125-29; SE-42 (April 24, 1953, ibid., 1160-62; SE-44 (April 30, 1953), ibid., 1168-69; NIE-65 (June 16, 1953, ibid., 1188-92; SE-46 (July 8, 1953), ibid., 1196-1205; NIE-99 (October 23, 1953), ibid, 2:551-62. On Solarium, see chapter 8. For the final Jackson Report, dated June 30, 1953, see ibid., 1794-1874. The relevant Planning Board and staff study drafts included, among others, NSC 148 (Far East, March 6, 1953), ibid., 12:285-93; 294-98; NSC 166 (Communist China, October 19, 1953), ibid., 14:278-82; 282-306; NSC 174 (Soviet satellites, December 11, 1953), ibid., 8:110-16; 116-25. For representative Bohlen memoranda and cables, see ibid., 1100-1102, 1108-11, 1156-59, 1162-66, 1193-96, 1205-6; July 10, 1953, 1207, 1210-12, 1218-20.
3. David J. Dallin, *Soviet Foreign Policy After Stalin* (Philadelphia, 1961), 125.
4. Philip E. Mosely, "The Kremlin's Foreign Policy Since Stalin," *Foreign Affairs* 32 (October 1953): 20-33.
5. Most scholars now believe that Stalin's death had a greater influence on the Communists. See Rosemary Foot, *A Substitute for Victory: The Politics of Peacemaking at the Korean Armistice Talks* (Ithaca, 1990); and William Stueck, *The Korean War: An International History* (Princeton, 1995).
6. *FR*, 1952-54, 8:96-100.
7. Dallin, *Soviet Foreign Policy*, 171-79; James Richter, "Reexamining Soviet Policy Towards Germany during the Beria Interregnum," *Woodrow Wilson International Center for Scholars' Cold War International History Project Working Paper* 3 (December 1992), analyzes the Soviet May/June decision regarding East Germany in the light of memoirs of key figures and relevant archives recently released in the U.S.S.R. and the former Democratic Republic of Germany.
8. *FR*, 1952-54, 2:551-62.
9. Ibid., 96-100, 1156-59, 1193-96, 1218-20, 1223-25.
10. Vladislav M. Zubok, "Soviet Intelligence and the Cold War: The 'Small' Committee of Information, 1952-53," *Woodrow Wilson International Center for Scholars' Cold War International History Project Working Paper* 3 (December 1992): 17. On pp. 9-10 Zubok stresses the Soviet leaders' fear of war as the "decisive reason" for the "peace offensive." He places equal stress on political infighting in his revised "Soviet Intelligence and the Cold War: The 'Small' Committee of Information, 1952-53," *DH* 19 (Summer 1995): 453-72.
11. *FR*, 1952-54, 2:579.
12. Ibid.
13. Ibid., 580.
14. Ibid., 8:116-20; Dallin, *Soviet Foreign Policy After Stalin*, 166-97.
15. Ibid., 2:580.
16. *FR*, 1952-54, 12:294.
17. Ibid., 285-93, 298-300.
18. Ibid., 14:282-305.
19. Ibid., 2:580; ibid., 14:279. See also ibid., 283-91.
20. Ibid., 279.
21. Ibid., 280, 265-66.
22. Ibid., 8:1189, 553.

23. Ibid., 2:579.

24. *FR, 1951*, 8:449–58. See also chapter 1.

25. *FR, 1952–54*, 8:551, 554. See also ibid., 2:1800.

26. Ibid., 2:580–81.

27. Ibid., 579, 581.

28. Ibid., 1800.

29. Ibid., 581.

30. Ibid., 841.

31. Ibid., 1800.

32. Ibid., 1801–5; ibid, 8:1191.

33. Ibid., 2:581, 1805–6; 1809–11.

34. Ibid., 231.

35. See ibid., 1806–9.

36. Ibid., 581.

37. Ibid., 8:101.

38. Ibid., 85.

39. Ibid., 2:581, 594–95; ibid., 8:111–12, 116–21, 124–27; Gaddis, *The Long Peace*, 188–94.

40. *FR, 1952–54*, 14:296–97; 280. See also ibid., 401–7.

11 Strategic Objectives: Rollback?

1. *FR, 1952–54*, 2:457.

2. See chapter 4.

3. *FR, 1952–54*, 2:441.

4. Marc Trachtenberg, "A 'Wasting Asset': American Strategy and the Shifting Nuclear Balance, 1949–1954," in Trachtenberg, *History and Strategy* (Princeton, 1991), 140–42; David Alan Rosenberg, "The Origins of Overkill," *International Security* (Spring 1983): 30–34.

5. *FR, 1952–54*, 2:594–95. While the phrasing differed from earlier drafts, the substance was the same.

6. Ibid., 595.

7. Ibid., 580–81. See also the discussion of Soviet vulnerability and relevant citations in chapter 10.

8. *FR, 1952–54*, 2:512.

9. Ibid., 513.

10. Ibid., 513.

11. Ibid., 492, 580.

12. Ibid., 493, 580–81.

13. Ibid., 499, 495, 586, 583.

14. Ibid., 496–97, 584–85.

15. Robert Amory, memorandum to director, Central Intelligence on paragraph 43 of NSC 162, October 1, 1953, Lot 54D563, S/P.

16. The positions taken in the Planning Board by the JCS advisor are reflected in the JCS memorandum for the secretary of defense, "Review of Basic National Security Policy (NSC 162)" and Appendix, October 6, 1953, OSD.

17. Ibid., 2–3.

18. Appendix to ibid., 2–3.

19. Appendix to ibid., 9; *FR, 1952–54*, 512.

20. Appendix to JCS memorandum to secretary of defense, 10.

21. *FR, 1952–54*, 2: 514. JCS proposed italics.

22. Ibid., 529.

23. See ibid., 512n.17.

24. Ibid., 529.

25. Ibid., 529–30.

26. Ibid., 530.

27. Ibid., 534.

28. Ibid., 565–67.

29. Ibid., 568–69.

30. Ibid., 595.

31. Ibid., 560–63 (emphasis in original).

32. Ibid., 696.

33. In addition to chapter 8, see Glenn H. Snyder, "The 'New Look' of 1953," in Warner R. Schilling, Paul Y. Hammond, and Glenn H. Snyder, *Strategy, Politics, and Defense Budgets* (New York, 1962), 407–8.

34. *FR*, 1952–54, 2:642.

35. Ibid., 397, 642.

36. Ibid., 804. See also *HD*, 69.

37. *FR*, 1952–54, 2:636.

38. Ibid., 641.

39. Ibid., 806 (emphasis in original).

40. *FR*, 1952–54, 12:285–98.

41. Ibid., 298–300.

42. Ibid., 300–302.

43. *FR*, 1952–54, 14:278–306, 307–30.

44. *FR*, 1952–54, 14:260, 270; ibid., 2:580.

45. Ibid., 14:280–82; ibid., 2:580.

46. Ibid., 14:296–97; ibid., 2:580.

47. Ibid., 14:281–82, 239–40, 268, 273, 409–12.

48. The background and substance of Project Control are well described by Tami Davis Biddle, "Handling the Soviet Threat: 'Project Control' and the Debate on American Strategy in the Early Cold War Years," *The Journal of Strategic Studies* 12 (September 1989): 273–302. We are indebted to Professor Biddle for making available to us the documents cited below regarding the project.

49. Briefing of Weapons Systems Evaluation Group (WSEG), 24 August 1954, PC.

50. In order to justify the first strike, the report argues for redefining aggression to include evident preparation of the capacity for atomic attack by an adversary whose doctrine includes ultimate military aggression.

51. "Strategic Atomic Offensive," Research Memorandum No. 4.10 (June 1954), 18, PC.

52. This brief sketch of Project Control is based on the Final Report, June 1954, except as noted.

53. Quotations are from memoranda for the record of the various briefings made by Colonel Sleeper, Colonel S. B. Hardwick, Jr., and Colonel G. V. Davis, all in PC.

54. Rosenberg, "The Origins of Overkill," 34; Trachtenberg, "Wasting Asset," 141.

55. *FR*, 1955–57, 19: 24–38 (see in particular paragraph 35, p. 33).

56. *FR*, 1952–54, 2:649, 655, 659.

57. Ibid., 2:675; *HJCS* 5, 42–44; *FR*, 1952–54, 2:595 (our emphasis).

58. *FR*, 1952–54, 2:680–86.

59. Ibid., 681.

60. Ibid., 684.

61. Ibid., 685.

62. Ibid., 694–95.

63. Ibid., 697.
64. Ibid., 698.
65. *HJCS* 5, 46.
66. Ibid., 47.
67. *FR*, 1952–54, 2:711; *HJCS* 5, 47.
68. *FR*, 1952–54, 2:772–76.
69. Ibid., 785–87 (emphasis in original).
70. Ibid., 788–90.
71. Ibid., 790.
72. Ibid., 791–92 (emphasis in original).
73. Ibid., 792.
74. Ibid., 794–96.
75. Ibid., 799–800.
76. Ibid., 808–12.
77. Ibid, 813–14.
78. Ibid., 814.
79. Ibid., 812–16.
80. Ibid., 818–19.
81. Ibid., 828.
82. Ibid., 829–30. No such special group was ever established.
83. Ibid., 832–36.
84. Ibid., 836–38.
85. Ibid., 839–40.
86. Ibid., 840.
87. Ibid., 840–41.
88. *FR*, 1955–57, 19:24–38. See also ibid., 6–9, 9–24.

12 Military Strategy

1. *MC*, 449.
2. John Lewis Gaddis, *Strategies of Containment: A Critical Appraisal of Postwar United States National Policy* (New York, 1982), 35.
3. *Nuclear Notebook* (December 1993): 57.
4. *FR*, 1952–54, 2:641–2, 804–6.
5. *HD*, 31.
6. *FR*, 1952–54, 2:601. Compared to America's 832, in 1952 the Soviet Union possessed only 50 warheads. And although it successfully tested a hydrogen bomb in 1953, its stockpile still totaled only 120. *Nuclear Notebook* (December 1993): 57.
7. *FR*, 1952–54, 2:367–70.
8. Frank Nash memorandum for the secretary of defense, May 5, 1953, CD 091.7 (Europe) 1953, OSD; Wilson memorandum to the president, June 2, 1953, ibid.
9. Omar Bradley memorandum for the secretary of defense, July 30, 1953, CD 092 (Germany), OSD; *FR*, 1952–54, 5:711–15. The State Department's estimate was as stark as Bradley's. "It should be emphasized that the survival of the Governments (if not the peoples) of our allies depends upon the success of the forward strategy," wrote Dulles's deputy assistant secretary for European affairs. "Should the other deterrents fail or disappear, and the NATO force prove inadequate as a barrier to the aggressor, they do not survive." Ibid., 443.
10. Memorandum of discussion at the NSC meeting of February 18, 1953, February 19, 1953, "132nd Meeting of the NSC," NSCS, AWD.
11. Eisenhower quoted in *HJCS* 5, 284–85.

12. *FR*, 1952–54, 5:440–43.

13. JCS 2124/98, September 12, 1953, 092 Germany (5–4–49), sec. 17, JCS; JCS 2121/108, September 24, 1953, 092 Germany (5–4–49), sec. 19, ibid.; Radford memorandum for the secretary of defense, Sept. 30, 1953, CD 350.05 (Europe) 1953, OSD.

14. *FR*, 1952–54, 5:430–31.

15. On the Korean War's effect on Truman's commitment to Taiwan, see Nancy Bernkopf Tucker, *Patterns in the Dust: Chinese-American Relations and the Recognition Controversy* (New York, 1983).

16. *FR*, 1952–54, 14:165.

17. The military agreement between America, Australia, and New Zealand (ANZUS) was the sole collective security pact.

18. *FR*, 1952–54, 14:1523–26, 1526–29, 1530–31, 1538–39, 1539–42, 1549–50. On the controversies surrounding Japanese rearmament, see Martin Weinstein, *Japan's Postwar Defense Policy, 1947–1968* (New York, 1971).

19. Memorandum of discussion at the NSC meeting of February 18, 1953, February 19, 1953, "132nd Meeting of the NSC," NSCS, AWD; *HD*, 132–37, 138–42; Samuel F. Wells, Jr., "The Origins of Massive Retaliation," *Political Science Quarterly* 86 (Spring 1991): 31–52.

20. For evidence that the Bradley-led JCS were wedded to the status quo, see JCS 1883/33, April 24, 1953, CCS 370 (5–25–48), sec. 11, JCS; N. E. Halaby to the director for mutual security, April 18, 1953, 334 NSC (1953), OSD.

21. Glenn H. Snyder, "The 'New Look,' of 1953," in Warner R. Schilling, Paul Y. Hammond, and Glenn H. Snyder, *Strategy, Politics, and Defense Budgets* (New York, 1962), 411.

22. Jeffrey G. Barlow, *Revolt of the Admirals: The Fight for Naval Aviation, 1945–1950* (Washington, 1994), 56–57, 243–59; 273–83; Douglas Kinnard, *President Eisenhower and Strategy Management* (Lexington, Kentucky, 1977), 21. Eisenhower comments on the feud between the Navy and Air Force in his entry for January 27, 1949, in *ED*, 154–56.

23. Legislation enacted in 1952 gave the commandant coequal status with the JCS in Marine Corps–related matters.

24. *HJCS* 5, 31–32.

25. *FR*, 1952–54, 2:231–34.

26. Ibid., 213–14.

27. Ibid., 1067, 1083–84.

28. The fiscally conservative NSC 149/2 stated the administration should "*increase* emphasis" on "protection of the continental United States from enemy attack." Ibid., 308 (emphasis in original). Similarly, after revisions NSC 153/1 stated that the policy of the administration was to "[e]mphasize the development of a continental defense system, including early warning, adequate to prevent disaster and to make secure the mobilization base necessary to achieve U.S. victory in the event of general war." Ibid., 382.

29. Ibid.; 328–49, 367–70.

30. In July the NSC Planning Board's Continental Defense Committee sent Cutler a long report, which Lay circulated on July 22 as NSC 159. On August 14 the Interdepartmental Intelligence Conference and Interdepartmental Committee on Internal Security submitted a joint report, designated NSC 159/1, which was followed the next month by a JCS report—NSC 159/2. The NSC discussed the Planning Board's synthesis, NSC 159/3, on September 24, which with slight revisions Eisenhower approved as NSC 159/4 the next day.

31. *FR*, 1952–54, 2:464–75, 475–89. The quotes appear on p. 478.

32. Ibid., 583.

33. *HJCS*, 5, 16.

34. Except for Twining, whose term began on July 1, the new JCS were on "standby" status until mid-August. Nevertheless, Eisenhower instructed them to attend the July 16 special NSC meeting when the Solarium task forces presented their reports.

35. Matthew B. Ridgway, *Soldier: The Memoirs of Matthew B. Ridgway* (New York, 1956), 265; *HJCS* 5, 16–17; Arthur W. Radford, *From Pearl Harbor to Vietnam: The Memoirs of Admiral Arthur W. Radford*, ed. Stephen Jurika, Jr. (Stanford, 1982), 318–20. This published version of Radford's memoirs is true to the admiral's own unedited manuscript, which provides slightly more detail. "A Brief Resume of the Life and Experiences of Arthur W. Radford, Admiral, United States Navy (Ret.) — February 4, 1966," Volume 2, AWR.

36. Radford, *From Pearl Harbor to Vietnam*, 320–21.

37. *HJCS* 5, 17–20; Radford, *From Pearl Harbor to Vietnam*, 321.

38. Memorandum by Radford, Ridgway, Carney, and Twining to the secretary of defense, August 8, 1953, our possession. We thank David Rosenberg for supplying us with a copy of this document, on which we base our discussion of its contents.

39. Prior to Eisenhower's departure for Denver, Radford personally briefed the president on the "new concept." One can infer from the JCS chief's verbatim reading of the memorandum at the start of the NSC meeting, moreover, that in a departure from normal procedure, few if any of the members had previously received copies of it. Radford, *From Pearl Harbor to Vietnam*, 321–22; *FR, 1952–54*, 2:443–55.

40. *FR, 1952–54*, 2:444–45, 447.

41. Ibid., 448. Prior to the *Sequoia* exercise Twining wrote to all the newly appointed service chiefs, "[I]nsufficient account has been taken of new weapons and their effect on the composition and employment of our forces, particularly in the field of atomic and thermonuclear weapons." Twining recommended that "we should accept these weapons as accomplished facts and employ them more fully ourselves while preparing to cope with them if they are used by the enemy." Quoted in *HJCS* 5, 17. The alternative, he explained shortly thereafter, would be to "arrive at a situation in which we will have entrusted our survival to the whims of a small group of proven barbarians." Quoted in Scott D. Sagan, "The Perils of Proliferation: Organization Theory, Deterrence Theory, and the Spread of Nuclear Weapons," *International Security* 18 (Spring 1994): 79–80.

42. Radford, *From Pearl Harbor to Vietnam*, 327.

43. *FR, 1952–54*, 2:445.

44. Roger Dingman, "Atomic Diplomacy During the Korean War," *International Security* 13 (Winter 1988/89): 50–91; Rosemary J. Foot, "Nuclear Coercion and the Ending of the Korean Conflict," ibid., 92–112.

45. Robert A. Wampler, "NATO Strategic Planning and Nuclear Weapons: 1950–1957," *Nuclear History Program Occasional Paper No. 6* (July 1990): 9–11.

46. Frank Nash memorandum for the secretary of defense, May 5, 1953, CD 091.7 (Europe) 1953, OSD; Wilson memorandum to the president, June 2, 1953, ibid.

47. *FR, 1952–54*, 2:447. Radford later suggested that Ridgway would not have signed the memorandum had he not wanted "to get home to his young bride for the weekend." Radford, *From Pearl Harbor to Vietnam*, 321.

48. *FR, 1952–54*, 2:446, 450, 452.

49. Ibid., 454.

50. Cutler memorandum on August 27/53 NSC meeting, September 1, 1953. Obtained through the FOIA, authors' possession.

51. *FR, 1952–54*, 2:455–56.

52. Ibid., 457–60, 460–63. This exchange will be discussed in the next chapter.

53. Memorandum of discussion of NSC meeting of September 9, 1953, September 10, 1953, "161st Meeting of the NSC," NSCS, AWD. The account of this meeting in the JCS of-

ficial history, which says that the secretary "gave assurance that the strain on US foreign relations [resulting from the redeployment] would not be fatal," is misleading. *HJCS* 5, 21.

54. *FR*, 1952–54, 2:491, 501, 505, 510.
55. Ibid., 514–26.
56. Ibid., 503. This section became section 1 of NSC 162/2. See ibid., 578.
57. Ibid., 578, 588–89, 591, 593–94; 501–2, 505, 510.
58. Ibid., 545–49.
59. Ibid., 494, 505–6; 582, 591; 477; memorandum by Radford, Ridgway, Carney, and Twining to the secretary of defense, August 8, 1953.
60. *FR*, 1952–54, 2:562–64 (our emphasis).
61. Ibid., 570. See also *HD*, 133.
62. *FR*, 1952–54, 2:571–74.
63. Ibid., 495–96.
64. Ibid., 496–99.
65. Ibid., 494.
66. Ibid., 497–98, 585.
67. Ibid., 569.
68. Memorandum by Radford, Ridgway, Carney, and Twining to the secretary of defense, August 8, 1953.
69. *FR*, 1952–54, 2:506.
70. Memorandum by the JCS to Secretary of Defense Wilson, October 6, 1953, 61 D 167, S/P–NSC.
71. *FR*, 1952–54, 2:563.
72. Ibid., 454.
73. Ibid., 456–57.
74. Ibid., 508–9.
75. Ibid.
76. Ibid., 526–28.
77. Ibid., 528–29.
78. Ibid., 549–50.
79. Ibid., 570–73.
80. Ibid., 593.
81. Memorandum by Radford, Ridgway, Carney, and Twining to the secretary of defense, August 8, 1953.
82. Memorandum by the JCS to Secretary of Defense Wilson, October 6, 1953.
83. *FR*, 1952–54, 2:532–35 (our emphasis).
84. Ibid., 536–45. Shrinking the military forces after the Korean War had, ironically, been recommended by JCS chairman Bradley, who testified to Congress in 1951 that maintaining armed forces of 3.5 million on active duty would be too costly; in his view, "we would be much stronger" to keep smaller forces, readily available, and backed up by "well-trained reserves." Quoted in Snyder, "New Look," 494.
85. *FR*, 1952–54, 2:545–46.
86. Ibid., 546.
87. Ibid, 641–42.
88. Ibid., 546.
89. Ibid.
90. NSC 162/1, October 19, 1953, 61 D 167, S/P–NSC.
91. *FR*, 1952–54, 2:565–66.
92. Ibid., 563–64, 593.
93. Ibid., 534–49.

94. The following discussion of the preparation and approval of JCS 2101/113, "Military Strategy to Support the National Security Policy Set Forth in NSC 162/2," draws on *HJCS* 5, 26–34.

95. JCS 2101/113, December 10, 1953, CCS 381 US (1–31–50), sec. 32, JCS.

96. *HJCS* 5, 30–31.

97. Radford memorandum for Wilson and attachments, December 9, 1953, "Wilson, Charles 1953 (2)," Administration Series, AWF.

98. At the time Eisenhower expressed "his strong feeling that General Ridgway was sincere in his view of the need for balanced U.S. military forces rather than upon atomic retaliatory capacity" and "was not merely presenting a 'parochial' Army viewpoint." After the 1955 testimony to Congress, however, the president lost his patience. "Gentlemen, Ridgway is Chief of Staff of the Army," the president told his congressional leaders. "Each service has as its head and has traditionally had as a head people who think that their service is the only service that can ultimately save the United States." *FR*, 1952–54, 2:804.

99. *HJCS* 5, 32–34, 69.

100. Ibid., 67–69. Congress further reduced new obligational authority from $30.993 to $29.584 billion and estimated expenditures from $37.575 to $35.533. Tables 9 and 10, ibid., 85–86.

101. *FR*, 1952–54, 2:593.

102. Unsigned [sanitized] memorandum, "The Meaning of Paragraph 39b, NSC 162/2, as Understood by the Department of Defense," December 1, 1953, "Atomic Weapons, Correspondence & Background for Pres. Approval," NSC Series, Subject Subseries, WHOSANSA. As Radford wrote Dulles earlier, the JCS wanted the assurance that "The United States will use atomic weapons in military operations in repelling aggression whenever it is of military advantage to do so in the following order of priority: (a) Immediately against military forces operating against us or our allies. (b) Against targets that would support the build-up of enemy military forces for renewed operations. (c) Unrestricted atomic operations for such attack on the United States or its allies." Radford memorandum to Dulles, October 13, 1953, CJCS 040, Atomic Energy Commission Files, JCS.

103. Cutler memorandum for the record, December 2, 1953, "Atomic Weapons, Correspondence & Background for Pres. Approval and Instructions (1)," NSC Series, Subject Subseries, WHOSANSA.

104. Smith memoranda for the president, December 3 and 22, 1953, ibid. (emphasis in original); Strauss memorandum for Cutler, December 3, 1953, ibid; Lay memorandum for the president, December 16, 1953, ibid.

105. Lay memorandum for secretaries of state and defense and chairman, AEC, January 4, 1954, ibid. The text is identical in the Lay and Smith memoranda.

106. Radford, *From Pearl Harbor to Vietnam*, 326; *NYT*, December 15, 1953. See also interview with Admiral Arthur W. Radford, "Strong U.S. Defense for the 'Long Pull,'" *U.S. News & World Report*, March 5, 1954, 48–55.

107. Foster Dulles telephone conversation with Allen Dulles, December 28, 1953, "December 1953 [telephone calls] (2)," CS, DPEL.

108. Robert R. Bowie memorandum for the secretary, January 5, 1954, "Bowie, Robert R.," Selective Correspondence and Related Material, DPP; Dulles memorandum for the president, January 7, 1954, Eisenhower to Dulles, January 8, 1954, and Dulles to Eisenhower, January 8, 1954, all in "Dulles—January 1954," Dulles-Herter Series, AWF; Draft #8, Speech Before Council on Foreign Relations, January 7, 1954, "Re: 'The Evolution of Foreign Policy,'" Selective Correspondence and Related Material, DPP; Speech Before the Council on Foreign Relations, January 12, 1954, "The 'Massive Retaliation' Policy, 1954," ibid; *HD*, 7.

109. Representative even if somewhat delayed was Walter Lippmann's article in the *New York Herald Tribune*, March 18, 1954.

110. Foster Dulles telephone conversation with Allen Dulles, January 14, 1953, "January 1954 [telephone calls] (2)," CS, DPEL; Allen Dulles to Foster Dulles, February 9, 1953, "Re: Council on Foreign Relations," AWDP; Hamilton Fish Armstrong to Dulles, February 5, 1954, "Re: Article by John Foster Dulles," Selective Correspondence and Related Material, DPP.

111. Armstrong to Dulles, February 5, 1954.

112. The Berlin conference of foreign ministers lasted from January 25–February 18, 1954.

113. "Dulles memorandum of luncheon conversation with the president," February 24, 1954, "Meetings with the President 1954 (4)," WHMS, DPEL; Armstrong to Dulles, February 24, 1954, "Re: Article by John Foster Dulles," Selective Correspondence and Related Material, DPP.

114. John Foster Dulles, "Policy for Security and Peace," *Foreign Affairs* 32 (April 1954): 353–64.

115. Ibid., 355–56.

116. Ibid., 356.

117. Ibid., 356, 358, 362.

118. Ibid., 358.

119. Ibid., 358–59.

120. Ibid., 359, 362–63.

13   Strengthening the Noncommunist World

1. *PP–E*, 1953, 4.

2. *FR*, 1952–54, 2:581, 579.

3. Ibid., 588, 591–92, 595.

4. Quoted in Harold Stassen and Marshall Houts, *Eisenhower: Turning the World Toward Peace* (St. Paul, 1990), 361.

5. *FR*, 1952–54, 2:585.

6. Ibid., 579, 581, 586–87.

7. "Our Relations with the Free World," August 3, 1953, "NSC 161, vol. 1, Status of US National Security Programs on June 30, 1953 (1)," NSCS, Status of Projects, WHOSANSA.

8. *FR*, 1952–54, 2:457. On September 1 Dulles had discussed his thinking with Cutler, who "outlined" it to Eisenhower. Ibid., 455–56. Above the memorandum's original draft sentence concerning the "propitious" timing for "such a move" Dulles wrote, "This, I think, is important!" Draft memorandum, September 6, 1953, "Dulles/Korea/Security Policy," International Series, AWF. We will discuss later in this chapter the CIA's August 1953 orchestration of the ouster of Iran's prime minister Mohammed Mossadegh. On September 5, 1953, Adenauer scored a solid victory in the West German elections.

9. Dulles memorandum for Bowie, September 8, 1953, "White House Correspondence 1953 (2)," WHMS, DPEL.

10. The following discussion is based on *FR*, 1952–54, 2:460–63 (emphasis in original). Earlier drafts of this Eisenhower memorandum can be found in "Dulles, Korea/Security Policy," International Series, AWF.

11. Fred I. Greenstein and Richard H. Immerman, "What Did Eisenhower Tell Kennedy about Indochina? The Politics of Misperception," *Journal of American History* 79 (September 1992), 568–87.

12. Periodically over the next several years, however, Dulles would raise the prospect of a diplomatic initiative aimed at inducing the Soviets to withdraw their forces from Eastern Eu-

rope. The "big idea," he explained shortly before the July 1955 Geneva Summit, "is to get the Russians out of the satellite states and to provide these states with a real sense of their freedom." *FR*, 1955–57, 5:184.

13. On double—or dual—containment, see Thomas Schwartz, *America's Germany: John J. McCloy and the Federal Republic of Germany* (Cambridge, 1991).

14. Richard H. Immerman, ed., *John Foster Dulles and the Diplomacy of the Cold War* (Princeton, 1990), 109–32.

15. *FR*, 1952–54, 2:592.

16. John Gillingham, *Coal, Steel, and the Rebirth of Europe, 1945–1955: The Germans and French from Ruhr Conflict to Economic Community* (New York, 1991).

17. Dulles to Jean Monnet, May 23, 1950, "Monnet, Jean—1950," DPP; *FR*, 1952–54, 7:502.

18. *FR*, 1952–54, 5:374, 1623; Dulles to James B. Conant, November 20, 1953, "Germany 1953–54 (2)," Subject Series, DPEL (emphasis in original).

19. Saki Dockrill, *Britain's Policy for West German Rearmament: 1950–55* (Cambridge, England, 1991), 68–73. Eisenhower initially described the proposal for an integrated European army as, as "cockeyed an idea as a dope fiend could have figured out." Gunter Bischof and Stephen E. Ambrose, eds., *Eisenhower: A Centenary Assessment* (Baton Rouge, 1995), 216.

20. Quoted in Francois Duchene, *Jean Monnet: The First Statesman of Interdependence* (New York, 1994), 231.

21. *DSB* 25 (July 30, 1951), 163–65.

22. Entry for July 7, 1953, "Diary Notes 1953," EJHP.

23. *FR*, 1952–54, 7:510–20; ibid., 5:450–51; Saki Dockrill, "Cooperation and Suspicion: The United States' Alliance Diplomacy for the Security of Western Europe, 1953–54," *Diplomacy and Statecraft* 5 (March 1994): 138–82.

24. *FR*, 1952–54, 2:592; ibid., 5:1783.

25. "Building Strength in Western Europe," September 18, 1953, 42, enclosure to James S. Lay memorandum to the NSC Planning Board, October 12, 1953, "NSC 162, section 4," RG 273.

26. The six members of the ECSC and unratified EDC had been attempting since early 1953 to create an EPC to provide democratic control over these two and any future functional agencies. By March 1953 an ad hoc assembly had drafted an EPC treaty, which called for a supranational, federal-type political system with an elected parliament. Its submission produced protracted and inconclusive debate, mainly over the issue of supranationality. The FRG, Italy, and the Benelux countries strongly supported the draft. But France, torn by partisan jockeying, blocked agreement and deferred ratifying EDC. Finally, the French rejection of EDC in August 1954 also buried EPC.

27. *FR*, 1952–54, 5:1554; David Bruce to Dulles, July 7, 1953, "Strictly Confidential A–B (4)," General Correspondence and Memoranda Series, DPEL. In July 1953 Congress adopted a Republican proposal to withhold 50 percent of the FY 1954 Mutual Security Program appropriations from any European nation that refused to ratify EDC.

28. *FR*, 1952–54, 5:450–51.

29. *FR*, 1952–54, 7:691–92; ibid., 5:1716. See also Dockrill, *Britain's Policy for West German Rearmament*.

30. Psychological Strategy Board, "An Evaluation of the Psychological Impact in the United Kingdom of United States Foreign Economic Policies and Programs," January 28, 1953, "President's Papers 1953 (10)," Special Assistant's Series, Presidential Subseries, WHOSANSA.

31. *ED*, 207–8.

32. *FR, 1952–54,* 6:884; *ED,* 222–23.

33. *FR, 1952–54,* 2:486.

34. *EP,* 12:225.

35. *FR, 1952–54,* 2:585–86, 592–93.

36. *FR, 1952–54,* 1:1484–86; ibid., 2:592, 586.

37. "Building Strength in Western Europe," September 18, 1953, 20.

38. *FR, 1952–54,* 5:386; Nash memorandum to secretary of defense, April 7, 1953, C.D. 350.05 (Briefing) 1953, OSD. Wilson also attended the meeting.

39. "Our Relations with the Free World," August 3, 1953, "NSC 161, vol. 1, Status of US National Security Programs on June 30, 1953 (1)," NSC Series, Status of Projects, WHOSANSA; *FR, 1952–54,* 5:429; Colonel Harrison Gerhart memorandum for Frank Nash, August 5, 1953, 334 NATO (Annual Review), assistant secretary for defense, International Security Affairs, 1953 Files, RG 330; Gerhart memorandum for Najeeb Halaby, July 23, 1953, ibid.

40. *FR, 1952–54,* 2:585–86, 592–93.

41. "Building Strength in Western Europe," September 18, 1953, 31–32.

42. *FR, 1952–54,* 6:679. See also ibid., 891.

43. Ibid., 2:586.

44. Dulles, "The 'Big Three' Alliance," July 19, 1954, "Think Pieces—Drafts (1)," Subject Series, DPEL.

45. *FR, 1952–54,* 5:452. See also "United States Foreign Policy," May 16, 1954, enclosed to Dulles memorandum for Merchant and Bowie, May 15, 1954, "General Foreign Policy Matters (2)," WHMS, DPEL. Ironically, it had been the Europeans, most notably the British, who had initially championed the incorporation of atomic weapons into NATO's war plans as a means both to lessen the cost of and irrevocably tie the United States to the defense of the continent. Robert A. Wampler, "NATO Strategic Planning and Nuclear Weapons, 1950–1957," *Nuclear History Program Occasional Paper No. 6* (July 1990).

46. "Building Strength in Western Europe," September 18, 1953, 15. The quote is underscored by hand on the copy released to the authors through the FOIA.

47. *FR, 1952–54,* 15:769–70. Truman's casual press conference remark that the use of atomic weapons was under "active consideration" following the Chinese intervention in Korea provoked "shock and outrage" across the continent. Burton I. Kaufman, *The Korean War: Challenges in Crisis, Credibility, and Command* (New York, 1986), 111–12.

48. *FR, 1952–54,* 15:769–70. When at a postarmistice tripartite meeting in Bermuda Eisenhower and Dulles discussed the use of atomic weapons in the event of renewed Communist aggression, the British and French "exhibited very stubborn resistance." Ibid., 5:1816–18, 1847.

49. Ibid., 15:826–27.

50. Ibid., 5:451.

51. Ibid., 2:593 (our emphasis). On the administration's continuing difficulty in reaching an accord with the allies, see Bischof and Ambrose, eds., *Eisenhower,* 162–90.

52. Eisenhower to Alfred Gruenther, May 4, 1953, "December 1952–July 1953 (1)," Diary Series, AWF; *FR, 1952–54,* 1:593–95; ibid., 2:265–67, 278.

53. Ibid., 2:507, 525–26, 592.

54. Ibid., 1:273–278, 289; notes of legislative leadership meeting, April 30, 1954, "1953 (4)," Legislative Series, AWF; minutes of cabinet meeting, August 27, 1953, "August 27, 1953," Cabinet Series, AWF; *FR, 1952–54,* 2:436–38, 303.

55. Memorandum for Dodge, July 20, 1953, "Legislative Leaders Meeting, July 20, 1953," Legislative Series, AWF; *HJCS* 5, 205–9.

56. *ED,* 242–45, 249.

57. *PP–E*, 1953, 15–16.

58. *FR*, 1952–54, 2:592.

59. Eisenhower established the Commission on Foreign Economic Policy on August 7, 1953. A week later he appointed Randall the chair. Randall had recently published an homage to liberal trade, *A Creed for Free Enterprise* (Boston, 1952).

60. Commission on Foreign Economic Policy, *Report to the President and the Congress* (Washington, 1954). The transcripts of the commission's hearings and related documents are located in the U.S. President's Commission on Foreign Economic Policy Records, Eisenhower Library. See also Randall's own journal in CRP.

61. Burton I. Kaufman, *Trade and Aid: Eisenhower's Foreign Economic Policy, 1953–1961* (Baltimore, 1982), 15–31, esp. p. 24. In 1955 Congress extended the Reciprocal Trade Agreements Act for three years, and again for four years in 1958.

62. *FR*, 1952–54, 1:939–42, 1059–60. The Truman administration initiated the program to restrict Western trade with the Soviet bloc in 1948.

63. Ibid., 968–81.

64. Ibid., 939–40; entry for March 2, 1953, Hughes Diary, "Diary Notes, 1953," EJHP.

65. *FR*, 1952–54, 1:939–40, 1200. We take the liberty of using the 1954 quotes because they so explicitly capture Eisenhower's consistent thinking.

66. Ibid., 1004–9; Warren I. Cohen and Akira Iriye, eds., *The Great Powers in East Asia, 1953–1960* (New York, 1990), 125.

67. *FR*, 1952–54, 1:1009–11.

68. Ibid., 1012–14; ibid., 2:586, 592.

69. Commission on Foreign Economic Policy, *Report*, 65–68; Tor Egil Forland, "'Selling Firearms to the Indians': Eisenhower's Export Control Policy, 1953–54," *DH* 15 (Spring 1991): 221–44; Robert Mark Spaulding, Jr., "'A Gradual and Moderate Relaxation': Eisenhower and the Revision of American Export Control Policy, 1953–1955," *DH* 17 (Spring 1993): 223–49.

70. Appendix A to Rostow to Jackson, June 9, 1953, "Bermuda Conference Briefing Book [June–July 1953] (2)," CDJR.

71. *FR*, 1952–54, 2:583, 587.

72. Ibid.

73. "Building Strength in Regional Groupings in the Far East," September 18, 1953, NSC 162, sec. 4, NSCPB 14.

74. *ED*, 223–24. See also *HD*, 96–97.

75. *ED*, 223.

76. Representative of the immense literature are George C. Herring and Richard H. Immerman, "Eisenhower, Dulles, and Dienbienphu: The 'Day We Didn't Go to War Revisited,'" *The Journal of American History* 71 (September 1984): 343–63; Melanie Billings-Yun, *Decision Against War: Eisenhower and Dien Bien Phu* (New York, 1988); David L. Anderson, *Trapped By Success: The Eisenhower Administration and Vietnam, 1953–61* (New York, 1991).

77. *ED*, 223–24.

78. See especially Peter L. Hahn, *The United States, Great Britain, and Egypt, 1945–1956: Strategy and Diplomacy in the Early Cold War* (Chapel Hill, 1991).

79. *ED*, 223–24; *HD*, 142.

80. *FR*, 1952–54, 2:586.

81. Ibid., 587–88.

82. *FR*, 1952–54, 4:6–10; JCS 1888/34, July 20, 1953, Report by the Joint Strategic Survey Committee to the Joint Chiefs of Staff on the Review of the Current World Situation and Ability of the Forces Being Maintained to Meet United States Commitments, CCS 370 (5-25-48), sec. 11, RG 218. See also Stephen G. Rabe, *Eisenhower and Latin America: The Foreign Policy of Anticommunism* (Chapel Hill, 1988); and Thomas Zoumaris, "Eisenhower's

Foreign Economic Policy: The Case of Latin America," in Richard A. Melanson and David Mayers, eds., *Reevaluating Eisenhower: American Foreign Policy in the Fifties* (Urbana, Illinois, 1987), 154–91. Later, as noted in the conclusion, the administration placed more emphasis on providing Africa, and especially Latin America, with economic assistance.

83. *FR*, 1952–54, 2:593, 595.

84. Ibid., 524–26.

85. Ibid., 14:279.

86. Ibid., 2:580.

87. Ibid., 14:291–92.

88. Ibid., 12:287.

89. Ibid., 2:586.

90. Ibid., 14:301, 1523–24.

91. Ibid., 1474, 1523, 1438–40; ibid., 6:1116–17.

92. "Building Strength in Regional Groupings in the Far East, September 18, 1953, 3; *FR*, 1952–54, 14:301, 305–6.

93. *FR*, 1952–54, 14:1406–8.

94. Ibid, 2:312–13; "Building Strength in Regional Groupings in the Far East," September 18, 1953, 28; *FR*, 1952–54, 14:1449; ibid., 13:361.

95. *FR*, 1952–54, 14:1411–15, 1434–35, 1438–40; ibid., 6:199, 217–18. Significantly, Britain and other Western European nations opposed Japanese admission to the General Agreement on Trade and Tariffs until 1955.

96. Ibid., 14:1389–90.

97. "Building Strength in Regional Groupings in the Far East," September 18, 1953, 28; Sayurai Shimizu, *Creating People of Plenty: The United States and Japan's Economic Alternatives, 1953–1958* (Ph.D. dissertation, Cornell University, 1991).

98. "Building Strength in Regional Groupings in the Far East," September 18, 1953, 3; *FR*, 1952–54, 14:281.

99. *FR*, 1952–54, 14:1389–90, 1394–97, 1438–40, 1464–66.

100. Ibid., 1464–66, 1473–77, 1406–8, 205–6.

101. Ibid., 2:436.

102. "Building Strength in Regional Groupings in the Far East," September 18, 1953, 9–10.

103. *FR*, 1952–54, 14:302, 305–6, 282.

104. Ibid., 165, 180–82, 213, 1473–77, 1491–96, 1497–1502, 305–6, 312–15, 324–25.

105. "Building Strength in Regional Groupings in the Far East," September 18, 1953, 23.

106. *FR*, 1952–54, 12 (part 1):260–63, 335–36.

107. Ibid., 258–60, 318, 318–19.

108. Ibid., 335–36, 258–60, 339–40. It warrants mention that the British perceived America's prominence in their traditional sphere of interest as a blow to their prestige and an indicator of U.S. intent to "ease them out of the picture" and "replace them in a position of proctorship." See ibid., 328–30, 122–24, 141–43, 149–51.

109. Ibid., 260–63, 344–51, 141–43, 575–79, 564. Ramon Magsaysay's election as president of the Philippines at the end of 1953 represented the administration's best hope. In addition to the above references, see Nick Cullather, *Illusion of Influence: The Political Economy of United States–Phillipines Relations* (Stanford, 1994), 96–125.

110. *FR*, 1952–54, 2:587, 591–92.

111. Steven Freiberger, *Dawn Over Suez: The Rise of American Power in the Middle East, 1953–1957* (Chicago, 1992).

112. Peter L. Hahn, "Containment and Egyptian Nationalism: The Unsuccessful Effort to Establish the Middle East Command, 1950–1953," *DH* 11 (Winter 1987): 23–40.

113. Ibid.; JCS 1888/34, July 20, 1953, Report by the Joint Strategic Survey Committee to the Joint Chiefs of Staff on the Review of the Current World Situation and Ability of the Forces Being Maintained to Meet United States Commitments, CCS 370 (5–25–48) sec. 11, JCS.

114. *FR*, 1952–54, 9:147, 381, 384.

115. Robert J. McMahon, "United States Cold War Strategy in South Asia: Making a Military Commitment to Pakistan, 1947–1954," *Journal of American History* 75 (December 1988):812–40; McMahon, *The Cold War on the Periphery: The United States, India, and Pakistan* (New York, 1994), 80–170.

116. *FR*, 1952–54, 2:593.

117. Ibid., 837–38; H. W. Brands, Jr., *The Specter of Neutralism: The United States and the Emergence of the Third World, 1947–1960* (New York, 1989).

118. *FR*, 1952–54, 2:524–25, 837–38, ibid., 11:1838–39; ibid., 9:453–54.

119. McMahon, *Cold War on the Periphery*, 173–88, 207.

120. "Bloc Political Warfare Strengths," Appendix C to NIE-90, "Soviet Bloc Capabilities Through Mid–1955," approved August 11, 1953," CIA.

121. Omar N. Bradley for the JCS memorandum to the secretary of defense, March 4, 1953, CCS 370 (5–25–48) sec. 11, JCS; JCS 1888/33, April 24, 1953, ibid.

122. Peter Grose, *Gentleman Spy: The Life of Allen Dulles* (Boston, 1994), 332–38.

123. William M. Leary, ed., *The Central Intelligence Agency: History and Documents* (University, Alabama, 1984), 143–45; Rhodri Jeffreys-Jones, *The CIA & American Democracy* (New Haven, 1989), 70.

124. Raymond L. Garthoff, "Assessing the Adversary: Estimates by the Eisenhower Administration of Soviet Intentions and Capabilities," *Brookings Occasional Papers* (1991): 16–17.

125. Klaus Larres, "Preserving Law and Order: Britain, the United States, and the East German Uprising of 1953," *Twentieth Century British History* 5 (1994): 320–50; Valur Ingimundarson, "The Eisenhower Administration, the Adenauer Government, and the Political Uses of the East German Uprising in 1953," *DH* 20 (Summer 1996): 381–409; and Christian F. Ostermann, "'Keeping the Pot Simmering': The United States and the East German Uprising of 1953," *German Studies Review* 19 (February 1996): 61–89.

126. *FR*, 1952–54, 2:438–39, 440. Eisenhower's cautious response to the Hungarian uprising in 1956, of course, remains controversial.

127. Kermit Roosevelt, *Countercoup: The Struggle for Control of Iran* (New York, 1979); John Prados, *Presidents' Secret Wars: CIA and Pentagon Covert Operations Since World War II* (New York, 1986), 92–98. See also Mark Gasiorowski, *U.S. Foreign Policy and the Shah: Building a Client State in Iran* (Ithaca, 1991).

128. AJAX inspired SUCCESS, the CIA operation against Guatemala's Jacobo Arbenz Guzmán the next year. Richard H. Immerman, *The CIA in Guatemala: The Foreign Policy of Intervention* (Austin, 1982), 135.

129. *FR*, 1952–54, 9:334–40 (our emphasis). See also ibid., 399–400; Some Comparable Data on the Soviet Bloc as of Mid–1954 (Prepared by the CIA), August 18, 1954, "NSC 5430 (7)," NSC Series, Status of Projects Subseries, WHOSANSA.

130. *FR*, 1952–54, 2:593, 595, 592.

131. "Progress Report on Foreign Intelligence Program," enclosed with Allen W. Dulles memorandum to executive secretary, February 6, 1953, "Background Documents on NSC 142," NSCPB; Sig Mickelson, *America's Other Voice: The Story of Radio Free Europe and Radio Liberty* (New York, 1983), Evidence suggests, however, that the influence of Radio Free Europe and Radio Liberty on discontented East Europeans was not as great as was once thought. See *Cold War International History Project Bulletin* 5 (Spring 1995).

132. Report of the Psychological Strategy Board on the Psychological Program (Part 6 of NSC 142), January 21, 1953, "Status of U.S. Programs for National Security as of December 31, 1952 (5)," NSC Series, Status of Projects Subseries, WHOSANSA.

133. Robert H. Lounsbury memorandum to William H. Jackson, March 8, 1953, "JC Numbered Documents (7)," PCIIA; R. W. Tufts memorandum for Mr. Jackson, May 19, 1953, "Rockefeller Committee Report," ibid. See also Townsend Hoopes, JC114, "Some Thoughts on the Problem," February 6, 1953, "JC Numbered Documents (7)," ibid.; Charles E. Bohlen testimony to PCIIA, Feb. 24, 1953, "JC Numbered Documents (3)," ibid; "Non-Military Factors Affecting Bloc Capabilities," Appendix A to NIE-90, "Soviet Bloc Capabilities Through Mid–1955," approved August 11, 1953, and Appendices, approved September 29, 1953, CIA. FR, 1952–54, 1823–34.

134. Report of the Department of State, Annex A to Psychological Strategy Board, Report on the Psychological Program (part 6 of NSC 142), January 21, 1953, "NSC 142, Status of U.S. Security Programs for National Security, December 31, 1952 (5)," Status of Project Series, NSC Series, WHOSANSA; FR, 1952–54, 9: 399–400.

135. Psychological Strategy Board, Report on the Psychological Program (part 6 of NSC 142), January 21, 1953.

14   Reducing the Nuclear Danger: Arms Control

1. Dwight D. Eisenhower, *The White House Years: Waging Peace, 1956–1961* (Garden City, New York, 1965), 467.

2. *FR*, 1952–54, 2:1455.

3. Ibid., 1321–22, 1342.

4. Joseph F. Pilate, Robert E. Pendley, and Charles K. Ebinger, eds., *Atoms for Peace: An Analysis after Thirty Years* (Boulder, 1985), 27; Richard G. Hewlett and Jack M. Holl, *Atoms for Peace and War* (Berkeley, 1989), 1–16.

5. *PP–E*, 1953, 5.

6. *DSB* (April 14, 1952): 572–79.

7. Quoted in Lewis L. Strauss, *Men and Decisions* (Garden City, New York, 1962), 336 (emphasis in original).

8. Eisenhower, *Waging Peace*, 653.

9. *FR*, 1952–54, 2: 1091–96, 1103–8.

10. Ibid., 1056–91.

11. Ibid., 1059–63.

12. Ibid., 1075–76.

13. Ibid., 1063. The reference to America's commitment to atomic retaliation was based on the pre–New Look Truman policy.

14. Ibid., 1073.

15. Ibid., 1074–77.

16. Ibid., 1077.

17. Ibid., 1081–88.

18. Ibid., 1088–91.

19. Ibid., 1107.

20. Ibid., 1107–8.

21. Ibid., 1110–14.

22. *ED*, 261–62; *FR*, 1952–54, 2:1309–10; Eisenhower, *Waging Peace*, 467–68.

23. Eisenhower to Milton Eisenhower, December 11, 1953, "Atoms for Peace," Administrative Series, AWF.

24. Eisenhower, *Waging Peace*, 469.

25. *FR*, 1952–54, 2:1455.

26. Emmet John Hughes, *The Ordeal of Power: A Political Memoir of the Eisenhower Years* (New York, 1975), 102–4. See also Walt W. Rostow, *Open Skies: Eisenhower's Proposal of July 21, 1955* (Austin, 1982).

27. *FR*, 1952–54, 2:1107–8.

28. This directive was issued by the Executive Committee on Regulation of Armaments (RAC), composed of the secretaries of state and defense and the chairman of the AEC, on May 26, 1953. See *FR*, 1952–54, 2:1160–69. See also ibid., 1175–76.

29. Ibid., 1190–1201.

30. Ibid., 1210–12, 1214–15, 1216–18.

31. Ibid., 584–85.

32. Ibid., 584–95.

33. Ibid., 512.

34. Ibid.

35. Ibid., 529–30.

36. Ibid., 680–86; *HJCS* 5, 45–46.

37. *FR*, 1952–54, 2:656.

38. *FR*, 1952–54, 2:687–88.

39. Ibid., 715–16.

40. Ibid., 818–19, 829.

41. Ibid., 818–19.

42. Ibid., 831.

43. Ibid., 833–44. The revised Basic National Security Policy was approved as NSC 5501 on January 7, 1955. See *FR*, 1955–57, 20:24–38. Paragraph 40 concerning negotiations is on p. 36.

44. Ibid., 2:1150–60, 1169–74.

45. Jackson memorandum for the files, September 30, 1953, "Chronology—'Atoms for Peace' Project," *Time*, Inc. File, CDJP; *FR*, 1952–54, 2:1223–24.

46. *FR*, 1952–54, 2:1224–26.

47. See chapter 13. For evidence that Dulles's "package" arose from consideration of his September 6 memorandum, see Dulles memorandum for Bowie, September 8, 1953, "White House Correspondence 1953 (2)," WHMS, DPEL; Dulles memorandum for the president, May 12, 1954, "White House Correspondence, 1954 (3)," ibid.

48. Dulles memorandum for Bowie, September 8, 1953; Dulles to Bowie, October 9, 1953, attached to Draft #1, October 4, 1953, "Candor Speech, December 8, 1953 (1)," Draft Presidential Correspondence and Speeches Series, DPEL.

49. Ibid.; "Material for Second Half of Atomic Speech," "Atoms for Peace—Evolution (3)," *Time*, Inc. File, CDJP.

50. *FR*, 1952–54, 2:1227–32, 1232–33, 1233–34. See also Frank Nash memorandum for Cutler, October 17, 1953, CD 388.3, OSD.

51. Dulles memorandum for the president, October 21, 1953, "General Foreign Policy Matters (4)," WHMS, DPEL. The Tripartite Foreign Ministers Meeting in London was held from October 16–18, 1953. Following it Dulles met with representatives of the Federal German Republic and North Atlantic Council.

52. *FR*, 1952–54, 2:1234–35.

53. Ibid., 1309, 1213.

54. Ibid., 1219. See also Strauss, *Men and Decisions*, 357.

55. *FR*, 1952–54, 2:1235–40, 1244–46.

56. Pilate, Pendley, and Ebinger, eds., *Atoms for Peace*, 22; Charles A. Appleby, Jr., *Eisenhower and Arms Control, 1953–1961: The Balance of Risks* (Ph.D. dissertation, Johns Hopkins University School of Advanced International Studies, 1987), 32.

57. The phrases in quotes are from the UN General Assembly resolution of ten days earlier urging the Disarmament Commission to adopt such a procedure.

58. *PP–E*, 1953, 813–22.

59. *ED*, 261–62.

60. *FR*, 1952–54, 2:1286–87, 1287–88.

61. Ibid., 1312–14, 1314–16, 1321–22.

62. Ibid., 1322–23, 1324–30.

63. Ibid., 1342–43.

64. See ibid., 1235–40, 1244–46.

65. Ibid., 1378.

66. Ibid., 1383–84.

67. Ibid., 1386.

68. Ibid., 1379–80, 1380–82, 1383.

69. Ibid., 1423–29.

70. Ibid., 1437–40, 1457–58.

71. Ibid., 1452–55.

72. Ibid., 1463–67.

73. Ibid., 1467–72.

74. "Summary of the Current United States and USSR Positions on Disarmament and of Significant Developments Since NSC 112" and "The Technical Feasibility of International Control of Atomic Energy." See ibid., 1540n.4.

75. Ibid., 1537–40.

76. Ibid., 1537–38.

77. Ibid., 1538–40. The reference is to the Working Group of the Special Committee.

78. Appleby, *Eisenhower and Arms Control*, 41–44, 65–67.

79. *FR*, 1952–54, 2:1563–64.

80. Ibid., 1564–66.

81. In addition to the reports already cited, these included a synopsis of the Defense member's position of November 24, a December 2 report by the State member, and a statement by the AEC member on December 2. See ibid., 1580.

82. Ibid., 1581–82, 1582–84. Wilson noted that he sent this identical letter to Strauss.

83. Ibid., 1585–86.

84. Ibid., 1586–88.

85. Ibid., 1588.

86. Ibid., 1588–89.

87. *FR*, 1955–57, 20:1–7, 15–20.

88. Ibid., 1–5.

89. Ibid., 5–6.

90. Ibid., 6–7.

91. Ibid., 15–16.

92. Ibid., 16–17.

93. Ibid., 17–18.

94. Ibid., 18–20.

95. Ibid., 29–30.

96. Ibid., 30 (emphasis in original).

97. Ibid., 31–32.

98. Ibid., 32–34.

99. Ibid., 58. See also Harold Stassen and Marshall Houts, *Eisenhower: Turning the World Toward Peace* (St. Paul, 1990), 275–91.

15   The Eisenhower Legacy

1. McGeorge Bundy, *Danger and Surival: Choices About the Bomb in the First Fifty Years* (New York, 1988), 287.

2. *PP–E*, 1960–1961, 421.

3. Richard G. Hewlett and Jack M. Holl, *Atoms for Peace and War* (Berkeley, 1989), 172–82; Bundy, *Danger and Survival*, 320.

4. *HD*, 102.

5. *C–EC*, 125.

6. Quoted in Bundy, *Danger and Survival*, 259.

7. See especially Peter J. Roman, *Eisenhower and the Missile Gap* (Ithaca, 1995).

8. David A. Rosenberg, "The Origins of Overkill: Nuclear Weapons and American Strategy, 1945–1960," *International Security* 7 (Spring 1983), 64–65; Fred Kaplan, *The Wizards of Armageddon* (New York, 1983), 266–70. We would suggest that the explanation for Eisenhower's lack of attention to targeting plans was that throughout his administration his focus was on avoiding general war, not planning how to fight one (which, as noted, he believed would be an unmitigated catastrophe under any circumstances).

9. Vladislov M. Zubok and Constantine Pleshakov, *Inside the Kremlin's Cold War: From Stalin to Krushchev* (Cambridge, Massachusetts, 1996), 188–89; David Holloway, *Stalin and the Bomb: The Soviet Union and Atomic Energy, 1939–1956* (New Haven, 1994), 335–45.

10. *PP–E*, 1955, 728.

11. Marc Trachtenberg, ed., *The Development of American Strategic Thought: Basic Documents from the Eisenhower and Kennedy Periods, Including the Basic National Security Papers from 1953–1959* (New York, 1988), 187–90.

12. Roman, *Eisenhower and the Missile Gap*, 193; Bundy, *Danger and Survival*, 319. Moreover, at Eisenhower's initiative in late 1958 a "Conference of Experts" was convened in Geneva for the "Study of Possible Measures Which Might be Helpful in Preventing Surprise Attack."

13. Eisenhower address in San Francisco, California, October 8, 1952, "September 26, 1952," Speech Series, AWF (our emphasis).

14. *FR*, 1952–54, 2:219–20.

15. David Alan Rosenberg, "The End(s) of American Strategy: Lesson from Plans and Budgets from America's Nuclear Revolution, 1945–1960," paper presented to the U.S. Army War College Conference on "Strategy for the Lean Years," April 27, 1995. We are indebted to Professor Rosenberg for providing us with a copy of his paper.

16. *FR*, 1952–54, 2:146, 213.

17. Rosenberg, "The End(s) of American Strategy."

18. Gerard C. Smith, *Disarming Diplomat: The Memoirs of Gerard C. Smith, Arms Negotiator* (Lanham, Maryland, 1996).

19. See Robert R. Bowie's foreword to "The North Atlantic Nations Tasks for the 1960s: A Report to the Secretary of State, August 1960, [The 'Bowie Report']" *Nuclear History Program Occasional Paper* 7 (1991): v–vii.

20. *ED*, 223–24.

21. *FR*, 1952–54, 2:592 (our emphasis).

22. This process is analyzed in detail in Burton I. Kaufman, *Trade and Aid: Eisenhower's Foreign Economic Policy, 1953–1961* (Baltimore, 1982), on which the following discussion draws.

23. Audrey and George McT. Kahin, *Subversion and Foreign Policy: The Secret Eisenhower and Dulles Debacle in Indonesia* (New York, 1995).

24. *PP–E*, 1957, 60–65.

25. Stephen E. Ambrose, *Eisenhower: The President* (New York, 1984), 376–81.

26. Russell Edgerton, *Sub-Cabinet Politics and Policy Commitment: The Birth of the Development Loan Fund* (New York, 1970).

27. Kaufman, *Trade and Aid*, 207–11.

28. Zubok and Pleshakov, *Inside the Kremlin's Cold War*, 193–94.

29. Smith, *Disarming Diplomat*.

30. On the [Pierre] Harmel Report, see Lawrence S. Kaplan, *NATO and the United States: The Enduring Alliance* (Boston, 1988), 121–27.

31. Fred I. Greenstein and Richard H. Immerman, "What Did Eisenhower Tell Kennedy about Indochina? The Politics of Misperception," *Journal of American History* 79 (September 1992), 568–87.

32. Irving L. Janis, *Groupthink: Psychological Studies of Policy Decisions and Fiascoes* (Boston, 1982).

33. Alexander George, "The Case for Multiple Advocacy in Making Foreign Policy," *American Political Science Review* 66 (1972): 751–85. See also George, *Presidential Decision-making in Foreign Policy: The Effective Use of Information and Advice* (Boulder, 1980), esp. chapter 1.

34. *FR*, 1952–54, 2:804–5.

Index

Printed in the United States
135353LV00005B/58/A

9 780195 140484

8444595R0

Made in the USA
Lexington, KY
04 February 2011